One and many mirrors: perspectives on graphic desi

Edited by Luke Wood and Brad Haylock

Occasional Papers

This book is dedicated to our teachers and students,
past, present and future.

Contents

- 6   **Introduction**
  Luke Wood

- 14   **What is design?**
  Jonty Valentine

- 24   **Care and inclusion**
  Sheila Levrant de Bretteville, interviewed by Ellen Lupton

- 32   **The most dangerous design school in the world**
  Lucille Tenazas, interviewed by Europa

- 42   **The critical turn: education of a design writer**
  Teal Triggs

- 62   **A refractive (re)view**
  Paul Bailey, Tony Credland, Katie Evans, Ricardo Goncalves, Gabriela Matusyck, Bryony Quinn, Carlos Romo-Melgar, Naomi Strinati, Jia Xiao and Roxy Zeiher

- 72   **School days**
  Rob Giampietro

- 86   **Parse and iterate**
  Rob Giampietro, interviewed by Vincent Chan

- 96   **A terminal degree**
  Stuart Bertolotti-Bailey, interviewed by Luke Wood

- 114   **Graphic design counter-education**
  Joe Potts, interviewed by Jon Sueda

- 130   **Arriving and landing: perspectives on the Werkplaats Typografie**
  Na Kim, Radim Peško and Lu Liang, interviewed by Megan Patty

- 136   **Chasing curiosity: inquiry-led practice in communication design**
  Lisa Grocott

- 148   **The ghost of a practice**
  Matthew Galloway

- 154   **The Leipzig style**
  Constanze Hein

- 162   **Norman Potter's teaching spaces**
  James Langdon

- 180   **It's rather an attitude**
  Richard Hollis, interviewed by Brad Haylock

Contents

194 Stripping down and dressing up
Corin Gisel and Nina Paim

220 Two schools of thought
Fraser Muggeridge, interviewed by Paul Mylecharane

230 Typography as a university study
Michael Twyman

**238 Communicating design studies:
a peripheral dialogue about transnational design pedagogies**
Noel Waite and Richard Buchanan, in conversation

246 Problem formulation is the problem
Brad Haylock

260 What matters for future practice?
Laurene Vaughan and Bonne Zabolotney, in conversation

267 Contributor biographies

276 Colophon

Introduction
Luke Wood

This book has been in development for a few years now, involving many practitioners, academics and students from different parts of the world. As we finalise it for publication, we all find ourselves in the same situation — working from home in various states of lockdown as a result of the COVID-19 pandemic. This international crisis has forced people to rethink what the future might look like. The closure of borders, restrictions on travel, and being thrown into online-only teaching environments have forced those of us in education to quickly reconfigure how we teach, and have made it quite clear what we lose when we can no longer meet in our communal spaces for learning. This book, the starting point for which was a more localised disaster, outlined below, cannot account for this situation, but might, we hope, contribute usefully to ongoing conversations about the future of graphic design education.

Teaching was something I fell into. It wasn't something I had ever seriously thought about doing. I had been working as a graphic designer for almost ten years and found myself wanting to move into another field entirely. Not sure what that something else might be, I took a job teaching graphic design, imagining I'd only do it for a year while I figured out what to do next.

Now, fifteen years later, I've taught at four very different design schools in New Zealand and I have completed postgraduate study in Australia. I have also, for various reasons, visited schools in Europe, the UK and the US. I've seen a lot of different (admittedly Western) approaches to teaching graphic design, but, funnily enough, I'd never really been particularly interested in education. Teaching had become my main source of income, but I'd never considered myself a teacher. If someone asked me what I did, I would say that I was a graphic designer, which I still was (and still am, sort of). My nonchalant attitude towards teaching changed, though, as a result of a series of earthquakes that all but destroyed the city of Christchurch in February 2011. That disaster, in a roundabout way, was really the catalyst for this book.

'Under review'
I have been teaching in the School of Fine Arts at the University of Canterbury in Christchurch on and off since 2003. The school had already been suffering from decreasing institutional support prior to the catastrophic earthquakes. There had been ongoing and significant cuts to budgets, facilities and staffing since the early 2000s; by 2010, the school was officially 'under review'. The situation was already ominous enough and so, in the days immediately following the earthquakes, paranoid staff were of course speculating that this new crisis would be used as a catalyst to close the school for good.

The earthquakes practically destroyed the centre of the city. Although the Canterbury campus is not in downtown Christchurch, there was damage to some university buildings. The biggest and most immediate problem for the wider university, though, was that students had left the city in droves, and international students were now too scared to come to Christchurch. The university was hurting financially and the Vice Chancellor's response was, predictably, to quickly downsize — to shut down certain departments and

Damage in the Central Library at the University of Canterbury, Christchurch, following the earthquake on 22 February 2011. Photograph by Stacy Squires for *Stuff / The Press*.

lay off a large number of staff. Early on, he proposed, in all seriousness, that we might imagine a university without the arts and humanities, including the fine arts and design. The arts, as he saw them, were unprofitable and, worse, not vocationally relevant.

To be fair, such changes had been in the air, and had been implemented by many other education providers around the country. The move towards purely vocational qualifications (once the preserve of high-quality technical institutes) and quick-turnaround coursework postgraduate degrees (rather than longer-duration research qualifications), a focus on the student as a customer (someone who gets what they've paid for, regardless of performance), and the prioritisation of resourcing for science and technology subjects were all well known elsewhere, as was the increasing lampooning of arts and humanities disciplines as unnecessary frivolities in a contemporary, fully monetised world.

The effects of neoliberalism on education are well known, felt internationally, and discussed in depth elsewhere.[1] I outline the situation at the University of Canterbury's School of Fine Arts because this was the context in which I met Melanie Oliver, then director of The Physics Room, a contemporary art project space in Christchurch that had narrowly survived the earthquakes. I was considering my options and joked that we might 'start our own bloody school' — one free from the bureaucracy and endless restructuring that seems endemic in all large educational institutions. Melanie immediately pointed me to a number of then-recent alternative/temporary/experimental art schools that had been established around the world, so-called 'schools' that didn't have buildings, such as the Mountain Art College in Los Angeles, or schools that eschewed official accreditation, like SOMA in Mexico City. It excited me to see a plethora of different types of schools trying to do different kinds of things, and so it was with some sense of urgency and naïve radicalism that I took up Melanie's offer to use The Physics Room to run a temporary design school of some sort.

(Graphic) Design School School

From 14 July to 24 August 2014, in collaboration with Brad Haylock, I ran a temporary design school at The Physics Room. That project, which was titled *(Graphic) Design School School*, spawned this book.[2] Both the project and the book have been the result of ongoing, spiralling conversations in and out of design, art, education, politics and culture. Brad came on board with this project through The Physics Room's artist-in-residence programme, and he brought a completely different perspective with him, from the School of Design at RMIT University in Melbourne, reminding me that the world is bigger than New Zealand.

Given the situation at my university, and my perception of what was happening elsewhere in design education, I was particularly interested in using the project to perform a return-to-zero restart of my own assumptions and expectations regarding education. It was upon Brad's suggestion, based on curriculum redesign work he was doing at RMIT at the time, that we decided to involve my students from the university in co-designing an entirely new curriculum from the ground up, and this became a pivotal guiding concept for the project at The Physics Room. The idea was that the students should have as much agency in the project as possible, as well as a good sense of individual and collective responsibility. This sense of responsibility in relation to one's own learning, and in relation to the social function of education in general, is something that has been significantly diminished since the introduction of the user-pays approach to education in New Zealand in the early 1990s. When students become 'customers', they understand that they are purchasing a product or service, rather than participating in a collective effort. This project, this 'school' at The Physics Room, was to be as much theirs as it was ours.[3] And so our immediate concern, when relocating to the gallery for a whole academic term, was to establish a setting in which graphic design students would be encouraged to think about their own education in an open-ended but critically informed way.

(Graphic) Design School School therefore began with a series of lectures, reading groups and discussions that aimed to expose the history of pedagogical conventions that we (students and staff) tend to take for granted. We put everything up for discussion and debate—the schedule, assessment regimes, modes of teaching and learning, and so on—anticipating radical and even problematic proposals. I remember expecting that we might well end up running classes late at night, and how interesting that might be, how that might shift things if we moved from a 9:00am – 5:00pm mindset to a 9:00pm – 5:00am mindset. This wasn't a popular notion, of course, as students had other things to consider—jobs, families, body clocks, etc. The students' concerns were all legitimate, but pointed to what I felt, at the time, was one of the major failings of the project: from early on, I worried that we were in most respects simply reproducing what the students were already used to, just in a different physical location. I also became vaguely uncomfortable about the fact that the project quickly became *not* about some idealised, utopian graphic design school—which is what The Physics Room staff were, I think, expecting—but very much about the specific institution we had come from. In hindsight, I can see I should have expected this. The students were, after all, still my students, and still students of the University of Canterbury. And so, in this sense, our project departed significantly from the plethora of radical, self-organised and aggressively anti-institutional schools that I had looked to for inspiration.

But our project, our school, was, in many ways, a genuinely valuable opportunity for us to step away from the institution for a short while, following a period of very real crisis. We needed a break—the students and I alike. And we were able to use that physical distance to more objectively reflect upon and reconsider the problems, but also the opportunities, that were presenting themselves to us in our very small graphic design department inside a fairly old, fairly conservative art school—problems and opportunities that, for my part, at least, framed my interest in attempting to put a book like this together.

One and many mirrors
This book is the result of my continuing these conversations, often abstract and epistemological in nature, with Brad and inviting others to contribute their specific and often more concrete perspectives. As such, it has turned out to be a compilation of quite different, sometimes competing points of view—

different reflections on contested conceptual terrain. A hybrid discipline since its inception, graphic design was already an amorphous subject, but, in recent years, what it is that graphic designers do has expanded in a myriad of different directions. In part, this has been in response to technology — developments that have led to the rise of new design roles, such as user experience (UX) designer, user interface (UI) designer, interaction designer, visual designer and front-end developer. But, at the same time, we have also seen graphic designers attempt to move in the opposite direction, away from specific skills-based work and into more open-ended roles, like design thinking and service design. These are areas in which the designer — in principle, at least — has more agency to make significant change, not just to the way things look or feel, but to the ways in which businesses, communities, organisations, institutions and governments might work.

And while all of this has been gaining momentum, we have also seen a plethora of ambitious designers abandon the so-called 'industry' — work in the service of a commission — in favour of more self-initiated, culturally oriented work. The exhibition *Graphic Design: Now in Production*, curated by Andrew Blauvelt and Ellen Lupton, first shown at the Walker Art Center in 2011, focused on the outputs of designers who are, in various ways, taking control of the means of production, designers who are 'becoming producers: authors, publishers, instigators, and entrepreneurs employing their creative skills as makers of content and shapers of experiences'.[4] In keeping with the proliferation of titles in the world of professional work, there have also been attempts to name these errant practices. In 2007, the exhibition *Forms of Inquiry: The Architecture of Critical Graphic Design*, curated by Zak Kyes, thrust the term 'critical design' into the broader lexicon of the discipline. Rick Poynor quickly pointed out that there was a history of such practice in the discipline, citing its rightful progenitors.[5] Later, in 2014, another exhibition and its attendant publication, *All Possible Futures*, sought to explore the increasingly popular and similarly deployed term 'speculative design'.[6]

Whatever we call the practice, the roles our graduates move into or the types of work they do, there is one thing we can be sure of: gone are the days when our highest-performing students unanimously dreamed of working for large corporate clients. But how have schools accounted for and responded to this expanding field of practice? Perhaps not very well, judging by the proliferation of small, alternative and experimental schools starting up around the world, all of which embody some form of critique of the larger, traditional educational institutions we know so well. This tendency is represented in Jon Sueda's interview with Joe Potts (pp. 114–129 in this book), founder of The Southland Institute, a new unaccredited interdisciplinary postgraduate typography programme in Los Angeles. It is a trend that is explored and articulated in greater depth in Jacob Lindgren's recent book on self-organised learning and education in graphic design, *Extra-Curricular*.[7] Significantly, many of these alternative, often temporary projects that seek to rethink our schooling and its systems are also motivated by the rapidly rising costs of tertiary education around the world. Matters of relevance and cost are at the heart of a growing questioning of education across all sectors. In September 2018, the Fourth Istanbul Design Biennial, *A School of Schools*, opened as a focused interrogation of design schooling today. The resulting publication, *Design as Learning: A School of Schools Reader*, is intentionally provocative, pointing out that 'conventional methods are no longer enough',[8] and that, in many instances, institutional education might be seen as 'a system predicated on producing efficient and obedient workers, and issuing qualifications as access- and status-control'.[9]

Universities and technical institutes of art and design — usually large-scale, long-running, traditional and conservative institutions — are the primary targets of these new critical perspectives. And rightly so. Slow-moving and constrained by sprawling webs of bureaucracy, these institutional behemoths struggle with change. And yet, like our project at The Physics Room, the task of putting this book together has often led to conversations that, strangely enough, point back to the values of an institutional education. Despite constant budget cuts, seemingly endless restructuring, increasingly precarious contractual arrangements for many staff, and the various other disruptions that result from being thrown into a free-market economy, such institutions, when operating well, still facilitate cultures of learning, teaching and research that are hard to find elsewhere.

This year, 2020, the School of Fine Arts at the University of Canterbury is 138 years old. Over its history, it has, like all schools, seen its ups and downs. It has by now clearly survived the financial and political fallout of the catastrophic 2011 earthquakes, and has, in fact, flourished. More recently, staff and students returned to the studios following the entire second term of our 2020 academic year being taught entirely online. We were happy to discover that we did not lose a single student as a result of the COVID-19 lockdown — an indication, perhaps, of the bonds that form between participants in a studio-based education.

While 'stability' is a relative term, especially in education, there is at least a sense of potential longevity that is critical to the development of approaches to teaching and research that aren't simply reactive or instrumental. When the institution works, it does still offer a unique space and time in which to think and act. In New Zealand, the Education Act of 1989 expressly states that universities must accept the role of the 'critic and conscience of society'.[10] I didn't know that prior to the earthquakes, but I'm very drawn to it now. It sounds quaint and a bit old-fashioned, but there it is, enshrined in national law.

There are many ways in which education might be understood to reflect the so-called 'real world'. To take a broad view is to walk through a hall of mirrors and see ourselves, and our disciplines, distorted in different ways, refracted by differing perspectives, histories and ideologies. The university is often criticised for being out of step with the real world; however one might argue — and many have — that the job of the university is not to replicate the real world, but to reflect upon it. Every pedagogy constructs its own world and each has its right place.

Thanks

My utmost gratitude goes, of course, to Brad Haylock, who has played the alternating roles of co-pilot and devil's advocate over the last few years. His breadth of experience in design education, editing and publishing has proved invaluable in the process of putting this book together, but also in regard to the development of my own thinking as a teacher and as a designer. This book would also never have existed without Melanie Oliver, who, during her tenure as director at The Physics Room, was the catalyst for all of this — the project we ran at the gallery, Brad's coming on board as the artist-in-residence, a small symposium we ran at a lodge in the Southern Alps, and eventually making contact with Occasional Papers about the possibility of publishing this book.

The publication has received considerable financial and administrative support from The Physics Room, and we are especially grateful for the efforts of Fiona Simpson over the course of the project, and for the support of Jamie Hanton, who took over as director following Melanie. This project also received significant financial support from the University of Canterbury's 'Ilam' School of Fine Arts, and in particular I am especially grateful for the support of Aaron Kreisler, Head of the School of Fine Arts, and Paul Miller, Head of the School of Humanities and Creative Arts.

My colleagues and students at the School of Fine Arts have played a significant role in my thinking about pedagogy, as have my ongoing conversations with Jonty Valentine and Aaron Beehre over many years. It also makes sense that I might now acknowledge my own teachers here, people whose efforts and ideas I appreciate in a much more tangible way these days: Tim Neale, Steve Gibbs, Gerard Murray, Max Hailstone, Lisa Grocott and Laurene Vaughan — thanks!

This book really only exists because of the work of our generous and patient contributors, to whom we are eternally grateful. Finally, and significantly, we must acknowledge the critical support of the team at Occasional Papers: Antony Hudek, Sarah Horn and particularly Sara De Bondt, who has stuck with us and kept us on track as life has pulled us all in different directions over the last couple of years.

1   Pascal Gielen and Paul De Bruyne, eds., *Teaching Art in the Neoliberal Realm* (Amsterdam: Valiz, 2012).
2   Our project was preceded by a conference/workshop at the University of Derby in March 2012, which we have since discovered had a similar title — 'Redesigning (Graphic) Design Education' — and shared interests. See: Yvan Martinez and Joshua Trees, 'Redesigning (Graphic) Design Education', in *Thought Experiments in Graphic Design Education*, edited by Yvan Martinez and Joshua Trees (London: Booksfromthefuture, 2013), 03:03–03:13.
3   Our immense thanks must go to the students who participated in and contributed to the experiment that was *(Graphic) Design School School*: Alice Bush, Gemma Banks, Tiggy Cameron, Millie Clarke, Sophie Cullen, Narelle Denmead, Laura English, Matt Fennell, Georgia Guilford, Sarah Jones, Klaudia Krupa, Lisa Maloney, Danica Nel, Kelsey O'Hagan, Cameron Ralston, Jose Sanchez, Tony Su, Jess Tabke and Emma Tuohy.
4   'Graphic Design: Now in Production', Walker Art Center, https://walkerart.org/calendar/2011/graphic-design-now-in-production, accessed 5 April 2019.
5   Rick Poynor, 'Critical Omissions', *Print*, 1 June 2008, http://www.printmag.com/article/observer_critical_omissions/, accessed 5 April 2019.
6   Jon Sueda, *All Possible Futures* (London: Bedford Press, 2014).
7   Jacob Lindgren, ed., *Extra-Curricular* (Eindhoven: Onomatopee, 2018).
8   Deniz Ova, 'The Ever Expanding Concept of a Biennial', in *Design as Learning: A School of Schools Reader*, edited by Vera Sacchetti (Amsterdam: Valiz, 2018), 35.
9   Jan Boelen, Nadine Botha and Vera Sacchetti, 'A School of Schools: Doubting a Biennial, Doubting Design', in *Design as Learning: A School of Schools Reader*, edited by Vera Sacchetti (Amsterdam: Valiz, 2018), 44.
10 Education Act 1989 (NZ), http://www.legislation.govt.nz/act/public/1989/0080/latest/DLM183668.html, accessed 5 April 2019.

What is design?
Jonty Valentine

Originally a talk presented for the Spark conference at the Wintec School of Media Arts in Hamilton, New Zealand, in 2012, this essay sees Jonty Valentine reflect on three very different schools that have shaped his development as a practising designer and educator. Valentine highlights the ideologies implicit in these educational programmes, his attempts to assimilate them, and the ways in which they have worked together to prompt him to continue asking the question: 'what is design?'

The title of this essay is taken from the first chapter of Max Hailstone's book *Design and Designers*, which was published in 1985 by Griffin Press and the New Zealand Industrial Design Council.[1] Max was my tutor. I would like to address his question but refine it to ask, more specifically, 'What is *graphic* design?'

I will reflect on how I might have answered Max's question differently over a few periods of my own design career, by writing about three different design schools I have been involved with and influenced by, first as a student, then as a teacher, and then as a student again: the University of Canterbury's Ilam School of Fine Arts (Christchurch, NZ), Wintec School of Media Arts (Hamilton, NZ) and Yale University School of Art (New Haven, USA). Each of these presented a different take on graphic design, prompting a reassessment of my assumptions about the discipline each time. They are all in some way incomplete or problematic, but my hope is that with my sketch of these schools I may somehow approach an answer to Max's question.

Problem solving: Ilam School of Fine Arts

My undergraduate study was undertaken at the Ilam School of Fine Arts. Max was the primary tutor there, and he was — perhaps questionably, in the early 1990s — still delivering the high-modernist programme of Typo-graphic Design (Max's spelling) that he had been instrumental in promoting at the school when he arrived from England in 1973.[2] Through Max's projects, we were immersed in the modernist myths of 'form follows function', 'relational composition', 'drawing as abstraction', 'the grid', and so on. In class critiques, we were indoctrinated into accepting the belief that design is a process of 'problem solving'.

Although others would be better placed than I to tell the full story of Max's design education influences from 1960s England, I would like to contextualise my reflections by explaining a little about where Max was from. Max possibly borrowed the title for his introduction to *Design and Designers* from Norman Potter's book *What is a Designer*, first published in 1969.[3] Max had a first edition of this book in his office, shelved next to his 'preliminary version', from 1968, of Herbert Spencer's *The Visible Word*.[4] In *Design and Designers*, Max was reiterating the priorities of English designers and educators of the 1960s, such as Spencer, Potter, Ken Garland and Anthony Froshaug. A well known document that reflects the spirit of this period is the 'First Things First' manifesto, written by Garland and published in 1964. A call to arms for graphic design, it criticised the profession of advertising, and encouraged designers to use their skills for more 'worthwhile' forms of communication, such as design for street signs, buildings, instructional manuals, educational aids, etc.:

> We do not advocate the abolition of high pressure consumer advertising: this is not feasible. Nor do we want to take any of the fun out of life. But we are proposing a reversal of priorities in favour of the more useful and more lasting forms of communication. We hope that our society will tire of gimmick merchants, status salesmen and hidden persuaders, and that the prior call on our skills will be for worthwhile purposes.[5]

What is design?

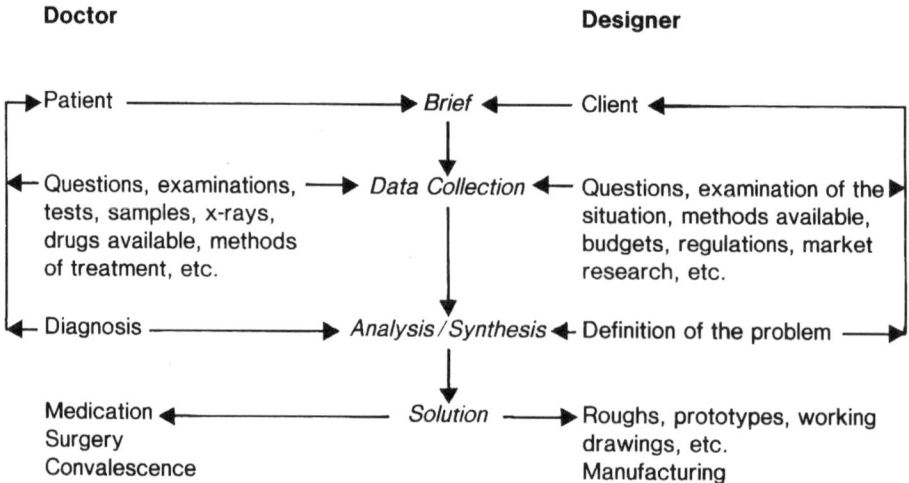

'Doctor/Designer' diagram by Max Hailstone, from *Design and Designers* (Christchurch: New Zealand Industrial Design Council and Griffin Press, 1985), 20.

This separation of advertising from graphic design is important. The idea of asserting the legitimacy of graphic design as an independent and socially accountable sphere of study had taken root in the then recently established degree-level courses at places like the London College of Printing — and also at the Manchester College of Art and Design, where Max did his postgraduate studies. While at Manchester College, he was engaged as a 'design consultant' to Germano Facetti at Penguin Books.[6] Also during his time there, he undertook research into the legibility of type, which resulted in a paper on the design of pharmaceutical labelling, which was published in the third issue of the first volume of *The Journal of Typographic Research*.[7] What I want to highlight here is the fact that the world of Typo-graphic design that Max introduced to the parochial outpost of Christchurch was taking itself pretty seriously.

As undergraduate students, we never directly asked the question 'what is design?' But, at the time, I was drawn to Max's reassuringly objective way of thinking about this profession, which was new to me. In critiques, Max liked to use the analogy that graphic designers are like doctors, and that our clients are like patients whose problems we must diagnose. The argument went that the reason a diagnosis fails (or a design fails) is because the doctor (or designer) has simply not succeeded in ascertaining the correct question. The analogy was attractive because it suggested that graphic designers have some kind of specialist knowledge, that they must be trained well, and that they are uniquely qualified to do what they do.

The 'scientisation' of design at the time was also evident in the New Zealand Industrial Design Council's periodical *Designscape*, in which designers were often pictured dressed in lab coats.[8] The shift towards scientific thinking in design may be partly attributed to the influence of some European design schools, perhaps most notably Ulm School of Design (Hochschule für Gestaltung Ulm). This saw graphic design aligned less with art and more with the social sciences. HfG Ulm was one of the first design schools to begin to articulate how the 'science' of semiotics could be adopted as a way of understanding graphic design (or 'visual communication', as they called it). Max owned a copy of issue five of *Uppercase* journal (1961), a special issue featuring work from HfG Ulm, in which Tomás Maldonado and Gui Bonsiepe published an influential series of articles on visual sign systems.[9]

This way of thinking did help me to make and critique work. Although I now know it was flawed, it proposed a rationale that was reassuring and seemed to have a clear aim: to simplify, align, clarify, reduce options, assume there was a system, and assess your work in relation to that system. So, then, an important part of my answer to the question 'what is graphic design?' was that it is an independent visual language, a language that most fundamentally promises expertise in articulating formal relationships. Because this language was often poorly understood, it could risk excluding people who were not literate in it. (But perhaps this is why I liked it.) It was as compelling as any language, a bit unstable if you wanted to say something complicated, and, although in some ways contrived, it was in other ways coherent, predictable and clearly circumscribed.

Taken negatively, this formalist, modernist teaching regime privileged dominant Western narratives, created fake or flawed authorities, reified contrived codes and procedures, and promoted problematic canons, most notably a narrative that privileges the 'great white men of history'.

In the early 1990s, when I was at Ilam, Max's projects had a lineage that might be traced back to the Basel School of Design and to the pedagogy of Wolfgang Weingart. Weingart visited us at Ilam in 1991. We all read his article in *Octavo*, a transcription of his 1972 lecture series on his approach to teaching in Basel.[10] I don't think I recognised it then, but my education with Max had been almost entirely about the syntactic dimension of Typo-graphic design — which was the article's main focus. This focus was fantastic for the design of sublime publication grids and pictogram systems. Weingart's account of the *semantic* dimension of typography, however, was less convincing. It didn't satisfy the promise of an account of purely visual semantic expression — rather, the examples seemed a bit dumb, as if merely illustrations of linguistic meaning.

I should mention that, by the early 1990s, writers, artists and critics in New Zealand had been questioning such modernist, formalist myths for quite some time. From at least the early 1980s, Wystan Curnow, for example, was writing about the postmodern rejection of art that was essentially inward-looking, and calling into question any visual art that proposed form as its primary 'content':

> Obviously, content [has] moved house, but where to? Instead of being in the work, firmly framed and recessed there, it has been 'forwarded', 'projected' into the territory it literally shares with us. Content is to be discovered not in the work, but in our interaction with the work. All observations are participations...[11]

Curnow was thinking and writing about art in a larger cultural context; he was outward-looking. By contrast, although Max was well travelled, took part in international design discourse, and was ahead of most graphic designers in New Zealand in his thinking at the time, he was still talking only about graphic design, and delivering projects to his students through an essentially modernist perspective — inward-looking, formalist projects *about* graphic design. He wasn't ignorant of art discourses, but he seemed not to care much about them. He was taking part in another discourse. His library was full of other books. In Max's defence, although we undergraduate design students all studied Art Theory, the matters of concern were worlds apart. For example, I particularly enjoyed reading Rosalind Krauss's rejection of the formalist ambitions of the modernist art world in her essay 'Grids', but I simply did not think that it was relevant to graphic design.[12] Although historically related, we in graphic design talked about the use of grids and content very differently to our art comrades.

Process and intermedia: Media Arts

After graduating from Canterbury University, I was appointed to my first job, working as the designer at the Waikato Museum of Art and History in Hamilton. Through that experience, my understanding of graphic design shifted to accommodate the less idealistic 'real world' of design — a world of restricted budgets, disorganised clients and seemingly uneducated audiences.

Unfortunately, after I had been there for five years, the Waikato Museum followed the trend in the museum world of the time, and became more market-focused. This meant an 'opening up' of the museum, and a change in focus from established curatorial and artistic concerns to questions of audience engagement and to exhibitions with a broader popular appeal. Consequently, half of the gallery staff resigned, myself included, and I began teaching at the local art school, the Waikato Institute of Technology, aka 'Wintec'.

In the mid-1990s, the School of Media Arts at Wintec was, as its name suggests, well ahead of its time in the New Zealand context, and was developing a curriculum that questioned the compartmentalisation of art school departments. When I joined, we were all talking about what we thought were postmodern theories of deconstruction, pluralist discourse, and so on. In the graphic design department, we looked to the work of designers such as Vaughan Oliver, Allen Hori, Lucille Tenazas, Lorraine Wild, Tomato and Studio Dumbar. And, of course, we were collecting — and reading — *Emigre* and *Eye* magazines. We were interested in collaboration and in unconventional ways of making. We talked about 'process' a lot. I was trying to contrive a new way of working that was documentary in method. I liked the conceit that I would no longer have to make up 'original' stuff in my work. This required an introspective attitude, trying not to impose a style, but instead looking at formal and material qualities as a 'natural' outcome of an interrogation of digital or mechanical media.

However, despite our best intentions, this 'media process' myth was, I think, still essentially formalist — like Max's ostensibly objective 'form follows function' approach. We were interested in the visual, material quality of our design work, and were not that interested in its cultural or social contexts. Whereas Max thought there was a right and a wrong process, we at Media Arts at the time wanted to intentionally mess with the making process. The object and the designer had not become less important — they had just become less *self-important*.[13]

The most interesting part of the course, for me, was that while we were talking about interdisciplinary collaboration, we were also paradoxically compelled to clarify what we were doing *within* our specific 'home' discipline. So, it was not so much about looking outwards and promoting cross-disciplinary mash-ups — or 'quackery', to echo Max's doctor analogy — but more about encouraging all of us to reflect on and be critical of the differences and similarities between disciplines. I realise now that this was an attitude that was still essentially modernist at heart.

What I mean by that is that it is essentially a modernist notion to want to differentiate between *any* disciplines or fields of knowledge. In fact, it may be the very definition of modernism, at least by one formulation. The social theorist Scott Lash explains that the primary shift from pre-modern to modern thinking started with a process of beginning to 'differentiate between cultural spheres'.[14] The dominant cultural spheres are, say, politics, religion, business, science, law, etc., but of course the same process of differentiation is at work when one distinguishes between the artistic spheres of literature, music, fine art, graphic design and advertising (as Ken Garland did).

While at Wintec, I read Johanna Drucker's book *The Visible Word*.[15] In it, she writes about the rift between the linguistic and the visual arts in the middle of the twentieth century — in a way that echoes Lash's account of modernist differentiation. Drucker's book is about the work of Dada and Futurist writers and artists of the 1910s and 1920s, whose typographic productions came from a tradition that was a synthesis of the literary and visual arts spheres:

> The challenge put forth by these complex aesthetic projects was to develop a critical method which was not derived exclusively from either literary criticism or visual arts theory and which would build on the sources and positions that had informed the original typographic work.[16]

This relationship became estranged for a whole lot of complicated reasons, resulting in a separation of linguistic and visual artistic practices. The aspect of the book I remember most fondly is Drucker's suggestion that the sphere of modern typo-graphic design took over the in-between space produced by this split — like the child of a broken family.

So, does graphic design really have any grounds for claiming to be a unique cultural practice? I'm no longer sure. Does it have its own history and mythologies? For some time, designers have questioned whether or not graphic design is an independent discipline. For example, the blurb on the inside flap of the dust jacket of Herbert Spencer's *Pioneers of Modern Typography* (1969) reads:

> Modern typography does not have its origins in the conventional printing industry. Its roots are entwined with those of twentieth-century painting, poetry and architecture, and it flowered quite suddenly and dramatically in the twenty years following the publication of Marinetti's Futurist manifesto in 1909.[17]

Part of the issue here is the question of whether any cultural sphere can really have its own unique knowledge, isolated from other influences. Scott Lash would also explain that *post*-modernisation is characterised by another shift — one towards a '*de*-differentiation of cultural spheres'. This implies a denial of autonomous disciplinary knowledge. And, to bring it back to my story about design schools, that is precisely the shift that I was still resisting, I think, at Wintec.

Intertextual browsing: Yale University

Anyway, I left Hamilton for postgraduate studies in the US in the early 2000s. And this is where it gets interesting… because I hadn't anticipated the culture shock I would experience, or the extent to which everything I had come to value in design would be discouraged. Just when I had begun to understand the documentary working method, I entered a programme that seemed to have no interest in students experimenting with, or discussing, graphic design as making.

Instead, I had to reorient myself to a course that expected us to account for the broader cultural and literary references in our work. I was pretty poor at this when I arrived at Yale, and in awe of everybody else's ability to perform design critique as discursive parlour games, full of intertextual quotations of big ideas. We looked at everything but the visual qualities of the work pinned on the wall. Instead, we would discuss references to Georges Perec, Roland Barthes or Walter Benjamin, and only obliquely talk about graphic design, which was implicitly recast as a poor cousin of higher cultural forms.

In hindsight, Yale was the perfect antidote to my previous experiences. Design for design's sake is even less rewarding than art for art's sake. And the once-new digital tools that were interesting to the previous generation of designers had become ubiquitous and were no longer worth experimenting with. We were expected to build graphic intertextuality by making work, as a prompt to develop outward-looking design projects that could reflect bigger ideas and more important content.

We watched Jean Cocteau's film *Orpheus* as a primer for a class. The story is about a poet who travels between the 'real' world and the underworld, through a mirror. A great mysterious message is transmitted from the underworld via transistor radio, 'The Mirrors would do well to reflect further'. It strikes me that this echoes a very Yale-style caution about the role of graphic design as a mirror of culture. At least, this is how it felt to me when I was there: mirrors reflect their surroundings but should not overstate their place.

Yale's introduction of intertextuality was fantastic but also flawed because it seemed to encourage us to become literary theorists or writers. At the start, Yale appeared to present an anti-aesthetic turn, whereby the critique was transferred from a material object to a discussion of imaginary content, and an intertextuality of ideas. At the time, this seemed to be a frustrating process of deflection, continually pointing elsewhere just as you landed on some seemingly stable content: 'Interesting, but what about this too?' … 'Haven't you read this?' … as if we could somehow get to the urtext. This did not help me make work. In fact, it had the opposite effect. For me, it became too open-ended, too opportunistic and too reliant upon verbal articulation.

In this discursive mode of practice, we didn't ever question the source or value of what we were drawing on. If we weren't going to talk about graphic design, how were we being assessed? There was no doubt a hierarchy at play. Popular culture and literary references were good. Art was fine. Film too. Music was good. Well, rock and roll was good… classical music was not so good, for some reason. Unfortunately, I came from a hippy upbringing, not punk, which was not so cool. Politics? Religion? I was troubled at the time by what I saw as a lack of critique surrounding our choice of content, and the politics of that choice.

I realise I am critiquing a postmodern approach with modernist assumptions. Am I conflating idioms? Probably. I found myself on the periphery of a new world that was problematising the role of graphic design in the production and exchange of content, where designers collapsed the typically separate roles of editor, designer, printer, etc., so that the development of linguistic, visual and material content could be negotiated. This world tested and questioned a graphic designer's ability to help translate, communicate and disseminate messages in an engaging way. Allow me to repeat this line from Curnow:

Content is to be discovered not in the work, but in our interaction with
the work. All observations are participations...[18]

I gradually gained an understanding of what visual or material intertextuality might be — although perhaps I only understood it fully after I graduated. The idea that a combination of the linguistic and the visual can say more than the linguistic alone is what the faculty at Yale were going for. As Michael Rock explains, it is crucial to see or *read* design as visual text:

> the designer's purview is to shape, not to write. But the shaping itself is a profoundly affecting form. ... This seems to be a rather mundane point, but for some reason we don't really believe it. We don't believe shaping is enough. So to bring design out from under the thumb of content we must go one step further and observe that treatment is, in fact, a kind of text itself, as complex and referential as any traditional understanding of content.[19]

All of this seems less fraught to me now. It has never been enough for me to merely style other people's content. This insight, once I was disabused of my need to be an expert in anything in particular, led to my realisation that, today, designers should be assessed on the grounds of the integrity of their ongoing investigations, their long-term, continually developing bodies of work — their having a 'practice'. Over the ensuing years, I came to appreciate the work of graphic designers who have developed sophisticated enquiries: Paul Elliman, Stuart Bertolotti-Bailey and David Reinfurt of Dexter Sinister, and Daniel van der Velden and Vinca Kruk of Metahaven. The work of these practitioners is, I am compelled to say, more rich than that of the design heroes of previous generations. These are, to my mind, the key protagonists for a community of graphic designers whose work aspires to be thoughtful, complex and speculative, as well as rich in references, interests and influences.

Design does not solve the darkness[20]

> 'I don't want to bother you much with what happened to me personally', he began, showing in this remark the weakness of many tellers of tales who seem so often unaware of what their audience would like best to hear; 'yet to understand the effect of it on me you ought to know how I got out there, what I saw, how I went up that river to the place where I first met the poor chap. It was the farthest point of navigation and the culminating point of my experience. It seemed somehow to throw a kind of light on everything about me — and into my thoughts. It was sombre enough, too — and pitiful — not extraordinary in any way — not very clear either. No, not very clear. And yet it seemed to throw a kind of light.[21]

So, what is design? I am interested in thinking about how the answer keeps shifting for me, or in reflecting upon the meta-question of what it means to ask that question. Perhaps the question is too big, too disingenuously finite-sounding, too seemingly objective and too ambitious. I hope my answer can be more modest and personal than that. And while I still want to defend graphic design, to differentiate between 'design' and 'graphic design', and even defend 'my New Zealand-accented Typo-Graphic Design', I also want to link graphic design to a bigger, richer and more complex discourse. Perhaps the answer lies in more questions.

Can I propose, then, an ironic, postmodern promotion of the unique cultural sphere of graphic design, where the subject I focus on is graphic design? Can I mythologise it in opposition to other cultural spheres? Can I circumscribe it tightly and link it to other things outside of itself at the same time? Does that have to be a paradox? Do you mind?

1. Max Hailstone, *Design and Designers* (Christchurch: New Zealand Industrial Design Council and Griffin Press, 1985). 'Design and Designers' is also the name of an exhibition that Luke Wood and I curated to accompany the launch of issue 8 of *The National Grid* at Ramp Gallery in Hamilton, New Zealand, in 2012, as part of the Wintec Spark conference.

2. Modern graphic design was introduced to Ilam by Maurice Askew, who established the design department in the art school. He was also influential in getting Max over from the UK to continue that trajectory.

3. Norman Potter, *What is a Designer: Education and Practice*, edited by John Lewis (London and New York: Studio Vista and Van Nostrand Reinhold, 1969).

4. Herbert Spencer, *The Visible Word* (London: Royal College of Art, 1968).

5. Ken Garland, 'First Things First', http://www.designishistory.com/1960/first-things-first/, accessed 18 December 2019.

6. From a reference letter for Max Hailstone by Germano Facetti, from Max's archive, held in a private collection.

7. Max Hailstone and Jeremy Foster, 'Studies of the Efficiency of Drug Labelling', *Journal of Typographic Research* 1, no. 3 (July 1967): 275–284.

8. Far more problematic was the journal's representation of women and its division of roles along gender lines: it seemed necessary for the mostly male designers to study ergonomics by photographing mostly female subjects without any clothes on, apparently in order to diagnose the success of a work of design, such as a chair. See: 'Sizing up our bodies', *Designscape* 69 (May 1975), 10–12.

9. Theo Crosby, ed., *Uppercase* 5 (London: Whitefriars Press, 1961).

10. See: Wolfgang Weingart, 'How Can One Make Swiss Typography?' *Octavo* 87.4, edited by Simon Johnston, Mark Holt, Michael Burke and Hamish Muir (London: Eight Five Zero, 1987). But some of Max's projects came via Rhode Island School of Design. At Ilam, we had a yearly 'Winter Session' exchange with RISD students and Max often visited Rhode Island.

11. Wystan Curnow, 'Postmodernism in Poetry and the Visual Arts', *Parallax* 1, no. 1, 1982. I quote from: Wystan Curnow, *The Critic's Part: Wystan Curnow Art Writings 1971–2013*, edited by Christina Barton and Robert Leonard (Wellington: Victoria University Press, 2014), 149.

12. Rosalind Krauss, 'Grids', in *The Originality of the Avant-Garde and Other Modernist Myths* (Cambridge, Mass. and London: MIT Press, 1985), 1.

13. This is paraphrased from Robert Morris, via Wystan Curnow. See: Wystan Curnow, 'Writing and the Post-Object', in *The Critic's Part: Wystan Curnow Art Writings 1971–2013*, edited by Christina Barton and Robert Leonard (Wellington: Victoria University Press, 2014), 385.

14. Scott Lash, 'Postmodernism: Towards a Sociological Account', in *Sociology of Postmodernism* (London, Routledge, 1991).

15. Johanna Drucker, *The Visible Word: Experimental Typography and Modern Art, 1909–1923* (Chicago: University of Chicago Press, 1994).

16. Ibid., 2.

17. Herbert Spencer, *Pioneers of Modern Typography* (London: Lund Humphries, 1969).

18. Wystan Curnow, 'Postmodernism in Poetry and the Visual Arts', *Parallax* 1, no. 1, 1982. I quote from: Curnow, *The Critic's Part*, 149.

19. Michael Rock, 'Fuck Content', in *Multiple Signatures: On Designers, Authors, Readers and Users* (New York: Rizzoli, 2013).

20. This is a quote from Paul Elliman during a panel discussion at Wellington's TypeSHED11 conference in 2009, organised by Catherine Griffiths and Simone Wolf.

21. Joseph Conrad, *Heart of Darkness* (London: Penguin Books, 1989), 32.

Care and inclusion
Sheila Levrant de Bretteville,
interviewed by Ellen Lupton

Sheila Levrant de Bretteville graduated with an MFA from Yale in 1964 and returned twenty-six years later, in 1990, as Director of Graduate Studies in graphic design. The first woman to be awarded tenure at Yale School of Art, de Bretteville is today still there, as the Caroline M. Street Professor of Graphic Design, and has over the last three decades championed diversity and inclusivity in the broadest sense. Her interrogation of modernist myths and her disruption of perceived norms in design education helped lay a new foundation for pedagogy moving into the twenty-first century. In this interview by Ellen Lupton, originally published in *Eye* magazine in 1993, de Bretteville's concerns and motivations are prescient — and enduringly relevant.

In 1990, Sheila Levrant de Bretteville became the new director of studies in graphic design at Yale University School of Art. Since the late 1950s, the Yale programme had been a bastion of modernist theory, a conduit between designers in the US and the programme in graphic design at the Kunstgewerbeschule in Basel, directed by Armin Hofmann. For more than thirty years, graduates of both programmes have profoundly influenced American design through both their professional work and their teaching.

Presiding over Yale's long and productive history was Alvin Eisenman, whose retirement in 1990 prompted a committee of faculty and design alumni to appoint a new head, a decision which will shape the programme's direction for the decades to come. The committee selected Sheila Levrant de Bretteville, who had attended Yale in the early 1960s and has since become an influential and outspoken designer and educator. As a feminist who participated in the rebirth of the women's movement in the 1970s and its critical refinement in the 1980s, de Bretteville believes that the values culturally associated with women are needed in public life. She wants designers to begin to listen to different voices, and to forge more attentive and open structures to provide opportunities for others to be heard. She wants to move design towards proactive practice instead of focusing on corporate services.

While most faculty and alumni have supported de Bretteville's inclusive definition of design, others have been outraged. Paul Rand, a member of the faculty since the late 1950s, resigned on principle, and encouraged his long-time colleague Hofmann to do the same. In an angry manifesto published in the American Institute of Graphic Arts *Journal of Graphic Design*, Rand railed against the violation of modernism by screaming hordes of historicists, deconstructivists, activists and other heretics.[1] Behind each of these recent challenges to modernism, one can name a powerful woman whose voice threatens the stability of Rand's carefully guarded ideals: behind deconstructivism stands Katherine McCoy; and behind activism stands de Bretteville. Perhaps de Bretteville's philosophy reflects an overall shift in the design profession, or perhaps it will be a catalyst for such a shift, just as the programme of Eisenman, Rand and Hofmann helped to redirect the currents of American design practice earlier in the century.

EL   How is the new programme you have instituted at Yale different from what preceded it?

SLB   When you ask a question like that, I feel reluctant to locate the differences, because notions of 'difference' have been invested with so much positive thought on my part. Also, I have a great respect for Eisenman, and for the forty years of work he did here, and for the intelligence and ecumenical spirit he brought to the endeavour.

But it is important to me that this programme be person-centred. The students are encouraged to put and find themselves in their work; my agenda is to let the differences between my students be visible in everything they do. In most projects — not just in thesis work — it's the students' job to figure out what they want to say. Emphasising the students' desire to communicate, and focusing on what needs to be said and to whom they want to say it — that's what I mean by person-ocntredness. While they may have existed before, it is even stronger now.

EL   Some faculty who were here for many years left in a spirit of protest. What resistance have you encountered from faculty or alumni or from your own students?

SLB   I think you should talk to the people who are upset. I am not upset. I am delighted. When students say they chose to come here because it scared them, because it was the most unfamiliar and most challenging programme, I consider that a positive place to start from (I think that comfort is a highly overrated emotion). It means they're beginning a journey that allows them not to become representatives of a single, unifying, totalising view that would make all their work look the same.

   I didn't need to end anything that was happening here; I needed to add what I felt had been left out. There are people for whom diversity and inclusion are terrifying and inappropriate, and they have absented themselves from teaching here. I am hoping that the students who come here are attracted by the open-minded attitude and by the opportunity to frame their own way of being in the profession.

EL   Do you think people are surprised by what you have done?

SLB   Some people have said that I should be less visible, that I should be in the background, that I should simply and invisibly support the people who are here and whom I brought. But don't those recommendations too closely match old female role notions?

   In truth, as a woman designer, no one would have known about me if I hadn't spoken out in the 1970s with a feminist reappraisal of the design arts. Focusing on one stratum of myself — gender — provided me with other ways to look at graphic design that anticipated the 1980s deconstructivism critique of the International Style. I feel aligned with Robert Venturi, Denise Scott Brown and other people who in the late 1960s and early 1970s were criticising the universalising aspects of design and the notion that there was one high, single truth that would improve the lot of everyone.

   'To be seen and not heard' was not a good thing to be told. I was not told that by the majority, however, and I was not told that by David Pease, Dean of the Art School, who was 100 percent supportive. The group of faculty and alumni that chose me, chose to send a signal to the design community about the kinds of changes they wanted to see at Yale. Since what I've done before is known, what I would do here can't have been a total surprise. No one should be surprised that I would look at things from multiple perspectives, that I would be involved in the community or that I would care about the personal voice of the designer.

EL   What do you think are the most important intellectual tools for young designers today?

SLB They need to learn about the different ways to interpret graphic design, the many different perspectives. Students should know the names and languages that go with each of these perspectives — not because jargon is useful, but because knowing about these issues enables them to participate in the debates should they choose to do so. I believe that a productive tension comes from diverse points of view, and that students should grapple with diverse points of view for any act of design.

We have given students readings from various critical perspectives, including psychoanalytic, semiotic, postmodern feminist and formalist. And we encourage them to take classes at the university, from people whose daily work is thinking from different perspectives. Our students take academic courses every semester; it's now a requirement. When I was a student here thirty years ago, we didn't have seminars with readings that allowed us to discuss different perspectives. We took courses at the university, but bringing that material back to the act of doing, and thinking about, and writing about and analysing design didn't occur in design seminars.

You asked about other kinds of tools. In order for designers to know whether the appropriate way of communicating to a particular audience is a poster, a billboard, an exhibition or an interactive hypermedia experience, they need to know what those tools can do. The choice of which format to communicate in should occur after you know whom you want to talk to, and what you want to tell them. This plays into our notion of proactivity, which is to go out into the community with issues that have meaning for you, find out who else is affected by these issues, what organisations already exist, what they are already doing, what needs have not been met and then look for what ways graphic design could communicate to those audiences who don't have access to the information that's out there for them.

EL The person focus of your programme concerns not just the designer, but the audience. The audience has a new centrality.

SLB That's correct. Because the audience is not an audience; it's a co-participant with you, and it's also your client. You bring skills, they bring their own knowledge and you are both agencies of knowledge — your knowledge as a designer, their knowledge as a person in need and the community as a group of people in need. It's a parallel construction rather than a top-down mechanism. The students here have had an experience of being alongside the client/audience/user, because they themselves are part of the group that makes up the client/audience/user.

EL How does form-making relate to these problems of addressing an audience? You talked about the format, the institutional frame of communication. How do you fill up that frame?

SLB I'm providing a variety of parallel experiences of coming to form. I personally believe in delaying form-making until you know what you need to say, to whom you need to say it and how it should be said. On the other hand, there is a hunger among our students for purely aesthetic exploration, where there is no need to communicate, where we take away the audience,

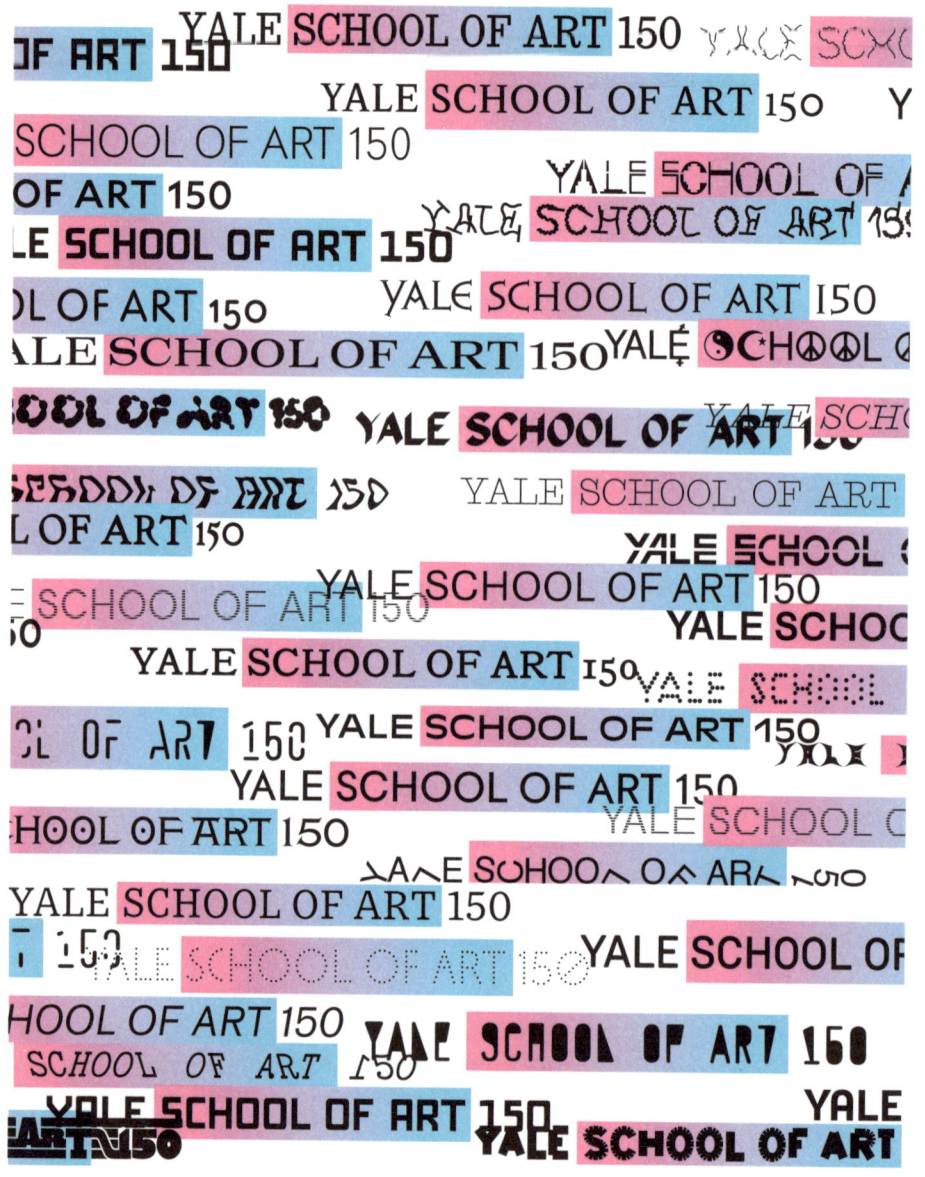

To commemorate its 150th anniversary, the Yale School of Art commissioned Sheila Levrant de Bretteville, Caroline M. Street Professor of Graphic Design and a 1964 alumnus of the Graphic Design programme, and Laura Coombs, 2017 Graphic Design alumnus and Senior Designer at the New Museum of Contemporary Art in New York, to create an anniversary mark that both celebrates and conveys the profound history of the School. Rather than creating a singular symbol, the designers collected a range of 150 interchangeable marks constructed with typefaces made by students, alumni and faculty of the School of Art. The designers include: Kyla Arsadjaja (2020 alumnus); Martin Bek (2016); Julian Bittiner (2008, and Senior Critic in Graphic Design); Matthew Carter (Senior Critic in Graphic Design); Laura Coombs (2017); João Doria (2014); Ben Fehrman-Lee (2016); Tobias Frere-Jones (Critic in Graphic Design); Moonsick Gang (2016); Ben Ganz (2017); Emma Gregoline (2019); Yotam Hadar (2015); Tiff Hockin (2013) and Stefan Thorsteinsson (2013); Shira Inbar (2014); Willis Kingery (2019); Sean Kuhnke (2014); Weiyi Li (2012); Martha Kang McGill (2014); Nate Pyper (2018); Tim Ripper (2015); Hrefna Sigurðardóttir (2018); Nina Stössinger (Critic in Graphic Design); Dirk Wachowiak (2005); Other Means (Ryan Waller, 2009); Yuanbo Wang (2020); Bryce Wilner (2018); Matthew Wolff (2018); and Christine Zavesky (2018).

where it doesn't matter if we can understand it. We just play with the materials because we can bump into a new form of expression that we could apply where it's appropriate. Pure aesthetic exploration of this kind is something I'm personally less comfortable with, so I invite people to teach here who are comfortable with it.

EL   In your 1983 essay 'Feminist Design', you describe feminist design as a set of formal, tactical moves.[2] What is 'feminist design'?

SLB   First, what is feminism? In my understanding, feminism acknowledges the past inequality of women, and doesn't want it to continue into the future. And the issue of equality broadens beyond women to involve the equality of all voices. Feminist design looks for graphic strategies that will enable us to listen to people who have not been heard before.

Thinking about myself from a gendered perspective — even if gender is a fiction — meant separating those experiences that relate to me as a gendered figure from other aspects of myself: from being from New York, being Jewish, being skinny. For me, the processes of childbearing, parenting and reading feminist writings brought social inequalities into sharper focus. There is a prevalent notion in the professional world that only if you have eight or more uninterrupted hours per day can you do significant work. But if you respond to other human beings — if you are a relational person — you never really have eight uninterrupted hours in a row.

Relational existence is not only attached to gender by history — not by genes, not by biology, not by some essential 'femaleness'. A relational person thinks about other human beings and their needs during the day. A relational person allows notions about other people to interrupt the trajectory of thinking or designing — I used to call it 'strudeling', because strudel is a layered pastry. I don't think strudeling is an exclusively female way of thinking, but I might call it a feminist way of thinking because to valorise this attitude is to separate it from gender and free it from the nineteenth-century notion that women's culture belonged entirely to the private, domestic realm.

My grandmother, my mother, my sister and I all work. In my family, private and public spheres are not separated. I could easily take on the values of the work world, since I had to work, there was no choice. The kinds of work habits that are part of this public sphere — that deny relational experience — are precisely the ones I want to challenge. Feminism has allowed me to challenge them; thinking about myself as a woman has allowed me to challenge them. When women are in the workplace, women do as the workplace demands. Part of feminism is about bringing public, professional values closer to private, domestic values, to break the boundaries of this binary system.

EL   In other conversations, you've used the word 'care' to describe feminist design. How is this relational spirit manifested in design?

SLB   In the early 1980s, I came upon a set of strategies which I thought manifested that care. These include asking a question without giving the answer, so that viewers feel their own thinking is a value. Another strategy is to have multiple perspectives, which creates a tension that enables critical thinking in a viewer. Having the words and images contradict one another also creates a productive tension, by asking the viewer to resolve the conflict and thus bring his or her thinking process and point of view into play. Another principle is to be there in the street of your audience, who can give you feedback on how they understand it. Once you've experienced this, you are transformed in your notion of who the client is. Last year a group of our students designed a pro-choice billboard for a course taught by Marlene McCarty and Donald Moffett. (Marlene and Donald work together in the design studio Bureau, and they're members of the AIDS activist group Gran Fury.) They gave the students a newspaper and asked them to locate an issue they felt was important. A group of students who chose reproductive rights analysed US laws, looked at what local and national organisations are doing, and finally decided to provide a fact: '73 per cent of Americans are pro-choice'. By providing a statistical fact that most people didn't know, they would allow viewers to think that perhaps they were being manipulated by media coverage of pro-lifers.

EL   The formal language of the billboard is the expected language of mass media. It doesn't have a 'design' look.

SLB   That's intentional. The students didn't want the aesthetic position to be the primary reading. They don't want you to think how nice it looks and wonder who designed it before receiving the information.

EL   A lot of contemporary writing about design, especially writing influenced by postmodernism and contemporary literary theory, suggests that when images and messages become completely layered, a political challenge occurs, because the design forces the viewer to discover the meaning. In the situation you've just described, a decision was made to be clear and direct. What do you think about the aesthetics of complexity?

SLB   These ideas are not mutually exclusive. On a billboard, which you have about three seconds to understand, a caring and inclusive design strategy can only be enacted in certain ways. On the other hand, when there's more time for the audience to be in front of the design communication, then more complex strategies that provoke a thinking audience to feel and resolve the tension are appropriate.

EL   A lot has happened since you studied at Yale thirty years ago — the protest movements of the 1960s, the feminist revolution of the 1970s, the theoretical research of the 1980s. How have the conditions changed that once made modernism seem viable?

SLB   I will never, never, never forget to include people of colour, people of different points of view, people of both genders, people of different sexual preferences. It's just not possible any more to move without remembering. That is something that modernism didn't account for; it didn't want to recognise regional and personal differences.

People who have given their whole lives to supporting the classicising aesthetic of modernism feel invalidated when we talk about the necessary inclusiveness, but diversity and inclusiveness are our only hope. It is not possible any more to plaster over everything with clean elegance. Dirty architecture, fuzzy theory and dirty design must be there.

EL   Many younger women are afraid of the word 'feminism', though they might support its principles. You've suggested that feminism is not just for women, but that it's an attitude for including everybody. Do you think that feminism could be a design philosophy for the 1990s, an aesthetic and ethical attitude that could help fill the void left by modernism?

SLB   I believe that gender is a cultural fiction, not a biological given. But while there have been many achievements in the last twenty years, racism and sexism are still rife. Some responses to my presence here really do come because people attach what I do to the fact that I am a woman. Those things have to become detached. But until we are able to detach gender from the ways we are in the world, it's important for us to move towards equality. Moving towards equality is what the word feminism means. Until we've achieved that, we can't give up the word. Feminist design is an effort to bring the values of the domestic sphere into the public sphere; feminist design is about letting diverse voices be heard through caring, relational strategies of working and designing. Until social and economic inequalities are changed, I am going to call good design feminist design.

This interview was first published as 'Reputations: Sheila Levrant de Bretteville' in *Eye*, no. 8, vol. 2, 1993.

[1]   Paul Rand, 'Confusion and Chaos: The Seduction of Contemporary Graphic Design', *AIGA Journal of Graphic Design* 10, no. 1 (1992).

[2]   Sheila Levrant de Bretteville, 'Feminist Design', *Space and Society* 6, no. 2 (1983): 98–103.

The most dangerous design school in the world
Lucille Tenazas, interviewed by Europa

Throughout the 1980s and 1990s, the influence of a small graduate programme in Michigan was felt not only across the US but internationally. Under the leadership of Designer-in-Residence Katherine McCoy, the 2D Design programme at Cranbrook Academy of Art during that era drew theoretical and social concerns into practice in new ways, and was a key player in the challenge to the hegemony of the modernist tradition in American graphic design. Lucille Tenazas is one of the most influential designers to have graduated from Cranbrook during that time. In this conversation with Robert Sollis of London-based studio Europa, Tenazas reflects upon the significance of the Cranbrook model, the ways in which she discovered her own voice as a graphic designer, and her convictions as a design educator today.

RS I wanted to start without any assumptions and ask you to talk us through the defining creative moments in your career, be that as a graphic designer or as an educator. Were there significant creative shifts that you recognise?

LT The turning point for me was trying to go beyond the formal — going from syntax to semantics, and I mean semantics in the sense of linguistics, which to me is really about meaning. There are people who are intuitively very good makers and craftspeople, they have a very good understanding of material and form, and I was very good with that. When I arrived in the US, my approach was still very formal. At the time, Californian design was moving through a flurry of colour, led by people like April Greiman, and I was swept along with that. But when I moved over to Cranbrook, I started to look beyond form. My design studies in the Philippines did not include anything about design history, so I had to go back and try to understand the antecedents of this discipline. All I knew was there was Swiss design and then there was Milton Glaser.

I had two epiphanies as a graphic designer. The first was at Cranbrook, moving away from strict formalism towards a deeper understanding of typography, extending to semantics and considering nuance and meaning. During that period in the late 1970s and early 1980s, Swiss design was widely regarded as the model, but people like Wolfgang Weingart and Bruno Monguzzi were approaching design as something more than just straight Helvetica; there was a kind of flourish to the work — and, as design students, we blindly copied that. We looked at them as our idols, thinking Univers never looked so good!

The second epiphany also relates to Cranbrook. I graduated in 1982 — nearly thirty-five years ago. We had no computers and none of the tools students have now. I look back on my experience at Cranbrook, putting all the tools away, and ask: what did graduate school give me? What, specifically, did Cranbrook give me? For me, it was this acknowledgement that there is this constant reinvention, a constant adaptation, so that you always feel relevant, regardless of how one is producing work.

RS My students and I recently revisited Sheila Levrant de Bretteville's text 'A reexamination of some aspects of the design arts from the perspective of a woman designer', in which she says: 'designers are often taught to reduce things to their essence, but in fact that process too often results in the reduction of the ideas to only one of their parts'. This statement still resonates with me today. Is this something that you have explored at any point in your career?

LT A reductivist design approach does not mean that its visual meaning is compromised. My husband is a photographer and an artist who works with very direct, singular images. Before we met, I was working with a very complex, layered approach. There are many layers of reading that you can return to and try to decipher — there's a lot of nuance. I would describe my work as layered, but it's not cluttered, it's quite disciplined. As I started to consider de-cluttering my work, I became interested in the idea of conceptual layering, as opposed to formal layering. And what that meant was a reduction of unnecessary elements, so that the remainder was thoughtfully considered, while amplifying meaning. I realised that restraint was also very much about structure. My father was a civil engineer and my mother a history and social studies teacher, so the dichotomy of left brain/right brain thinking was present in me from an early age. I think my father had an influence on me: my work has always had this kind of architectonic quality that relies a lot on underlying structures and systems.

RS   So you felt that as the work became more conceptually layered it should simplify formally?

LT   The most simple modern architecture is the most difficult to achieve because you can't hide anything, everything is exposed. I consider my own approach to be similar, taking a reductive standpoint and working intensively on the elements that make it rich — things like the typography, the printing method, the weight of the paper, a certain colour and lots of attention to production details. In the past, I didn't have to be careful about the paper stock because the layered image was the most important element. In my previous work, you could look at it and be drawn in, try to lift some of the layers. With my later work, I felt I could still achieve this, decoding layers of meaning as opposed to layers of form, making the approach more intellectually enriching, less reliant on form.

RS   What are you working on now?

LT   I'm working on my monograph, which has been in process, off and on, for the last seventeen years, by which I mean the contract has been sitting in my files, unsigned for that long. Over the years, I would have bursts of ideas and try to design my book in sections, but I was never fully convinced that the approaches represented my authentic experience. I was ambivalent about what kind of book it should be, since I was not interested in a traditional monograph, in the conventional approach to a design portfolio, dictated by chronology. I wanted to make a book about my evolution as a designer, taking into account my cultural background as someone born and raised in the Philippines, which provided a rich underpinning to my work, without the obvious cultural and visual signifiers. It was through ongoing conversations with colleagues in the UK — Teal Triggs and Adrian Shaughnessy, in particular, both from the Royal College of Art in London — that I was able to determine the conceptual framework of my book, synthesising my thinking as a designer, influenced by my rich cultural narrative and my role as a design educator.
    Growing up in Manila, we were taught English in school, so I am bilingual, as well as conversant in one of the 120 regional dialects spoken in a country of over seven thousand islands. I have crossed these linguistic frontiers constantly and automatically, so my knowledge of the constructions of grammar is often combined with the delicate nuances of hidden meanings that open themselves up to association. I wanted to free myself of the colonial nature of my relationship with the English language, to subdue it and make it my own. So when people ask, 'what about the Philippines is in your

work?', I say, 'well, it's not visible immediately, there are no hallmarks of tropical colours, palm trees, etc., but it goes deeper than mere visual signifiers'.

I've been working on the book about once a week between other commitments, and I've made a conscious decision to create new work that addresses some of these issues, to create a kind of genealogy. For example, I have these tribal hair combs that were given to me in the Philippines, which I used to wear for many different occasions. I think I can unravel a whole cultural history with these kinds of objects. So I'm thinking: how to show extant work as a theme? How can this story unfold over a 200-page book?

RS It's fascinating to take on your monograph in such an active and creative way. It sounds scary to be asked to work on your own monograph, almost like writing your own obituary. It's great that you're bringing life to something that is so often associated with the end of a career.

LT When I was young, graphic design to me was about creating something: it was about producing a body of work that you can handle, that you can touch, that you can see. I was so married to the idea that design equals artefact. But then, when I became an educator, I realised that something had to give. I've always seen teaching and designing as very fluid and seamless, I've never made compromises with either, but in some ways the teaching work seemed less quantifiable. As an educator, you have to be perpetually relevant — that's a consciousness that you have in your work and you need to be able to give that to your students. The kind of passion you possessed when you were young has to be maintained. It's an ongoing journey.

A friend recently pointed out that my contribution to the discipline of design is not always an artefact, but is often walking around on two legs. These students and what I have ingrained in them will live on into the next generation. My past students are themselves now teaching, and whoever they're teaching will, in turn, pass on the values and ideas I taught — it's become this exponential process. It was disconcerting for a while, because I was so tied to the idea of making things — yet another book, yet another object. But I see teaching as the creation of an environment that is generous and hospitable.

RS I think the creativity it takes to be a teacher is often underestimated. It's almost thought of as a less creative discipline than design, but, for me, it just feels like a complete creative practice.

LT Exactly — for the good teachers, at least. There are teachers who have 'retired', who have become dead wood at their institutions. It's those people who, I think you're saying, give education a bad name. I meet a lot of these people at education conferences — people who are in a position to inspire but they are not inspiring.

RS It's terrible to have someone in that position who has completely lost the joy of discovering new things for themselves. The students need that so strongly. Do you feel that the cultural starting points that fed a lot of your work also come into your teaching? Are you asking your students to consider their cultural backgrounds?

LT   Definitely. Parsons has a big international population, and I also give workshops all over the world. Even if I don't speak the language of the country I am in, design can transcend that. I like to hear students speak in their native language, I try to read in their body language what they're saying. But of course I can also see the work, I can 'read' that.

On the first day of teaching a new class, I go through the roster, asking each student to raise their hand when I call their name, and I ask if there is a name they would like to be called. Some people stick to their legal names, and I try very hard to pronounce it correctly. That first effort is very important to me and to them.

As an educator, I encourage my students to use their cultural background as a filter — to look back on who they are, but without nostalgia. Some of them are uncomfortable with that approach; they think that design is about a service and a response to a problem posed by a client. But I think there's a universality to design that can transcend anything that is culturally specific. We try to encourage that in the work. For example, I've given this project to choose a person, place or thing that I would never encounter in a guidebook, that will be my entry point into an unfamiliar place, that will provide an authentic experience of your city. Typically, the first thing they come up with is a place; 90 percent will talk about a specific location. But then I will encourage them to dig deeper. What about that grandmother who makes the most authentic pasta? That neighbour who happens to have this amazing calligraphic hand? Isn't that more unique? So, of course, on the second day around 50 percent are talking about people. It's about shifting away from a predictable approach, beyond what a guidebook offers. I talk about very close observations, looking at each other, looking at things that are not necessarily prescribed, not in a book, not because somebody told you, but something that you know yourself, that is your authentic voice.

RS   At what point did you feel comfortable using your own 'authentic' voice?

LT   After being rejected by Cranbrook twice, I had set my sights on finishing my second degree in San Francisco. But coincidentally I have an aunt who lives in Michigan, ten minutes away from Cranbrook. I visited her during the Christmas holidays, with my portfolio, and she suggested that I try to show my work to the programme directors at Cranbrook again. It was the winter break, but I called anyway. Katherine McCoy, who was the Designer-in-Residence at that time with her husband, Michael McCoy, happened to answer the phone and I managed to set up a meeting. It went really well and I was offered a place, despite it being the middle of the academic term.

At the time, I was still in my mindset (though slowly weaning myself off of it) that the Western attitude was better. After studying for six months at California College of Arts and Crafts (CCAC), which is now California College of the Arts (CCA), in San Francisco, I came to the realisation that my design work was less and less inferior. I think my time in California showed me that

I was on equal footing with these other students. When I started at Cranbrook in spring 1980, the current students returned from their winter vacations and noticed this newcomer they didn't know, occupying one of the studios — obviously a foreigner. I think they thought I probably didn't speak English.

RS   Were they mostly American students? Or were there other international students there?

LT   Cranbrook is small and selective, with only 120 graduate students in nine programmes, of which 10 percent are international students. There was a student from Hong Kong, and another from Tokyo. They gave me a studio next to these two men, so we considered ourselves the Asian contingent. When I was there, some students in the design programme were from Germany, Lebanon, Canada and Taiwan. But it was mostly Americans, who were from all over the country. In fact, there was only one person from Michigan. People came from New York, the Midwest, Texas. As I started to get acclimated to the new studio environment, I developed confidence in my work and in my ability to interact, to articulate my design process and to give feedback to my colleagues. People were often amazed by my facility with the English language and how I could communicate effortlessly. For me, this was a chance to talk about the cultural history of the Philippines, the influence of language in a country colonised by the Spanish and then the Americans — it was an opportunity to teach.

RS   I'm interested to find out more about Katherine McCoy. It sounds like she was taking strong and deliberate decisions at Cranbrook. Could you say anything more about what she was like and the atmosphere she created?

LT   Cranbrook has a unique system, in that the programmes are run by Artists- or Designers-in-Residence. Ostensibly they are the mentors for the duration of a student's two-year graduate study. Kathy was in charge of 2D Design, and Mike McCoy, 3D — the students were split up that way, although the openness of the studio layout made for fluid and ongoing discussions and interactions. In this environment, students learned from each other. There was no structure, we only met officially once a week. We could go into our studios, which were accessible twenty-four hours, at any time; there were no classes, no grades. We would be given a project and then on Thursdays, critique day, everybody went crazy. Because that's the one day you were required to really put in the work and be committed and engaged. They didn't care what you did the rest of the week. For those of us who were there working, we relied on each other's opinions and ideas, it was very porous. You could go into somebody's studio and just discuss what was on the wall, or go to a museum, or discover a new Chinese restaurant. It was as if life was prescribed like that by the school, by the parameters of the project as well as the days of the critique. If I think about it, there was no mentor per se — the McCoys *were* our mentors, we were answerable to them because they gave the projects, but it was not the kind of traditional classroom or studio environment that other academic institutions have.

Lucille Tenazas, *Street Signs project: Woodward Avenue*, 1981. This assignment, undertaken during Tenazas's studies at Cranbrook Academy of Art, was pivotal in her development as a designer. The assignment consists of several visual and typographic compositions documenting a street block near Detroit, one of which is shown here.

RS   Were they very tough on those critique days?

LT   We were tough on each other. Kathy would come around a couple of days before so that she was in the loop with what we were doing. She would look at our progress, going from one studio to another. She was very opinionated, and would suggest lots of books and references. The studios are just separated by the bookcases, and so sometimes other students would overhear what was going on; people just felt free to come over and join in the conversation. We were all recognising things in each other. I think we felt that we had a certain sense of responsibility to each other, to help and inspire one another. My relationships with the people who went to Cranbrook are still strong: we were embedded in the ethos and know what we've all been through.

RS   It's really fascinating how these dynamics are created. Do you think part of the intensity was that it was just twenty people in a class? Do you think if the student group was much larger it wouldn't have worked in the same way?

LT   Exactly. Every year, ten people graduated and then ten people came in. And because of my unusual situation of arriving in the middle of the academic year, I straddled three sets of student groups and feel lucky to have known more than the usual number of student overlaps. But your assessment is right: people couldn't disappear, you were so visible, and the McCoys also expected that your voice would be heard.
   We were also encouraged to go to the different making studios, i.e., ceramics, metalsmithing, fibre; to interact with students and faculty in architecture; to see what students in photography and printmaking were working on. Because of the small number of students in the whole academy, divided among nine disciplines, we knew we were a select few and took advantage of this small, intimate environment.

RS   Were you working on the same assignments as the people in the year group above?

LT   We would overlap; it was very fluid. We had our own projects, but we had the option to participate in the same assignments should we be interested.

RS   For me, it's really fascinating to understand the dynamics of different educational structures. Slight structural shifts in the way things are set up create such different experiences for students.

LT   I think that, for many institutions, Communication Design is looked at as a cash cow, so they are less selective in their admission processes. When I look back on my experience at Cranbrook, I think it's unique. Cranbrook was modelled after the Bauhaus, a laboratory where students lived and worked together, having this very close interaction with a few people. Cranbrook was located seventeen miles outside of Detroit, amidst an idyllic setting of three hundred acres designed by Eliel Saarinen, father of Eero Saarinen, who was a contemporary of the mid-century designers Charles and Ray Eames. In a way, this insular, concentrated environment was the perfect context for design ideas to develop and germinate.

But I also think it was very serendipitous to be back there visiting my aunt, and this leading to my acceptance into Cranbrook. I have always believed in circumstances that align to one's advantage, perhaps seen as luck by others. I gave a lecture recently on luck, and about meeting opportunity halfway, being open-minded and receptive without necessarily anticipating an outcome. This attitude relies on a certain level of trust in what you are capable of doing, and anticipating that others can support you in those endeavours that lead to fruition.

After graduating from Cranbrook, I came to New York as a young designer, where I encountered art directors who were sceptical about my portfolio, which included several experimental projects. At the time, people thought a graduate degree was unnecessary; there were very few Masters programmes in design. I thought my work was strong, and that I could articulate my design process. But most art directors couldn't look beyond the work in a professional context; they thought the aesthetic was inappropriate for their work, which relied on a commercial approach. The more I got those comments, the more firmly I felt that they were so conventional in their thinking. I had encouragement from my Cranbrook classmates, and from the McCoys. They said I should believe in the work that I was doing.

RS   How long did these kind of exchanges last before you found work?

LT   I'll give you a little bit of a side story. I went to sixty-five interviews in New York in early 1982, spanning five months. The first interview was with Michael Beirut, who was then a young designer working at Vignelli, and he arranged for me to meet Massimo Vignelli. I dropped off my portfolio in advance of the meeting, but the interview was cancelled at the last minute.

In spite of this disappointment, I went through my list of studios, continued my search, calling to schedule interviews and thought nothing of this cancelled appointment. Then, years later, when I was looking through my archives, I came across a copy of a letter I sent to a classmate where I lamented the fact that Massimo cancelled the interview when he found out that I went to Cranbrook. So that was the reason. I had totally forgotten about it.

Around twenty years ago, Massimo said that Cranbrook was 'the most dangerous design school in the world'.[1] For a designer who uses just five fonts, perhaps the work from Cranbrook was disconcerting. But, even so, labelling Cranbrook as a dangerous school did not make sense. Isn't the role of schools to encourage experimentation and the creation of new knowledge? I realised then that there are those who have reached the pinnacle of their careers and cannot be accepting of or generous towards those who come after them.

RS   By this point, he was such a significant figure who was clearly confident in his work, why should he feel threatened? Shouldn't he be excited by these new approaches?

I stumbled upon a phrase in reference to some of the experimental typographic work of the 1980s and early 1990s — it said that it represented a 'devolution of communication'. I find this subject of hierarchy and power in design really interesting and wondered if you saw this work as a way of devolving power or perhaps resisting the hierarchies of modernism?

LT   The clarity and hierarchies that characterised modernism were bound to be questioned and disrupted by those who wanted to decentralise power and break away from the tenets of a prevailing school of thought. I came upon these dogmatic approaches as a somewhat naïve young designer, arriving in a new country and eager to try new approaches. In reaction to this, I was easily seduced by the California New Wave movement practised most notably by April Greiman and Jayme Odgers, as well as the famous flock of designers named 'Michael' in San Francisco. This shift in focus effectively moved the centre of design gravity away from the east coast, where the norm was corporate and conservative, to the west — and it slowly permeated the rest of the country, with the design boom in key cities in the south and the Midwest.

It felt like a natural extension of my cultural background, which was characterised by a more intuitive and craft-based sensibility, with no foundation in Western design history. If anything, the process was a freeing methodology, offering a way out of the straitjacket of Swiss modernism. It was visually engaging and a stark departure from the shackles of the grid and prescribed typography. What made my work different from other designers who were eager to take this on, perhaps indiscriminately, was that I was able to effectively use principles of fragmentation in both image and text in my work, but also reinforce it with an architectonic quality that had an underlying systematic structure. My interest in the importance of content and the accessibility of the text was the overarching priority.

1   See: Laurel Harper, *Radical Graphics/Graphic Radicals* (San Francisco: Chronicle Books, 1999), 65. [Editors' note: Following a hunch that Vignelli's comment had perhaps been captured in an early interview in *Emigre* or *Print*, the authors and editors asked Katherine McCoy if she knew its source. She offered the following insights and context: 'As I recall, Massimo made this pronouncement during a design conference panel discussion, perhaps organized by the New York City AIGA chapter. I'm not sure if Massimo repeated it again or if it was ever quoted in print by a writer who heard it first-hand. As you can imagine, back at the time, it provoked much comment and hilarity in the Design Department. We've always considered it a compliment and a significant credential. Some background: Massimo and I enjoyed a long connection that included affection, admiration, disagreement, and debate. My first design critique came from Massimo, about my first printed piece at age 22, while I was a junior designer at Unimark International and Massimo was Executive Vice President: "Too contrived!" Through the years we crossed paths many times. He visited Cranbrook c. 1977 and he hired at least two of our graduates. I treasure the memory of our last visit in his handsome NYC home two weeks before his passing.' Katherine McCoy, in an email to Brad Haylock, 9 April 2019, printed with permission.]

The critical turn: education of a design writer
Teal Triggs

In the mid-1990s, in the early days of the internet, graphic designers lamented the 'end of print'. However, the first two decades of the twenty-first century have seen an explosion of activity from graphic designers discovering their own agency to publish — often independently and, significantly, in print. A logical parallel development has been a growing interest amongst graphic designers to research and write about their own discipline. Drawing upon her experience as a design writer and educator, Teal Triggs reflects here upon her own infuences, upon recent developments in critical writing in design, and upon what a 'critical turn' might mean for graphic design education.

I have been revisiting a few of the key articles and books about art criticism that at one time provided me with insights into the subject's history. My introduction to criticism emerged in the mid-1970s as a student in the Art Department at the University of Texas at Austin. I remember studying the American art critic Clement Greenberg's writings with some interest, but also mulling over the pages of *Artforum* — the then-cutting-edge contemporary American art magazine, which was designed in a distinctive square 10½-inch format. Over the decades, a roll call of notable contributing editors of *Artforum* (such as Philip Leider, John Coplans, James Monte, Max Kozloff, Barbara Rose and Rosalind Krauss) built upon or reacted against Greenberg's formalist art criticism. His perspective and those of his fellow critics (some of whom were practising artists), clearly shaped the discourse of contemporary art.[1] As the founding editor of *Artforum*, Leider, argued: 'what a critic can do is influence *you* as to what to look at — what to take seriously — and what not to take seriously'.[2]

When I reflect on the publications produced in the field of graphic design, a similar relationship between the editors, critics and practitioners emerges, as does a distinct discourse. *Emigre* and *Eye* magazines are pivotal influences. I would not be the first to suggest that the development of criticism as a practice in graphic design still lags behind that of other arts-related disciplines, such as fine art and architecture. In 1983, Massimo Vignelli observed in his keynote address for 'The First Symposium on the History of Graphic Design' that 'We need to produce continuous criticism which will push us forward into the right place, showing us the appropriate directions… Do you think we can go on without criticism? Without criticism we will never have a profession.'[3] Over a decade later, in 1995, the American designer Michael Rock and the British design critic Rick Poynor took a similar stance in relation to criticism as a practice and argued that 'for graphic design criticism to exist in the sense that it does in other disciplines, and with the same variety of perspectives, it will need dedicated writers'.[4]

In the 2000s, a handful of select academic institutions responded to an increased interest in the role of writing and criticism in the design profession by establishing new Master's programmes. The School of Visual Arts in New York, the London College of Communication and the Royal College of Art in London, for example, shaped curricula in order for designers and writers to come together and develop their writing skills and critical thinking about design.[5] In part, these programmes emerged out of debates around graphic authorship, where new voices, some highly politicised, were searching for relevant platforms to instigate critical discourse. Designers such as the Amsterdam-based duo Metahaven pointed to new articulations of graphic design as embracing theoretical and critical perspectives on, for example, notions of branding and identity.[6] Their work followed in the footsteps of designers such as Jan van Toorn, Ken Garland and Richard Hollis, who have successfully taken a critical position on the contexts in which they are operating — whether it is in the format of provocations or through visual essays set to change a viewer's perspective. Along with initiatives such as the 'First Things First Manifesto 2000', a resurgence of the politicisation of design emerged and captured the imagination of graphic design students who were discovering ways to make an impact on the world. It was within this context that we began to see the articulation of design writing and the roles of criticism and critical practice as serious topics for academic study.

This essay seeks to speculate on what might happen next with design writing, criticism and recent explorations into critical practice. It asks: what is the critical turn in graphic design and where is it located? And, ultimately, what impact might this have on graphic design education? Before we continue, it is worth defining some of the key terms and recognising some of the nuances of how writing and criticism are used in design. Design writing describes a process by which the resulting texts and/or visuals locate 'design' as its primary focus, whether this focus is on objects, issues, etc., as conveyed through an authorial positioning. Whilst a design critic might also be a writer, the assumption is that design writing is a sustained 'distinctive style and voice'[7] that conveys an interpretation, opinion or judgment upon design.[8] In addition, a definition of critical practice argues for the idea of 'improving' something through design, engaging with reflective practice as a way of challenging the designer's process or contexts, resulting in a focus on 'discursive and propositional ends'.[9]

My own experiences as a design educator and writer are inserted into the discussion at various points in this essay to elucidate the ways in which my pedagogical approach has been informed not only by my own practice but also, importantly, by the students, academics and designers I have the privilege to know. By way of examples, this essay identifies three independently produced, academically led journals. Whilst the field has had only a handful of notable mainstream publishing avenues for design writing and criticism, alternative platforms have emerged and will continue to emerge within an academic context. The three publications highlighted in this essay have in some way contributed to a timeline of independently produced and academically led publications that continue to run parallel to mainstream graphic design magazine publishing. Their significance resides in their capacity as experimental platforms for emerging writers and editors to publish and for new kinds of critical perspectives to evolve. The publications I will focus on in this essay are: *Zed: A Journal of Design* (1994–2000, hereafter *Zed*), edited and designed by Katie Salen; *That New Design Smell* (2011–), produced by Michèle Champagne; and *Modes of Criticism* (2015–), edited and designed by Francisco Laranjo. *Zed* sought to promote design in relationship to cultural theory, design artefacts and digital technologies, whilst *That New Design Smell* and *Modes of Criticism* focus on the critique of design, often in relation to social and political contexts. I am also interested in the move away from journalistic accounts *about* graphic design practice, towards introducing distinct editorial and critical inquiries *into* graphic design practice and the environment in which it operates. And, whilst Leider's definition of the role of the critic establishes criticism as a position of influence, it is also necessary to expect that criticism should stimulate 'new forms of practice and expression'.[10]

I selected these publications because they all embody aspects of approaches to design writing and critical practice that have a place in my own pedagogical thinking. *Zed* was, from its inception, a design journal that set out to 'identify and embrace the margins' and to focus on 'the fundamental issues of concern to practitioners, educators, and students as a group' in the field of visual communication. *Zed* was produced in the 1990s, when designers, academics and students could have 'access to visible forums'. The journal was unique at the time in its intent to bridge both printed and digital formats for experimental writing. *Zed* embraced the broader context of cultural theory and 'critical issues addressing technology'.[11] Nearly two decades later, the subsequent two publications, *That New Design Smell* and *Modes of Criticism*, also emerged out of the academy but signalled a welcome shift from an entirely Anglo-American perspective and indeed they include a critique, in some cases, of that perspective. For example, to their critical understanding, Champagne and Laranjo bring individual educational and cultural perspectives fostered by their experiences as students and designers in the Netherlands and Canada and in the UK and Portugal, respectively. The publications also exhibit other qualities that offer a way of looking to the future — not only for writing but also in how we approach graphic design practice.

As the discipline of graphic design has evolved, we are slowly coming to understand and appreciate the significance of the practitioner as editor, writer, critic, historian and curator. We might raise questions as to what the design practitioner brings to the shape of design writing and criticism that those who have trained outside the subject do not. In a similar way to *Artforum*, where many of its writers began their careers as practising artists, graphic design criticism, too, has evolved out of the practice of the subject. The practitioner's role as writer and critic is an established tradition in graphic design, from the early writings of Bauhaus members to recent online publishing ventures by contributors to design magazines such as *Design Observer*. The practitioner-critic provides graphic design with another and equally valid critical lens and, I would argue, one that impacts not only written criticism, but the very notion of critical design practice itself. Jessica Helfand, for example, had a clear-cut response to Poynor's *Design Observer* piece, 'Where are the Design Critics?',[12] when she said: 'but one thing I do know, and that is this: to the degree that everyone sees design as their business — and they do — design criticism needs designers as critics'.[13] And, if the example of *Artforum*'s successful entry into commissioning practitioners as critics is anything to go by, there is hope yet for a similar pathway to be forged in graphic design criticism.

Part I: The critical turn

To begin, we need to define the concept of the 'turn' — a term that suggests a shift from one paradigm to another. This phrase means 'to affect' and is often used to explain new directions in disciplines ranging from tourism studies and critical theory to language and intercultural communication. In design, Bruce Archer described this succinctly in his foreword to Klaus Krippendorff's treatise, *The Semantic Turn: A New Foundation for Design*, where he argued that any paradigm shift requires 'a new generation of proponents, a fertile cultural climate, but also significant technological advances'.[14] Although focusing on the 'semantic turn' in product design, Krippendorff provides a clear indicator as to the ways in which we can 'reconceptualise the world' to encourage new practices. He explains: 'a requirement for introducing changes in a discourse is that the discourse remains *rearticulable*, that its users can understand, practice and speak about these changes'.[15]

Two years later, the curator and art theorist Irit Rogoff revitalised the phrase 'educational turn', which originated in the mid-1990s, and applied it to curatorial contemporary art practice. She described the turn as a shift from object-orientated display to a practice that focusses on the production of processes. She argued that this turn was represented by the development of new formats and methods, especially those found in 'conversations' — a process that for Rogoff became central to the articulation of knowledge.[16] These conversations took the form of 'public' declamations and were centred on discussions around the theme of education — a process itself considered to be transformative.[17]

Both Krippendorff and Rogoff have something to offer in terms of the ways we might describe the 'critical turn' in graphic design. Graphic designers increasingly find themselves operating within a condition of perpetual change, responding to unstable cultural, political, economic and technological environments. For example: the economic impact of Brexit, the polarising effect of the forty-fifth American Presidency, a generalised sense of the threat of terrorism, and the recent focus on information leaks and cybersecurity. For designers, this climate presents a real need to develop new strategies for addressing such wicked problems and contributing towards positive global and social change. This challenge was not lost on Richard Buchanan in his conference keynote for 'New Views 2: Conversations and Dialogues in Graphic Design' (2008), where he stated his concern: 'I'm worried about graphic design. It's at a critical turning point. The window of opportunity is about to close.'[18]

The complexity of wicked problems has led to designers asking what it means to be critical and to identify and propose effective design responses. It may be argued that the contemporary demands on design practitioners have, to some extent, taught graphic designers to be 'critics' — that is, to adopt a critical design practice that reframes the boundaries of design as an integrated part of the process of making. Thus, it is through critical practice that designers are reflecting, iterating and innovating graphic design solutions. Whilst graphic designers continue to be obsessed with graphic artefacts (such as arguing that print is certainly not dead), designers have also considered the role of the 'critical' in speculative processes (for example, in design fiction, or as in the work of designer and educator Denise Gonzales-Crisp and her term 'designwrights'),[19] and new methods of social design practice (for example, the discipline known as 'transition design'). At the same time, sites for critical practice have also expanded over the last decade to include: exhibitions, such as Zak Kyes's *Forms of Inquiry: The Architecture of Critical Graphic Design* (2007); alternative sites of critical production, such as Dexter Sinister's 'The Serving Library' (2006–); and specific design criticism conferences, such as 'AIGA Blunt: Explicit and Graphic Design Criticism Now' (2013). This is also the context in which *That New Design Smell* and *Modes of Criticism* have been making their intervention and which *Zed* predicated a decade before — a discussion of which follows.

As a sidebar, we might also be able to draw closer parallels with the field of architecture, since graphic designers often look to the theoretical and historical traditions offered by architectural criticism to locate frameworks for design. Architect and educator Markus Miessen, for example, in an interview for a special issue of *Archis*, 'Ways to be Critical' (2013), described the ways in which architectural criticism has 'changed from verbal or written criticism, to the attempt to actually practice that criticism'.[20] Similar parallels may be drawn in how we are seeing not only a shift from writing to graphic design outcomes, but also a focus on the ways in which critical practice may be fully integrated into the process of design. Educator Tara Winters elaborates upon this in her essay 'The Practitioner-Researcher Contribution to a Developing Criticism for Graphic Design', by arguing that 'critical exchanges from the community of practice and practitioner-produced writing and theory offer an alternative to the model of the outside critic looking in'.[21]

Design Writing Criticism: a pedagogical approach
As part of the Master's of Design Writing Criticism course, which I led from 2008 to 2012 at the London College of Communication, University of the Arts London, I sought to enable exploration of writing *about* design, writing *into* design, and design *as* writing.[22] The students were primarily from design or architectural backgrounds and were keen to expand their 'point of view', building upon the skills they brought to their studies as designers. The curriculum was written to promote the use of critical reflection as part of the 'making' process in order to establish authorial positioning, and, by doing so, bring different kinds of insights to the process of writing, criticism and design practice. This was achieved through a series of short exercises and longer projects emphasising different elements of the craft and techniques of writing, exploring new methods for design writing research, and applying a critical lens to design and cultural artefacts and processes. The role of historical research and theoretical understanding were also deemed significant to the totality of the process. This process yielded interesting and innovative explorations in both written and practical outcomes.

An example of the approach taken to design writing within the Master's of Design Writing Criticism can be found in a collaborative project that ran with two consecutive student cohorts (2011–2012) and with the programme's core staff and the archivists from the British Telecom (BT) Archives.[23] BT is the world's oldest communications company. Its archives preserve the company's documents, photographs and films that reflect the social, political, cultural and design history of networked, electric and digital communications from 1846 to the present day. The archive became the focal point through which students were encouraged to engage with history in writing about contemporary design practices and to explore design methods and processes that would enhance an understanding of the archive materials. Each of the two project cohorts produced an exhibition and two edited publications. The aim was to explore how to make visible the objects from the collection and the narratives that surrounded them — an objective that BT Archives were keen to pursue because it brought something 'new' to the collections. Each student took an artefact or an idea from the archive and interpreted it within the social, cultural and design history of telecommunications. This included objects such as phone boxes, telegrams, disabled rights promotional material, telegraphy, 'Personality Girl' advertising,[24] letters from General Post Office (GPO) exhibition designers, and so forth. The narrative genres chosen reflected the diversity of the student-authors: documentary, critical commentary, fiction, essay and academic, among others.

At the end of the year-long project, the students summed up the process: 'By going back to original source material, we find "authenticity" and raw stories to tell. We learn that narratives lie in every archive and every object. They can speak to us, and we can listen.'[25] For BT Archives, this was a new kind of archive user and, as a result, the project addressed their interest in widening the archive's reach. Importantly, the project presented fresh, critical insights into the materials housed in the collection. In the context of design writing, this meant that students were introduced to the role of the archive in exploring contemporary authorial positions. The public exhibition that followed provided a secondary forum for students to explore visual and aural ways of communicating these narratives. The often-invisible research process was made visible and the importance of critical reflection in the act of making was considered as a practice in its own right.

The experience also laid the foundations for some of my pedagogical thinking, which I later applied to my teaching at the Royal College of Art (RCA) towards the development of the Book Test Unit (BTU) project. BTU is an experimental forum for student projects under the remit of the RCA's research group 'Book Futures Lab', which I had the privilege to lead. As with the BT Archives collaboration, student cohorts took part in four iterations of BTU projects: 2015/16, 2016/17, 2017/18 and 2018/19.[26] In 2017, for example, the Book Test Unit hosted a collaboration of fifteen design students from the School of Communication's Master's of Research Communication Design pathway and Master's of Visual Communication students, who joined a handful of RCA alumni to explore 'the future of the library and the production of knowledge'. The resulting book, titled *'Oh, Wow, I had no idea I could get that from the library!'*, provided documentary evidence of the research collaboration through photographs and short critical essays that interrogated topics such as contemporary publishing and dissemination modes, both analogue and digital, political discourse in social media, public and private spaces, multimodal literacy practices, and the experiential relationship between sound, reading and technology. The central role that writing took in this iteration of the project emerged from the BTU collaborators who were unambiguously engaging with design writing as a creative and critical practice.

In summary, both projects developed the students' specialist research interests but also encouraged the exploration of different critical approaches to design writing and practice. By bringing a design-led perspective to these projects, students were introduced to a range of theoretical as well as practical insights to the work, methods and processes. This resulted in a deeper understanding of such things as manufacturing and printing production processes, the practicalities of communication and messaging for audiences, close readings of images, and so forth. In other words, designers brought a nuanced understanding of their role as 'makers'; when designers apply this to writing, they understand deeply what that process entails.[27]

The role of the independent publication in graphic design criticism
Like Massimo Vignelli before him, design writer and curator Andrew Blauvelt called for a unification of the discipline of graphic design. Writing in 2003, Blauvelt remarks: 'an important way out of the conditions of a commensurate pluralism is for graphic design to reclaim a position of critical autonomy'.[28] He goes on to propose that graphic design 'must be seen as a discipline capable of generating meaning on its own terms' and that 'such actions should demonstrate self-awareness and self-reflexivity'.[29] Critical practice, he argues, is key to this process of discipline formation. Whilst graphic design critics such as Rick Poynor and Steven Heller have kept the debate foregrounded within mainstream design publications, a great deal of the more experimental critical writing has been published in alternative, independent publications, often by younger designers.

Throughout the history of graphic design, writing and criticism has found a unique forum within the pages of independent magazines and trade publications produced by professional societies. Examples include: *Das Plakat* (1910–1921), which was produced by the commercial art collector Hans Sachs and the collectors' association Verein der Plakatfreunde (Society of Friends of the Poster);[30] *Emigre* (1984–2005), founded and designed by Rudy VanderLans; *Dot Dot Dot* (2000–2011), founded and designed by Stuart Bertolotti-Bailey and Peter Biľak (with David Reinfurt replacing Biľak in 2006); and *Eye: The International Review of Graphic Design* (1990–present), led first by founding editor Poynor, later edited by Max Bruinsma (1997–1999) and John L. Walters (1999–present).

Small print runs of self-published magazines or journals produced by students and/or faculty within an academic environment are also part of this historical trajectory. For example, *Typographica* (1949–1967), published by Lund Humphries, was edited by Herbert Spencer who in 1966 joined the Royal College of Art, and *Typos* (circa 1980–1983), published by London College of Printing, was edited by LCP staff member Frederick Lambert.[31] *Typos* was a constant source of inspiration for me when I was teaching on the MA Typo/Graphic Studies at the London College of Communication. Lambert had been adept at successfully connecting students' learning experiences with contemporary professional practice. Then there is, of course, the well-established journal *Visible Language*, which began publishing in 1967 under its original title *The Journal of Typographic Research*. It was founded by Dr Merald Wrolstad and was supported by Rhode Island School of Design and the Illinois Institute of Technology, under the watchful editorship of Sharon Poggenpohl. Mike Zender, who is based at the University of Cincinnati College of Design, Architecture, Art and Planning, took over the editorship in 2013. Poggenpohl and Zender have been influential in fostering design research and interdisciplinary studies. This ongoing interest is reflected in a dedicated special issue of *Visible Language*, published in December 2015, which explores ideas surrounding 'critical making' and the boundaries between design and the digital humanities.[32]

The self-produced design studio publication has been another avenue for design writers. For example, *Open Manifesto* (2004–), produced by designer Kevin Finn in Australia, has been an attempt to 'democratise' design writing and criticism by welcoming contributions from students, academics and designers. In addition, Armin Vit and Bryony Gomez-Palacio founded *Speak Up* (2002–2009) — an online graphic design blog-magazine whose intent was to 'spark a good debate'. *Speak Up* had a regular column titled 'Critique', where guest writers would critically comment on different aspects of design.[33] In 2007, the blog became a controversial focus for a debate between Poynor and blogger/designer Mark Kingsley, who took opposing views on the merits of the role of editors and the format of blogging. The ensuing debate led to a passionate critique by the two authors on the virtues of 'amateur' and 'professional' modes of design writing and criticism. Although still inconclusive, the points raised by both writers (and the authors of comments on the exchange) are still noted as part of the emerging discourse in graphic design.[34] Around the same time, *Design Observer* took criticism into a professionalised online environment with founding editors William Drenttel, Jessica Helfand, Michael Bierut and Poynor (2003–present, under the editorship of Helfand and Bierut). *Design Observer* has provided a significant platform for design writing, whilst at the same time exploring a broader remit of visual culture. Poynor, for example, expanded the relationship between the critic and the 'critical' reader in his provocative blog posts for the online publication: in a 2012 post titled 'The Closed Shop of Design Academia', he wrote of 'the cloistered quality of academic life' and criticised academics for not participating in the public discourse on design. The article sparked a substantial number of responses from designers and academics, which appeared in the comment boxes between 13 April and 22 April 2012. The comment boxes formed the basis of a dialogue between Poynor and readers, but also among readers with one another. For a moment, the graphic design community interacted in a passionate and participatory critical intervention.[35]

These publications have often been produced and edited by design professionals, academics, writers or even specialist enthusiasts. Such a range of critical voices is laudable and desired — it evidences how members of a profession are keen to raise the level of discourse. Such variety of criticism has also generated debate as to the purpose and function of writing, as well as the voice through which it is presented: journalism, critical journalism, academic writing, critical writing or critical practice. For example, Gonzales-Crisp coined the term 'designwrights' in her essay 'Discourse This! Designers and Alternative Critical Writing' to describe the process by which design writers have adopted rhetorical positions of fiction in order to 'evaluate [and] elucidate practices, cultural forces and artifacts'.[36] She acknowledges the work of historical figures such as William Morris and W. A. Dwiggins, as well as more contemporary examples including Diane Gromala (aka Putch Tu), Bertolotti-Bailey and Bruinsma, amongst others, who have flirted, if not directly engaged, with a more literary and semi-fictionalised positioning. Through this process, the role of speculation is foregrounded, thereby presenting a critical freedom for experimentation and exploration.[37]

Further problematising the current state of criticism is designer and educator Kenneth Fitzgerald, who, in his piece 'Fuck All' (a title that proposes a critique of Michael Rock's seminal article 'Fuck Content') for *Modes of Criticism* 1, addresses the potential conflict of the role of the designer who is also a critic. He writes:

a simple disclaimer must accompany practitioners' writing: *Warning: may contain ulterior or mixed motives*. This is a significant issue in design writing, where practice-related and practice-centric writers predominate.[38]

This is where the three publication examples I have cited — *Zed*, *That New Design Smell* and *Modes of Criticism* — come into their own. I am aware that the claim for special significance may seem premature since only six issues have been published to date for the latter two: one issue of *That New Design Smell* and five issues of *Modes of Criticism*. Yet, the trajectory indicated by these publications evidences what we might hope for in a new generation of graphic designers who place criticism firmly at the heart of an integrated practice of production. The designer-critic is now operating across a broader range of roles as producer (for example, as designer, writer, critic, editor or social media expert), as well as publisher and distributor. Is this what may be described as the critical turn in graphic design? And what insights and understanding are brought to design writing by practitioners that are absent from the writing of their counterparts who are not in design practice? In the next section of this essay, the publications above are discussed in some depth to illustrate ways in which critical writing and critical design have been informed by designers bringing a new kind of 'lens' to an editorial positioning.

Part II: The critical examples

In Part I of this essay, I discussed how academic institutions have often published experimental editorial design and writing platforms for students and tutors, independently of the mainstream. The proposition of situating a critique within the process of design has the potential to stimulate new kinds of practice — whether through writing or designing. This moves criticism beyond defined conventions of having a role of 'influence' into a practice where reflection and critique are an integral part of the design process. In Part II, my intent is to focus on the three publications as examples that have bridged writing, criticism and practice to bring new approaches to perspectives on graphic design. The editors of all three publications are also designers and are involved in the academy. The first issue of *Zed* hails from the 1990s and was instrumental in bringing the idea of the 'value of debate' in graphic design to stimulate a reconnection between what had been a disparate design community of students, academics and designers. Continuing in a similar tradition, *That New Design Smell* and *Modes of Criticism* reflect a period of production in the 2000s that fostered exploration of graphic design writing/criticism as an academic pursuit.

Zed: A Journal of Design

During the 1990s, design criticism and writing was often the domain of experimental platforms, with enough proliferation of work for Poynor to remark 'a substantial body of critical writing has been amassed'.[39] With this, we experienced an increase in the founding of new graphic design publications that helped to foster and shape an emerging critical design discourse. The designer as editor became instrumental in the creation of new experimental forums and innovative editorial positioning for the field.

One publication that informed my approach to design writing and criticism as a contributor was *Zed*. The journal launched in 1994 and ran for seven volumes until 2000 under the Center for Design Studies, Virginia Commonwealth University, where its founding editor, Katie Salen, was an associate professor. The remit of each of the seven themed volumes, according to Salen, was to deal 'with fundamental issues of concern to practitioners, educators, and students as a group, and [to acknowledge] the impact of these issues on society'.[40] *Zed* provided a forum for critical debate in the form of 'questioning' and engaged with broader themes where design was integrated into discussions on politics, objects, semiotics, pedagogy, morality, graduate education and experimentation. The journal was slanted towards writings on design as a broader cultural artefact. *Zed*'s designs under Salen's editorship subtly posited alternative ways of reading texts — in some cases through the inclusion of a CD-ROM, or through typographic experimentation and play. For example, the second issue of *Zed* (1995) withdrew the vowel 'i' each time it appeared in the text and re-introduced 'I' to the margins in homage to the experimental works of Georges Perec, a member of the twentieth-century literary group Oulipo, who coined the lipogram to designate texts constructed with the omission of a given letter.

The seventh and final issue of *Zed*, titled 'public + private', was edited by myself and Siân Cook under the aegis of the Women's Design + Research Unit (WD+RU) — a loose-knit collective co-founded in 1997 with Liz McQuiston to raise awareness about women working in visual communication. Our own political intentions as a design collective — with political concerns including gender, women's visibility in the workplace, and so forth — aligned with *Zed*'s main aim to be a 'vehicle for divergent viewpoints and new voices'.[41] WD+RU has given and will continue to give voice to women who aren't normally heard. To this end, *Zed* was perfect as a discursive space for making visible contributors' interdisciplinary perspectives in text and image on the theme of 'public + private'. The issue was divided into four main 'zones' or juxtapositions: navigating/mapping, hiding/revealing, ritual/sexualisation and culture/boundaries. Our contributors included: writer and photographer Rosa Ainley, designer Jonathan Barnbrook, artists Angela Forster and Anne Wilson, design writer Kristina Samagyi, filmmaker Maureen McCue, designer Andrew Slatter, photographer Jennifer Small and designer Niall Sweeney. We collaborated with the artist Marysia Lewandowska to include sporadic insertions of photographic images of 'public matter' in the form of newspaper and magazine cuttings collected from the private apartment of the film critic Misia Oleksiewicz in Warsaw. The resulting effect was a mirroring of the 'unexpected encounters' the critic herself had created in the placement of clippings into books, medicine cabinets and show boxes, each 'assimilated into the living space'.[42] The notion of a 'discursive space' has always been central to my own practice as an educator, and accordingly the opportunity to be involved in *Zed* provided a further testing ground for the ways in which design and writing conversations could be catalysts for probing social, political and cultural issues.

That New Design Smell

That New Design Smell was conceived as 'an experiment in smart and fun

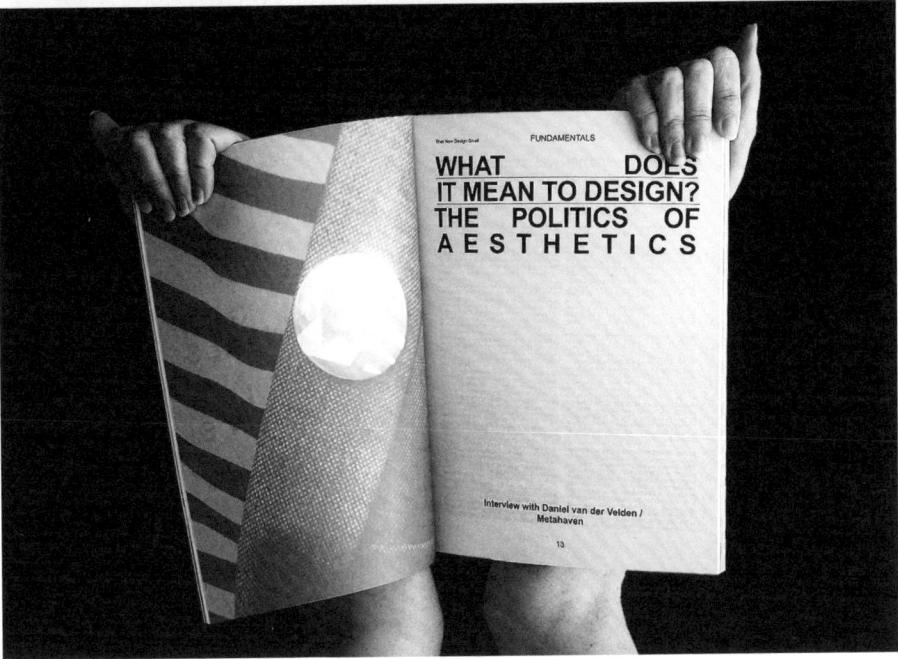

Top: *Zed: Public + Private*, issue no. 7 (September 2000). The Center for Design Studies, Communication Arts and Design Department, Virginia Commonwealth University. Guest edited by the Women's Design + Research Unit (WD+RU). Edited and designed by Katie Salen. Cover design by Bethany Johns. Image courtesy of the author.

Bottom: *That New Design Smell*, issue no. 0 (June 2011). Edited by Michèle Champagne. Amsterdam, The Netherlands. Photograph by Jason Mortlock, courtesy of Michèle Champagne.

Top: *Modes of Criticism: Critical, Uncritical, Post-critical*, issue no. 1 (February 2015). Edited and designed by Francisco Laranjo. London, England. Photograph courtesy of Francisco Laranjo.

Bottom: *Modes of Criticism: Critique of Method*, issue no. 2 (May 2016). Porto, Portugal. Edited and designed by Francisco Laranjo. Photograph courtesy of Francisco Laranjo.

conversations on design' and was part of Michèle Champagne's thesis at the Sandberg Instituut, a postgraduate programme of the Gerrit Rietveld Academie, the Netherlands. Only one issue (no. 0) was produced, in an A4 magazine format.[43] The print run of *That New Design Smell* was limited to only fifty copies, but the accompanying website remains online and so its written content is still accessible.

Champagne's editorial intent for *That New Design Smell* was to introduce 'an independent venue for design criticism and dialogue in a post-medium fashion'.[44] *That New Design Smell* is presented as 'documentary-style design criticism'. Articles and images reflect the publication's political leaning in reportage, including, for example, photographs of the Toronto G20 Summit, archive images of decision-makers gathered around political round tables, and observations of the future of city living. At the same time as articles in the magazine question the role of criticism, the design of the print magazine presents 'a visual argument' that Champagne describes as 'design is a disgrace'.[45] This, she argues, is in itself 'critical design', interrogating the rules of what 'good design' should be. The design of the publication is a catalyst for debating questions around design aesthetics or, in this case, a seemingly anti-design aesthetic. Champagne, as if to emphasise this point, includes in the first issue an interview with Daniel van der Velden — co-founder, with Vinca Kruk, of the collective Metahaven and a tutor at the Sandberg Instituut. In her interview with van der Velden, he remarks: 'if you don't address the politics behind the aesthetics, there will be no real change'.[46]

What is distinctive about this publication is the editor's special formula by which content generated from the website is then curated into a printed format. Champagne adopted an open content submission policy, 'where contributors engage with an active online public' to facilitate 'dialogue rather than monologue'.[47] This is not dissimilar to what Rogoff proposes in her definition of the 'turn', where new platforms encourage 'public utterances'.[48]

Modes of Criticism

Modes of Criticism is an ongoing research project produced by Francisco Laranjo, which formed part of his submission towards a PhD at the University of the Arts London in 2016.[49] In his thesis, titled 'Design as criticism: Methods for a critical graphic design practice', Laranjo argues that 'in order to develop a critical practice, a designer must approach design as criticism'.[50] His ideas are explored through an applied practice — the production of *Modes of Criticism* — citing as a key influence the work of Dutch critical designer and thinker Jan van Toorn. As practice-led research, Laranjo's intent is laudable in highlighting the potential of new critical methods and processes through which to explore the designer as a reflexive agent of change.

Modes of Criticism too has a limited print run — of three hundred copies — whereas the online journal provides an additional forum to expand the selection of writings to reprints or specifically commissioned texts in a timely fashion. Here, the visual takes a predominant role in introducing each text to the reader. Laranjo seemingly found inspiration in the design of the last six issues of *Emigre* (issues 64–69), where VanderLans had intentionally changed the publication's format from a magazine to a reader-friendly paperback version. This was a radical shift from the earlier issues, in which *Emigre* had displayed highly experimental visual and typographic layouts, to a more traditional, review-style paperback. The first issue of *Modes of Criticism* used only a few images; in some articles, the design is reminiscent of earlier *Emigre*-like typographic page layouts. For example, the essay by Ahmed Ansari, 'Politics & Method', in *Modes of Criticism* 2, exploits this to good effect where the text is split into two columns — one for 'A Method in Politics' and the other for 'A Politics in Method', whilst references are printed vertically in the margins, breaking from a top-to-bottom reading. By the third issue, Laranjo has achieved a greater sense of visual balance between image and text in the publication's layout, reflecting, perhaps, the theme of 'design and democracy' and its author's critical and dialogical positioning.

As an editor, Laranjo has carefully curated *Modes of Criticism*, inviting a select group of contributors including some familiar practitioners and academics who have written about criticism throughout their careers, such as Anne Bush, Kenneth Fitzgerald, Noel Waite, Els Kuijpers and Jan van Toorn, as well as new voices, such as Ahmed Ansari and Matthew Kiem, both PhD students, at Carnegie Mellon University and Western Sydney University respectively. At the same time, Laranjo introduces writers from areas related to graphic design to evidence the increased blurring of disciplinary boundaries, such as Cameron Tonkinwise, a theorist who taught previously at Carnegie Mellon University, and who is a strong advocate of the emerging field of transition design.

The debates that Laranjo highlights resonate with earlier writings, such as those by Poynor and Fitzgerald, on the role of criticism. For example, designer and educator Bush observes in her piece for *Modes of Criticism* 2 that critics have seemingly avoided tackling criticism head-on in their writing. She remarks: 'vacillating between a desire for stable foundations as well as a need to address change — graphic design critics have tended to both embrace and resist authority through a range of manoeuvres which foreground personality, sidestep history, or prioritize description over analysis'.[51]

Speculative design and design fiction are also contemporary themes addressed in the publication, the early exploration of which Laranjo attributes to Anthony Dunne and Fiona Raby, among others. Yet it is only recently that graphic design has begun to adopt some of the techniques and strategies offered by these narrative design methods. Waite reflects on his practice as exemplified through his own teaching in showing to his students 'the value and relevance of history and its methods'.[52] He draws from Tony Fry's book *Design Futuring*,[53] citing the role 'critical fictions' might play in 'enabling the contemplation of what would otherwise not be considered'.[54] An equally valid approach is proposed by James Langdon, designer and creator of the project A School for Design Fiction. Langdon elucidates his use of the term 'design fictions' and explores in his teaching 'how artefacts speak to us, sometimes in ways that can be shaped by design, but also in ways that a designer cannot control'.[55] His reference to historical design fiction, as Laranjo points out, is an alternative to the legacy of science fiction on which Dunne and Raby relied.

The third issue of *Modes of Criticism* reflects a maturity in the publication's approach to critical writing, interweaving established and emerging voices in graphic design. The theme of 'design and democracy' suggests a broader critical view of the field, including discussions of the socio-political and technological contexts in which designers operate and of neoliberal models of education in art schools. Here we see a nod to the rise of norm-critical design. The role of critique in design (whether theoretically or through practice) takes on a greater sense of urgency in the problematisation of design moving forward, revealing many design practices as steeped in historical hegemonic discourse. For example, the article titled 'Design Activism: A Conversation by the Decolonising Design Group' reflects the diversity of perspectives on the politics of design (e.g., political design, design activism, etc.) and 'how design expresses its agency beyond and often against the terms of Design'.[56] The fourth issue of *Modes of Criticism* extends the critical impetus of the third, but with a specific focus upon radical pedagogy.[57]

Such debates are essential. Even as initial published outcomes, *Modes of Criticism* and *That New Design Smell* propose new dialogic platforms for broader discussions around design criticism and critical practice, made more evident by the cross-fertilisation of ideas between the two publications. In 2012, Laranjo interviewed Champagne about *That New Design Smell* and her approach to 'critical thinking and designing' for its source website. Through this exchange, Champagne proposes that for her there are three types of 'critical': critical thinking, design criticism, and critical design. And, all three positions, she argues, are incorporated into *That New Design Smell*. She explains that the publication 'was trying to present a piece of "critical design" (in terms of its visual argument) all the while engaging "critical thinking" and publishing "design criticism"'.[58] Equally, Champagne proposed that a 'visual argument' was at play through her design choices for the magazine — 'Arial, justified titles and pixelated images'.[59] The questioning of what might be seen to be breaking the rules of 'good design' in turn leads us to ask: does engagement with the critical necessitate an 'ugly' aesthetic?

Such questioning is not necessarily new in graphic design. One precedent, for example, emerged out of a series of student-led experimental publications called *Output* (1990–1991), where emphasis was placed on an 'integration of its content with its visual structure'. Initiated by design educator Joani Spadaro, who hailed from the Herron School of Art at Indiana University, the project's intent was to create a platform for students to work outside the commercial context that normally defines the outcome of their studio projects. The collaboration encouraged critical reflection on the state of graphic design practice and the opportunity to reflect those through the publication.[60] *Output* also found a place amongst students at Cranbrook, The University of Texas, and in the creation of an international issue between North Carolina State University and Ravensbourne College of Art and Design in London. In this later collaboration, with which I was involved, students came together via fax machines and video conference calls to foster an understanding of their positions in relationship to cultural, social and political contexts in the UK and the US. *Output* was a publication in which students could calibrate its final form with the intentions of its content.[61]

Each version of the publication drew upon a range of production techniques, such as overprinting, letterpress, video and fax machine technology, which reflected the students' critique of their postmodern condition. The resulting aesthetic led Heller to castigate them for representing 'the cult of the ugly'. He described in *Eye* magazine in 1993 a 'critical ugliness' that he accused of being 'self-indulgent' and which 'could be considered a prime example of ugliness in the service of fashionable experimentation'.[62] Such musings on an 'aesthetic critique' have now entered the canon of graphic design history. At the beginning of the new millennium, a paradigm shift was underway. Debates centred on the post-critical as proposed by Blauvelt and others, who called for 'graphic design to reclaim a position of critical autonomy' and a position of 'self-reflexivity'.[63] The emphasis shifted from the production of graphic expression and, by the mid-2000s, to that of critical agitation.

There is no doubt that the academy provides a 'safe' space for critical dialogues to be shared and interrogated, arguably untouched by Fitzgerald's concern for 'ulterior motives'. Yet, despite the danger of producing work that is only discussed within the academy, *Modes of Criticism* and *That New Design Smell*, as student-led publications, have made attempts to bring their critiques into the wider design community. Both editors have been regular guest speakers and presenters at AIGA conferences (for example, Champagne was a keynote at the AIGA's 'Blunt: Explicit and Graphic Design Criticism Now' in 2013, and Laranjo was a guest at the 'Undesign Symposium' at the University of Applied Arts Vienna in 2016). Their publications are distributed internationally, in print and online. The editors are also active on social media, which is used as another type of critical space, thereby greatly increasing their visibility and potential discursive impact on the wider graphic design community. This reach aligns with Krippendorff's criteria of the *rearticulable*, which extends the 'conversation' (as proposed by Rogoff) to generate an ongoing dialogue.

My proposal here is that, despite it still being early days for *Modes of Criticism* and *That New Design Smell* (and even if they don't publish any further than these first issues), their significance resides in the curation of writings focused on criticism and critical practice. Much in the same way that *Zed* had done in the 1990s, these publications provide useful evidence of a 'critical turn' in graphic design, further shadowing the writings of 1970s artists who provided the impetus for critical arts practices. The 'turn' reads like the creation of a new paradigm.

Postscript

I have been asked to reflect on the education of a design writer, partly because I have been involved in the field for such an extended period, but also because of my experiences in the development of writing as a critical practice within the context of graphic design education. Yet I am in the position of being inside the academy, where my perspective on design writing and criticism has been informed in part by academic convention. It is axiomatic in the academy that the learning environment necessitates an engagement between students, colleagues and the wider profession. This is a position of privilege: the new perspectives, contexts and intentions foregrounded by such engagements often yield opportunities for innovative practices. New ways of considering the 'how' and 'why' are being played out 'live' in the postgraduate classroom. I continue to be inspired by students and alumni who are taking cues from their learning experiences and developing these into new kinds of critical design practice.

1. Amy Newman, *Challenging Art: Artforum 1962–1974* (New York: Soho Press Inc., 2000), 2.
2. Newman, *Challenging Art*, 128.
3. Massimo Vignelli, 'Keynote Address', in *The First Symposium on the History of Graphic Design: Coming of Age*, edited by Barbara Hodik and R. Roger Remington (Rochester: Rochester Institute of Technology, 1983), 9.
4. Michael Rock and Rick Poynor, 'What is this thing called graphic design criticism?', *Eye*, vol. 4, no. 16, Spring 1995, 58.
5. The School of Visual Arts (2008–present) has refocused, with a newly titled Master's course in Design Research, Writing and Criticism positioning research at the heart of its offer, whereas the Royal College of Art's Master's of Critical Writing in Art and Design (2010–present) maintains a focus on the creative practice of writing and criticism with 'their own techniques, ethics and technologies'. As the first of its kind in Europe to focus on design, writing and critical thinking, London College of Communication's Master's of Design Writing Criticism ran from 2008 to 2012. When the College re-evaluated its offering, the course had graduated four cohorts of students, many of whom are now working as design writers or educators, or continuing their studies in criticism at PhD level. See also: David Crowley, 'Head of Programme Welcome', Royal College of Art website, www.rca.ac.uk/schools/school-of-humanities/cwad/head-of-programme/, accessed 22 October 2015.
6. Rick Poynor, 'Borderline: Profile: Metahaven', *Eye*, vol. 71, no. 9, Spring 2009, 25.
7. Rick Poynor, 'The Death of the Critic', *Icon* 033, March 2006, www.iconeye.com/404/item/2527-the-death-of-the-critic-%7C-icon-033-%7C-march-2006, accessed 9 September 2017.
8. Grace Lees-Maffei offers another definition in the introduction to her edited volume *Writing Design: Words and Objects*: 'although writing on design often analyses design *after the fact*, or after the processes of briefing, conception, design and manufacture have occurred, design criticism and design reform discourses critique what exists with the aim of improving what will follow'. See: Grace Lees-Maffei, 'Introduction: Writing Design', in *Writing Design: Words and Objects*, edited by Grace Lees-Maffei (London: Berg, 2012), 4.
9. Matt Malpass, *Critical Design in Context: History, Theory and Practices* (London: Bloomsbury, 2017), 18.
10. Maurice Berger, 'Introduction: The Crisis of Criticism', in *The Crisis of Criticism*, edited by Maurice Berger (New York: The New Press, 1998), 11.
11. Katie Salen, 'Introduction', *Zed 1: The Politics of Design*, 1994, 11–12.
12. Rick Poynor, 'Where Are the Design Critics?', *Design Observer*, 25 September 2005, accessed 2 August 2016.
13. Jessica Helfand, 'Comments' for 'Where Are the Design Critics?', Rick Poynor, *Design Observer*, 25 September 2005, http://designobserver.com/feature/where-are-the-design-critics/3767, accessed 2 August 2016.
14. Bruce Archer, quoted in Klaus Krippendorff, *The Semantic Turn: A New Foundation for Design* (London: Taylor & Francis, 2006), xiii.
15. Krippendorff, *The Semantic Turn*, 12.
16. Irit Rogoff, 'Turning', *e-flux Journal*, #00, November 2008, www.e-flux.com/journal/turning/, accessed 2 August 2016.
17. Ibid.
18. Richard Buchanan, quoted in Rick Poynor, 'It's the End of Graphic Design as We Know It', *Eye*, vol. 18, no. 69, 2008, 76–77.
19. Denise Gonzales-Crisp, 'Discourse This! Designers and Alternative Critical Writing', *Design and Culture: The Journal of the Design Studies Forum* 1, no. 1 (2009): 105–120.
20. Markus Miessen, quoted in Brendan Cormier and Arjen Oosterman, 'From Written Word to Practiced Word: Marcus Miessen', *Archis*, Special Issue: 'Ways to be Critical', no. 36, 2013, 100.
21. Tara Winters, 'The Practitioner-Researcher Contribution to a Developing Criticism for Graphic Design', *Iridescent: Icograda Journal of Design Research* 2, no. 2 (2013), tandfonline.com/doi/abs/10.1080/19235003.2012.11428506, accessed 22 October 2016.
22. Teal Triggs, 'Writing Design Criticism into History', *Design and Culture: The Journal of the Design Studies Forum* 5, no. 1 (2012): 33–38.
23. A full listing of students and staff involved in the project is provided in the second project publication: *Telling Tales: Revealing Histories in BT Archives* (London: London College of Communication, 2012). I continue to work periodically with David Hay, Head of Heritage, to promote the value of the archive collection for designers.
24. 'Personality Girl' was the name given to actresses who represented the ideal consumers in BT promotional materials and advertising campaigns selling phones as fashion statements.
25. Teal Triggs, Brigitte Lardinois and Anna Gerber, *Seeing Voices: Inside BT Archives*, Field Study 13 (London: London College of Communication, 2011), 3.

26 The Book Test Unit is part of the curriculum delivery for the Royal College of Art's MRes Communication Design pathway and is intended to foster collaboration between Master's students and industry partners.
27 This is not to diminish the non-designer writer. Design historian and writer Alice Twemlow remarks in an interview with Steven Heller for *The Atlantic*: 'But a writer who really loves design will immerse themselves in the design process and learn to approximate this natural familiarity with the various facets of form-making.' See: Steven Heller, 'Writing is Design, Too', *The Atlantic*, 26 July 2012, www.theatlantic.com/entertainment/archive/2012/07/writing-is-design-too/260342, accessed 10 September 2017.
28 Andrew Blauvelt, 'Towards Critical Autonomy or Can Graphic Design Save Itself?', *Emigre 64: Rant* (Sacramento and New York: Emigre and Princeton Architectural Press, 2003), 41.
29 Ibid.
30 Steven Heller, 'Graphic Design Magazines: Das Plakat', first published in *U&lc*, vol. 25, no. 4, Spring 1999, and reprinted in *Typotheque*, www.typotheque.com/articles/graphic_design_magazines_das_plakat%20, accessed 22 October 2016.
31 *Typos* was intended to be produced three times per year, edited by Frederick Lambert and produced by design and printing students and staff at The London College of Printing. Only six issues were published, although an advertisement for a subscription to issues 7, 8, 9 appears in one later issue to suggest an ongoing commitment for the project from the College. A previous iteration of *Typos* was published by The London School of Printing and Graphic Arts in the 1960s, edited by G. R. Garland with Tom Eckersley as art director.
32 Jessica Barness (Kent State University) and Amy Papaelias (State University of New York at New Paltz) were guest editors of the themed issue: 'Critical Making: Design and the Digital Humanities', *Visible Language* 49, no. 3 (December 2015).
33 Armin Vit, 'An Interview with Armin Vit: December 2003', *Emigre 66: Nudging Graphic Design* (Sacramento and New York: Emigre and Princeton Architectural Press, 2004), 7.
34 This is a point not lost on design writer Alice Twemlow, who dedicates a chapter to the debate and the role *Speak Up* has played in design criticism in her book *Sifting the Trash*. See: Alice Twemlow, *Sifting the Trash: A History of Design Criticism* (Cambridge, MA: MIT Press, 2017), 250.
35 See: Rick Poynor, 'The Closed Shop of Design Academia', *Design Observer*, 13 April 2012, http://designobserver.com/feature/the-closed-shop-of-design-academia/33658, accessed 4 September 2017; and Matt Soar, 'Rick Poynor on Design Academics: Having His Cake and Eating It Too', personal blog, 13 April 2012, www.mattsoar.com/2012/04/19/rick-poynor/, accessed 10 September 2017. Radio, on the other hand, provided popular platforms for graphic design. For example, Adrian Shaughnessy presented the programme 'Graphic Design on the Radio' (2007–2011) for London's Resonance radio station, in an hour of interviews and music from graphic design's luminaries. In the US, Debbie Millman's podcast Design Matters (2005–present) equally showcased 'luminaries of contemporary thought' from a broad range of cultural practices. And, more recently, Jarrett Fuller's podcast *Scratching the Surface* (2016–present) with notable designers and educators addresses the intersection of criticism and practice.
36 Gonzales-Crisp, 'Discourse This!', 106.
37 James Langdon, on the other hand, argues that his definition of design fiction is 'not primarily about the impossible, or the futuristic, but about the multiplicity of possibilities in any ordinary decision making process'. Here there is an emphasis on the 'imaginary'. James Langdon, in James Langdon and Francisco Laranjo, 'A School for Design Fiction: Interview', *Modes of Criticism 1: The Post Critical*, 2015, 80.
38 Kenneth Fitzgerald, 'Fuck All', *Modes of Criticism 1: The Post Critical*, 2015, 88.
39 Rock and Poynor, 'What is this thing...?', 56.
40 *Zed*'s format reflected contemporary debates on technology and publishing by including in the printed version of the journal a CD-ROM, components that Salen proposed 'were designed to be read as a single conversation'. Katie Salen, 'Editor's Note', *Zed 1: The Politics of Design*, 1994, 6.
41 Katie Salen, 'Introduction', *Zed 1: The Politics of Design*, 1994, 11.
42 Maryisa Lewandowska, 'Intellectual Property', in *Zed 7: Public and Private*, edited by Teal Triggs and Siân Cook, 2000, 18–19.
43 *That New Design Smell* issue 0 was edited by Michèle Champagne, with web concept and design by Lennart Bruger and contributions from Daniel van der Velden, Gert Dumbar, Cedric Flazinski, Anja Groten, Femke Herregraven and Jason Mortlock.
44 Michèle Champagne, 'About', *That New Design Smell* website, 2011, http://thatnewdesignsmell.net/all-about-page/, accessed 7 August 2016.
45 Modes of Criticism, 'Interview: That New Design Smell | Modes of Criticism', *Modes of Criticism* website, 26 October 2012, http://modesofcriticism.org/that-new-design-smell/.

46 'The Politics of Aesthetics: What does it mean to design? Interview with Daniel van der Velden/Metahaven', *That New Design Smell*, issue 0, 2010, http://thatnewdesignsmell.net/daniel-van-der-velden-explains-himself/, accessed 14 April 2019.
47 Ibid.
48 Irit Rogoff, 'Turning'.
49 Here, I declare my interests as Director of Studies for Laranjo's PhD, titled 'Design as Criticism: Methods for a Critical Graphic Design Practice' (2016), awarded by the London College of Communication, University of the Arts London.
50 Francisco Laranjo, 'Design as Criticism: Methods for a Critical Graphic Design Practice' (PhD diss., London College of Communication, University of the Arts London, 2016), 5.
51 Anne Bush, 'Double Vision: Graphic Design Criticism and the Question of Authority', *Modes of Criticism 2: Critique of Method*, 2016, 15.
52 Noel Waite, 'Learning Design Histories for Design Futures: Speculative Histories and Reflective Practice', *Modes of Criticism 2: Critique of Method*, 2016, 52.
53 Tony Fry, *Design Futuring: Sustainability, Ethics and New Practice* (London: Berg Publishers, 2008).
54 Tony Fry, cited in Waite, 'Learning Design Histories', 52.
55 Langdon and Laranjo, 'A School for Design Fiction', 79.
56 Matt Kiem, quoted in 'Design Activism: A Conversation by The Decolonising Group', *Modes of Criticism 3: Design and Democracy*, 2017, 62.
57 *Modes of Criticism 4: Radical Pedagogy*, edited by Francisco Laranjo (Eindhoven: Onomatopee, 2019).
58 Modes of Criticism, 'Interview'.
59 Ibid.
60 Joani Spadaro, 'Letter to the Editor: Output Explained', *Eye*, vol. 3, no. 10, Autumn 1993, 3.
61 Teal Triggs, 'Letter to the Editor: Need to Experiment', *Eye*, vol. 3, no. 10, Autumn 1993, 4.
62 Steven Heller, 'Cult of the Ugly', *Eye*, vol. 3, no. 9, 1993, 52–59.
63 Blauvelt, 'Towards Critical Autonomy', 41.

A refractive (re)view
Paul Bailey, Tony Credland, Katie Evans,
Ricardo Goncalves, Gabriela Matusyck,
Bryony Quinn, Carlos Romo-Melgar,
Naomi Strinati, Jia Xiao and Roxy Zeiher

When examining the relative merits of different schools, we can sometimes forget that graphic design education programmes are themselves objects of design. In this collaboratively authored essay, current participants, staff and recent graduates of the MA Graphic Media Design course at London College of Communication, University of the Arts London, collectively consider the ways in which the shaping and reshaping of a course can influence participants' practices and their publics.

This essay asks: what can it mean to approach graphic design education as a piece of design today? It does so through a collective review of practices underway and emergent on the MA Graphic Media Design (MA GMD) course at London College of Communication (LCC), University of the Arts London (UAL). Members of the course team, current participants and graduates came together to think through the contexts, conditions and concerns that emerge in and through a course design, speaking to and from distinct standpoints, histories and ambitions.

We adopt *refraction*, rather than *reflection*, as a metaphorical device to help us recognise and discuss some of the core priorities of the MA GMD course design: the cultivation and maintenance of critical practices in and through graphic design, socialisation of practice in progress, and making design research public. We share examples of 'designed' actions, from small to big, in reference to these priorities.

The text follows a line of questioning and reasoning, interspersed with commentary gathered during a roundtable discussion comprised of graduates and current participants, which revealed different perspectives on recognition, progression, community and language. We hope to mobilise further discussion on how the design of a graphic design course may support participants, graduates and course teams in determining their own interrelationality and territory of action in the world today.

What can it mean to approach graphic design education as a piece of design today?

Participant: If we talk about [design education] as a piece of design, then it's definitely a piece of design co-authorship. It feels like a piece of design where there are different authors shaping the education.
Participant: If you plan, then it's a piece of design. I would say [the MA] is designed by me. I'm taking information from different places, with me at the centre, and trying to put everything together.
Participant: I never thought of [the MA] as a piece of design, but saw it as part of the process in relation to what happened before — as an expanded piece of education itself.
Graduate: I started thinking about education as a piece of design when introduced to Nina Paim's book *Taking a Line for a Walk* (2016), seeing a course as something that is shared, and which can be reproduced and experimented with, rather than something developed in a linear way.

MA GMD is a fifteen-month postgraduate course, launched in October 2015 at LCC, UAL. The course, which is situated within the Design School, builds upon the legacy of the MA Graphic Design, MA Design Writing Criticism and MA Typo/Graphics courses before it, but with a renewed focus — to explore the use of graphic design as a critical tool to investigate the complexities of contemporary society.

The course has been active during a period of considerable uncertainty in the UK: ongoing mayhem of national governance, continuing (looping) revisions to the engagement between the UK and Europe, incremental and notable increases to the cost of studying in higher education, precarity of future employment, the climate crisis, and much more besides. Change is nothing new or surprising in educational contexts. In fact, according to Anja Groten, the educational space is one in which we are confronted with the 'temporality of constantly changing relations'.[1] This period of uncertainty, however, is significant in terms of its direct impact on the requirements and potential of postgraduate graphic design education. Design educators and institutions are being called to action. We specifically ask: what can a Master's course in the subject/practice of graphic design do to speak to these complex conditions and times? How do we mobilise action within and beyond current institutional parameters (such as validation processes, budget negotiations, shifting cohort dynamics and profiles)? How can we design and deploy a curriculum for a practice (and discourse) that is seen to be 'truncated by the limits of its own criticality'?[2]

The course approaches these questions by inviting engagement with, and interrogation of, key critical perspectives of our time. We ask what it means to seek, gather, analyse, interpret and materialise propositions into/through/for (or as/from/against/in) graphic design research practice(s).[3] We acknowledge that these are large ambitions and difficult tasks. We realise this approach requires an examination and revision of our practices as educators, researchers, designers and otherwise. It requires a consideration of *how* we learn, as much as *what* we learn. We realise that we cannot approach our practices alone. We believe there is a need to find a shared language and to establish reciprocal modes of working. We cultivate a site of participation, to work with one another. For this reason, the statuses of 'student' and 'tutor' are rethought and are recast simply as 'participants', where we work alongside and in relation to one another. We are enacting this to alert participants to the constructed (i.e., designed) nature of the institution, to motivate among participants a critical assessment of the distribution of power and agency in their prior academic histories (which, typically, are characterised by a top-down, 'banking system of education'),[4] and to introduce the practice and potential of 'languaging' as a tool to build new realities for and through design.[5]

How can we address replication in and through a course design?

Participant: **Is there such a thing as graduating with a singular MA?**
Graduate 1: **No way.**
Participant: **Is it a fallacy to say that you're graduating with your own practice?**
Graduate 1: **You already had the practice when you came here.**
Graduate 2: **Yeah? I didn't know that!**

Light is a familiar metaphor for knowledge, and a mirror — as a device used to reflect light — extends the metaphor to helpfully describe the ways in which education can direct and reposition knowledge. However, we don't see education as a purely reflective exercise — as one intended to replicate the image of a given curriculum or student body, or to direct light on or from a fixed point. We need to acknowledge that the lived realities of many people are not currently reflected in the institution, due to increasing issues of access and privilege. This problem extends the point beyond the institution, into contemporary design practice. We argue reflection risks replication, and omits that which sits outside of the frame.

On MA GMD, rather than reflecting knowledge, we choose to refract it. With a basic definition of 'refraction' — the phenomenon of light or sound breaking up, only to be deflected along oblique lines through and between mediums of varying density — we understand that the trajectories that bring our participants to us are omnidirectional and that they move at different speeds. Instead of installing 'mirrors', we set up 'prisms' throughout the course that have some ability to reflect, but which, more crucially, continue to refract the routes of individuals. These prisms represent 'mediums of varying density' and provide conditions that every participant will encounter differently, via their own research and experimentation, and which they will pass through on their own terms or according to their own lines of inquiry. By consciously and recurrently 'breaking up' to move through the system in a divergent way, our participants find greater possibilities for intersection and collaboration, as well as the opportunity to transgress the edges of the framework altogether. This approach speaks to the views shared in 'An Ecology of Practice', in which Isabelle Stengers states: 'approaching a practice then means approaching it as it diverges, that is, feeling its borders, experimenting with the questions which practitioners may accept as relevant, even if they are not their own questions, rather than posing insulting questions that would lead them to mobilise and transform the border into a defence against their outside'.[6]

How is a refractive approach enacted through a course design?

Participant: **You come here thinking the education is on the paper, on the brief, but it's not.**
Graduate: **It's about finding allies, but also about finding people that challenge your view and what you're doing.**
Participant: **We all recognise we've developed a common sense of language. That is something that has changed a lot — the way we frame ourselves — the vocabulary we use now to talk about our work. And it keeps changing…**

The course design initiates various moments for participants to think through their place in practice. Below, we set out two significant examples, which behave as prisms within and beyond the course: The Reciprocal Studio and *A Line Which Forms a Volume*.

Each year, The Reciprocal Studio takes form through a series of commissioned collaborative workshops authored and led by guest practitioners in response to a negotiated socio-political concern of the time. Our guests and participants are invited to work with a learning and teaching model based on reciprocity — to use this period to collectively investigate and to further their own, and one another's, knowledge through the procedures of a research-oriented graphic design practice. We refer to the work of author bell hooks here, as we aim to build community 'in order to create a climate of openness and intellectual rigour … to receive actively knowledge that enhances our intellectual development and our capacity to live more fully in the world'.[7]

In 2018, we hosted '(Re)distributed Media: Leakage',[8] a set of workshops that called for a review of our increasingly polluted information-scapes. We were interested in how design research could be used to articulate insights about the governance, provenance and authority of information. Our guest practitioners FRAUD, Ruben Pater, Marwan Kaabour and David Benqué approached these concerns through distinct methods to make sense of specific issues concerned with 'leakage'.[9]

FRAUD put forward a proposition for design-as-conflict: a framework that presents strategies of design-led inquiry to reveal coercive and operational modes of conflict. Unlike approaches that seek conflict resolution, they viewed conflict as a desirable and productive force. David Benqué initiated an exploration of the graph as a site for critical investigation and speculative imagination. The participants' graphs were not to be seen as an end in themselves but as a grounding for critical practice and discursive research, with the aim to unpack, comment on or propose alternatives to existing systems and narratives. Marwan Kaabour called for a close reading of the significance of language in political discourse. Sifting through the complex landscape of political rhetoric across media platforms, the participants explored the ways in which verbal and visual language is used by politicians (and celebrities) to shape the narrative and to define the context around pressing issues today. Working on-site within specific localities, but with reference to open-source datasets, Ruben Pater and the participants operated as citizen journalists to devise and distribute hyper-local disaster risk reports through mapping design.

More recently, in 2019, a workshop series titled 'The Reciprocal Studio: On Distraction' inquired into moments of distraction as a strategy to think into (and against) a set of perceived requirements of design — to clarify, to simplify, to render knowable, and so on. This series invited contributions from a number of guest practitioners: Confusion of Tongues with Susan Schuppli, Demystification Committee with Tony Sampson, FRAUD with Anna Santomauro, and Francisco Laranjo with Laura Gordon.[10]

Departing from a thorough image reading of the Frontex Photo Competition archive,[11] Confusion of Tongues and the participants staged a performative exhibition and published a catalogue asking questions regarding the visual rhetoric of contemporary EU border governance that touched upon meta-themes such as the privatisation of public services, verticalisation of power and curating within security politics. Initially drawing insights from the extreme case of the financial trader, The Demystification Committee led the participants through a process of de-optimising and re-optimising the self, managing and reducing the conditions of distraction. FRAUD invited participants to perform a décollage of key factors embedded in surveillance technology and migrant flows,[12] critically tracing links between political, climactic, technological and legal aspects of borders in the Gibraltar region. Finally, Laranjo's provocation — 'we live in an age of distraction because distraction is profitable' — motivated the participants to examine the political, social and cultural dimensions of design, and their place within a critical practice.

Positioning Practice 2, published by MA GMD to coincide with the '(Re)distributed Media: Leakage' public programme for the *Hope to Nope: Graphics & Politics 2008–18* exhibition at the Design Museum, London (June 2018).

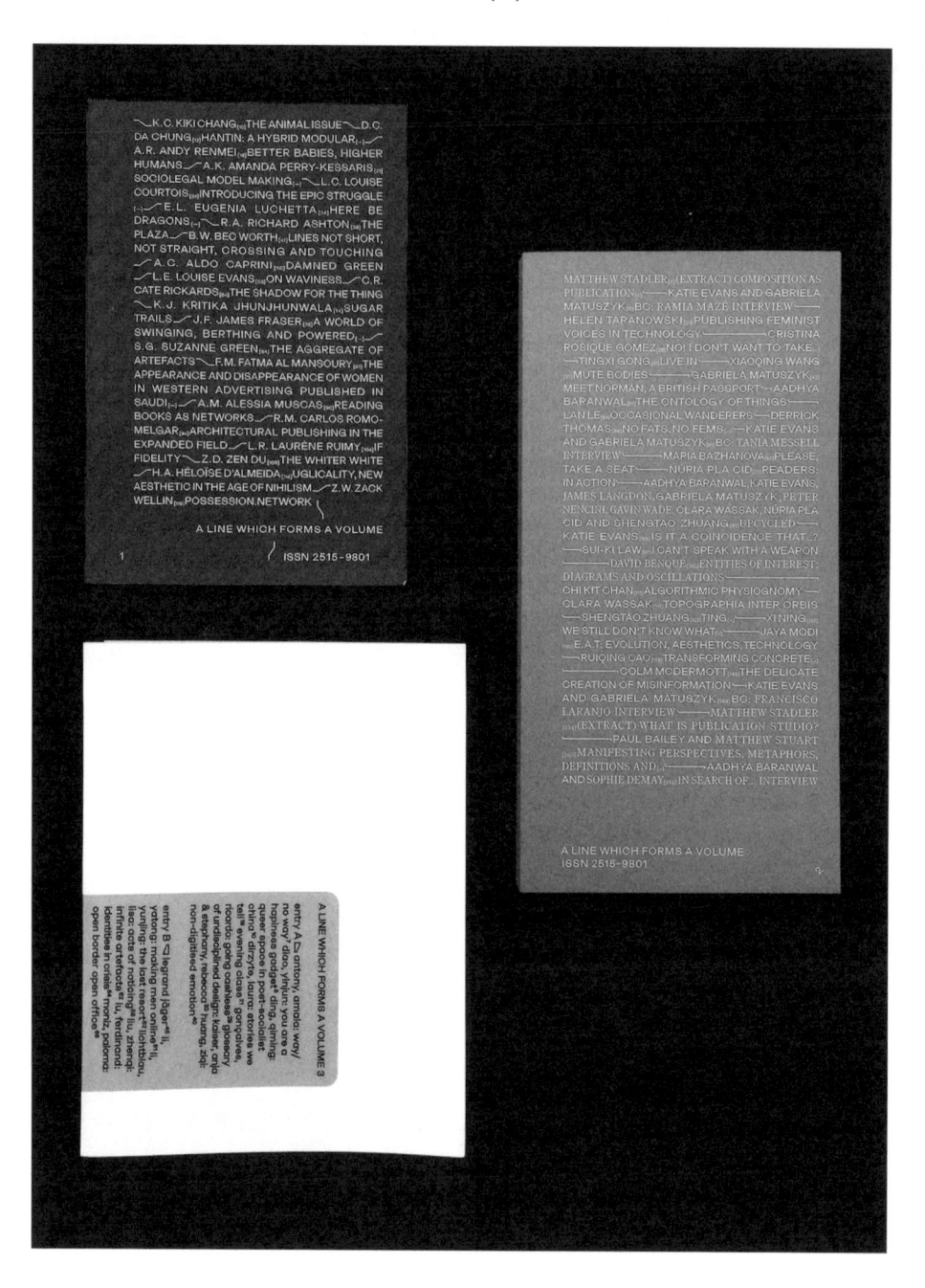

A Line Which Forms a Volume 1 (2017), *A Line Which Forms a Volume 2* (2018) and *A Line Which Forms a Volume 3* (2019), published by MA Graphic Media Design with support from London College of Communication.

Recognising a growing interest in the potentialities of design writing and collective publishing from, through and beyond the institution, in 2017 the MA GMD worked with Bryony Quinn (editorial advisor) and Daly-Lyon (design advisors) to establish *A Line Which Forms a Volume* (*ALWFAV*), a critical reader of design research authored, edited, designed and published by course participants.[13] It set out to investigate strategies to make graphic design research public — to make it voluble — and to make it resonate with multiple publics across LCC, UAL and beyond. It has become a space devised to sit outside of the core curriculum — to transgress the institutional frame — supported by an advisory team of guest editors and designers, taking form in an annual publication, in print and online, as well as a curated symposium hosted at LCC.

Each year, MA GMD participants are invited to seek out their public(s) and to re-imagine their collectivity through design. The contributions, taking form as critical texts, visual essays, poems, interviews, articles, biographies, scripts, instructions, indexes and more are captured in varied states of becoming. *ALWFAV 1* editor Gabriela Matuszyk explains how the editorial model considers various states of research in an interview with *Grafik* magazine:

> The editorial model we constructed for *ALWFAV 1* derived from Michel Butor's 'The Book as Object', an essay where he referred to book publishing as a 'freezing' method for preservation of language. This was an important consideration when approaching our material, as the research is not only of its time contextually, but it also represents varied stages of research in practice — for some MA participants the act of publication symbolised an end to a project, for others it was a prompt for continuation, or a marker for establishing new design-led inquiries.[14]

As each volume materialises, the frame of collectivity is extended and diffused in a manner that supports the participants in identifying their place in the design and construction of a community itself. *ALWFAV 2* contributor Matthew Stadler reminds us 'it is imperative that we publish, not only as a means to counter the influence of a hegemonic "public" but also to reclaim the space in which we imagine ourselves and our collectivity'. Contributions from 'allies' whom the participants have identified or incorporated in their practices, such as Stuart Bertolotti-Bailey, Eleanor Vonne Brown, Sophie Demay, James Langdon, Ramia Mazé, Peter Nencini, Jack Self, Matthew Stuart and Gavin Wade, offer visibility and locality for an otherwise invisible or illegible community of expanded practice.

(Re)view

Participant 1: I don't know where I stop. I don't know the border.
Participant 2: If there is a border?
Participant 1: If there is no border, how are you going to make progress?

Oscillating from micro to macro, institutional to personal, this exercise in collectively approaching the MA GMD course as a piece of design has offered an opportunity for the participants and graduates of the course to come together to think through various contexts, conditions and challenges affecting design education today. We noted the complexity of the challenges at the outset and sought to identify moments within the design of the MA GMD course where we can observe action underway.

The Reciprocal Studio has developed into a framework for the course to seek out and support a plurality of practices, and to collaboratively investigate critical concerns of our time through design. We observe new modes of working, expanded methodologies and a consideration for alternative models of practice seeping into the culture of the course.

A Line Which Forms a Volume emerged from a concern, observed in participants' practices, to make graphic design research public. Shifting constellations (design, editing and publishing teams), expanding networks (contributors, collaborators and producers) and divergent modes of address (events and distribution channels) provoke a concern for laying claim to a shared space that supports and socialises critical practices of design.

The move towards refraction prompted us to question replication and to work towards a sharper consideration of everyone and everything that presently sits outside of the institutional frame. As we progress onwards, we are reminded of the imperative to work towards practices of inclusion, interruption, resistance and action, by way of refraction or otherwise.

1. Anja Groten, 'Design Friction', in *Modes of Criticism 4: Radical Pedagogy*, edited by Francisco Laranjo (Eindhoven: Onomatopee, 2019): 74.
2. Anne Bush, 'Double Vision: Graphic Design Criticism and the Question of Authority', in *Modes of Criticism 2: Critique of Method*, edited by Francisco Laranjo (Eindhoven: Onomatopee, 2016), http://modesofcriticism.org/double-vision/, accessed 21 October 2019.
3. On the 'into/through/for' formulation, see: Christopher Frayling, 'Research in Art and Design', *Research Papers*, vol. 1, no. 1 (Royal College of Art, 1993/4). On 'as/from/against/in', see: Graphic Design Educators' Network, *Beyond the Margins: tools, strategies and urgencies transforming graphic design research*, https://www.graphicdesigneducators.network/events/beyond-the-margins-tools-strategies-and-urgencies-transforming-graphic-design-research/, accessed 21 October 2019.
4. Paolo Friere, *Pedagogy of the Oppressed* (London: Penguin Modern Classics, 2017), 72.
5. 'Languaging Glossary', metadesigners, https://metadesigners.org/Languaging-Glossary, accessed 28 October 2019.
6. Isabelle Stengers, 'An Ecology of Practice', *Cultural Studies Review* 11, no. 1 (March 2005): 184.
7. bell hooks, *Teaching to Trangress: Education as the Practice of Freedom* (New York: Routledge, 1994): 40.
8. This workshop series was extended to formulate a weekend-long public programme for the *Hope to Nope: Graphics & Politics 2008–18* exhibition at the Design Museum, London (June 2018).
9. FRAUD (Audrey Samson and Francisco Gallardo) is an art-research duo based in London. Ruben Pater is a graphic designer, writer and tutor based in Amsterdam. Marwan Kaabour is a graphic designer based in London. David Benqué is a designer and researcher based in London.
10. Confusion of Tongues (Marthe Prins and Benedict Waishaupt) is an artist-affliation based in Amsterdam and Berlin. Susan Schuppli is Reader and Director of Centre for Research Architecture, Goldsmiths. Demystification Committee (Oliver Smith and Francesco Tacchini) is chaired in London and Berlin. Tony Sampson is a critical theorist and Reader in Digital Media Cultures at University of East London. FRAUD (Audrey Samson and Francisco Gallardo) is an art-research duo based in London. Anna Santomauro is Program Curator at Arts Catalyst. Francisco Laranjo is a graphic designer, writer and researcher based in Portugal. Laura Gordon is a designer, researcher and lecturer based in London.
11. Frontex is the semi-private governing agency held responsible for the management of all border control in the Schengen area.

12 Décollage is an artistic method that inscribes itself within critical technical practice, concerned with uncovering obfuscated material conditions of production.

13 *A Line Which Forms a Volume* borrows its title from a subheading in Michel Butor's essay 'The Book as Object', in *Inventory* (London: Jonathan Cape, 1970). Under this heading, the French novelist explores how writing records threads of speech and thoughts by dividing and stacking this continuous stream: 'every word follows one other, precedes one other. As a result, they take their places along a line activated by a meaning, along an axis.'

14 Theo Inglis, 'Line Dance', *Grafik*, 22 February 2018, grafik.net/category/feature/line-dance.

School days
Rob Giampietro

Originally commissioned by Andrew Blauvelt and Ellen Lupton for the catalogue *Graphic Design: Now in Production* in 2011, this essay by Rob Giampietro compares the emergence and proliferation of graduate programmes in graphic design to similar developments in creative writing education. Asking the question 'how are designers produced?', and following the lead of Mark McGurl's 2009 book, *The Program Era*, Giampietro discusses the systematisation of creativity and the rise of personal experience and self-examination as central tenets of graphic design education today.

'And you may ask yourself, well, how did I get here?'[1]

A few years ago, after being invited to serve as a critic for final reviews at an MFA graphic design programme, I found myself riding home with two designers and an architecture critic. Each designer had an MFA from a different programme, and the architecture critic was working on a PhD. I have a BA. All of us teach at the graduate level while working actively in the profession. After catching up a bit with one another, our discussion returned to the critique. 'Why do the students talk about their personal lives so much in explaining their work?', the architecture critic asked. 'What do their biographies have to do with it?' While it is certainly valid to question the place of personal histories in a professional context, to talk about ourselves and our stories, it nevertheless seems a persistent inclination among designers to do so. We hardly know we're doing it — look, I've opened here with an anecdote drawn from my own life story.

Perhaps part of this is that there is no one else to write these stories for us. Whether overtly biographical or simply self-referential, design remains even today in the peculiar position of having its history and criticism written largely by and for its own practitioners. Since most of us are involved in making things, we write quite naturally of the hows and whys of making them in a collective effort to evaluate a design's production. But what's gone into our own production? How are designers produced?

There are, of course, many ways, many paths — possibly as many as there are designers. Designers can certainly produce themselves as self-taught designers, often through equal parts passion, necessity and aesthetic brute force. Or designers can be produced by hands-on training through internships and on-the-job experiences. Or designers might arrive from other disciplines and professions. Here's a cross-section drawn from Rob Roy Kelly's account of the early days at Yale University in the 1950s:

> Most faculty members were well-schooled in art and design history, although several were educated in fields other than art or design. [Alvin] Eisenman, a Dartmouth graduate, studied typography with Paul Nash and had a book design and publishing background. [Lester] Beall had been educated in art history. [Alvin] Lustig did not have a formal education in art or design. [Leo] Lionni was educated as an economist in Italy and was a self-taught graphic designer. [Herbert] Matter studied painting at the Ecole des Beaux-arts in Geneva and the Academie Moderne in Paris under Leger and Ozenfant. [Bradbury] Thompson was a graduate of Washburn College, a small liberal arts school in Kansas. He had been a cartographer during World War II. Paul Rand, largely self-taught, was influenced by European painters and designers. He attended night classes at Pratt Institute, took some courses at Parsons School of Design and studied with George Grosz at the Art Students League.[2]

While there may be many routes into a life in design, recent years have found one path in particular on a steady rise: the graduate programme. And as more designers return to school for graduate degrees in graphic design than ever before, they fuel a growing list of graduate graphic design programmes. Beginning with just a few of these in the 1940s and 1950s, including the founding of the first MFA programme at Yale in 1951, the National Association of Schools of Art and Design (NASAD) now lists approximately 300 accredited institutions as its members, the great majority of which offer both graduate and undergraduate degrees in design, and, while the AIGA and other design organisations don't have precise numbers on record, there are published estimates of up to 2,000 graduate and undergraduate graphic design programmes in the US alone. By any measure, the design school business is booming.

Consider the example of the School of Visual Arts (SVA) in New York, which opened its Designer as Author (now Designer as Entrepreneur) MFA programme in 1998. Since then, SVA has entered a period of rapid expansion, opening one new graduate programme every two years, including programmes in Branding, Design Criticism, Design for Social Innovation, Interaction Design, and Products of Design. (I have been fortunate to teach, lecture, or visit in several of these programmes.) During the same period, designers Karel Martens and Wigger Bierma founded the influential Werkplaats Typografie (WT) (1998), Bruce Mau worked with Toronto's George Brown College to create the Institute without Boundaries (2003), and IDEO's David Kelley founded Stanford's d.school (2005).

This growth is hardly unique to design. Other creative disciplines have experienced a similarly steady increase in new programmes, particularly in graduate programmes, along a similar timeline. One of the most significant, both in terms of expansion and in terms of cultural impact, has been creative writing, which, starting with a handful of programmes in the 1940s, had increased this number to over 350 accredited institutions offering both graduate and undergraduate programmes by 2004.

The rise and impact of creative writing programmes in the postwar period is studied by UCLA English Professor Mark McGurl in his thoroughly illuminating book *The Program Era* (2009). McGurl takes my architecture colleague's earlier question about personal histories quite seriously:

> [The] category of 'personal experience' has over the course of the twentieth century, and in the postwar period in particular, achieved a functional centrality in the postindustrial economies of the developed world. These economies in turn inhabit what Ulrich Beck, Anthony Giddens, and others have described as a 'reflexive modernity'.[3]

The reflexively modern society, unlike the conventionally modern society, looks forward to the new *and* backward to its modern past, a modernity whose impact has been total and whose influence reverberates in every sector of culture. Instead of the dismantling and overtly critical strategy employed by postmodernism, the reflexively modern society seeks to examine and correct itself in order to keep placing itself back on track. The result is a heightened sense of self-awareness and self-preservation leading all the way back to the individual. McGurl writes that the utility of reflexive modernity as a concept 'leaps off the page, suggesting that literary practices might partake in a larger, multivalent social dynamic of self-observation', which includes 'the self-monitoring of individuals who understand themselves to be living, not lives simply, but *life stories* of which they are the protagonists'.

It is not simply the unexamined life here that is not worth living, but the unnarrated life — and far from a nostalgic examination, that narration is increasingly essential and increasingly likely to occur in real time. Far from narcissistic, McGurl writes, this instinct is decidedly self-preservational and potentially even an unwanted burden, like a kind of punishment:

> [As] Beck puts it, modern people 'are condemned to individualization'. To be subject to reflexive modernity is to feel a 'compulsion for the manufacture, self-design, and self-staging' of a biography, and, indeed, for the obsessive 'reading' of that biography even as it is being written. And in this project there are a host of agencies, including schools, waiting to help.

It would be quite natural to stop here and ask if graduate programmes in graphic design and creative writing can really be compared. While the writing programme has remained relatively consistent in its structure and steady in its evolution since its earliest days in the 1920s and 1930s at Bread Loaf in Middlebury, Vermont, and at the Iowa Writers' Workshop at the University of Iowa, graphic design programmes have changed and adapted to new currents in the profession. The first schools embraced the Bauhaus's original workshop structure (Josef Albers founded the Yale University School of Art and Mies Van Der Rohe directed the architecture programme and designed the campus at the Illinois Institute of Technology), but the model was soon restructured to include a more programmatic and analytical approach drawn from architectural training. Other schools throughout the 1960s and 1970s (like CalArts, founded by Walt Disney in 1961) popularised design through the lens of applied art training. When Katherine McCoy was appointed co-chair of the graduate design programme at Cranbrook Academy of Art in 1971, she combined an interest in architectural theory with the more language-based techniques drawn from the writings about deconstruction and post-structuralism by Barthes, Derrida and others. Sheila Levrant de Bretteville's arrival at Yale in 1990 extended these ideas to include postmodern notions of identity and a public-minded social awareness, giving design the broadened sense of a humanistic discipline sited at a major research university. Jan Van Toorn's arrival at the Jan van Eyck Academie in 1991 signaled a similar shift in the Netherlands. The end of the 1990s found design education having come full-circle, from Dan Fern's studio-practice-driven model at the Royal College of Art (RCA) in London to the Werkplaats Typografie's reintroduction of the workshop model in the Netherlands.

On this level, graphic design and creative writing programmes might be considered distant cousins at best. Both are creative pursuits sharing certain structures, like critique and peer review, but many more of these structures remain distinct to each. What McGurl's book offers to a designer reading it closely is not a set of examples to follow in explaining design education, but rather a methodology to adapt for investigating it. What if we play the old 'designer as author' metaphor in reverse, describing authorship not as an input or mode of creation, but as an output or model of practice: the designer as cultural influencer, identifiable persona and creator of a distinctly voiced body of work. This, perhaps, is how an author's training and a designer's training are linked.

And this is how the 'Program Era', a term that McGurl adapts from literary critic Hugh Kenner's earlier 'Pound Era', might resonate with designers today. 'The rise and spread of the creative writing programme over the course of the postwar period has transformed the conditions under which American literature is produced', McGurl writes, adding:

> It has fashioned a world where artists are systematically installed in the university as teachers, and where, having conceived a desire to become that mythical thing, a *writer*, a young person proceeds as a matter of course to request *application materials*. It has in other words converted the Pound Era into the Program Era.

Once dedicated to mastering basic skills of the craft, the school has become, in design's Program Era, tied instead to the production of a professional, the creation of a designer as a whole self, an individual with a self-actualised practice in which student work, not client work, often forms the basis for an introduction and ongoing access to the design sphere. Compare this to Lorraine Wild's description of the graduate school environment at Yale in 1982 that, she writes, functioned like a kind of boot camp where 'correct typography' consisted of 'using only one font with one weight change'. In this context, Wild wonders,

> Could you be forgiven, perhaps, for beginning to suspect that what you were being taught was not actually modernism at all, but habit? Or bizarre fraternity rituals? The similarities to frat hazing were alarming; if you did what you were told you would be let 'in'. ... If you asked questions, there were no sensible answers and you definitely risked rejection.[4]

Today, students' design work is less learning by rote than practice through self-examination. The resulting work, shared online and through institutions, events, talks, collaborations, extracurricular projects and other generally pedagogical methods, becomes, in effect, an advertisement for its accompanying self, the designer whose interests and academic path of inquiry shaped it, framed it and offered it into the context in which it now resides.

'For the modernist artist', McGurl writes, 'the reflexive production of the "modernist artist" — i.e., the job description itself, is a large part of the job'. These reflexive professional efforts, he suggests, are not all that 'radical' or even 'deconstructive' but instead 'perfectly routine', part of a system of self-reference that extends past the making of literature and to the making and organising of all things. McGurl describes this self-constitution of systems using a concept drawn from systems theory called 'autopoesis'. Designers know these efforts, under slightly different circumstances, as so-called 'self-initiated work', which comprises a good portion of what's done as an MFA student. And just as McGurl prepares a list of 'signature genres of the Program Era' — which includes the campus novel, the portrait of the artist, the workshop story collection, the ethnic family saga, meta-genre fiction and meta-slave narratives — we might attempt a designer's list along the same lines, including the thesis book, the process poster, the experimental typeface, the urban map, the data visualisation exercise, the group portrait photograph, the image archive, the slide talk, the meta-exhibition and the project-as-class performance.

Especially this last genre owes a debt to the recent 'pedagogical turn' in art, which suggests that education is itself a form of art, a facilitator of artist development, and a method for activating art in the public sphere. Among the key projects in this movement is Manifesta 6, which announced the creation of an art school in Nicosia, Cyprus, in place of a typically 'temporary, drop-on-a-city' exhibition.[5] Artist Anton Vidokle notes in the catalogue *Notes for an Art School*,

> The Bauhaus, in its brief period of activity, arguably accomplished what any number of Venice Biennials have not (and at a fraction of the cost) — a wide range of artistic practitioners coming together to redefine art, what it can and should be, and most importantly, to produce tangible results. All this in the face of Walter Gropius's famous assertion that 'art cannot be taught'. An art school, it would appear, does not teach art, but sets up the conditions necessary for creative production, and by extension the conditions for collaboration and social engagement.[6]

Vidokle's essay concludes with an 'Incomplete Chronology of Experimental Art Schools' beginning with the École national supérieure des beaux-arts (1671) and continuing through the Bauhaus (1919), Black Mountain College (1933), Skowhegan School of Painting & Sculpture (1946), Nova Scotia College of Arts & Design (1966), Whitney ISP Program (1968), Beuys's Free International University (1974), General Idea (1977), the Vera List Center for Art & Politics (1992), Mountain School of Art (2005) and beyond.

While Manifesta 6 did not come to be, it did serve as a catalyst for organising many groups including Dexter Sinister, who 'proposed to establish a print workshop as part of the [Manifesta] school, which would explore existing modes of art publishing and possibly suggest new ones'. In addition to the Bauhaus, Dexter Sinister looked to Toyota's 'just-in-time' production process as a model for their workshop. The spirit of this pragmatic academic/commercial workshop fit well with Manifesta's hybridised exhibition/academy format. Dexter Sinister, who designed *Notes*, also contributed the school's iconic blazon, a slashed shield that Steve Rushton likens to a typographic slash marking the tenuous boundary between terms like love/hate, speech/writing and, perhaps, art/school.

As art's 'pedagogical turn' seeks to dissolve or at least refashion this last boundary, so too does McGurl undertake an effort to frame writing as a distributed, multifocal and highly structured creative effort. With this, he completes the second of two substantive transformations of standard-issue Program Era criticisms. The first, as we have seen, is to dismiss the idea that programme work is narcissistically *self-involved* and instead suggest that it is enlightenedly *reflexive*. McGurl's second transformation is to dismiss the idea that programme work is 'generic', 'assembly-line' and basically *unoriginal* and instead suggest that it is deeply *systematic*.[7]

But how can a creative discipline be systematically taught? The question is pervasive. Earlier, we saw Vidokle nod to Bauhaus founder Gropius's assertion that 'art cannot be taught'. McGurl quotes the Iowa Writers' Workshop's official history in the same vein: 'though we agree in part with the popular insistence that writing cannot be taught', it states, 'we continue to look for the most promising talent in the country, in our conviction that writing cannot be taught but talent can be developed'. It's a careful balancing act of populism and elitism, allowing for the popular notion of individual genius on one hand while underscoring Iowa's legacy and prestige on the other. Neither Gropius nor Iowa doubts the possibility of the creative individual, but both seem at best anxious and at worst dismissive of a creative system. Creativity, especially in the last century, has been characterised as something that breaks from the pack; how, then, can it be broken down, spread out and passed on?

To the extent that there are systems in place to teach writing and other forms of creativity, they are not the same systems that are in place throughout the rest of the university. At Iowa, for example, one participant recalls that her teachers 'commented on what they liked or didn't like about a particular story, offered isolated bits of advice about technique, but most of us got through two years of instruction without any formal discussions of theory or craft'. The description might apply to many design classes as well. And while there was much debate, especially in the early 1990s among a new generation of design educators, of the potential for adapting theoretical systems in the teaching of design, 'slowly', notes Andrew Blauvelt in his essay 'Towards a Critical Autonomy', 'the debates subsided'.[8]

'Graduate schools', Blauvelt continues, 'whether celebrated or scorned, were once seen as the source of "the problem"' of design's reduction 'to its commodity form — simply a choice of vehicles for delivering a message: ad, billboard, book, brochure, typeface, website, and so on. Implicit in this reductive understanding is the denial of graphic design as a social practice and with it the possibility of disciplinary autonomy.' Here a new question has emerged: not 'can it be taught' but 'to what end'?

Lorraine Wild asks a similar question, writing in 2004 that 'for a time, some of the design schools were more responsible for creating a space where a little more perspective and independence about the practice and the "profession" could occur than anywhere else. The formal investigations produced by students and teachers were produced against this context, which utilized, and was enabled by, a reading of critical theory, and had large targets.'[9] But soon, she writes, these forms 'were so alluring (and so specific to a younger audience) that, like every other formal expression of a cultural idea in our consumer-based society, they entered the life cycle of visual style; that is, they were marketed'.[10] In Blauvelt's formulation, the project of teaching design is tied to the project of teasing design apart from other disciplines; in Wild's formulation, the project of teaching design is tied to the potential of the school's position as a space outside the commercial aims that design typically must serve.

But school was changing too. As McGurl notes, the increasing commodification of everyday goods (including those design objects that Blauvelt and Wild describe) required the marketing of 'the experience of being marketed to' as a reflexive thing unto itself. After a brief nod to Joseph Pine and James Gilmore's late 1990s business classic *The Experience Economy*,[11] McGurl quotes landscape architecture scholar Dean MacCannell's book *The Tourist* from a decade earlier to help illuminate this shift in our cultural understanding of school.[12] MacCannell, he writes, surveyed this new landscape of experiences and compared it to a 'generalised tourism' in which 'the value of things such as programmes, trips, courses, reports, articles, shows, conferences, parades, opinions, events, sights, spectacles, scenes, and situations of modernity is not determined by the amount of labor required for their production. Their value is tied to the quality and quantity of the *experience* they promise.'

What may have first looked like a shift away from the idea of including theory in the classroom was instead a shift towards the classroom as a lived experience in which people, places and real-world projects come together in a pragmatic whole — an idea that was advanced by the Werkplaats Typografie with its arrival in the late 1990s. In its prospectus, founders Karel Martens and Wigger Bierma describe the idea of 'Workshop as Meeting Place':

> For typographic designers who are just starting to practice — in this case, the participants of the Typography Workshop — it is vitally important that they become familiar with the standpoints and considerations of other typographic designers. The best way to do this is literally to enter into a conversation with them. Moreover, it is important that participants are offered the opportunity to *present* themselves to future colleagues.[13]

The prospectus goes on to describe the idea of carrying out real-world assignments alongside individual research as participants inhabit a fully-equipped studio where other participants, advisers and outside experts are all available to discuss and develop creative work.

And though its prospectus doesn't exactly describe a classic master/apprentice system, the Werkplaats's outside experts do seem to function in a similar way. McGurl notes a similar dynamic in the creative writing classroom, where the relationship between student and teacher is more of a creative 'apprenticeship' and knowledge is delivered informally via practice rather than systematically via syllabus. Perhaps, like the teaching of writing, the teaching of design at the graduate level has this kind of informal system at its root.

McGurl extends this idea further still, past the classroom and into the writing itself:

> Creative writing issues an invitation to student-consumers to develop an intensely personal relation to literary value, one that for the most part bypasses the accumulation of traditional cultural capital (that is, a relatively rarefied knowledge of great authors and their works) in favor

of a more immediate identification with the charisma of authorship. ... Part of the value of the modern literary text, quite apart from the 'relatability' of its characters, is the act of *authorship* that it records, offering readers a mediated experience of expressive selfhood as such.

Rather than separate the teaching of writing from the autopoetic act, the experience economy bundles them together. 'Is such a thing [as systematic creativity] possible?', McGurl finally asks. 'Or is it, rather, perfectly normal?' Isn't declaring a passion for a creative pursuit and making time for it in our busy lives, selecting to be in a group of similarly passionate people led by a mentor who has been successful at that effort, improving our work through discussion and debate, and developing a sense of ourselves and our role in the wider field of cultural production — isn't that a system? Isn't it one that allows us to grow and be more creative? Isn't it one that asks us to teach and learn, lead and follow, remain who we are and be changed by our surroundings? Don't our deepest lived experiences change us? And isn't school one of them?

Setting aside the anxieties that naturally surround discussions of systematic creativity in this way is just one of McGurl's many useful insights into the world of creative training and how we might reflect differently about it — to reevaluate (and to crib a favourite author) What We Talk about When We Talk about Education. The key question is not, as McGurl so lucidly observes, 'Programs: pro or con?' Instead, he suggests, we need studies that seriously examine the influence of these programmes on literary production and interpretation in the post-war period. What, he asks, are the social factors that gave rise to these programmes? How, in their sheer magnitude, have these programmes reorganised creative production in our time? And how might we seek a new and more nuanced awareness of the creative products they produce?

Perhaps around the bright sun of design we have, during the last few years of our own Program Era, added more planets, more moons and comets, more elliptical orbits, more complexity and more interconnectedness to our disciplinary universe as it expands ever-outward. This idea ran through part of a Rhode Island School of Design (RISD) MFA syllabus that I wrote several years ago called 'Graphic Design & Critical Thinking', which, if I can indulge in a second autobiographical moment, I will quote here:

> Designers are asked to have a tremendous number of technical and analytical skills at our disposal to communicate information that is unfamiliar to us. Borrowing from Alice Twemlow's book *What Is Graphic Design For?*,[14] a few of the forms that designers regularly use include: typefaces, motion graphics, music and sounds, games, signage and wayfinding systems, posters, magazines and periodicals, books, information graphics, interactive systems, identity systems, advertising, writing, software programs, and more. All of these forms require very different skills, different critical tools for understanding them, and different expectations from audiences in terms of which forms suit certain kinds of content best.

Rather than seeing design as a single paradigm practised in a uniform way by canonical figures, this 'universal' model of design — McGurl would note the similarity to 'university' — sees a multiple, shifting set of polarities with highly influential individuals and institutions acting as centres of gravity. The task for emerging designers is to first enter an orbit and then, if they wish, increase their gravitational pull over time. A wider variety of schools and programmes naturally help to foster this exercise in self-definition. As more types of people described as 'designers' arrive, however, skillsets can grow more distinct and distant from one another.

One of the effects of this broadening has been that design has, in recent years, become noticeably less like a trade and more like a humanistic discipline than ever before. As part of this shift, designer and professor Gunnar Swanson authored a call in 1994 to reconsider 'Graphic Design as a Liberal Art'.[15] He writes,

> We must begin to believe our own rhetoric and see design as an integrative field that bridges many subjects that deal with communication, expression, interaction, and cognition. Design should be about meaning and how meaning can be created. Design should be about the relationship of form and communication. It is one of the fields where science and literature meet. It can shine a light on hidden corners of sociology and history. Design's position as conduit for and shaper of popular values can be a path between anthropology and political science. Art and education can both benefit through the perspective of a field that is about expression and the mass dissemination of information. Designers, design educators, and design students are in a more important and interesting field than we seem to recognize.

In Swanson's formulation, design as a discipline acts as a kind of guide between disciplines, adopting and adapting specific theoretical concerns of each and passing them through the lenses of form, communication and distribution. To this process, Blauvelt adds the important quality of reflexivity:

> Graphic design must be seen as a discipline capable of generating meaning out of its own intrinsic resources without reliance on commissions, functions, or specific materials or means. Such actions should demonstrate self-awareness and reflexivity; a capacity to manipulate the system of graphic design.

If humanistic disciplines bridge the analytic, critical, and speculative impulses in understanding ourselves and our world, then design is increasingly engaged in all three of these impulses. It always has been analytic, attempting to understand and solve problems in both the commercial and cultural spheres. But, with the support of academic institutions like schools and museums, design has explored a critical role as well. 'Critical design' is a term associated with a growing set of designers, including the RCA's Anthony Dunne and Fiona Raby. 'Speculative design', another alternative practice model and cousin to critical design, has sprung up with methods allowing designers to unpack new scenarios of technology, citizenship, communication and power. Metahaven, who teach, lecture and publish widely, are frequently cited as touchstones for speculative design and practice.

The subdiscipline of 'design research' has been launched as well. In his preface to one of the first collections on the topic, UCLA's Peter Lunenfeld begins by stipulating that 'the territory is vast' but cites Rem Koolhaas as one possible model for design practice in three ways: 'first, to understand the context of any building project he might wish to undertake; second, to develop the building's program itself; and third, in a reflexive way, as a selling tool for the research and the building themselves'.[16] Research, in this model, is not only an analytic method but also a cultural product unto itself.

And there's 'design thinking', a kind of re-envisioning of problem-solving itself, less didactic and more open-ended, less specifically about problems and solutions and more of a method for observation and analysis, particularly within larger corporations and institutions. Its name is a curious mash-up of forming things and formulating ideas, which are both separated ('designing' and 'thinking') and intertwined ('design thinking'). It may, in the minds of many, be more easily associated with a set of advocates than a set of concepts, as Helen Walters wrote in early 2011 for *Fast Company*:

> I joined [BusinessWeek] back in 2006, which was a time when design thinking was really beginning to take hold as a concept. My old boss, Bruce Nussbaum, emerged as its eloquent champion while the likes of Roger Martin from Rotman, IDEO's Tim Brown, my new boss Larry Keeley and even the odd executive (A. G. Lafley of Procter & Gamble comes to mind) were widely quoted espousing its virtues.[17]

Other than Walters and Nussbaum, who are journalists, each of these figures is associated with a postgraduate educational institution: Martin became Dean at Rotman School of Business in 1998 (before that, Lafley was his client at Monitor, a consulting group), Brown at Stanford University's d.school, and Keeley at Chicago's Illinois Institute of Technology. Walters's article continues:

> Still, in the years that have followed, something of a problem emerged. ... When we stopped and looked, it seemed like executives had issues rolling out design thinking more widely throughout the firm. And much of this stemmed from the fact that there was no consensus on a definition of design thinking, let alone agreement as to who's responsible for it, who actually executes it, or how it might be implemented at scale.

With its collection of faculty-advocates, its self-evolving set of methods, its position as a primarily theoretical rather than practical structure, and, above all, its assertion that — unlike the more action-oriented, collective 'doers' of business cultures past — this process defined by a more contemplative, individual 'thinker', 'design thinking' is in every way more the kind of movement that emerges from a school than the kind that emerges from a typical boardroom.

And it is the kind of movement that's funded like a school as well, complete with the grants, fellowships, prizes and an expanding base of institutional support. As programmes grow, many designers may also rely on teaching to support their practices, and many grad students may look to teaching as a way to remain engaged in the more reflexive practice of design they currently study. 'Like most writers these days, I support myself by preaching what I practice', jokes John Barth in his 1966 novel *Giles Goat-Boy; or, The Revised New Syllabus*[18] (which appears nearby Chip Kidd's *The Cheese Monkeys: A Novel in Two Semesters* from 2001 on Wikipedia's illuminating list of 'the school and university in literature').[19]

But before we settle too comfortably into this system of increased support, there are those who take a more cautionary tone. As historian and theorist Thierry de Duve notes in the book *Art School (Propositions for the 21st Century)*:

> Art schools have not always existed, and nothing says that they must always exist. Their proliferation is perhaps a *trompe l'œil*, masking the fact that the transmission of art today from artist to artist is very far from occurring directly in schools.[20]

In de Duve's version of events, the growth of art schools is not a steady trend but an illusory and temporary event. This is the 'school experience' as goldrush, like a kind of speculative bubble about to burst — with dozens of ad-hoc schools, for-profit trade academies and educational ventures jockeying for a piece of the student loan industry pie. There is now more education-related debt than credit card debt in the US.

And there may be overeducation, too. While there has never been a more important goal than universal access to a college education, the US Bureau of Labor Statistics nonetheless reports that seventeen million Americans with college degrees do jobs that do not require them. In the sciences, the number of PhDs given has grown by nearly 40 percent during every year since 1998, reaching 34,000 doctorates in 2008. In her essay 'The PhD Problem', science writer Kate Shaw cautions that 'the workforce cannot absorb all these highly trained graduates', most of whom 'are fully funded through research assistantships, teaching opportunities, and fellowships. With so many graduates these days taking jobs they are overqualified for, some educators and economists believe this money is simply being wasted.'[21] These developments suggest that education may need to adopt a more streamlined attitude in the years to come.

During an interview in *Eye magazine* from 1997, Paul Elliman noted that:

> It almost doesn't matter that it's graphic design I'm teaching. There must be equivalents in all academic areas of people who teach through a sense of passion. ... The World Wide Web — an environment where, for better or worse, connection is everything — suggests, among other things, new possibilities for design and its education.[22]

Elliman continues,

> This space allows both practice and reflexivity. For the 'school', both as extension to the old model and in the transition to a new one, the

Internet will offer a more continuous dialogue with practicing designers, and with other specialized areas, in ways that could counter some of the problems and complexities found in the institutional teaching of design.

To tweak Gropius's assertion once more, the question here is not 'can it be taught', but rather 'can it be taught in school'? Because just as art is a frame for a certain kind of aesthetic practice, school is a frame for a certain kind of pedagogical practice. And just as there are types of aesthetics that are not called art or are coming to be known as art, so too are there types of pedagogy that are not called school or are coming to be known as school.

Vidokle notes in his essay that his research into the Manifesta 6 school project unearthed 'an amazing range of schools in the past 100 years' that suggest an ever-changing field. 'Art education is not in stasis', he writes. 'It is being constantly rethought, restructured, and reinvented.' De Duve calls the extracurricular teaching and learning of artistic practice 'transmission' and suggests, along with its deprofessionalisation, that it be made available to everyone, not just art students. As Raymond Williams's *Keywords* project teaches us time and again, what we call things now may be different than what we call them in the future.[23]

But whatever we call design school next, our design schools now have undoubtedly produced the design culture we share today, and perhaps this is exactly the point. As more designers go to school, go back to school, and return again to teach in school; as there are more postgrad 'lifelong learning' environments like conferences and meetups; as there is more discussion and debate online, in after-work lectures and weekend book fairs and degree shows; as designers seek to make themselves better, learn more, and define a life in design as an unfolding lived experience — as all this happens, then the culture of design becomes increasingly more like the culture of school. As we look back on this period in the years to come, these may be design's school days indeed.

This essay was first published in *Graphic Design: Now in Production*, edited by Andrew Blauvelt and Ellen Lupton (Minneapolis: Walker Art Center, 2011), 212–221.

1. Talking Heads, 'Once in a Lifetime', *Remain in Light*, Talking Heads and Brian Eno, Sire Records, 1980, sound recording.
2. Rob Roy Kelly, 'The Early Years of Graphic Design at Yale University', *Design Issues* 17, no. 3 (2001).
3. Quotations from McGurl in this essay are from: Mark McGurl, *The Program Era: Postwar Fiction and the Rise of Creative Writing* (Cambridge: Harvard University Press, 2009).
4. Lorraine Wild, 'Castles Made of Sand', *Emigre 66: Nudging Graphic Design*, edited by Rudy VanderLans (New York: Princeton Architectural Press, 2004), 111.
5. Emily King, 'Wouldn't it be nice...', interview with Dexter Sinister, 25 October 2007, http://www.dextersinister.org/index.html?id=123, accessed 30 May 2011.
6. Anton Vidokle, 'Exhibition as School in a Divided City', in *Notes for an Art School* (Nicosia: Manifesta 6 School Books, 2006).
7. Steve Rushton, 'Sinister/Bastard', in *Notes for an Art School* (Nicosia: Manifesta 6 School Books, 2006).
8. Andrew Blauvelt, 'Towards a Critical Autonomy', in *Looking Closer 5: Critical Writings on Graphic Design*, edited by Michael Beirut, William Drenttel and Steven Heller (New York: Allsworth Press, 2007).
9. Wild, 'Castles Made of Sand', 119.
10. Ibid.
11. Joseph Pine and James H. Gilmore, *The Experience Economy: Work is Theater & Every Business a Stage* (Cambridge: Harvard Business Press, 1999).
12. Dean MacCannell, *The Tourist: A New Theory of the Leisure Class* (Berkeley: University of California Press, 1999).

13 Karel Martens and Wigger Bierma, 'WT Prospectus', in *In Alphabetical Order: File Under: Graphic Design, Schools, or Werkplaats Typografie*, edited by Stuart Bailey (Rotterdam, the Netherlands: NAi Publishers, 2003).
14 Alice Twemlow, *What is Graphic Design For?* (East Sussex: Rotovision, 2006).
15 Gunnar Swanson, 'Graphic Design as a Liberal Art', in *The Education of a Graphic Designer*, edited by Steven Heller (New York: Allsworth Press, 2005).
16 Peter Lunenfeld, Preface to *Design Research: Methods and Perspectives*, edited by Brenda Laurel (Cambridge: MIT Press, 2003).
17 Helen Walters, 'Design Thinking Isn't a Miracle Cure, but Here's How It Helps', *Co.Design*, 24 March 2011, http://www.fastcodesign.com/1663480/helen-walters-design-thinking-buzzwords, accessed 23 May 2011.
18 John Barth, *Giles Goat Boy* (Harpswell: Anchor, 1987).
19 Wikipedia, 'School and University in Literature', http://en.wikipedia.org/wiki/School_and_university_in_literature, accessed 23 May 2011.
20 Thierry de Duve, 'An Ethics: Putting Aesthetic Transmission in Its Proper Place in the Art World', in *Art School: (Propositions for the 21st Century)*, edited by Steven Henry Madoff (Cambridge: MIT Press, 2009).
21 Kate Shaw, 'The PhD problem: are we giving out too many degrees?', *Ars Technica*, 25 April 2011, http://arstechnica.com/science/news/2011/04/the-phd-problem-what-do-you-do-with-too-many-doctorates.ars, accessed 23 May 2011.
22 Rick Poynor, 'Profile: Paul Elliman', *Eye*, no. 25 (1997).
23 Raymond Williams, *Keywords: A Vocabulary of Culture and Society* (Oxford: Oxford University Press, 1985).

Parse and iterate
Rob Giampietro, interviewed by Vincent Chan

Rob Giampietro's practice spans designing, teaching and writing. His influential essay 'School Days', originally commissioned for the catalogue for *Graphic Design: Now in Production* in 2011 and also reproduced in this book, reflects on the rise of graduate programmes in graphic design since the late 1990s. In this conversation, Vincent Chan picks up on lines of thinking in 'School Days' to explore Giampietro's own experiences and methods as an educator, and how these intersect with his parallel practices as a designer and writer.

VC   One idea I'm interested in unravelling with you is the relationship between education and vocation. In your essay 'School Days', you make the point that design schools have produced design culture today. What are your thoughts on how institutions and industry should relate to one another? Is their influence mutual, or should each maintain some autonomy? Should educational institutions propose new paths, or should they simply provide work-ready graduates?

RG   My essay takes Mark McGurl's book *The Program Era* and uses a close reading to adapt it for a design context. McGurl is talking about a 'pure art form', creative writing, and design is more often considered an 'applied art form', so there isn't a perfect correlation; it's more of a translation than a mirroring.[1] What I found really interesting is the way he looked at how a writer develops. In the 1920s, a writer went to Paris, experienced the city, did a lot of writing and became a cultural figure. Then this shifted, and at a certain point a writer needed to go to school and be trained and kind of produce themselves as a writer. The grad schools were in charge of that production, so that the writer arrived on the scene fully formed. Nowadays, this is increasingly the case with MFAs for artists as well. Recently graduated artists will have a gallery show, more or less of their MFA work, and arrive on the scene professionalised. It's interesting to see how, in these 'pure art forms', the professionalisation of the emerging practitioner is handled by the graduate programmes.

If we look at the history of how design schools arose, there were a lot of different models. There's the Bauhaus model, which is, to an extent, a workshop or apprenticeship model, but basically as you move west across the US to California, design school becomes more professionalised and more like a kind of preparatory school. There's this history of becoming a professional through your work, but I think a lot of designers now go to school to make work that they couldn't make somewhere else, or to uncover new pathways in their work that simply doing commissioned work wouldn't allow them to do. It's important for school to be a place where people can take those risks.

VC   You have used the term 'professionalise' a couple of times. Michael Rock, in his essay 'Deprofessionalization', writes, 'the current state of deprofessionalization means we must jettison the dream of a singular definition of design practice. Why should design have some unified field theory anyway?'[2] Could you comment on the notion of design as a profession? And perhaps a second quote that might have some relevance is from Raqs Media Collective, regarding the education of an artist:

> Being someone, and learning to be someone are seen as two distinct moments, with the first following the successful completion of the second. While this might be true generally, it is difficult to sustain this understanding of art education as a phase that merely seeks its posthumous completion in the career of an artist. Artists undertake to transform themselves continually through their practices and throughout their working lives. For an artist, there can be no rigid

separation between being someone and learning to become someone. The reason to continue to be an artist lies in an everyday rediscovery of what remains to be said or done. Being an artist is no different from learning to become an artist.[3]

RG Both quotes are apt. There has been talk in educational circles over the years about the concept of 'deschooling', popularised by Ivan Illich in *Deschooling Society* (1971), which advocates shifting learning out of an institutional structure and re-centring it on the learner. Illich writes,

> The current search for new educational funnels must be reversed into the search for their institutional inverse: educational *webs* which heighten the opportunity for each one to transform each moment of his living into one of learning, sharing, and caring. We hope to contribute concepts needed by those who conduct such counterfoil research on education — and also to those who seek alternatives to other established service industries.[4]

There's a balancing act that happens in an MFA: an artist who is being taught in that context is absolutely being professionalised and acclimated to the gallery scene, and to curatorial practice, and at the same time they're being taught how to be an artist. McGurl observes the same thing as Raqs Media Collective when he writes that, for a modernist artist, the production of the artistic self is part of the job. That self-production can be continuous. Rock, meanwhile, is talking about the danger of professionalisation. In the architectural context, for example, where you become a member of an architectural association and there are certain skills you're tested on, that then risks becoming normative instead of encouraging design to draw from other disciplines in a continuous attempt to reformulate and critique itself.

VC You've been involved with pedagogy in various ways, at institutions like the School of Visual Arts (SVA), Rhode Island School of Design (RISD) and Parsons, but also in projects like the 'Teacher's College' workshop at the Free University of Bozen-Bolzano and Dexter Sinister's Banff project, 'From the Toolbox of a Serving Library'. The last two are unique in that they asked what design education could look like outside of existing frameworks. Could you speak about these two specific experiences? Were they purely speculative, or did they have pragmatic and transferable outcomes?

RG 'School Days' ends with this image of taking the school apart, both in the sense that a school is more than four walls, and also through Paul Elliman's idea of the 'free listener', a student who is 'able to wander at will and determine his or her own educational needs'.[5] Those are interesting and important images to keep in mind. There's also a section of my essay that talks about a continual re-normalisation of what school is. So we might now describe school as a series of YouTube videos, like the videos Salman Khan uploaded for his cousins on that platform as homework help starting in 2007, a startup we now know as Khan Academy — before, we might have always imagined school as a building or physical classroom. So I approached both workshops with that kind of spirit of mediation and disembodiment, to some extent. The best thing about being a design writer is that you put writing out into the world and you find friends who are interested in what you're talking about, and that was the case with David Reinfurt and Stuart Bertolotti-Bailey in Banff, and also in Bozen-Bolzano with Georgio Camuffo. With Georgio, it was interesting to learn about the Italian system of the *maestro*, where you trace your intellectual heritage back to an individual. This goes all the way back to the Renaissance, to the model of the painter's workshop, which is interesting.

VC   The way you pitched your Bozen-Bolzano workshop, 'Teacher's College', seemed reminiscent of Manifesta 6, as a place to imagine what's possible without any boundaries. I recall that there was a Github repository at one point, which acted as a kind of open-source curriculum.

RG   Sadly, I think the Github repo just went down. I just imagined it would always exist. But I do have a screenshot of it, so I can prove its existence!
   After I introduced the workshop in Bozen-Bolzano, and talked about why I cared about the subject, we talked about learning, and the students had a passionate discussion about the right way to teach design. Then they divided up into teams and did some short research and basically re-formatted the class so that the students became the teachers, which is exactly what I wanted to happen. I don't know if I would say that we left that experience with a sense of a new possibility of school, but we definitely left feeling like we shared a lot of different perspectives on education.
   To circle back to the Banff workshop: David and Stuart are long-time collaborators of mine, so when they got the residency in Banff it was natural to get the band together to do it. I was always going to talk about networks and mediated technology, so the idea of doing a chat with me, both in terms of scheduling and in the spirit of what I was talking about, made sense. I wrote this chat titled 'I am a handle', which was delivered as a lecture via iMessage.
   I was assigned the 'handle' from the Photoshop toolbox by David and Stuart, without too much explanation as to why I should take that on. At the time, I had been thinking a lot about riddles. What I love about a riddle is that the object speaks for itself, and I really wanted to write something like that in the first person. I had this idea for a while and somehow it just came up through being a chatbot that it could both be a riddle about what a handle is, and this metaphor that I was going to make. Soon after that, I saw a friend, David Cole, who is an interaction designer and who also designs a lot of games, both analogue and digital. He was talking to me about the 'desktop metaphor' and I was really excited about this idea that would somehow bring these two things together. And, really, the whole workshop was a metaphor, taking a Photoshop toolbox and taking those tools, using them metaphorically as teaching exercises or as teaching prompts. It was very much in the style of Josef Albers. The way he taught colour was very metaphorical. What was nice about the Toolbox project was that it produced a lot of writing and research from a lot of different people, and all of that was shared publicly. I guess it could be compared with the traditional educational model of the symposium,

but it took down the walls of the school. It was a much more open context. I really enjoyed that.

VC Alongside more conventional design subjects like typography, publication design and branding, you've taught workshops and classes on topics such as 'Circuitry', the 'Content Management System' and 'Antithesis'. I imagine that writing these classes involves wrestling with the topic yourself, and that your students become interlocutors, to a degree. Here I'm also specifically thinking of Jacques Rancière's *Ignorant Schoolmaster*, in which he writes: 'it's the explicator that needs the incapable and not the other way around. To explain something to someone is first to show him that he cannot understand it by himself.'[6] Can you describe how, in your experience, teaching, learning and practising relate? Are they distinct modes that occur in a virtuous cycle, or can they — or *should* they — be conflated or collapsed somehow?

RG It's certainly been a lot more interesting to me, the longer I've been a teacher, to try to blur teaching and learning as much as I can. The 'Circuitry', the 'CMS' and the 'Antithesis' workshops were through the RISD MFA grad programme — which is the longest-running job I've ever had! — and so I feel very connected to the programme that we've built there with Bethany Johns, who is Graduate Program Coordinator in Graphic Design, and our other colleagues. In working with grad students, I needed to shift my teaching, because teaching undergrads, which I did at Parsons for several years, really has a lot to do with a certain parsing of the assignment into smaller, more easily executable bits. And then there's also the insistence that those things get done, to instil a sense of discipline, which more advanced students may not need.

There was a point at which I realised that I didn't want to play that role with my grad students: they were adults, at a different point in their careers. Also, they were very capable of co-creation, of creating things *with* me rather than *for* me. I got a lot more out of the classes by bringing a problem to them and working on it together, rather than by giving them this rehearsed assignment that I knew 'would work'. I mean, I'm very comfortable with things not working. Essentially, the way I teach at RISD is I have two three-day weekends in the fall and two in the spring that focus on the grad thesis, and then in the middle of that there is a winter session, a period in between the two semesters, and I always get to do a workshop. The projects we make at that time form a fork in the road, a suggestion of some kind of other path that the students might need. For example, in 2015, we did a project around the Eameses' multi-screen work for IBM at the 1964 New York World's Fair, *Think!* — my class was titled 'Re-think!' The students had to make an explanatory work for multiple screens, and essentially the reason I assigned that is because the students had made very wordy presentations that didn't take into account the fact that they were being read aloud, and which showed very little imagery, and I wanted to open up a channel. I was thinking a lot about explanation and about how all the students are always wanting to be very metaphorical and poetic in their work, but that metaphor and poetic approaches sometimes mask weak reasoning, or keep the students from just saying what they really mean.

At the time, I was also working as a Design Manager and Creative Lead at Google, and I was thinking a lot about the Eameses in relation to my work there — thinking about what they did for IBM, the way they created an intellectual agenda for the company on a mass scale, and the rich possibility of that historical moment. I wanted to explode that and unpack it with my students. Every year, I change the workshop, and every year it's very targeted and functions as a metaphor for the class's exploration. The last two years, 2017 and 2018, we've been looking at the structure of writing.

VC It sounds like the 'Antithesis' workshop was a nice way to shake up some of the tired ways of working that your students may have settled into.

RG Each group is different. Long-term projects can languish sometimes, so we designers need to be reminded of the different potentials presented by working quickly. We sometimes complain about people not recognising how much time design takes, but we can publish work quickly — much faster, for example, than the time it takes an architect to build a building. This is a meaningful aspect of graphic design work. With the workshop, I wanted to remind the students of that, and to force them to make things quickly rather than overly plan and pre-verbalise their projects, so speed is always also a component of these short workshop-style classes.

VC I'm aware of a class you taught titled 'Graphic Design and Critical Thinking'. The first iteration was built on the first branches of philosophical inquiry, and the second, with Luke Bulman, was pitched as a platform for thinking about design as an engaged cultural practice. In Bertolotti-Bailey's 'Towards a Critical Faculty', he also champions this idea of educating for a progressive reflexivity, teaching students to observe their practice from both inside and out.[7] Can you speak to the outcomes of those two classes, and do you see critical thinking or philosophical inquiry as fundamental, transferable skill sets that design educators should promote?

RG To take the second part first, I think yes, absolutely, particularly reflexivity. If there's one key message in 'School Days', it's about the power of reflection on one's practice and that that, in a way, is the best teacher. That is the way forward for any designer to continue to iterate and develop work. Those classes were really early sketches of that philosophy, which has borne itself out over the next dozen or so years of my teaching. And the legacy of those two classes does live on. A hybrid of them is still taught at RISD with a similar syllabus and many of the same reading materials. I inherited my class from Alice Twemlow and I just gently manoeuvred things around based on ideas I'd introduced in *Dot Dot Dot* and other things I thought students should read. Then I got a lot of feedback on the course, changed some things again, and then invited Luke Bulman to co-teach with me, and he brought a great level of rigour and different ideas from his training as an architect at Rice University. Then I was able to become a thesis advisor and I was excited about that, because I love working closely with the thesis and graduating students. It's a nice thing because they care more about their thesis than anything else, so you get the students at their highest point of investment. There's some emotional work you have to do to mitigate the anxiety that accompanies that level of attention, but, in terms of the work the students are producing, it's really amazing.

VC   It seems like you have quite a sensitive barometer to being stagnant. You're always moving. You were at Winterhouse originally, and then you started your own studio with a partner, then you went to Project Projects as a principal, then Google, and most recently you have moved to working as Director of Design at the Museum of Modern Art. I get the impression that you're always curious and always trying to push yourself, aiming for something slightly out of your reach.

RG   Yes, I think there have always been changes in context, and in terms of how I make work — but, at the same time, there have been the constants of writing and teaching that have gone alongside those things. I really like the Rem Koolhaas formulation of the 'critic in the studio'. No one would ever say he doesn't design his own buildings, but in a way he and OMA are also creating contexts and fostering a group of people that is always changing, spinning off and re-shifting. And Koolhaas edits, shapes, motivates or cajoles that work to happen. As a critical person, that's a model I feel I can really embrace. When it first came out, I got *S, M, L, XL* as a gift from my parents, who were puzzled and asked, 'why do you want this massive book?' Koolhaas was always someone I was curious about in terms of how he works. More and more, I go back and re-read certain things he has written.

VC   Okay, two more quotes for discussion. Richard Hollis writes that 'graphic design constitutes a kind of language with an uncertain grammar and a continuously expanding vocabulary',[8] and Andrew Blauvelt has characterised the field as a 'vast, formless body, able to absorb any blows delivered to it, lacking coherency and increasingly dispersed'.[9] Graphic design seems to be in a state of expansion and fragmentation, both swelling to encompass neighbouring domains of activity while also splintering into discrete coteries. Can you speak to this tension?

RG   Graphic design is still a young discipline — maybe 150 years old, at the most, if you see it as deeply connected to industrial production, as I do. So I think that it was — or is — due for expansion, and also for more radical forms of inclusiveness and diversity, and I think these are all things to be applauded.
    The other thing is the 'Dunbar number' effect, that upper limit of how many social relationships you can keep in your head at one time, and that keeps a group of people connected to one another.[10] As design grows, you always have new subsets: motion designers, brand designers, interaction designers, user experience designers, and so on. Then they synthesise and blur together again. I do see this effect at work, but I don't see it as something to worry about.

VC I guess I'm thinking about Blauvelt writing what might be understood as a call for disciplinary autonomy. To me there's a tension there, in trying to consolidate while you also have this outward swelling, and I wonder if those can both happen at the same time.

RG I don't think you can establish a programme that purports to teach graphic design without establishing a certain degree of disciplinary autonomy — perhaps this is the appeal of 'de-schooling' as I mentioned earlier — but in establishing a specific programme you make the articulation of whatever discipline you've made autonomous the subject of critique as well. In a very small, focused way, that's exactly what 'Teacher's College' was. The workshop I did was essentially saying: this is a class that will become autonomous and articulate itself. In doing that, a huge range of critiques of what design can and should be emerged, and ultimately that's very productive and generative.

VC Related to this discussion is a quote from Yvan Martinez and Joshua Trees, from a publication titled *Thought Experiments in Graphic Design Education*. In the foreword, we read:

> Graphic Design education can be considered an ongoing thought experiment forever performing a triple paradox: (a) transcending disciplines while seeking respect as a discipline, (b) being simultaneously ubiquitous and invisible as a field/process/profession/subject and (c) being simultaneously vital and inconsequential to the so-called real world.[11]

Does this seem like an accurate assessment to you?

RG I guess I would say I agree with 'a' and 'b' and maybe take issue with 'c'. I think design's vitality is undisputed, while its inconsequentiality is simply the product of designers being too humble with regard to the impact they think they can make.

I do think that transcending disciplines while simultaneously trying to seek respect *as a discipline* is difficult. We live in an information economy and the jobs within an information economy are primarily about the manipulation of information and the successful shifting of information from one place to another to create value. When I was working at Google, we wouldn't define the shape or the size of the screen, the cropping of an image, the specific layout of the page, or even the colours on the page. All of those things could basically be generated algorithmically, based on a set of rules the designer might define. I think these kinds of methods are going to push us into generating new forms and they are going to push our work into new realms of possibility, and so I'm going to chase them. I'm going to run headlong into these opportunities — although it will make it harder for me to say exactly what I made!

VC I suppose you're designing systems, and when I think of a manual counterpart to that, I think of Conditional Design.

RG   Absolutely, I had Luna Maurer, one of the authors of the 'Conditional Design' manifesto and partner at the firm Moniker, speak at SPAN 2015, Google's design conference in London. It was interesting to bring someone like her to a group of developers, and to see how much her work resonated with them. She got a standing ovation! That was an important part of my role and time at Google: building bridges and introducing different worlds of practice to one another, in order to create some new sparks of possibility. There's something deeply human about Moniker's work, even though they are very interested in algorithmic processes, and I think that was inspiring to a group of very excited humans who nevertheless work on algorithms. Moniker show us that an algorithm can be a method or an approach to the world. And that's what Stuart's article 'Only an Attitude of Orientation' talks a lot about, the approach.[12]

VC   It seems that, for you, thinking programmatically is quite a prevalent lens. Often in this conversation you've used terms like 'parse' — this kind of logic seems to be a productive way to think through design systems.

RG   When I graduated from Yale as an undergrad, I designed mostly books and some identity work, both of which are very systematic, and so I think once I found web and interactive design, I found this whole body of knowledge on how to approach systematic work that was super rich for me, and which continues to be very rich. And it also feels like it's not set. It's not that there's a set way to make a book, but the landscape of how to make interactive work is changing every day and that is really fun to be a part of, to see the research happening, and having things coming off the line and being able to play with them right away. As a designer, that is very fun, and it is a privileged place to be. You asked about shifts in my career and they honestly and truly are a surprise to me. I try to keep interested in myself. It's sort of a game of not getting bored of who you are — an endless and lifelong self-education.

1   Mark McGurl, *The Program Era: Postwar Fiction and the Rise of Creative Writing* (Cambridge, MA & London: Harvard University Press, 2011).
2   Michael Rock, 'Deprofessionalization', in *Multiple Signatures: On Designers, Authors, Readers and Users* (New York: Rizzoli, 2013), 226.
3   Raqs Media Collective, 'How to be an artist by night', in *Art School (Propositions for the 21st Century)*, edited by Steven Henry Madoff (Cambridge, MA: MIT Press, 2009), 74.
4   Ivan Illich, *Deschooling Society* (New York: Harper & Row, 1971), xix–xx.
5   Rick Poynor, 'Other Spaces', *Eye*, vol. 7, no. 25, Summer 1997, http://www.eyemagazine.com/feature/article/other-spaces.
6   Jacques Rancière, *The ignorant schoolmaster: five lessons in intellectual emancipation* (Stanford: Stanford University Press, 1991), 6.
7   Stuart Bertolotti-Bailey's 'Toward a Critical Faculty' is a 'short reader concerned with art/design education' compiled for the Academic Workshop at Parsons School of Design, The New School, New York, Winter 2006/7, available at: http://www.dextersinister.org/MEDIA/PDF/criticalfaculty.pdf.
8   Richard Hollis, 'Introduction', in *Graphic Design: A Concise History* (London: Thames & Hudson, 1994), 10.
9   Andrew Blauvelt, 'Towards Critical Autonomy or Can Graphic Design Save Itself?', *Emigre 64: Rant* (Sacramento and New York: Emigre and Princeton Architectural Press, 2003), 38.
10 R. I. M. Dunbar, 'Neocortex Size as a Constraint on Group Size in Primates', *Journal of Human Evolution* 22, no. 6 (1992): 469–493.
11 Yvan Martinez and Joshua Trees, 'Thought Experiments in Graphic Design Education', in *Thought Experiments in Graphic Design Education*, edited by Yvan Martinez and Joshua Trees (London: Booksfromthefuture, 2013), 3.

12 'Only an Attitude of Orientation' is 'another pamphlet concerned with art/design education', compiled by Stuart Bertolotti-Bailey as a sequel to 'Towards a Critical Faculty', edited and published by Office for Contemporary Art Norway, Oslo, Winter 2009/10, available at: http://www.dextersinister.org/MEDIA/PDF/OaAoO.pdf.

A terminal degree
Stuart Bertolotti-Bailey, interviewed by Luke Wood

This interview is an edited version of a sprawling email conversation conducted in 2015, shortly after Stuart Bertolotti-Bailey had completed a practice-based PhD at the Reading School of Art, University of Reading, UK. Bertolotti-Bailey initially studied graphic design at Reading in the early 1990s, and then became one of the first students to attend the Werkplaats Typografie in Arnhem, NL (1998–2000). Following this, he co-founded and edited twenty issues of the maverick design journal *Dot Dot Dot*, until 2010, when this publication was ended and replaced by the online-and-in-print *Bulletins of The Serving Library*. Bertolotti-Bailey has taught on and off at various design schools all over the world, and his essay 'Towards a Critical Faculty' (2006/7), originally written for an academic workshop at the Parsons School of Design, NYC, was an influential reading for the project, *(Graphic) Design School School*, which spawned this book. Since the mid-2000s, the practice-based PhD has emerged as the new 'terminal degree' for academically-minded artists and designers alike, and we were keen to hear about Bertolotti-Bailey's experiences engaging at this level of study.

LW I'm interested in the institutionalisation of design practice, and what we might call 'research', because I've been a (sometimes sceptical) participant in it myself. And now, for example, as a full-time teacher at a university, there is increasing pressure on me to enrol in a PhD. I know you've just completed a PhD, so maybe we could just start with the obvious: when did you start, and what were your motivations to do something like this?

SBB Basically, I was invited to do it. A doctorate is not something I'd ever considered before. I had, and still have, no academic ambitions that would require a formal qualification such as this — which isn't to say it mightn't be useful in some future situation I haven't yet anticipated. It came with a stipend, roughly the same as what I'd be paid to teach somewhere, and being paid to write seemed like a good idea after fifteen years or so without that having ever really happened.

That said, there were at least a couple of non-mercenary motivations too. At the point of being asked in 2011, I'd co-founded, -edited, and -published the journal *Dot Dot Dot* for a decade, and was about to embark on its successor, *Bulletins of The Serving Library*. Most of the writing I'd done over the years was published in *Dot Dot Dot*, in which case it never had to meet with any sort of third-person approval beyond immediate colleagues. On one hand this was a positive thing, in that it gave the journal its very particular idiosyncrasy and independence, but the lack of objective overview also allows and fosters obscurity and opacity without question. And so I was interested at this point in trying to write along the same lines, knowing it would have to be peer-approved, argued against and, in the process, ideally worked over into something more rigorous and answerable.

Secondly, for years with the journals, as well as my work with David Reinfurt as Dexter Sinister, we'd only ever responded to circumstances without any masterplan. Again, this was helpful and hugely responsible for sustaining the energy behind a lot of the work — working blind and attempting to register situations on the fly. But it felt like time to stop and reflect on what it was we thought we were doing in order to realise a more considered direction. We were anyway simultaneously taking stock of *Dot Dot Dot* and Dexter Sinister, and trying to shapeshift both into something new with the same sense of longer-term projection. This is what led to The Serving Library, an attempt to take several kinds of activity that had developed over the years — the printed journal, an online library, parallel collections of objects and books, and a pedagogical programme — and synthesise them under a single coherent umbrella institution. This involved tinkering the journal's publishing mechanism into something more digital, and making its subject matter even more free-ranging than before. All to say that it was generally a period of reflection for us, and so assembling a concerted body of writing as a 'practice-based' thesis seemed fitting.

There was also the fact that the school doing the asking happened to be where I'd studied as an undergraduate, the University of Reading, just west of London. Interestingly (for me), I was a student in Typography & Graphic Design (on a very *proper* course of the kind that's since been felled by the corporatisation of education — PhDs and 'research' being part of the general thrust, of course). The invitation, however, was from the Fine Art department next door. Apart from a significant number of literally romantic entanglements, there had never been much communication between the two departments, however obvious and productive such a connection would seem to be. And given that I'd ended up working in the grey area between these fields, it seemed appropriate to return to do this at the rival department, so to speak. It was almost entirely coincidental that the invitation came from the same place, and I intuited that this could usefully shape what I might do.

Practice-based art PhDs were still a new enough entity to preclude any clear models, and this, too, seemed conducive to my, and our, way of working. At the time, I was very taken with a book by Umberto Eco from the early 1960s, *The Open Work*, which seemed to dovetail with a lot of what we'd been up to with the journals and Dexter Sinister. All I could propose at the time was to take Eco's thinking as a kind of springboard, in order to consider how our work relates to his ideas, and perhaps in the process update those ideas some fifty years on. In particular, I was attracted by the title of one chapter from *The Open Work* called 'Form as Social Commitment', which seemed to promise an explanation of how our concerns might have relevance beyond the art and design coteries that *Dot Dot Dot* and Dexter Sinister tended to, and still tend to, operate within.

So this was how I started. I applied, forgot about it, then unexpectedly found I'd been accepted. I should add that, having been in Melbourne lately, there isn't (yet) the same sense of inevitability that people in our field end up doing this as an extension of teaching or that it's a good way to pay the rent in lieu of any more meaningful work. It's in the post, though.

LW I've been slowly digging into your thesis and it's interesting because it becomes difficult, if not impossible, to separate the *doing* of the PhD (the structure and process) from the content of the thesis (the 'working ethos' you're trying to articulate). Which is also probably exactly as it should be — that 'self-reflexive oscillation' between form and content you describe in the thesis.

That said, though, in terms of those non-mercenary motivations, how has the structure and process of the PhD — the peer review, the arguing against, the working towards something more rigorous and answerable — how has that paid off? Has it worked out more or less how you thought it would? Or did you meet with unexpected shifts in your thinking or outcomes as a result of being enrolled? If we leave out the obviously very valuable financial support of the stipend, do you think your practice would've developed very differently over the last nine years if you *hadn't* been doing the PhD? I ask this mainly because, from my perspective at least, those 'immediate colleagues' you mention were already a group of very astute, critical thinkers/practitioners anyway.

SBB The promise of peer review didn't play out at all as I'd anticipated: both the department in general and my supervisors in particular were very casual about the whole thing. Whenever I was required to submit bits and pieces along the way, I'd generally receive broadly approving comments and a few suggestions for further reading, but very little beyond that. I think this was

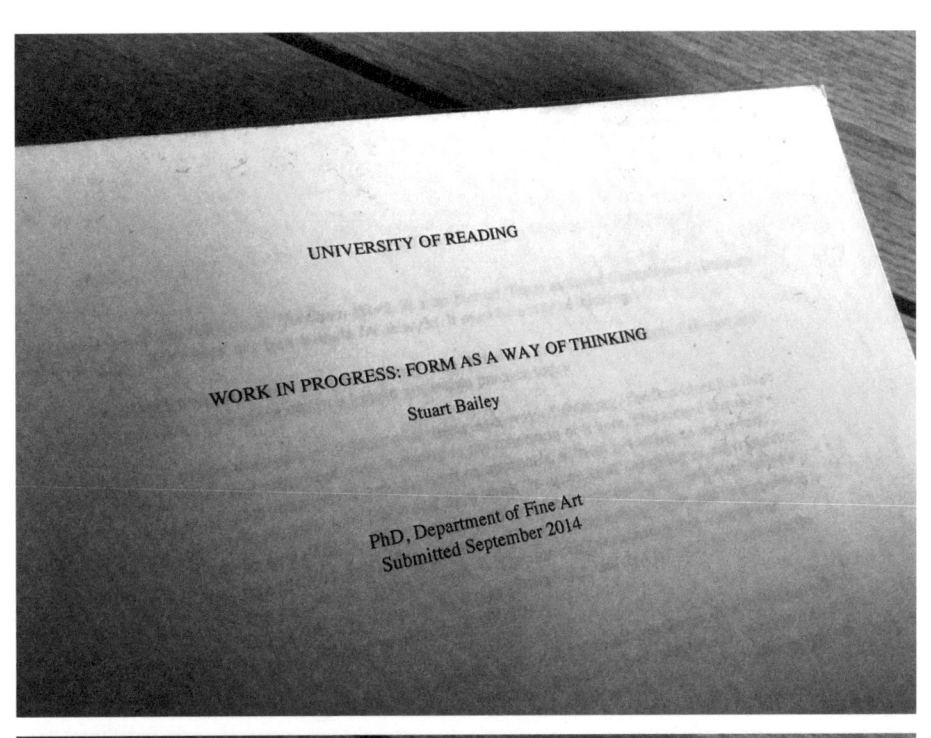

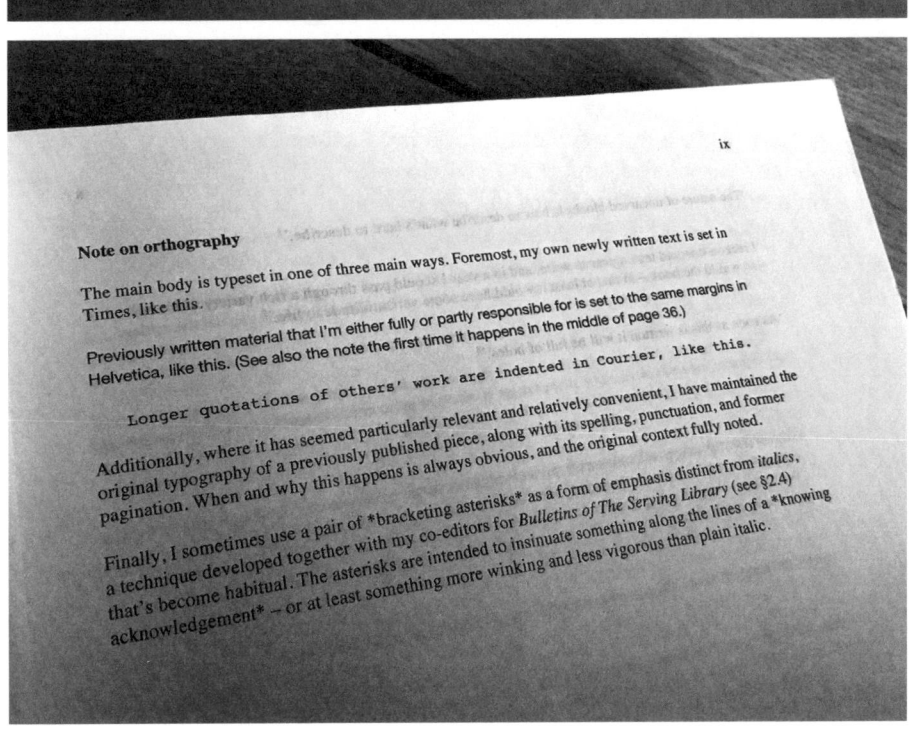

Work in Progress: Form as a Way of Thinking,
PhD thesis of Stuart Bertolotti-Bailey, University of
Reading, September 2014.

partly by design, in that they trusted me to find my own way and didn't want to impose anything that might hinder that, and partly because the sorts of things I would send were so long and unwieldy that they could barely get through it all before we'd meet up to discuss things, so anything 'official' always felt incomplete and pending. This wasn't helped by the fact that I didn't write it as a series of progressive chapters, where each completed part would logically feed the next. It was more like a tornado. I'm clearly not an academic writer in the normal sense, and fortunately the department was trying to get as far away from that as possible anyway. In this sense, it was a good match: right place, right time.

That's not to say it was completely unsupervised. The main points of contention related to my use of very general terms like 'aesthetic' without any proper recourse to their involved histories, though it always seemed clear to me that I was using such terms in their most obvious, prosaic senses, and was happy enough to declare as much in the text. That's to say, contesting what 'aesthetic' might mean wasn't really part of my point, and a rudimentary definition along the lines of 'the form by which an idea is communicated graphically or verbally' was adequate enough for my needs.

There's a small section near the start of the thesis that briefly accounts for my use of the words 'aesthetic', 'poetic', 'art' and 'design'. The first two are anyway derived from Eco's usage and so are straightforward enough to summarise from his writing, but it was actually very useful to grapple with the last two. I tried to force myself to describe what these terms meant to me right now, without referring to historical lineage or received wisdom. This brought into focus my own sense of the distinction, and why I tended to prefer to refer to a more general 'work' rather than classify stuff as 'art' or 'design' per se. I realised, too, that Eco also referred to a general open 'work', rather than considering openness in view of a single domain.

The other thing I recall during those early drafts is my chief advisor expressing alarm at what he perceived as my slipping into propagating what he semi-seriously called 'Christian values' — honesty, goodwill, authenticity, and so on. This made me duly self-conscious, and I set about trying to articulate such notions in more concrete terms, but it also made me realise that I was indeed out to advocate what are basically 'humanist' values, and so reflect on what that word means relative to art and design nowadays. There's a paragraph on the first page of the introduction that attempts a kind of deadpan definition of the summary idea I'm trying to articulate throughout, namely 'form as a way of thinking'. This fragment will give you an idea of the nature and the point of deconstructing the vocabulary:

> Now, if in their most general senses 'form' means a lasting encounter between atoms that hold good together, and 'thinking' the process of relating two or more discrete ideas in order to yield new ones, then 'form as a way of thinking' in its most skeletal and pedantic sense describes the process of manipulating sensory matter — whether verbal or graphic — by juxtaposing, connecting or configuring already existing ideas with a view to generating new ones. It is a fundamentally constructive, progressive process.

Strangely, I found myself reading loads of those little Oxford Short Guides to Philosophy on anything that might seem loosely relevant — Nietzsche, Wittgenstein, Derrida, Heidegger, and so on. I think this was my version of the kind of crisis of confidence I suppose most people experience at the beginning of a doctorate, a response to the fear of having to start from scratch and suddenly read every book you were ever 'supposed' to. But I did wonder why my impulse was to focus on philosophy. Then a friend said, 'well, you *are* doing a philosophy degree…'. I'd never consciously registered that that's what PhD stands for! So, again, as absurdly obvious as it might seem now, this was a good lesson in paying attention, in really thinking things through, and in sharpening the reflex to account for every single word you're using.

Following this early flailing about in philosophy, there was a big gap before I discovered what I should be doing, meaning the overall shape and form of the thesis. This was also a result of painfully realising I couldn't write in what I understood to be a typically academic manner — that it just killed any of my interest in the subject. I squeezed out a semblance of a first chapter, more or less a summary of the aspects of Eco's book that interested me, along with a synthesis of related ideas from a string of heavy hitters like Benjamin, Adorno, Badiou, Sontag and Latour — which was a version of the usual 'literature review'. Then I wrote an equivalent chapter conceived of as a kind of parallel introduction, more or less a literature review of the past ten years of *Dot Dot Dot*, including fragments from all the parts that explicitly dealt with that 'oscillation of form and content' you mentioned.

It dawned on me that the whole thing could be structured along these parallel lines, alternating between chapters of so-called 'theory' and so-called 'practice', which I supposed might ideally demonstrate the blurring of the distinction between the two that I was hoping to convey. At the time, I also wrote a convoluted meta-intro about this, i.e., the thesis demonstrating its proposition, which my supervisor quickly told me to cut, as pretty much every practice-based PhD explicitly or implicitly claims as much — and that of course it's far more efficient and convincing to demonstrate it than to 'cleverly' (i.e., tediously) point out that you're demonstrating it. It took a while to get out of such snake-eating-its-own-tail thinking, which in a similarly spiralling way also happened to be what I was trying to get out of my system with the final, *very* self-reflexive issue of *Dot Dot Dot*.

This zigzagging practice-theory-practice-theory structure was the first time I had any sense of an overall shape, and from there everything got a bit easier.

The next key thing I understood was that, as the Dexter Sinister projects I'd inevitably be writing about (inasmuch as the thesis was categorically practice-based) typically generated a lot of mannered writing, it would make a lot of sense to incorporate it into the whole. I began to think of any new text for the practice chapters as a kind of glue that could stick together the existing stuff, and that I might profitably maintain the original formatting in each case. As you might imagine, in our work, such formatting — typesetting, layout, distribution channel, etc. — is generally intended to say as much as the text itself. For this reason, such fragments would serve as illustrations as much as quotations. I saw, too, that I could achieve something similar with the theory chapters by incorporating certain auxiliary talks, interviews, letters and essays, and start writing for upcoming events with the PhD in view. If I squinted, I could just about conjure the ghostly outline of a last practice chapter based on some piece of work we hadn't yet imagined, to be written in pronounced real time, which again was precisely one of the qualities of the way of working I was out to grasp. So that's when it all coalesced as a single idea, though it was still a whole other story to actually do it.

    I'm well aware that the procedures I'm describing here are fairly commonplace: the majority of people working on lengthy doctorates write bits and pieces for journals and conferences, etc., and use the occasions to shape and hone the work. Nevertheless, I did have the sense of having arrived at this point by trial and error, by working through it rather than having been told what to do, which I'm sure makes all the difference. Otherwise put, it felt inherent and organic rather than applied and artificial — which is once again the nature of the work the thesis attempts to account for.

LW I've talked to quite a few people who express concern that this thing, the practice-based PhD, could go either way. The formal processes and requirements of the institution could support, provoke or cajole you into developing your work in beneficial ways. But the weight of the institution, the structure, the formality, might equally crush a practice's motivating spirit. There's a lot of cynicism about PhD-level study in art and design, which comes from that sort of perspective.

SBB I don't think the PhD format crushed the sort of active spirit you mention, because eventually I came to treat it just as I, or we, would any other piece of work, whether an exhibition or essay or issue of the journal. Probably the main stumbling block in my case was that I'd become so used to working with David as Dexter Sinister, with all the benefits that brings in terms of security: strength in numbers, quality control, a certain propulsive hilarity in dealing with other people, and so on. Even if the thesis was fundamentally based on our work together, suddenly I was solely responsible for all the decisions, and that was hard.

LW I'm interested in the potential significance of this thesis being done at an art school rather than a design school. The 'grey area' between art and graphic design is something your thesis addresses quite specifically, and yet you point out that there was no real practical or academic relationship between the two departments at the University of Reading. Do you think this PhD could have been done in a graphic design department? Or was the art school context necessary?

SBB I don't think I could have done the PhD in the Typography department at Reading (which is really a general Graphic Design department, just one with an enduring bias towards book design and the niceties of typesetting) — at least not in the way I ended up doing it. That's not because it's a design department per se, just that that *particular* department has more entrenched old-school academic expectations than its Fine Art neighbour. This is partly historically determined, and partly a consequence of the current staff. In this sense, the two departments conform to the stereotypes: the Typography department would have been far more strait-laced and uptight, where the Fine Art department was more speculative and searching.

To generalise wildly now, I often think that designers and design departments tend to get bogged down in details that aren't as important as they assume, while artists and art departments are just as prone to airy abstraction and imagining their work communicates far more than it actually does. Part of my thesis argues for a merging of the best of both — towards a freer-thinking attempt to genuinely connect.

LW   When you wrote that 'I'm clearly not an academic writer in the normal sense, and fortunately the department was trying to get as far away from that as possible anyway', can I ask you to describe where you think they (the department) were trying to get to instead? I'm interested to know more about what that might mean, to eschew the traditional academic narrative? I guess I ask because to some extent I think I yearn for some formality, to be forced, more or less, to submit my usually very woolly thinking to a strict framework of some kind — a scaffold. But then your comment about trying to write in a 'typically academic manner' killing your interest in the subject also makes total sense to me.

SBB   As I said, rethinking how to approach an academic thesis outside the regular decorum seems part and parcel of the whole point of 'practice-based' PhDs right now. But how might we account for the *extra* benefit of what we're rather reductively calling 'non-academic'?

Regarding both my own and the Reading Art Department's view on practice-based academic work, my provisional answer is precisely that the *form* of the thing can add to (or multiply or supplement or reinforce) the 'hard' meaning of the writing itself. Trouble is, this is already a bit of a knot, because to my mind such 'extra-textual' qualities don't only allude to the typography or layout, but to the writing too: the rhetoric, the style, the *way of writing*. Being exaggeratedly casual, for instance, admitting a bit of humour, or adopting and bending genre conventions. This is why I decided to include a number of fairly contrived conversations, letters to people, lectures and other 'set pieces' that are pretty clearly outside the regular academic gamut.

In any case, for me this is the 'extra' aspect that a typically freewheeling art or design temperament might bring to a typically uptight mode of academic inquiry. No one at Reading ever confirmed this directly; it was an unspoken assumption that became clearer to me through doing it. Of course, many people in more overtly academic fields — science, maths, philosophy, art history — might well be just as loose and inventive and by no means stick to what we imagine to be The Rules. The point is only that the practice-based model is an immediate license to think more speculatively from the outset, that conventional forms of inquiry are called into question as a matter of course, and this suits the particular talents and interests of those involved in the arts. None of which is to say that a more regular academicism is outdated or lacking; on the contrary, it has fairly obvious benefits (peer approval, etc.)

in those other domains. All of this is surely tied up, too, with the fact that it's easier to determine what science or maths are, as compared to art and design.

I think there were two main academic conventions that troubled me, that made me uncomfortable to a degree that outstripped any positive sense of having to answer to a relatively strict framework, which I looked forward to in the abstract as much as you. The first was the obligation to synthesise others' writing. I became very self-conscious about this, perhaps because my impulse was to look outside my own founding domain of design to bits and pieces of philosophy, aesthetic theory and sociology — areas in which I have no grounding whatsoever. Although all the stuff I wanted to incorporate was absolutely helpful, to stick it all together formally felt like: 'in 1960 person X said this, two decades later person Y said more or less the same thing, and recently person Z has written something similar, which is more or less what I want to say too'. It felt tedious to me — as if I might as well just give anyone a list of references and let them do the patchwork themselves. This was less the case when I forced myself to paraphrase rather than simply quote, but still. I think there are people who can do this sort of thing and manage to conjure something greater than the sum of parts, but for me it felt like it was just the parts. Spare parts. Over time, I realised that such synthesis is something David and I do all the time, but with the benefit of not immediately *appearing that way*.

So that was my first sticking point — the starchy quality of academic synthesis. The other was being obliged to write in a formal voice. I didn't so much mind affected phrases like 'what I want to do in this chapter is...', or 'as I argued in chapter four...', as I could see easily enough that they were genuinely necessary to keep anyone oriented in such a sprawling piece of work, myself included. The problem was trying to write without contractions. After fifteen years of habitually having written 'it's' and 'I'll' and 'he'd' in *Dot Dot Dot* and *Bulletins*, having to suddenly adopt 'it is' or 'I will' or 'he would' felt out of character to such a degree that it outstripped any positive notion of answerability to the academic community. Simply put, I felt like a fraud, and more pointedly that I was doing something I wasn't very good at with no discernible benefit.

On one hand, I can readily dismiss such informality as a contemporary tic, increasingly ubiquitous as written language tends more and more towards the relative laxity of speech, which equally permeates social media and serious journalism. On the other hand, I can also see that such nonchalance is analogous to the casual drift between fields that marks our work. In some obscure sense I can't fully articulate, it seems appropriate to me that this blurring of borders requires an equivalent blurring of language. This has never been too conscious: we never sat down with a flip chart and said 'okay team, how are we going to embody our disciplinary looseness in language?' But as I think I say in that last theory chapter, it's both *what* you do *and* the way you do it — or it can be.

LW I really liked what you wrote about working out 'what these terms meant to me right now, without recourse to historical lineage or received wisdom'. Which is sort of anti-academic in the traditional sense, but, of course, entirely useful in terms of locating a more practical resonance between language and practice. Anyway, that comment actually reminded me of something you'd written before — that funny sort of misappropriation of 'Design Thinking' in 'Towards a Critical Faculty'.[1] I know one of the people you were supposed to be working with/for at the Academic Project Office at Parsons, and I know that when they used the term 'Design Thinking', they would have been using it in the sense that it has become widely known and propagated by the likes of Richard Buchanan and IDEO. However, you completely ignored that usage and went after your own sense of the term, via an altogether different historical lineage and a sense of received wisdom.

SBB This brings to mind a radio conversation between Michael Silverblatt and David Foster Wallace on the NPR show 'Bookworm' that influenced me a great deal. Silverblatt introduces Wallace's essay collection *Consider the Lobster* and leads into his opening question by suggesting that whatever topic Wallace has been commissioned to write about — an article on conservative American talk radio, for instance — he'll generally spend a good bit of time upfront debunking received wisdom on and around the subject. He tries to lay bare the mechanics of what's *actually* going on, which are frequently contrary to the terms in which the subject is discussed by the mainstream media. This return-to-zero perspective, a kind of rebooting of the subject, makes apparent how much we're unconsciously swayed by the ways in which things are reported — even, or maybe especially, stuff we might not spend a lot of time thinking about. Wallace observes, for instance, that the standard liberal response to conservative talk radio is to be outraged by its right-wing sloganeering and political provocations, when its main motivation is not politics at all, but entertainment — and as long as its critics address it on political terms, they're missing its point, hence their counter-arguments miss their mark.

So this applies to my personal rebooting of 'Art' and 'Design', and of 'Design Thinking', too, in that earlier Parsons essay you mention — trying to think about those terms *on your own terms* to avoid contamination by consensus opinion. I think having the kind of time and space necessary to really think for yourself at this level of detail is one of the real luxuries of undertaking an extended thesis. Even if you end up back where you started and agree with the received wisdom, your work thereafter ends up far more nuanced and convincing for having put yourself through the mangle.

LW I brought up Design Thinking here because I've come up against it a bit in the last few years at different academic institutions, most recently here at the University of Canterbury, where they wanted to set up a d.school following the Stanford model. Many things bugged me about it, but one broader issue I had was with the way Design Thinking was being portrayed: a clear emphasis or prioritisation of the *thinking* over the *doing*. The 'dematerialisation of design' is, I guess, another way of putting it. It also seems to come packaged with euphemisms about design for social good, but only where there is money to be made. And, indeed, there was a sizable corporate interest backing its establishment as a programme at our university. There are two points here that I'd like to explore: graphic design as a practice of *form giving*, specifically, and the *social value* in that — both of which are critical components of your thesis. I've just read your 'Chapter 9: Grey Area', and through it are statements like this:

> Rather than the way things work, Graphic Design is still largely (popularly) perceived as referring to the way things look.
>
> The danger is that you read the form as though it sprang fully formed from the designer's mind, in which case you tend to read it as an exercise in style, as formalism...
>
> ...usually another euphemism for formalism...
>
> Graphic design then becomes simply — and boringly — an exercise in formalism.

It might sound naïve and maybe I'm misreading you a bit, but I wanted to ask about this scepticism regarding formalism. I mean, I know we're not supposed to make or read things superficially, but, more and more, I'm wondering why not? Why can we have a purely visceral engagement with, say, music, but not with graphic design? I listened to a Brian Eno talk recently,[2] in which he mentioned a scientist who claimed that one of the great questions of modern science could be 'Why do we like music?' In this same talk, Eno outlined his belief that art or culture, which he sees as one and the same, is simply 'everything we don't have to do'. The 'everything' he then talks about is 'styling'. The implication here is that there is very much more to these seemingly superficial activities than we might presume.

This leads me to the question of social value. At the very beginning of your Chapter 9, you write: 'the channels for a socially-oriented graphic design practice have been largely eradicated by an all-pervasive corporate sensibility that prioritises profit over culture — and hence bureaucratic concerns over aesthetic ones'. This sounds about right to me, but I know a lot of people would argue that this bureaucratisation of design — you mention 'focus groups, marketing, and public relations departments', and might we add Design Thinking to that list? — has been *for* the social good, *for* the benefit of a perceived audience, a user, or a public. *And*, that 'aesthetics' are just far too subjective and superficial to be worth any real interest or concern. This is what I come up against regularly, anyway. So, if design is supposed to be primarily concerned with a broader sense of problem solving and with the improvement of society in general, what role does aesthetics have to play?

And is there not a contradiction here, in the sense that you're concerned about graphic design being perceived as an exercise in formalism, but then lamenting that bureaucratic concerns have overtaken aesthetic ones? Am I misreading your use of the concepts of formalism and aesthetics here?

SBB Part of the problem is that these things are so general, the subject so expansive, and I tend to object to the term 'design' being bandied about without qualification, given that it can be used in so many senses. I think anyone dealing with the subject should be obliged to state precisely what they take the word to mean, otherwise it fosters confusion. This is why I wrote, in the 'Towards a Critical Faculty' piece for Parsons, that, for me, 'Design Thinking' is a tautology: to my mind, designing in its most general sense *is* thinking, not a *way* of thinking. In a casually under-formed way — partly because I can't bear the slightly creepy Design Thinking rhetoric — the IDEO-ish approach reads to me like a lot of hot air and self-justification for charging a lot of consultancy money for something that's actually pretty unremarkable, a means of making little more than common sense seem professionally particular. From what I gather, 'Design Thinking' supposedly means thinking outside the usual ways of doing things, with a bias towards 'iterating' different possible solutions and letting those iterations lead you to places you may not have readily conceived otherwise. Er, *thinking*. As my Wallace anecdote suggests, I support this. (Who wouldn't?) It's the glorification of the idea that bothers me. This is why, unfashionable as overkill and deification have made him at this point, Wallace was and still is such a touchstone for me: his resolve to get to grips with the root level of whatever subject he was dealing with, without making a big deal about doing so. The fact that he was so free-ranging in subject matter makes him all the more exceptional as a model.

    Anyway, if we're talking about formal aspects of graphic design as synonymous with 'style' in the sense of 'formalism', or form for form's sake, my sense is that style *in itself* no longer has the sort of meaningful power it had in the past. This is close to saying that I think 'everything's been done', though I hesitate at how reactionary that sounds. What I mean is, I can appreciate how throughout the relatively short history of graphic design there have been many moments when the surface appearance of, say, political protest posters, or punk record sleeves, or a classically designed book, or an isotype chart, have carried a certain quality in themselves (i.e., have carried meaning distinct from, if ideally as a reinforcement of, the raw content, the base material to be manipulated). These days, style inevitably refers to something already done. Perhaps the last of such vanguard styles occurred in the 1990s. I'm thinking of work by designers such as Tomato or Emigre or Jonathan Barnbrook or David Carson, a breed of conspicuously 'experimental' second-wave computer-based work involving the digital manipulation of type, which to me tended to obscure rather than articulate its 'base' content, as was often its stated aim. I had and still have no particular affinity with or appreciation for that stuff, but I can see readily enough that style was the primary point, towards what aesthetic philosophers call 'affect'. A favourite book of mine, Michael Bracewell's *The Nineties*, has a subtitle that sums this up beautifully: 'When surface was depth'. So I'm saying that, since the 1990s, surface no longer has such depth.

    I'm sceptical, then, about what we're calling formalism in graphic design today communicating very much as an end in itself. I'm less sceptical of this idea in the realm of fine art, which is a whole different matter with a different set of attendant problems. But I'm alluding specifically to the idea of form treated as something distinct from content, something that can be 'applied to' the raw materials of text and image. I know well enough you can't *not* have style. That's to say, pedantically conceived, everything has a style, 'non-style' is a style, etc., in which case, perhaps 'stylish' is a better word. But in the realm of graphic design, which I define in the PhD as 'the articulation of text and image, ideally according to meaning', stylish work no longer has much purchase. Certainly, I find the idea of teaching graphic design stylishness to students fairly pointless, not least because what tends to happen out in the world of work is that someone says, 'we want this (menu, T-shirt, billboard, web ad, homepage) to look something like that (fancy, minimal, distressed, baroque, ironic)'. To become proficient in this, you don't need to be taught how to think, you just need to look around and scavenge. It's possible, it's fine, it amounts to a certain 'vocational' education in that it makes you 'employable' — but it doesn't interest me. More dramatically put, it's complicit with our contemporary condition: homogenisation, blandness, monoculture, etc. I think in education and elsewhere, it's important to resist that and to open up other, more thoughtful and less predictable avenues.

So, for instance, I *do* think that there's a sense in which form can be appropriate to or *at one with* the internal meaning of its material in a way that's fundamentally different to the sense in which 'minimalism' might be considered appropriate to, say, Nike's Fall 2015 marketing campaign. And this, I suspect, is where you and I align in thinking that form giving is the sort of thing that can be usefully taught: a sensitivity to meaning and how to translate that meaning via other materials, formats and channels. This is very much a *social activity*, though fundamentally different from one that's only involved in trying to sell things by making superficial differences to more or less the same products or institutions.

Following Eno, you wonder why there should necessarily be a fundamental difference between the way we think about graphic design and music? In view of this question, what I'm saying, I think, is that graphic design no longer functions in an 'abstract' sense equivalent to music — at least in the way Eno conceives of it. Then again, my suggestion is not a million miles away from the way certain commentators argue that pop music has arrived at or is approaching a terminal point — not as some reactionary, middle-aged complaint, just as a kind of hard fact about the inevitable lifespan of a cultural phenomenon, like a used-up mineral resource. And so it seems endlessly more interesting and necessary to me to engage with graphic design not as a form of formalism but as a form of articulation. Trouble is, this requires material worth articulating. And, as far as I can see, the sheer number of people who consider themselves graphic designers combined with the sheer scarcity of third-party work worth working on has led to a state of confusion, hence the blurring of roles and activities that doesn't make things any clearer but has forged a lot of escape routes.

I challenge you to give me any counter-examples to what I'm saying about contemporary formalism in graphic design, and I'll be happy enough to stand corrected. It's maybe worth adding that I don't see new formalisms in graphic design — in the sense we've been using — happening in the realm of digital media. I think this is partly because the interfaces are so limited in scale and capacity, even though we may instinctively suppose that they're far more flexible and generative than print, and partly because the software monopolies always already short-circuit the potential of these new formats. Think, too, how difficult it is to ensure that anything out of the ordinary on a website will function properly across diverse platforms, browsers, etc.

As such, I think computer programming ought to be a foundational component of any design school today, simply in order to avoid immediately working within industry defaults. The better websites and the better forms of digital publishing today surely have little to do with graphic design style, and more to do with how intuitive they are to use, and how navigable they are.

Ultimately, I suspect that your university's penchant for immaterial Design Thinking and your own convictions about, um, 'material' graphic designing probably aren't that far apart; it's just the methodology and the rhetoric that are at odds. You're all for teaching people how to think *by making things*, in which they have to respond to limitations and contingencies and materials and make informed choices towards particular ends. And I'm sure that aligns with the sorts of skills the DT-ers want to foster via more conceptual means. My concern is that teaching Design Thinking remains uselessly vague until it's actually applied, that it requires an object to work in order to face the generally messy and unpredictable realities of a given situation. When the Parsons crew were initially explaining Design Thinking to me and going on about 'iterating', I thought, well, if I'm going to drive up to San Francisco from LA this weekend, don't I 'iterate' — in my mind, without a pen and paper, or even Google maps — which of the three likely routes I should take according to my knowledge of their various benefits, then choose one accordingly (and possibly get stuck in traffic for reasons beyond my control). Is this Design Thinking? I think it's common sense.

Moreover, I don't think that your methods being more material means they're any less 'social'. For me, the rational thinking that any mode of teaching might encourage can equally be directed towards social or anti-social (capitalistic?) ends. Like you, I don't see the inherent link between Design Thinking and social values. As you imply, too, I suspect it's more frequently directed towards economic ones.

One last thing here. A couple of years ago, I taught a seminar class to graduate graphic design students, and at some point asked them each to 'bring in' four or five websites they appreciated *for the design* — though I was careful to add that by this I meant in view of the way they work, rather than their stylish style. To my surprise, almost all of them pointed to the four or five most ubiquitous, high-traffic sites, often search engines, including Wikipedia, Craigslist, Reddit, even Google. It made me realise that such sites are barely graphic-designed in that overtly stylish sense, but extremely well designed in terms of user-friendliness, often in very smart, subtle, sophisticated and what seem satisfyingly inevitable ways. I thought, too, that in some sense this must be because they're designed, or at least refined, by large aggregates of people — including the users themselves, whether directly or indirectly. Moreover, being digital, they can be amended and updated any time in a way that's not possible with the relative fixity of print. For me, this is where the really interesting work is happening in graphic design — far more interesting, at least, than whatever might be the equivalent of the formalisms of the 1990s. It's work that's more concerned with the way things work than with the way things look (one doesn't rule out the other, of course; it's just a matter of priorities). As for the more 'musical' ways of working with form in Eno's sense: I think that's art. And graphic design usually makes for terrible art, which is to say, not art at all.

LW   This reminds me that in 'Towards a Critical Faculty', you stated that before we thought about *how* to teach we needed to know exactly *what* we were teaching. And so, given that your PhD was a 'movement towards the heart of the matter', as you say, I was interested to ask you about that. Can you tell me about your experiences of teaching, and about how your work towards the PhD might have affected that?

SBB   My first teaching experiences were in the graphic design department at the Gerrit Rietveld Academie in Amsterdam. Under the direction of Linda van Deursen in particular, it was regarded as a very 'conceptual' course, which meant something closer to an art practice, less concerned with teaching what we might think of as traditional design skills. Projects typically involved coming up with content as much as communicating it — or at least both were entangled in ways I didn't always find productive. I'd had such an opposite education at The University of Reading, where the whole class would typically be given the same raw material and a very specific brief in view of turning it into, say, a magazine, a book, a poster, a signage system, a timetable, or a webpage. (This was the early 1990s, so they were the very early days of the internet and of ideas of what digital publishing could mean.) What I noticed then, and which is far more common now, is that if you require students to fold their own interests into the brief — to be responsible for the content — they often spend at least half the project's run trying to work out what they're interested in, and by the time they'd sorted that out there was hardly any time to critique and refine it in view of anyone else receiving it. In other words, there was no time to sketch, to 'iterate', with actual material towards particular ends. This way of working presupposes that students are invested in subjects enough to bring decent material to the table, but I often felt that this simply wasn't the case, that they didn't care enough about what they were working with, and so came up with fake, temporary interests for the sake of the project, which is often what made the work weak and insubstantial. Their learning would have been far better served by having material carefully considered by a teacher and imposed after all. There was an air of personal therapy about the whole thing that I didn't like either.
    In a way, it didn't matter much, as I usually tried to do the opposite, imposing a bit of hardcore Reading-like specificity on the class. And this usually worked, because they were hungry for something else. It was probably a relief to them to relinquish responsibility for the content, but there were also those who just couldn't understand the lack of personal investment. In any case, all this instigated my minor crisis of not-knowing-what-I-was-teaching-to-what-end. I suppose it's quite normal.
    However, when I then moved to the US and started doing a few small things with equivalent schools there, I realised how relatively sophisticated those Rietveld students were. This is a massive generalisation, but to my mind the undergraduates at the Rietveld ended up far more capable and interesting than their graduate equivalents in the US. So it made me reconsider things, and I could eventually accept that the so-called 'conceptual' approach at the Rietveld did actually make them better and freer thinkers, more self-critical and questioning, less bound to conventions and ultimately more engaged. Still, I couldn't perceive how they might go about working on anything that

would promise the same level of engagement after school and simultaneously pay the rent. That's to say, I couldn't see the vocational benefit of a well-rounded humanities education. With the benefit of hindsight, I now think that was more a lack of imagination on my part, and that they'll figure it out — quite possibly in areas that have nothing to do with their base subject. I've come around to the idea that helping people to think critically is more important than helping people to be employable. This is a blindingly obvious idea, if a very unpopular one in some quarters. It certainly goes against the whole shift of education towards the quantitative, corporate-bureaucratic model.

So I eventually worked out I was more comfortable with the idea of helping people develop those 'critical faculties' than teaching them to be graphic designers in the old 'hard skills' sense, particularly as desktop publishing was ever more prevalent and so 'professional graphic design' was increasingly unnecessary, or at least deemed unimportant by whoever the equivalent of the previous generation of employers might have been. Today it would seem to me enough for anyone who wants to work as a graphic designer in a, let's say, 'standard' sense to simply learn Creative Suite and be aware of what's around them, because, as I've said, most regular work in typical design studios involves, more or less, the copying of things that already exist. Meanwhile, the more thoughtful types who find that sort of thing completely tedious forge their own working contexts in the same spirit as those Rietveld projects. It's not straightforward, it takes time to plot a course, but I think this is the path of those who have ended up assuming the wider roles that graphic design is now associated with — writing, publishing, selling, distributing, and so on.

As for how the PhD connects with this: I think the main thing is that the chapter called 'Grey Area' tries to account for what this supposedly 'thoughtful' wing of graphic design is up to, exactly — the sort of work that has no obvious commercial application, that's more 'philosophical', which doesn't fulfill an obvious brief, and which is largely if not exclusively self-generated. For instance, we publish essays on many different subjects through The Serving Library, but we're equally interested in publishing as a subject itself — and so the *ways* in which we channel things tries to draw attention to certain aspects of contemporary publishing in forms other than writing. I end up concluding that, like many artworks, they're 'tools for thinking' — or, better, 'tools for psychic survival', a favourite phrase of mine, though I can never remember who said it. But *ideally* these grey area equivalents are more oriented towards a public audience than I think a lot of 'straight' art is: directed outward, more generous, more cosmopolitan. And I propose, too, that the benefit of this art/design crossover *at best* is to bring the desire and talent for communication to bear on speculative, philosophical ideas in an age in which much contemporary art is emphatically uncommunicative, hermetic and, I think, spectacularly delusional about the extent to which it actually puts its ideas across.

LW   One more thing: your comment about the lack of 'material worth articulating' and how that has 'generated a lot of escape routes' — are these escape routes the same ones you talk about in your final theory chapter under the heading 'Orphaned Interests'? You're quite critical of the surge in independent art and design publishing and the attendant proliferation of book fairs. I don't necessarily disagree with your sentiments here, but am keen to ask you to elaborate. In particular, this part interested me:

> ...the uncommercial counterpart is generally drawn from someone's personal, niche interests with no real profit motive and no urgent need for an audience either. Such productions inevitably foster a certain amount of community and goodwill, and it would be churlish to see this as negative; but in being so self-serving they're not really 'socially oriented' in that former sense either.

SBB I think it relates to that trend of setting 'personal' projects I mentioned, where students are suddenly required to supply the content as well as the form. It's surely no coincidence that this happened around the advent and proliferation of social media: everyone's-a-publisher-artist-designer-whatever. In the PhD, I quote a teacher of mine who wrote quite plainly that progressive design — meaningful work that isn't only concerned with generating the superfluous differences that drive capitalism — can only take root as one facet of a general atmosphere and programme of social construction. It's hard to find any semblance of such a spirit nowadays, at least compared to, say, after the Second World War in the UK, which is the era in which that Reading University course I did was incubated, and that attitude was still mostly intact while I was there. In other words, graphic design there was absolutely considered a positivist project, with the idea that texts and images could be communicated in more or less correct ways, in order to share ideas publicly, towards making the world a better place: more navigable, more cultured. Notably, 'information design' was a key component of the course.

But, in a contemporary context, where that broader sense of social constructivism seems shut down, overtaken by such things as the ironically antisocial tendencies of social media and iProducts, there are individuals and groups sensitive to all the ersatz, infantilism and disconnection. They quite possibly ended up in areas like graphic design in the first place thanks to an interest in (and/or talent for) sharing ideas. These are the 'orphaned interests' I'm on about, the ones who step sideways into the broader roles attached to graphic design like writing, publishing, selling and distributing: an ever-increasing pool of design graduates dealing with an ever-diminishing supply of worthwhile work, who end up making work for themselves, who take the 'escape routes'.

On one hand, I see this as a positive thing, but it also makes me uncomfortable, as I'm still rooted in the humanist idea that graphic design is fundamentally about multiplying ideas for the common good — to generate thoughtful, meaningful, critical culture. This discomfort is due to seeing the sheer quantity of the stuff being produced (specifically the small, often exquisitely designed publications and other printed matter about fairly esoteric subject matter that flood the book fairs) and suspecting that the process of making it is the real point, as opposed to anyone else reading or looking at it. There's a horrible sense of this corner of culture being totally *unbalanced*, out of whack, that the idea of multiplying matter in the hundreds or thousands is being applied to stuff that really only requires one or ten for family and friends, as proof that something happened rather than as a vessel for transmitting ideas. Hence it all arrives with some pervasive sense of waste, like a food mountain — a depressing surplus. To borrow a term that always affected me as a student, this sort of work has no sense of *requiredness* — no standards, quality control or reason for existence beyond a bunch of people occupying their time. That's what bothers me: the mass solipsism it implies.

1 Stuart Bailey, *Towards a Critical Faculty (Only an Attitude of Orientation) From the Toolbox of a Serving Library* (New York: Dexter Sinister, 2015), 4.

2 Brian Eno, '2015 Brian Eno', *BBC Music John Peel Lecture*, BBC Radio 6 Music, 27 September 2015.

Graphic design counter-education
Joe Potts, interviewed by Jon Sueda

Tertiary education in most developed countries now leaves students with debilitating debt. In this climate, there is a growing interest in viable alternatives to the mainstream. In 2016, Joe Potts launched the Southland Institute — an evolving programme of workshops, activities and events building towards the establishment of a new, interdisciplinary, postgraduate typography school. In this interview by Jon Sueda, Potts discusses the ways in which the Southland Institute, side-stepping official accreditation processes, focusses on potential affordability for students and the fair compensation of educators' labour. Today, in addition to aggregating selected public resources and events, including lectures, screenings, exhibitions and rigorous-yet-accessible community college classes, the Southland Institute offers its own programming, including public talks, a series of in-depth conversations that take place in exhibitions within existing institutions, as well as a foundational sequence of courses at a local community college. While a physical space and a sustainable financial structure remain on the horizon, the Southland Institute is highly motivated in its search for a viable, egalitarian alternative to the increasingly elitist neoliberal education system.

The discipline of graphic design has expanded so significantly in the last two decades that the schools teaching it — art colleges and major universities alike — have had to respond rapidly and sometimes hastily to contend with changing disciplinary, cultural, commercial and technological conditions. Some have begun offering specialisations in typography, typeface design, design criticism, branding, packaging, UI/UX, interactive, motion, research, information design, and more. A handful have gone in the other direction and are strongly encouraging inter- or transdisciplinary practices. But the stalwarts of this landscape, at least in the US, have not changed much. The top four or five graduate programmes today are the same ones that dominated the field two decades ago.

Meanwhile, tuitions across the US continue to rise: a report by *US News & World Report* shows a 48 percent increase in tuitions and fees among private non-profit colleges between the years 2000 and 2015. Today, most private art schools cost students $40,000 to $50,000 a year. These conditions have resulted in a noticeable shift in how students view an advanced degree and how they imagine their futures post-graduation.

In response to all of this, Joe Potts, a Master's-level graduate from California Institute of the Arts (2009) and faculty member at Otis College of Art and Design and the University of Southern California (USC), launched the Southland Institute, a self-described 'unaccredited postgraduate graphic design workshop and evolving public repository of educational resources' located in Los Angeles. And while the Southland Institute is a deliberate counterpoint to the 'bigger is better' ethos of many larger tuition- and endowment-driven institutions, with their state-of-the-art equipment and limitless resources, it does also involve a deliberate and thoughtful effort to pack 'more into less', to infuse into its curriculum a rich history of radical art/design and counter-educational movements. In this conversation, I speak with Joe about his motivation for starting a new school, and what it offers as an alternative to existing models of contemporary graphic design education.

JS   What is the Southland Institute? And why do we need this option for graphic design in the context of today's educational landscape?

JP   The Southland Institute is a new, unaccredited, two-year, postgraduate typography workshop, and also an evolving public online repository of educational resources. It's built around the tools, processes, histories and discourses of typography and certain strains of what might be most conveniently summarised as post-conceptual art, and is intended to be a forum for inquiry into some of the processes, potentials and complications of higher education and its attendant structures and systems.

It's also an attempt to bring an affordable, high-quality offering to the landscape of graphic design education in the US. It distinguishes itself in that it foregrounds the uses and histories of typography and graphic design in a way that focusses on publication as a critical artistic practice, and addresses things from an angle of thinking about typography as a formal, physical and structural manifestation of language. It also looks at how the tools of graphic design have been, and can be, activated in the service of practices that might be more conceptually aligned with certain strains of critical art making.

Among the major aims of the Southland Institute are to activate and explore points of contact between disciplines and media, and to create a space for extended development, exposure and conversation, without the heavy debt burden that typically accompanies such study here in the US. It arises very specifically in response to several significant gaps that we perceive in the current landscape of higher education: a gap in dialogue between departments and discourses at existing institutions of all sizes; a lack of programmes that actively integrate strategies and pedagogy from both graphic design and post-conceptual art; a lack of programmes that enable and encourage rigorous and sustained study and practice without incurring long-term debt; and a lack of institutions in which faculty are paid fairly and sustainably for their contributions.

One component of it is very much in-person — reliant on conversation and interaction among enrolled participants and faculty. Another component is that these conversations, resources and documentation get put up on the website, creating a public resource for anyone who might be interested. And the participants themselves are required to teach at least one public workshop per year of their residency.

JS Is Southland Institute in any way a critique of the current state of design education or our larger educational issues as a country?

JP It's trying to look closely at both of these things, but it is worth noting that while an element of critique may be inherent in the Southland Institute's very existence, it's far from its sole purpose. The Southland Institute is, first and foremost, an attempt at a lighter-weight, nimbler institution of higher education that responds to a specific gap in the available offerings, and to what could reasonably be perceived as large-scale institutional failings at colleges, art schools and universities all over the country. I don't think that it's necessarily a critique of the content or curricula of current design education so much as maybe an articulation of the embeddedness and inextricability of some of the country's strongest programmes within institutions whose costs require their attendees — at least those without access to a certain level of financial resources — to effectively undertake upside-down debt obligations on their futures.

JS On the surface, the most divergent ideas that the Southland Institute represents are that you don't need to earn an accredited 'degree' and/or pay steep tuition prices in order to participate in and benefit from higher education. What are the other differences between what the Southland Institute offers in comparison to more traditional institutions?

JP It is our view that while accreditation may create a certain baseline of quality, and help ensure that predatory for-profit schools don't have access to funds from federally backed loans, the accreditation process and requirements can also have a limiting effect. And while it's well-intentioned, and in certain cases necessary, the emphasis on quantification, metrics, rubrics and front-loading curricula and syllabi with clearly articulated outcomes can actually preclude unconventional possibilities, unusual approaches and unexpected outcomes.

We also hope to offer an alternative to the student debt cycle in which students are permitted to take out extremely large federally backed and private loans, irrespective of their current or future ability to repay them. While accreditation definitely serves a number of useful purposes, and ideally prevents certain institutional abuses, it also seems worth questioning its role and complicity in this problematic cycle.

The Southland Institute also asks what would happen if a study of the connections between a school's curriculum and its institutional structure were themselves part of the educational experience. We are interested in examining what happens if part of an education that concerns itself with form, and the underlying structures of things, is about understanding and making visible the form(s) of the education and the educational institution itself.

This model (and in particular here we're talking about higher/post-graduate art and design education) — a rigorous but curricularly nimble, lightly administered, porously bordered, self-reflexive and flexibly structured model that costs students less and pays teachers more — is a proposition built from pieces that are neither new nor unique, but it's far from the norm, particularly in the US.

All of this is relevant because, as clichéd as it has become, there is a very real crisis happening in higher education, at both the private and the public level (and all of this is before we even figure out what effect the current administration in Washington will have on it). It's hitting the institutions themselves in enrolment and applicant numbers, and the fallout from it is happening in the financial lives of recent graduates. These problems aren't a secret, and there are certainly discussions within the departments and institutions about how best to address them, but a lot of these departments, and the institutions they're in, from what I've seen at least, aren't in a position to solve it because they've got massive overheads already: property costs, administrative costs, equipment costs, salaries, etc., and what are they going to do, roll back tuition? I don't think that's even close to being on the table.

So what we're proposing is to keep some of what we've learned, and what we value, from our involvement in some of these institutions — keeping the conversations, the atmosphere of permission and curiosity, the rigour, and the critique — but starting from scratch with the institutional scaffolding. We are asking: what are the most important parts of an educational experience, and what can be left out? What are interesting models from the past that could still be relevant today? What's the value of an instructor's time, and how can we build a budget around that? We're interested in how we can create an institution that's not built on ego or an ethos of perpetual expansion and exploitation, but on learning, cooperation, value and an ability to self-sustain.

JS Debt is certainly a topic of conversation among students not only today but when I was a student in the early 2000s. It certainly affects the range of opportunities post-graduation. Today I see fewer graduates embarking on self-directed, autonomous practices, and more who seem interested in joining established companies with greater resources. What do you hope your students will do after their experience at the Southland Institute? What types of practices will result from this experience?

JP   We hope that by choosing to participate in an education that doesn't require a large debt commitment, they might be less beholden to the banks, and to the kinds of careers and other sacrifices those debts can require. To say that paying off the loans inhibits certain ideal trajectories suggests, optimistically, that paying off these loans is actually possible. Part of what is making this problem so severe for a lot of people is that if you run the numbers on, for instance, paying off $100,000 in debt on a $50,000-a-year salary, while also covering housing, food, health insurance and transportation in a large US city, the numbers just don't add up.

I would love to see people who attend the Southland Institute publishing books, teaching at community colleges, starting bands, editing and designing magazines, running blogs, setting up co-ops, curating shows, starting non-profits, creating their own currencies, organising events. Some of them may decide to go into or back to conventional academia to get PhDs, in which case a hope would be that they bring some of the spirit of Southland to those endeavours.

For those who opt for a more entrepreneurial route, we hope that they might look for ways to build things in the world that chart a different course than some of the ones we're familiar with, but which also avoid Silicon Valley's problematic version of 'disruption' — that is, the so-called 'sharing economy' where the majority of people involved end up working for less than living wages in order to create value for shareholders and start-up founders. We want them to find the cracks in the system and not only make them visible, but cultivate practices in the spaces they create. We want them to be resourceful, astute, critical, socially responsible and imaginative. We want to show them, and hopefully also discover together, some tools and strategies that might enable this, but more importantly than that I think there's a hope that they'll show us things we can't imagine yet. Above all, the hope would be that they pursue a practice of making challenging, thought-provoking, conceptually and formally sophisticated work, in whatever form it needs to take.

JS   The landscape in graduate-level graphic design education is pretty different than it was even twenty years ago. Many more applicants today are 'career changers' with great knowledge or experience in another field, but limited or sometimes no design in their backgrounds. Most programmes now include a third preliminary year where they spend time up front teaching typography and image making, for example, and concurrently try to impart an understanding of history, theory and critical thinking. How do you prioritise different types of skills? Do you expect students to come in with them, or are you spending time skilling them up?

JP   We are operating on the premise that perhaps the ultimate skill is paying attention. Paying attention to what's going on around you, to what other people are doing, to how the surface of something provides information about what's going on behind the scenes, and to how many things that present as subtle, even ignorable, are actually affecting everything all the time. The skill of recognising and articulating these things is a priority. Another crucial skill of attention would be understanding different contexts.

Most specific to the Southland Institute, perhaps, and maybe more along the lines of what you're asking, would be typo/graphic skill, which is also in many ways about paying attention: to letters, to words, to space and proportion, and to the ways that these qualities can and do affect the meaning of text and language. Paying attention to history — how letterforms have been used to support and subvert language — and what the form of typography can mean and how it communicates. It's a balance of knowledge, openness and, to some extent, touch. You learn it by doing it and by looking at it and by talking about it — all things that you'll spend a good portion of your time at the Southland Institute doing.

So, with regard to skills: a certain baseline, as it were, of typography and graphic design skills is important coming in, but ultimately a capacity to look closely, process, contribute and absorb is paramount. If someone comes to us with a less developed set of formal skills, say, but an interesting analysis of the world, an awareness and attention to detail, the other skills will come, and the Southland Institute could be a great place to develop them.

JS Is the Southland Institute looking for a completely new audience/student, or is it aspiring to compete with the current US-based MFA graphic design programmes out there, like Yale University, California Institute of the Arts (CalArts), Rhode Island School of Design (RISD) and Cranbrook Academy of Art? And if yes to the latter, how do you compete with the enormous resources that tuition-driven institutions can provide?

JP While it is possible, and even likely, that the Southland Institute may appeal to certain students who would also be interested in some of those more traditional programmes (though it's interesting to note that the ones you mention, while traditional in a certain sense, are also built on their own traditions of experimentation, formal innovation and breaking with tradition), it's not meant so much to compete directly with them as to offer some of the positive things they do at a far, far lower cost. Some of these things include: a rigorous, intensive experience that unfolds over the space of a couple of years; access to ideas, minds, texts, prompts, conversations, situations, etc., with space to reflect on all of this; and the context of a programme that is structured yet open-ended, self-directed but also guided. So I guess you could say we're looking, in part at least, for people who would likely thrive at any of those places, but have been priced out. Or perhaps their practices don't fit as neatly into the departmental boxes that all those schools still have in place.

There are obviously certain things offered by the programmes you mention that we can't begin to compete with: campuses, resources, endowments, a menu of course offerings, name recognition, illustrious histories and, importantly (for now at least), degrees. But we also believe that some of these assets may, paradoxically perhaps, be the very things that are holding these institutions back from being able to function as they once did, as places to take genuine risks, to reimagine what's possible.

It isn't that they're not amazing places to learn, but at many of their current price tags, it's hard to defend them against the accusation that they've become luxury experiences. All of them are places that can change a person's life, can expand, refine and crystallise ways of working, thinking and making. It's just that they've passed a cost-benefit tipping point for many people; they've priced out anyone who's not at least upper-upper-middle class, but in doing so they've opened up a space for micro-institutions like Southland to come in and set up shop.

As the bigger schools have entered this strange new era of only being able to function at tuition-fee levels that are unattainable for anyone other than the affluent, this interesting void is being created for folks who might be looking for these kinds of conversations and experiences. And, in the meantime, some of these accredited schools are finding, unsurprisingly, that their applicant pools are shrinking, and thus they're not able to be as selective as they've been in the past. So, going back to your question, we're not looking so much to attract the same people that these schools might be attracting, so much as we're looking to attract the people they're leaving behind: people whom they are no longer able to effectively serve; people who are hungry for the kind of intellectual worlds that programmes like theirs can open, but who are prescient or fiscally cautious enough to see that the cracks in the current system are spreading; people who realise that the contingent faculty teaching them by and large aren't being paid a living wage; people who have been following the articles about the questionable business practices of Sallie Mae and Navient,[1] and don't want to get tangled in that web; people who have talked to graduates from the last ten years who (at best) can't qualify for mortgages because their debt-to-income ratio is too high or (at worst) have trashed their credit on defaulted loans.

So there's all of that. And we're also offering something to people who might be attracted to some of the European programmes but for whatever reason can't or don't want to spend a couple of years abroad. And, importantly, we're very interested in students who have a harder time shoehorning themselves into a specific discipline. We're looking for folks interested in the intersection of language, image, sound, material and time, who would like to investigate the powerful and complex role that typography and publication can play in articulating these points of contact. I think in that way — the active and willing looking outside of the discipline of graphic design, while keeping some of its core tools and approaches — the Southland Institute is looking for an audience/participants who are comfortable on the fringe, who are interested in cultivating practices in the margins and in-between spaces that some of the existing programmes have a harder time accommodating.

JS   An advanced degree seems almost an expected requirement in many fields. Today, a lot of students go directly into a Master's programme from their undergrad studies and see it as a requirement, not a decision based on some type of agenda fuelled by 'real' practice. What is the value of a Master's degree in 2017? Conversely, I've also observed very resourceful young designers using the internet as a way to create their own 'micro-community' that facilitates a heightened level of discourse among like-minded individuals from different parts of the world. This no-cost discursive community seems like a valid alternative to higher education today.

JP   Totally. That makes a lot of sense. For the hypothetical student you're describing, a person with a certain degree of technical and formal sophistication and/or training who feels confined and wants to explore or be exposed to things, a lot of that stuff is instantly accessible if you know where to look. Or even if you didn't know where to look but just spent enough time looking, you could figure it out and find things. And I think in addition to the increasing expectation of an advanced degree, graduate school could also come as an appealing option when the seeming alternative is indefinite unemployment, temporary employment, or endless hustling in the 'gig economy' with no health insurance, no security of any kind. The prospect of graduate school, which you can pay for later by doing something that you hopefully like more than what you're doing now, sounds pretty good.

I think your point of the well-considered decision is an important one, and one that the schools themselves are in a pinch with, because they're not in a position to be turning good students away, even if maybe that student would be better served doing something else.

JS   What about the 'summer school' model that has emerged recently in graphic design? Typography Summer School, Ventriloquist Summer School, etc. Are these now the venues for experienced designers who want this temporary escape from practice without the high price tag? Where do you situate the Southland Institute in this shifting landscape?

JP   I think these can definitely serve that purpose, to an extent. And there's certainly an overlap in our interests, particularly with regard to approaches to typography and publication as artistic practice, and a keen interest in questions of pedagogy — design and otherwise — and the space of the school as a fertile one for inquiry and formal exploration. Something I admire a lot about Ventriloquist is the importance they place on keeping it free for students, and in paying their instructors. The unfortunate downside of this is that when funding doesn't come through, cancelling the programme becomes necessary, as happened this summer, which is so unfortunate because what they're offering is really great.

I'm less familiar with the details of Typography Summer School beyond what's on their website and what I know of the faculty and guests, but it seems like it has similar concerns, and a lot of amazing people coming through. It also operates more self-sufficiently, with a monetary exchange/ tuition fee to support the costs of the operation.

I don't think it would be presumptuous or a stretch to say that all of us come from a place of being genuinely invested in typography and publication design as a creative practice, and also that teaching is an important part of what we do. And I obviously can't speak for them, but for me part of this investment comes from an ongoing interest in the history and discipline of typography and graphic design, and a feeling that a lot of the richest, deepest, most exciting work comes from the margins of the discipline, the points of contact with other fields, ideas, processes and ways of working.

And now I'm only speaking for myself, but part of what I think is so interesting about teaching is that it can be a relational space with varying degrees of structure and openness, fixed elements and variables. In certain ways, I think of it as one of the most 'alive' forms of design. So there's a similarity maybe in terms of approach and rigour, and the fact that all three are alternative schools that deal with the formal, visual manifestation of language — in other words, typography. And then another similarity is that all of us are unaccredited, existing outside the sanctioned systems of higher education, and yet clearly are all born from an intimate familiarity with these systems.

Where Southland differs perhaps the most from the summer schools is in the durational aspect. Part of the intended function of the Southland Institute is to provide the temporal space for ideas and practices to unfold, whereas by their very nature the summer schools are meant to be brief, condensed and action-packed. Southland Institute operates more on the premise that education is a slower burn, that ideas take time to develop, that you just can't pack as much space for risk and space for failure and space and time for practice into a compressed timeframe.

Another difference with Southland is the very intentional involvement of people who bring things from outside of graphic design, and the idea that bringing in other conversations, points of view, and approaches can be an amazing way of enlarging the practice, field of view, and both formal and conceptual toolboxes beyond those conventionally found within even the outer margins of the discipline.

JS   It's certainly a complex challenge to create the ideal context for interesting conversations and great work to be produced by students. Developing a great faculty, a good working environment, an excellent culture and a solid reputation takes time. How are you addressing people, place, facilities and legitimacy as an institution? How does a new programme compete with many other established programmes, like RISD, for example, with more than a century of proven excellence?

JP   Well, one thing I think that's happening is that these schools with the decades of proven excellence are opening themselves up to be challenged. How much is decades of proven excellence worth? Is it worth $80,000? $100,000? $150,000? Maybe. But also, if a person is willing to take that gamble of investing their time and resources into something, it might be worth considering a place like Southland that draws from those traditions but isn't beholden to them, and doesn't ask participants to commit to a foreseeable future of $1,200-per-month loan payments. And state-of-the-art equipment is great, but, on the other hand, we also live in a time when Hollywood movies and platinum records have been shot and recorded on iPhones. You can publish and distribute a book with Lulu. An $800 refurbished laptop will do anything and everything you could ever dream of and more.

So that still leaves us with place, community, thought leaders, access to less tangible resources. In most of these regards (with the unfortunate, but all-too-real, exception of the current cost of living here) I can't think of many better places to have access to all of that than Los Angeles.

And obviously you're right that a reputation takes time, but what we're hoping to do is to start with a foundation that a reputation can be built on, of people who look at and respond to the world in an attuned way, who make challenging, engaging work, and who are also committed to and curious about investigating the role that teaching plays in the development of a practice. And I think we're open to the idea of excellence potentially meaning a lot of different things, and a culture that doesn't necessarily strive for it, but hopefully comes to it naturally as a by-product of rigorous analysis and investigation.

It's interesting that you bring up RISD as a point of comparison, as I happened to be in Providence earlier this summer, at the same time as their end-of-year grad show of all the departments. I was struck by how so many of the works were pressing hard against the walls of their departmental containers. This has been the case there for a long time, but all these departments persist. So, along with the decades of proven excellence, which is undeniable, there also comes some structural baggage, particularly for those who might be looking for a more inclusive, connective, unconventional approach.

I guess, ultimately, the things we have on our side, in addition to affordability, are the energy and flexibility of institutional youth, a location of infinite possibility in the heavy sunspace of Los Angeles, and an understated but exceptional faculty who more than make up in substance for whatever they may lack in name recognition.

JS Who are the Southland Institute's faculty, and how did you decide on a core group to launch the programme? Are you also utilising visitors, and local experts outside the graphic design community?

JP For the first year, we have a core faculty of four people, including myself. Of the four, my educational and professional background is maybe the most conventionally aligned with graphic design and graphic design education, though my interests range well outside of those worlds. The other faculty are: Fiona Connor, whose practice moves between curating, facilitating and object-making, and who uses strategies of repetition to produce objects that interrogate their own form by engaging different histories embedded within our built environment; Lucas Quigley, who organises programmes concerned with images of the production and distribution of objects and goods, unusual threads within the history of technical image-making, and the social parameters that make these descriptions possible; and Aurora Tang, a researcher and curator with a focus on place-based practices, who is also a programme manager at the Center for Land Use Interpretation, and from 2011 to 2015 was managing director of High Desert Test Sites. I'm obviously biased, but I think it's a powerfully generative combination of people, whose concerns, interests and approaches are complementary, but varied

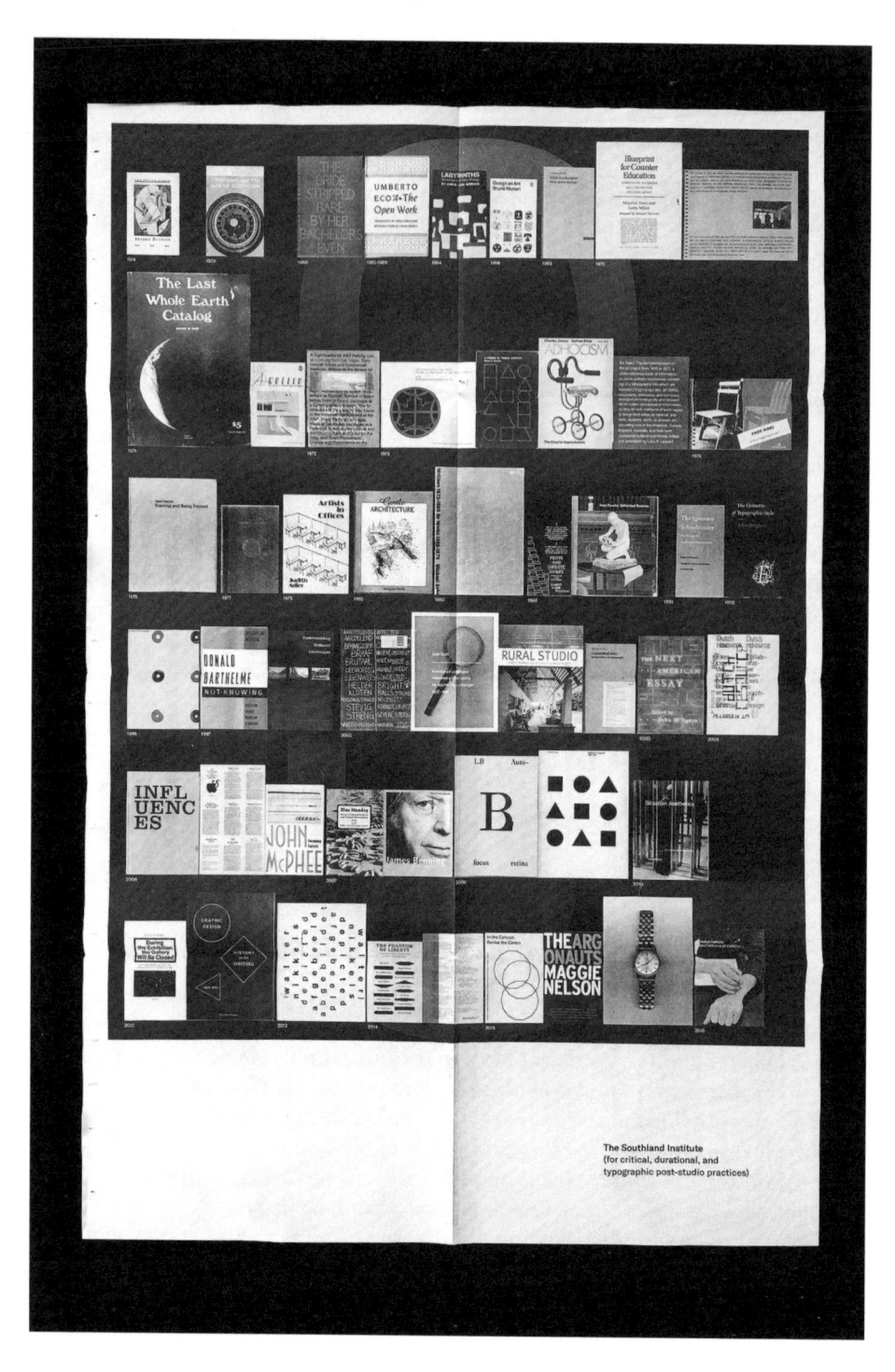

Southland Institute prospectus showing source
materials, 2017. Image courtesy of Joe Potts.

enough to provide a real range of perspectives. Each stands easily on their own, but combined we become even greater than the sum of our parts.

We also have some amazing people coming in from other schools to do shorter workshops and lectures, including, at the moment, Paul Soulellis (RISD), Shannon Ebner (USC), and Yasmin Khan (CalArts, Otis), as well as other folks as the programme grows.

Hopefully all of this will be attractive to students who are intellectually curious, critical, engaged and excited about building something new.

JS What is your curriculum based on, and how are you managing the 'residency' model? Is the programme highly structured, or based on each participant's engagement with their independent work?

JP The programme is very much based on its participants' individual investment in their own projects. What these projects can be is very open-ended. They might be self-initiated, or collaborative, or commissioned. In terms of the curriculum, it's intended to be very fluid. This definitely raises the question of curricular specifics and structure, that is: how do you create something that's open and fluid without it being completely amorphous or unmoored?

And I think that this is where the prospectus comes in. In addition to outlining some of the aims of the programme, the prospectus includes a list of fifty-two books. This list is by no means finite, but it gives a structure of sorts. It pencils in some lines, suggests some conceptual and strategic approaches. It's concerned with form, and the relationship between form and ideas, but it isn't formally prescriptive. It's not exactly a reading list (though it could be if someone was feeling motivated to engage with it in that way) so much as a collection of sources intended to provide a versatile series of something like modules, to create a base for a vast but interwoven combination of compelling curricula that look at language, typography, pedagogy, theory, documentation, institutional critique, architecture, reproduction, publication as critical practice, and alternative narrative strategies, among other things, but not in a way that's scripted. With all of this as a jumping-off point, much is left to the discretion and inclinations of the faculty — guided by their own work, explorations, interests and ideas about teaching — in active response to what the participants themselves bring to the table.

The residency question is one that may end up needing to play itself out. There's a tension at work between what's ideal and what's realistic, and a paradox, perhaps, in trying to create a programme that at once acknowledges the precarious fiscal realities of a majority of people, while at the same time distancing itself from the notion that higher education equals increased employability or earning potential. Thinking about the type of education that the Southland Institute aims to provide, and the conditions under which this might best occur, a more 'high-residency' model seems in many ways to be ideal.

But even with a very modest tuition fee, there's still the issue of cost of living. So what we're looking to achieve is something more, you could say, of a 'medium-residency' model. Something where there's enough time together, enough time for projects and relationships to develop, and also time for the other aspects of life to not only occur, but hopefully feed into the work as well.

In the beginning, we'll be itinerant, setting up shop where we can, in unused, borrowed and in-between spaces, in roughly six-week blocks of time, one block in each season. As time goes on and situations change, this configuration may also change.

JS A really successful 'alternative' school that you reference a lot in your materials is the Werkplaats Typografie. The WT is a great example of a programme that had very modest resources initially, yet was able to vault into the conversation with the best schools in the world in quite a short period. I think part of it was perfect timing — a counterpoint to the end-of-the-1990s postmodern wave, an iconic faculty member in Karel Martens who instantly sparked interest from many students, and a pretty great location in Arnhem, a city far enough away from Amsterdam to separate itself from the status quo and form its own identity. How is the WT — or other schools, for that matter — influencing you?

JP I agree with your observations about the elements that coalesced in the case of the WT, and obviously all of those are circumstances that don't exist here. Context is obviously a huge factor in everything, schools being no exception, and I have a lot of thoughts about the specific context of Los Angeles in 2017. But I'll talk a little bit first about some of the things, in the case of the WT, that I think might be translated or transposed from one context to another in a compelling way.

One of the most literal and direct ways in which the WT has been an influence is Paul Elliman's essay in their early 'In Alphabetical Order' book, which begins:

> Using even the barest design or programming tricks, it shouldn't be too difficult to set up a fledgling 'academy' for the internet. A basic school channeling available resources: dictionaries, search engines, mailing lists, chat-rooms; along with a collection of scholarly (or not) web-links; a loose assembly of contributing texts, workshops, lectures, 'slideshows', notes and correspondences. A content begins to take shape, presents itself as a space; people go there, a discussion begins.[2]

It's easy to see the connection between the approach outlined there and the Southland Institute website.[3] Some of the other things about the WT (or my interpretation of it, at least) that have been most inspiring, as someone who's been watching from afar — and that I think are relevant to some of the aims of Southland — are the self-directed and open-ended qualities, the use of graphic design and typography as jumping-off points for broader language, image, sound and situational explorations that may diverge from conventional practice, and also the cultivation of practices that incorporate elements of the extremely pragmatic (the commissioned, 'real projects' aspect) along with things that might be more speculative and/or oblique.

Other schools that have also been influential in various ways include the Nova Scotia College of Art and Design, particularly the era of the late

1960s and early 1970s, when they were bringing in, and publishing books by, people like Steve Reich, Hans Haacke, Yvonne Rainer, Dan Graham, Michael Asher, Allen Sekula and others. The relationships between the work, teaching practices and publications of these artists are definitely of interest.

And Black Mountain College, though clearly from a very different time, place and set of circumstances, has this line in its prospectus that I think is always worth revisiting:

> [A base principle] worth emphasizing (it is still generally overlooked in those colleges where classification into fields, because of curriculum emphasis, remains the law) is that Black Mountain College carefully recognizes that … it is not things in themselves, but what happens between things, where the life of them is to be sought.

Though rooted in graphic design and typography, there's also an element of the Southland Institute that is about this idea of a holistic educational experience that's not broken down into departmental categories, and where interdisciplinarity isn't just talked about or constructed after the fact, but built into the project from its conception.

JS   How does place — meaning the Los Angeles area — play into the plans for the Southland Institute? Is the agenda of the school in any way site-specific? Are you drawing from the area's rich history of art and design?

JP   Definitely. While it clearly derives a degree of institutional influence from places farther afield geographically, it's also very much a response to its own surroundings. And in addition to the region's history of art and design, there's also a history of pedagogical innovation. And then, on top of all of that, there's an interesting confluence of recent events that make it all very much a product of its own place and time.

These recent events that I'm talking about all took place around 2015–2016, and were localised, but also representative of a much broader set of concerns. One was the arrival of the *Leap Before You Look* Black Mountain College retrospective at the Hammer Museum. The resurgence of interest in one of the most influential educational experiments of the twentieth century speaks to a spreading sense that it might be worthwhile to step outside the institutional frameworks we've become familiar with and look at this historical model, not out of nostalgia, but more out of a sense of mining the past for information that we may have overlooked, that might be useful as inspiration for a version of the near future that's markedly different from the path we're heading down.

A second significant Los Angeles event was the USC Roski MFA class all dropping out at once in response to what they perceived and articulated as unacceptable and irresponsible institutional behaviour. There are conflicting accounts of what precisely transpired, but the fact remains that this was, to my knowledge, an unprecedented student response to the corporatisation of higher education.

The third Los Angeles event was the near-simultaneous efforts to organise faculty (contingent and otherwise) at CalArts, Otis College of Art and Design, Art Center and the University of Southern California, all of which were suppressed in various ways by their respective administrations, even in the cases of Otis and USC, both of which voted for faculty representation. That these kinds of behind-the-scenes institutional machinations would be a part of a curricular conversation about typography and the meaning of structural forms and images is a different way of thinking about an art and design education.

CalArts also factors into its lineage, but in a more fragmented, collaged way. We're thinking about the history of design there, not only the critical and post-structurally derived form-making of the 1990s and beyond, but also the early Victor Papanek days and Sheila Levrant de Bretteville's women's design programme.[4] But we're also interested in CalArts beyond its design history. We're thinking about Maurice Stein and Larry Miller's vision for the Critical Studies programme, outlined in *Blueprint for Counter Education* (1970) (another document that is enjoying a recent resurgence in popularity), and, importantly, the history of the 'post-studio art' class that was started by John Baldessari, and taught for thirty-five years by Michael Asher. Then a couple of other CalArts influences that are part of the Southland DNA are the art and pedagogical practices of filmmaker James Benning, photo-essayist Allan Sekula and composer Morton Subotnick.

Another influential contemporary practice is that of the architecture collective Assemble, who describe their work and studio as 'founded on the belief that an understanding of how things are made, of how materials are assembled, brings an intimate engagement with the problems and possibilities of the real world' (that quote comes from the catalogue for the *How We Build* show at Architekturzentrum Wien). Their strategic, conscientious and socially engaged architectural practice delves into questions of structure, form and material that go beyond the physical and into areas of history, economics, land trusts, housing, play, the public, conversations about contemporary art practice, and where and how these things connect. All of this is done with simple construction methods and inexpensive and easily accessible materials.

So there's a lot there, but the hope is that it all weaves together in a powerful and ultimately cohesive way, and that while we may not have name recognition, a long-standing reputation, or the financial resources that both enable and derive from those things, we have enough of the other pieces to begin to attract the kinds of folks who will help the project gain momentum and evolve into whatever it is going to become.

Coda

During the 2018–2019 academic year, the Southland Institute began a public events series, and also delivered a sequence of foundational courses at Los Angeles City College.[5] At the graduate level, a cohort of participants enrolled in a core curriculum of four courses: 'Typographies', 'Cf.' (discussion and critique), 'Close Reading' and 'Frame and Field' (curation). In 2019, the Institute additionally offered a series of in-depth conversations that took place in the context of public exhibitions within existing institutions,[6] and three public workshops: a paid type design workshop with Johannes Breyer and Fabian Harb of Dinamo, a free web typography workshop with Masato

Nakada, and a free workshop with Nicole Killian examining digital archives as a way to manipulate and build language.

This interview was first published on 9 August 2017 on *The Gradient*, the Walker Art Center's digital magazine: www.walkerart.org/magazine/southland-institute-jon-sueda-joe-potts. The coda is newly included here.

1. For more on Sallie Mae and Navient, see: Stacy Cowley and Jessica Silver-Greenberg, 'Loans "Designed to Fail": States Say Navient Preyed on Students', *New York Times*, 9 April 2017, https://www.nytimes.com/2017/04/09/business/dealbook/states-say-navient-preyed-on-students.html?_r=0, accessed 26 November 2019.
2. Paul Elliman, 'Otherschools' in *In Alphabetical Order*, edited by Stuart Bailey (Werkplaats Typografie, Arnhem: 2002), 77.
3. See: http://southland.institute/, accessed 26 November 2019.
4. Izzy Berenson and Sarah Honeth, 'Clearing the Haze: Prologue to Postmodern Graphic Design Education through Sheila de Bretteville', *The Gradient*, Walker Art Center, 26 April 2016, https://walkerart.org/magazine/clearing-the-haze-prologue-to-postmodern-graphic-design-education-through-sheila-de-bretteville-2, accessed 26 November 2019.
5. See: http://southland.institute/events.html, and http://southland.institute/LACCGD.html, accessed 26 November 2019.
6. These conversations are part of a programme called 'Discussions in Exhibitions', initiated in 2010 by Adam Feldmeth, who joined the Southland Institute in 2018 as programme director, bringing this and several other open, independent pedagogical initiatives into partnership with the Southland Institute. Another of these initiatives is a reading group called 'Ad Hoc', co-organised by Feldmeth and Carmen Amengual, who also joined the core faculty in 2018. See: http://southland.institute/openelectives.html, accessed 26 November 2019.

**Arriving and landing:
perspectives on the Werkplaats Typografie**
Na Kim, Radim Peško and Lu Liang,
interviewed by Megan Patty

Werkplaats Typografie (WT) is a two-year graphic design Master programme in Arnhem, the Netherlands. It was founded by designers Karel Martens and Wigger Bierma in 1998, and is now part of the ArtEZ University of the Arts. From humble beginnings, it has established itself as a centre of innovative practice in publication design and typography. Here, Megan Patty discusses the experience of studying at the WT with three of its high-profile graduates: Na Kim, Radim Peško and Lu Liang. We read about the challenges of relocating to study, the familial environment of the school, the particularities of the Dutch approach to design, and the lasting influence of the WT upon these three designers.

In my work as a publisher at a large public museum, I have seen many recent graphic design graduates arrive into the workforce. Their arrival is usually characterised by bright eyes, good intentions and much potential. Over the next year or two, they (and we) then grapple with their landing.

I use the terms 'arrive' and 'land', and I think of my migrant family, who arrived and who had to land in a foreign place. They came from the Netherlands to Australia, where few (if any) cultural tropes were familiar to them. They faced a new language, a new set of histories and a landscape that was like nothing they had seen before. But this place was full of potential.

Werkplaats Typografie is a two-year Master programme in Arnhem, the Netherlands, founded by designers Karel Martens and Wigger Bierma in 1998. In 2010, on a research trip, I travelled to Arnhem to spend some time there. I was looking at speculative forms of publishing. At the time, the publishing industry was greatly concerned with the rise of the digital and the apparently pending death of print. I had hoped the school would provide something of an antidote to those conversations. On arriving, I was immediately struck by how familiar and familial it felt. The school was so intensely Dutch.

The programme prospectus states that students will work with 'leading designers, artists, curators and peers from various countries in a small very particular building'. Indeed, it is a very particular building: a former radio broadcast facility turned into a school. However, it is not simply a school. The Werkplaats comprises a community of activities and things: a publishing house, a project space, a library, an archive and, naturally, a design studio. It curates exhibitions and provocations at major publishing events such as the New York Art Book Fair, and has alumni scattered around the globe.

Three of these are Na Kim, Radim Peško and Lu Liang, who respectively arrived in the Netherlands from Korea, the Czech Republic and China. All three now practise as designers, typographers, curators and educators. They came to the Werkplaats with different design backgrounds, and distinct personal histories and cultural knowledge. Given the 'Dutch-ness' of the school and its approach, how does a non-Dutch designer find themselves in this immersive environment?

Na Kim had studied industrial design, then a graphic design Master programme in Seoul, and had worked in a design agency before attending the Werkplaats from 2006 to 2008. She looked to Europe to continue her study and to leave Korea for a while.

> NK   I believe that the actual spaces — the surroundings and the atmosphere for studying and living — mattered a lot because I was there for two years. I loved the autonomous life of students at the school. It completely changed my concept of schooling at that time — having individual spaces and working on your own, self-generated projects without framed academic classes. Because it is open twenty-four hours a day, seven days a week, everyone can use the space as a personal 'werkplaats' and spend most of their time together — working, cooking and hanging out together.

Radim Peško graduated from The Academy of Arts, Architecture and Design in Prague in 2001. Dissatisfied and looking to continue his studies, he made a rather sudden and intuitive decision to apply to the Werkplaats after seeing an exhibition about Dutch graphic design and the work of Karel Martens at the Brno Biennial. He studied at the Werkplaats from 2002 to 2004.

Immersion is a distinguishing feature of the school. The students and educators form a close-knit group, and students spend a *lot* of time there during the programme. The school provides twenty-four-hour access, a kitchen and communal meals for only two Euro per person. This model is perhaps more reflective of 1960s art schools than contemporary design schools. But while Kim appreciated this atmosphere, Peško struggled with it.

> RP   Growing up in a communist country, socialist Czechoslovakia, I have an inherent resistance towards community activities. (Anybody with such a background would tell you a similar thing.) I had serious difficulties with partaking in the group lunches every day at the school. But now I am thankful to have met all those great teachers, mentors, colleagues and friends. I feel immensely lucky.

Students are encouraged to carry out 'research in applied art, on content and form, text and image and theory and practice'. This means studios with a great variety of facilities and conversation, rather than rows of computers and silence. Without a timetable filled with classes, students take on projects and self-directed research inquiries, and are largely left to their own devices. They must work through the challenges that this freedom inevitably brings.

> NK   I didn't know so much about graphic design in the Netherlands beforehand, but I realised the educational system has much more flexibility than Korea and a practical approach that enables designers to engage in multidisciplinary practices. Students are working independently, on commissioned projects. Within this structure, the relationships with tutors and other students are far from conventional — tutors and other students become more like professional advisors, collaborators, counsellors, or even family. Almost everything was done by autonomous decision and learning-by-doing. In the first year, I was quite perplexed by this freedom and needed some time to learn how to make myself busy. That was one of the most valuable experiences: being compelled to think about developing a sustainable practice and my own design language.

> RP   It was a very slow process for me, and not always pleasant. I did not understand what was meant by 'develop your own voice' or 'approach' and things like that. In Prague, it was all about dealing with tasks, so, at first, I found myself struggling in Arnhem. But it was a necessary struggle.

Lu Liang attended the Werkplaats from 2009 to 2011, after having completed a BA at Central Academy of Fine Art (CAFA), Beijing, then another BA at Gerrit Rietveld Academie, Amsterdam. The transition from the Rietveld to the Werkplaats was a natural one, after she met and was encouraged to apply by Karel Martens and current school director Armand Mevis.

LL   I was in a period of searching for my next step after school. It was a confusing time. Especially as a non-European student, it was tough in many ways. But they gave me the encouragement. I got accepted, but, more importantly, suddenly I felt safe and grounded, I felt protected, and I felt I had the space and time to fully develop myself.

Kim's and Liang's references to family are insightful. When a school aims to offer such an immersive experience, it surely has a duty of care to its students, especially if it has only a small cohort, many of whom take a risk in relocating across the world to undertake further study in a model that is significantly different from that of the design education they experienced prior. This immersion is not just about the time spent in the school or the strength of the communities built; it is also an immersion in Dutch design and in the rich histories of practice that influence education in the Netherlands.

LL   The Rietveld was my transition into being in the Netherlands, into a different type of education. It 'brainwashed' me. It taught me how to think, and paved a foundation for my study at the Werkplaats. If I'd come from China straight away, this would have been a different story. Without this foundation, I think I would have had a much harder time. The directness of the Dutch, their efficiency and pragmatism, has, in my opinion, shaped 'Dutch design'. It was not until later that I understood Dutch design better, after I really spent time learning the language; the Dutch language itself is quite straightforward. The Dutch directness is the total opposite of a Chinese way of thinking. As a designer, I am always attracted to beauty. But when I was in China, I never asked about the reason behind it. My education in the Netherlands has changed my practice, as well as my views on aesthetics. Since then, it has been hard for me to think of visual style before concept and functionality.

NK   On reflection, it seems like the Netherlands was a utopian cultural territory. At the time, Amsterdam was definitely attracting many foreign designers, and producing immensely interesting projects because of its abundant cultural funding and exchange programmes. In my view, Dutch designers are not only those from the Netherlands: they are designers who share values from a certain time and place.
      The Werkplaats is typically Dutch in its attitude to education — there is a freedom, an independence and a positiveness — but its Dutch-ness is not limited by language. The school was like a small stateless island in the Netherlands. Most participants were international; only one or two were from the Netherlands in my years.

With teachers at the school all practising designers, critics or curators, including Danny van den Dungen (Experimental Jetset), Constant Dullaart, Paul Elliman, Angie Keefer and Maxine Kopsa, learning from practice and practising learning is a key component of the school's pedagogical approach. For those who have grown up with similar values, or who have been in similar educational environments prior, this feels quite natural. For students from non-European countries, this shift in thinking can be quite pronounced and significant. The school's definitions of what a designer is and can do, and what their contributions might be, are speculative at best, and, further, the students are encouraged to navigate these matters themselves.

> RP   The Werkplaats opened my eyes to what the practice of a designer can be, and that it is in my hands to define it. It sounds obvious now, but it was something of a revelation to me at the time. In a formal way, I don't think my work has ever been very 'Werkplaats-like'. I realised that I have different preferences or sensitivities, which took over.

> NK   A clear definition of practice was not crucial, which enabled me to challenge my thinking with fewer limitations in terms of process, method and outcomes. But — ironically, I thought — the basis of this flexibility was the pragmatic Dutch attitude, which often set up the rules and limitations beforehand. The idea of 'playing with the rules' must be a core aspect of this approach.
>   I finished the first assignment and was quite proud of my work. But Karel immediately said that I needed to forget about what I used to think of as design rules. I realised that I often trusted those solutions or rules without any reflection. His advice allowed me to think about 'how to work', rather than about any particular technical approach to designing.

> LL   One thing I love about the Netherlands is that there's no hierarchy. It seems there is always this equality between everyone. The teachers never exercised any authority, but were mentors guiding the students to find their own way. This is not only at the Werkplaats, but in many Dutch schools. All the teachers have their own practices and teach part-time, which also brings a valuable aspect to education there. I don't believe in pure academic research without real practice in the creative field.

Language is a significant concern in an international design programme, not only in terms of the need to learn a new language of design, but also because students sometimes need to learn a new language simply to communicate. The school teaches in English, perhaps to democratise the cohort. For Peško, this wasn't particularly consequential: 'My English was really basic (more basic than I thought back then, as a colleague later told me!), but when you have to use it, you find a way.' But for others, language can be a site of possibility. Matters of language can hold much potential for an inquiring design practice when you are living in a country that uses not one but two languages that you do not speak.

> LL   It took me about a year to finally be able to express myself fully. But this language 'problem' eventually became a main topic of my research. I got really interested in the relationship between language and objects, words and things.

And so, after completing two years of 'in-depth theoretical research, in the form of critical reflection, excursions and a thesis, developing artistic, visual, discursive and practical skills', where does one land?

NK   In 2008, I initiated an exhibition in Seoul of ten years of work from Werkplaats Typografie, called *Starting from Zero*. It was just after I graduated from the Werkplaats and I wanted to share the special experience I'd had, in my home country. Moreover, it was a good occasion to have the ten-year anniversary event for the Werkplaats. Like many other projects from the school, this exhibition was autonomously planned by participants, but it became a notable turning point in my practice. *GRAPHIC*, a Korean graphic design magazine, proposed to collaborate on an issue based around the exhibition, and I worked as an art director and editor for this magazine for three years afterwards. During my time there, I changed the magazine to be bilingual, which opened it up for an international audience and distribution. I expressed my own enquiries through each issue and featured great practitioners whom I had known from my time in the Netherlands.

LL   If the Rietveld taught me how to think, the Werkplaats taught me how to make. Don't get me wrong, the Werkplaats is of course very much focused on a conceptual approach, but I already had that in my previous education. All I needed was to bring it out in practice, and eventually it made me ready.

RP   Being at the Werkplaats, I could not (and did not want to) resist being influenced by the teachers, whom I admire greatly. I was in total awe. But after this experience, the most important moment for me was to break out of that and realise what I myself could do — to 'develop my own voice'. That really happened after I graduated, over the course of many years and through a number of important opportunities. When I was in my first year at the Werkplaats, I got a commission from Mevis and van Deursen to create a typeface for the identity of the art museum Boijmans van Beuningen in Rotterdam, which they were designing. They were very pleased with the result, and since then we have done more work together. A few years later, Linda van Deursen asked me to teach at Gerrit Rietveld Academie, where I stayed for six years. My work for *Dot Dot Dot* magazine was a similar story, as was the story of my first studio space after studying at the Werkplaats: when I was graduating, Roger Willems (founder of Roma Publications, who was based in Arnhem at that point) offered me a 'temporary' desk space in his new studio space in Amsterdam. I stayed there for ten years!

And if Kim, Peško and Liang had not attended the Werkplaats Typografie?

NK   I have never thought about this.

RP   My practice would either be better or worse.

LL   I might have become a photographer.

Interviews conducted with Na Kim, January 2019, Berlin; Lu Liang, February 2019, Rotterdam; and Radim Peško, March 2019, London.

**Chasing curiosity:
inquiry-led practice in communication design
Lisa Grocott**

Once a graphic designer, Lisa Grocott is now a design researcher and academic. In this essay, she explores the role that self-directed inquiry plays in design by examining the integration of designing, writing and researching in her own work and in that of three of her colleagues. She argues that curiosity fuels the inquiries that propel evolution within a designer's practice. These inquiries transcend individual projects to drive a culture of learning and innovation in the discipline.

I began this writing with an open-ended question: what is the legacy of late-twentieth-century communication design? I was thinking about my own work and looking at that of my colleagues, Yoko Akama, Anne Burdick and Sean Donahue.[1] What the four of us have in common is that we belong to a tribe of academics who once called themselves 'communication designers', but we now practice in harder-to-define, interdisciplinary research spaces. As art and design became more integrated into academia in the late twentieth century, we gained tenures and began to contribute to the then-new field of design research, venturing into collaborations with colleagues in the fields of digital humanities, human and land rights law, educational psychology, literature and learning science.

I recognised a strong common thread across our practices: a commitment to life-long learning and thinking-through-doing. All of us work in higher education and we identify as design researchers, yet our research is driven by an intrinsic curiosity that has us following our individual lines of questioning. Design research might be understood as an outwardly motivated act of making a contribution to the field, but an examination of our practices reveals that our explorations are propelled forward by more personal threads. The interplay between research and design in our inquiry-led practices suggests to me that the bigger questions that designers are asking fuel the evolution of their work.

In this essay, I explore how the psychology of motivation, strategic design and pedagogy can help designers sustain generative inquiry. And I identify three key characteristics of our practices, which I suggest are central to sustainable inquiry-led practice: (1) inquiry is personally *meaning-making* for the designer; (2) externalised reflection brings a level of *sense-making* to the framing of future questions; and (3) projects themselves are *world-making* in their potential contribution.

Chasing a question

I began this project with a false start. Initially, I designed a series of visual prompts to scaffold our virtual conversation between New York, Los Angeles, Kampala and Melbourne, but I soon realised I was off course. In an effort to isolate common patterns, I set up an exercise in which we would map all of our past projects on a series of conceptual quadrants using binaries such as 'expeditionary–instrumental' and 'representing–discovering', but found we quickly became bored by the task and each of us made attempts to subvert and redesign the exercise. I noticed that my colleagues' rethinking of the exercise was an active strategy to make the questions interesting to themselves — this was evidence to me of a disposition towards 'remaining open to continuous learning'.[2] Thus I arrived at a central pivot, and I began to examine instead our practices through the lens of *learner* instead of *researcher*.

All of my colleagues have expressed, either in interviews with me or in their own published papers, their compulsion to locate design in relation to political, socio-cultural and environmental questions.[3] Burdick said in one interview that her sense of urgency around unanswered questions was a motivation for attending graduate school, and that her quest for new knowledge was not easily satisfied. Donahue wrote about how, for him, a great deal of possibility lies in using the qualities of design to construct new types of engagements, exchanges and understanding.[4] I myself have interrogated my own past practice as a way to 'sense-make' future practices.[5] Yet, for all the commentary on newfound understandings and insights, and new methodologies, we never mentioned our own 'learning'. Perhaps we thought that doing so would diminish our hard-won research profiles.

The anthropologist Mary Catherine Bateson speculated that we will 'cease to focus on learning as preliminary and see it threaded through other layers of experience' because she saw learning as an activity to be pursued throughout life — and she even saw it as necessary to our enjoyment of life.[6] Bateson's idea of *learning* writ large, combined with our first-person accounts of why the four of us chase *curiosity*, led me to see *inquiry* as fundamental to our practices.

This reshaping of my own line of questioning in this essay, through insight gathered in the process, illustrates the point I am making. It is this notion of an evolving line of inquiry that I want to hold up. The projects that the four of us undertake are almost secondary to our investment in learning. The will to discover, to answer a question with a question, and to be led by curiosity into design responses that could not be anticipated at the outset is what quickens our hearts.

Four design practitioners

My three colleagues and I all hold undergraduate degrees in communication design — from universities in the UK, New Zealand and the US. Between us, we now teach a range of students, from undergraduates in communication design to graduate students and PhD candidates in design more broadly. The reason I invited these particular designer/educator/researcher peers to collaborate on this study was due to our shared interest in zooming out from our own work in order to make sense of the field of design, a habit of mind that both interrogates and defines inquiry-led practice in communication design. By examining some of our individual projects, we can see the ways in which our careers have been animated by chasing questions.

Inquiry-based learning

I am situating inquiry as a subset of learning (since some learning does not embrace inquisitiveness) and research as a subset of inquiry (since not all inquiry is deemed research). I am proposing that a predisposition to inquiry was what set myself and my colleagues on a path to becoming researchers. Donahue's account of his practice as a platform 'to untether from the isolating canons of disciplinarity' sheds some light on how he steps sideways, away from capital-'D' design or capital-'R' research, while still valuing the unique qualities that design brings 'to an expanded field of issues, contexts and interrogations'.[7]

Advocates of inquiry-based learning argue that its potential to increase engagement and foster deep understanding is a consequence of authentic learning where the student is engaged in hands-on meaning-making. What might it mean to situate this within design practice? Might authentic discoveries come from a researcher engaged in a practice primarily motivated to pose questions rather than solve problems? Neil Stephenson, in his 'Introduction to Inquiry Based Learning', proposes how a 'research-based disposition' to learning can honour the complex, interconnected nature of knowledge construction.[8] I use the term *inquiry-led practice* here to describe an intentional practice of attuning to and negotiating the meta-questions that weave through one's practice. Viewing a practice as more than a culmination of decades of projects allows the designer to see that 'knowledge is created through the transformation of experience'.[9]

The characteristics of an inquiry-led practice

To explore this idea of inquiry-led practice, I interviewed my colleagues, I studied their work, and I reflected upon my own work and experiences. Interpretation of these sense-making activities unearthed three key insights as to what might drive the inquiry for the practitioner.

The first was the question of motivation. Through the interviews, it became apparent that we all understood our practices as a response to ongoing and ever-evolving questions. These questions fed the curiosity that fuelled the inquiry.

Second, there was a pattern in how our practices engaged with the perpetual evolution of our questions. It was difficult to determine how we interpreted new knowledge, but mappings of our practices hinted at a negotiation between different 'sense-making' activities. We moved between writing and designing, and between, on the one hand, exploratory projects that chased the right question and, on the other, instrumental projects that temporarily fixed propositions to questions.

Third came the role of design exploration in animating our inquiries. Design practice, as the primary mode of investigation, was a vehicle for our project-based reflection-*in*-action and our practice-based reflection-*on*-action.[10] Most significant was the intentional decision to frame projects as platforms for testing out new ideas and foreshadowing future practice questions.

While I will give only one example per designer of how these three characteristics play out within a project, they manifested consistently across all of our practices. Together, the three characteristics, which I refer to as *meaning-making*, *sense-making* and *world-making*, form the inquiry-led framework that I propose below.

Meaning-making: the question of motivation

At the heart of the four practices discussed here is a compulsion to follow a line of inquiry — a question that transcends your current project, which you feel compelled to explore. A current question for Akama is a concern for the ways in which participatory design might create dialogue and build awareness of local environments to help communities prepare for natural disasters.[11] My own question explores what the material and performative act of designing brings to interdisciplinary collaborations.[12] For Burdick, it is a question of the role of design in reconceiving knowledge production in the information age.[13] For Donahue, the inquiry is grounded in designers asking how we might support the human condition in the twenty-first century.[14] These practice questions illustrate that these designers have woven their experiences, expertise and proclivities into the inquiries that guide their practices. All practice involves sites of inquiry and the making of meaning; the distinction offered here is that sustained topics of inquiry *direct* the practice.

In *Before Happiness*, psychology researcher Shawn Achor translates goal-setting research into mental maps that make visual the psychological advantage to be gained from consciously orientating our lives around what we care about. In placing 'meaning markers' onto our mental maps, Achor argues that we learn to scan for opportunities (rather than predetermine the path), to acknowledge the rewards, and to foresee threats and setbacks.[15] Management and psychology researchers Amy Wrzesniewski and Barry Schwartz created a study to better understand how internal motivations (such as, 'I want to explore these practice questions') are more powerful than instrumental motivations (such as, 'I need to publish for promotion'). The assumption was that a combination of both kinds of motivation would be better than just one, but the evidence showed that people were more likely to succeed when their motivation was essentially internal. Counterintuitively, Wrzesniewski and Schwartz concluded that instrumental motives can hold you back.[16]

It is interesting, then, to cast personal learning as a primary motivation for the designers in this study (as opposed to the more instrumental and abstract motive of career progression). If, as professionals, we accept the volatile, uncertain, complex and ambiguous world in which we live as a permanent condition, then we also foresee the instability of our profession and of design education.[17] If we recognise the importance of practitioners being adaptive to new challenges and responsive to new opportunities, then a commitment to lifelong learning becomes a matter of self-sustainability. And so it is a self-preserving pursuit of knowledge. For us, the four subjects of this study, the decision to orient our practices around inquiry may have had instrumental consequences, such as promotions, recognition, awards, and so on, but the driving motivation was *learning* — our inclination to lean into challenges, overcome obstacles, embrace effort, seek feedback and learn from our peers.[18]

In his book *Making Learning Whole*, David Perkins presents the principles of authentic learning through the analogy of playing baseball.[19] Perkins's argument is that breaking knowledge into *elements* or learning *about* something does not serve learning well. He argues that deep learning comes from a sense of the big picture, and that through this integrated approach the learner develops the tacit knowledge that comes with active engagement. There are seven principles for Perkins's learning by wholes: play the whole game; make the game worth playing; work on the hard parts; play out of town; uncover the hidden game; learn from the team; and, lastly, learn the game of learning.

Perkins implies that, in the 'real world', we are always playing the whole game. However, many professional roles might narrow the way we play the game: the professor who, like the coach, doesn't play any more; or the creative director who, like the pitcher, can't bat; or the critic who watches from the bleachers and doesn't step onto the field. An inquiry-led approach to design practice potentially offers a strategy for playing the whole game: we challenge ourselves to discover new skills, explore opportunities, transfer our knowing and work on our weaknesses. All the while, we give meaning to our work, which motivates us to invest time and fuels our quest to learn.

Co-design for communities: Yoko Akama
Yoko Akama has been part of an interdisciplinary research team funded by the Australian Government to investigate communication obstacles and community preparedness for bushfire. Over the course of five years, rather than tunnelling into a single 'most effective' communication method, Akama sought to help a community understand their resources and risks. This led her to explore various community-centred processes that engaged residents and emergency management agencies. She developed educational workshops animated by everyday objects (or 'playful triggers'), such as buttons, toy animals and matchsticks, to guide conversation and planning among communities and neighbours in high-risk areas.[20]

By choosing the applied context, Akama was *playing the whole game*. The opportunity to design workshops for the local residents provided a rich learning experience distinct from the abstraction of academia or piloting workshops with civil servants alone. And even though her participation in this research project offered significant extrinsic motivations for her career, it was Akama's intrinsic motivations that *made the game worth playing*.

Another characteristic of whole-game learning consistent across all of our practices was the decision to collaborate with experts from other disciplines. Perkins argues that there is a significant opportunity for learning when *playing out of town*. Akama describes interdisciplinary collaboration as a significant and rewarding learning curve. Designers often enter these partnerships as — arguably — the least understood collaborator at the table. Akama spoke of the challenge to learn the culture and the vocabulary of emergency management in order to have her ideas heard, but she also acknowledges the deepened personal understanding that came with having to transfer her design knowledge into a new domain. She then sought to co-author papers with academics from other disciplines. She describes a shift from a traditional notion of designers as producers of products to one in which designers are 'builders of scaffolding for experiencing'.[21] Through this responsive design practice and her interdisciplinary collaborations, Akama extends the territory of her practice and in turn forges interdisciplinary collaborations that further fuel her motivation and deepen her practice.

Sense-making design: the question of synthesis
For any designer, the role of synthesis is an iterative process that happens across the course of a project, but I would like to consider how we make sense of our work at the level of our ongoing practices. Bryan Lawson and Kees Dorst propose a hierarchy that begins with the *project* at the base, moves through *process* to consider *practice*, and positions the *profession* at the apex of the triangle.[22] They describe the pathway to mastery as a procedure of moving through these phases, culminating with our contribution to a community of like-minded peers — our capacity to interpret our own practices, they argue, is central to our ability to contribute at the level of the professional community.[23]

An inquiry-led practice benefits from meta-reflection exercises that can help to unearth insights, refine research questions and propose next steps. Conceptually mapping a practice over time allows an observation of the underlying line of inquiry and can guide future directions. Instrumental motives might have inspired certain activities, such as academic writing, and yet the insights uncovered in the process of that writing may become the true driving force for the next phase of the practice. Similarly, the visual and verbal nature of conference presentations can provide a platform for the translation of nascent ideas into concrete insights.[24] Making sense of one's practice through designing, writing and sharing fosters the externalisation of an otherwise internalised process, ensuring that the practice inquiry can move beyond self-reflection and begin to model, advance and debate future directions for the profession.

Jon Kolko uses the term 'sense-making' to describe the design act of synthesis. Combining definitions from management and communication, he defines sense-making as 'an action-oriented process that people automatically go through in order to integrate experiences into their understanding of the world around them'.[25] The 'sense of getting it out' is about constructing an external view of things in order to find patterns and forge connections that, in turn, reveal unforeseen next steps.

Making sense through mapping: Anne Burdick and Lisa Grocott
In her work collaborating with writers as a 'design co-author', Anne Burdick's process keeps her constantly shuttling between the micro and the macro: from words in a sentence to the structure of an argument to the social construction of knowledge and back again. But it wasn't until she created a wall-scaled timeline of her design and writing projects that she was able to recognise a second layer of questions that she had been asking from early on. The visualisation showed her that, in addition to her interrogation of the relationship between writing and design, she was also posing questions about design itself, as a practice and as a profession.

Through this mapping exercise, Burdick came to understand that an essential part of her practice was to push into uncharted areas, so that her projects no longer sat squarely in any one discipline — they were part communication design, part linguistics, part literary science, part experimental fiction, part media criticism. She also saw that the market-based design practice models that existed were a poor fit for her concerns — she was more interested in scholarly knowledge production.

Additionally, Burdick realised that she had worked — and enjoyed working — to create the institutional structures, social configurations, dissemination networks, funding models and professional contexts within which her projects could thrive. And, importantly, her process of sense-making included writing. She then used what she had learned through the visualisation exercise to frame her projects, process and practice, using the term 'investigative design' to describe her approach.

Using this close reading of past projects, Burdick could reflect on her past practice to speculate about her future practice. Donald Schön has argued that designers engage in 'frame-making' to set their line of inquiry.[26] Schön is referring to a designer's capacity to shift perspective in order to see the familiar in unfamiliar ways and, through this reframing, to see new possibilities. Burdick was using the holistic view that mapping offers to reveal such insights regarding her own practice. It is important to note that she created the timeline as a process of discovery, through which she would uncover mental schemas, not as a representational or chronological exercise.

My own process of creating 'figuring diagrams' is a similar strategy for teasing out not-yet-formed ideas.[27] The graphic practice of 'figuring' seeks to enact an active state of insight through an interplay between the known and the not-yet-known. I draw ambiguous diagrams that are not 'figured out' in advance — the ambiguity is a tactic to draw others into the process of making meaning.[28] Similarly, the conceptual journey map I used in the discovery phase of this study was a hybrid narrative-timeline that amplified Schön's notion of 'back-talk' — the cognitive and performative conversation between the designer and the materials of the situation.[29] The process of mapping revealed that it wasn't the story of our projects but the story of our journeys through and between projects — the story of our inquiries — that was really worth telling.

On a granular level, the insights gained through these sense-making activities uncovered the ways in which we made meaning in our work, leading to further insights regarding ways in which we could configure our workplace projects to advance our inquiries. In our academic roles, Burdick and I have both come to see that our respective practice inquiries could also shape the immediate context in which we work. Burdick applied this knowledge to improving the graduate programme she chairs, whereas I applied my figuring practice to organisational change at my institution.

World-making projects: the question of exploration
All four designers have practices shaped by a commitment to learning and sharing new knowledge. This commitment is fostered by the cultural values of our roles as educators and researchers, but it is also possible to imagine ways in which design practitioners outside the academy might deploy active strategies for schematising their questions. Shana Agid, for example, champions the importance of designers learning from what we know of the world 'in order to make, represent and imagine new or differently designed things in the world'.[30] She offers feminist theories of world-making as a way to ground this call to action, but also as a way to destabilise assumptions we hold regarding power and politics. Donahue similarly investigates the ways in which design might catalyse these kinds of conversations. He uses his practice to understand how design might 'participate in and contribute to the politics, scale and sustainability of power, authority and access across multiple social agendas and positions'.[31]

Dan Hill, in his book *Dark Matter and Trojan Horses*, proposes a vocabulary for strategic design as an integrated practice.[32] Given the embedded social, political, environmental and economic forces that provide the context for design, it would be irresponsible, Hill argues, to see projects and ideas as isolated solutions. He presents the idea that strategic designers are constantly up against 'dark matter' that can only be perceived when it comes into effect in relation to other things. In fact, if an idea is too easily accepted, he argues, it is probably because a designer has not disrupted the dark matter enough and has made only an imperceptible difference. Hill's vocabulary makes explicit this call for designers to see each project as a world-making, territory-traversing opportunity.

Borrowing the concept of the 'MacGuffin' from film, Hill asks: what is the plot device that will drive a project? Here, he is pointing to the potential of a material, performative artefact that will 'motivate the various actors to create a richly rewarding experience for the audience, and enable strategic outcomes by also addressing the context'.[33] Within the grander narrative of an inquiry-led practice, revealing the artefacts, conversations, experiences and interrelationships of projects can offer insight into the meta-objective of the project. Where the MacGuffin represents what can be learned in the pursuing of a project (or practice), the concept of a Trojan Horse comes into play to refer to the intentional framing of a project that entices people to engage, to commit — a kind of stealth cover for the desired outcome. Donahue's project *LA Has Faults* provides an example of these devices within a project.

Spaces for dialogue: Sean Donahue

The project *LA Has Faults* explores how a series of design interventions might increase earthquake preparedness for under-resourced communities in the Westlake area of Los Angeles. For Donahue, this collaboration served as part of an ongoing investigation into how design can be used to create new kinds of community engagement, using conversation starters that have been shaped to invert, equalise or decentralise the default agendas, orientations and structures associated with existing models of community exchange.

Donahue's design team of faculty, alumni and students of Art Center College of Design in Pasadena conducted a large-scale design intervention in MacArthur Park, the social centre of Westlake, in order to introduce their topic to the community. During the day-long event, the team constructed three-metre high letters and used them to spell five different words. Built one at a time with each left standing for thirty minutes, these words — 'shake', 'shift', 'aware', 'alerta' and 'alto' — in English and Spanish, drew on familiar earthquake rhetoric, piquing the curiosity of passers-by. It was not so much the words themselves as the 'building' of the letters that generated interest and started conversations with park visitors, passing commuters and local residents. While ostensibly erecting 'messages' (the Trojan Horse), the team tactically deployed the extended, interactive construction time to engage local children and their families, serving to explore Donahue's ongoing practice questions around how designers can critically engage with communities (the MacGuffin). By using the formal qualities of design to engage passers-by to inquire into what was going on, Donahue was exploring a broader question about the world-making possibilities of design.

The park event was simply the introduction. The conversation began in earnest in a former retail space that the team had rented and transformed into a community dialogue centre for civic leaders, residents and service providers, with the intention of identifying and addressing the preparedness issues of the community. Conversation starters included catering in the form of small white boxes simply labelled 'food'. The absence of information on the packaging created uncertainty and so provoked discussion around how many boxes to take and what was inside. Further to this, in order to highlight the problem of community resource distribution in emergency situations, the team deliberately under-catered, provoking more debate around sharing or abstaining from the supply of cookies. The design of the situation, including the activities, furniture and catering, intentionally restructured conversations and destabilised expectations regarding 'who was the expert' and who had authority.[34]

Conclusion

At the outset, I understood the threads that connected our practices to be a background in communication design and an orientation towards research, but, over the course of this reflective investigation, through the generation and sharing of knowledge, I came to understand that our common ground was better located in the inquiring mindset we all bring to designing. This characterised our similar transitions from communication design to collaborative, interdisciplinary research and foregrounded us as learners determined to *play the whole game*.

In the discovery phase of this project, I noticed that our four design practices were united by an intrinsic and compulsive curiosity. Jordan Litman has reconciled decades of competing theories of curiosity, arguing that curiosity can be both a positive feeling of being 'stimulated by opportunities for learning something interesting as well as experiences of tension associated with feeling deprived of knowledge'.[35] We each held early memories of encounters with our personal curiosity that would account for our trajectories from students of design to the role of inquirers. This led to the investigation of inquiry-based learning and motivation and a broader question around sustainable inquiry-led practices.

I have suggested that the framework of *meaning-making*, *world-making* and *sense-making* makes up the cornerstone of inquiry-led practice. These activities enable us to contribute to the evolving field of design as well as the intellectual life of the academy. Examining the meanings and trajectories of design, we are able to expand the role of the designer, the partnerships we forge, and the scope of the projects on which we work.

A *meaning-making* practice addresses the importance of orienting and owning our internal motivations. This helps 'people focus on the meaning and impact of their work', and key to this is 'to structure activities so that instrumental consequences do not become motives'.[36] *World-making* refers to the potential of design to have meaningful impact outside the market, such as in community contexts, to expand the remit of design 'from simply problem-solving to context-setting'.[37] *Sense-making* is the process of writing, sharing and presenting, which leads to synthesis, which in turn enables the transfer of insights into the next stage of inquiry in a new domain,[38] and the sustainable progress of a practice.

If we limit the objective of academic research to primarily being about 'knowledge production', then it is interesting to consider how the motivation of 'lifelong learning' can underpin an inquiry-led practice and lead to more resonant research. The insights that come from the interplay between our practices, projects and professional communities inform our future moves and the spaces we carve out for our practices. As educators, we are also able to share the insights we gain through such an inquiry. By reframing our research practices around this notion of inquiry driven by curiosity and the will to continuously learn, we are able not only to make meaning, make new worlds and make sense of our chosen fields, but we might also help to foster critical shifts in practice that will have widespread implications for the field of design — in the classroom, in academia and in the market, and also in public and political spheres.

1. Yoko Akama is a participatory design researcher and Associate Professor in Communication Design at RMIT University, Melbourne, Australia; Anne Burdick is Chair of the MFA in Media Design Practices at Art Center College of Design in Pasadena, California; Sean Donahue is core faculty in the same Media Design Practices programme, and principal of RCD/LA; and I am a Professor of Design at Monash Art Design & Architecture, and director of WonderLab, a design and learning research lab.
2. Arthur Costa and Bena Kallick, *Learning and Leading with Habits of Mind: 16 Essential Characteristics for Success* (New York: Association for Supervision & Curriculum Development, 2008).
3. Yoko Akama, 'Passing on, handing over, letting go: the passage of embodied design methods for disaster preparedness', in *Service Futures: Proceedings of the fourth Service Design and Service Innovation Conference*, edited by Daniela Sangiorgi, David Hands and Emma Murphy (Linköping: Linköping University Electronic Press, 2014).
4. Sean Donahue, 'Unmapping', in *Design as Future-Making*, edited by Susan Yelavich and Barbara Adams (New York: Bloomsbury, 2014).
5. Lisa Grocott, 'Taking Action', presented at the AICAD Remaking Research Conference at Emily Carr University, Vancouver, 2012, http://vimeo.com/channels/remakingresearch/53954464, accessed 18 October 2015.
6. Mary Catherine Bateson, *Peripheral Visions: Learning Along the Way* (Toronto: HarperCollins, 1994).
7. Donahue, 'Unmapping'.
8. Neil Stephenson, 'Introduction to Inquiry Based Learning', http://www.teachinquiry.com/index/Introduction.html, accessed 7 February 2015.
9. David Kolb, *Experiential Learning: Experience as a Source of Learning and Development* (New York: Prentice Hall, 1984), 38.
10. Donald Schön, *The Reflective Practitioner* (New York: Basic Books, 1983).
11. Akama, 'Passing on, handing over, letting go'.
12. Grocott, 'Taking Action'.
13. Anne Burdick and Holly Willis, 'Digital learning, digital scholarship and design thinking', *Design Studies* 32, no. 6 (November 2011).
14. Donahue, 'Unmapping'.
15. Shawn Achor, *Before Happiness: The 5 Hidden Keys to Achieving Success, Spreading Happiness, and Sustaining Positive Change* (New York: Crown Business, 2013).
16. Amy Wrzesniewski and Barry Schwartz, 'The Secret of Effective Motivation', *New York Times*, 4 July 2014, http://www.nytimes.com/2014/07/06/opinion/sunday/the-secret-of-effective-motivation.html?_r=0, accessed 18 October 2015.
17. Bryan Lawson and Kees Dorst, *Design Expertise* (New York: Routledge, 2009), 224.
18. Carol Dweck, *Mindset: The New Psychology of Success*, 2nd edition (New York: Ballantine Books, 2007).
19. David Perkins, *Making Learning Whole: How Seven Principles of Teaching Can Transform Education* (San Francisco: Jossey-Bass, 2009).
20. Yoko Akama, Roslyn Cooper, Laurene Vaughan, Stephen Viller, Matthew Simpson and Jeremy Yuille, 'Show and tell: Accessing and communicating implicit knowledge through artefacts', *Artifact* 1, no. 3 (2007).
21. Elizabeth B. N. Sanders, 'Scaffolds for Experiencing in the New Design Space', in *Information Design*, edited by Institute for Information Design Japan (Tokyo: Graphic-sha Publishing, 2002); Akama, 'Passing on, handing over, letting go'.
22. Lawson and Dorst, *Design Expertise*, 61.
23. Ibid., 66.
24. Lisa Grocott, 'Design Research & Reflective Practice: The Facility of Design-oriented Research to Translate Practitioner Insights into New Understandings of Design' (PhD diss., RMIT University, 2010).
25. Jon Kolko, 'Abductive Thinking and Sensemaking: The Drivers of Design Synthesis', *Design Issues* 26, no. 1 (Winter 2010).
26. Schön, *The Reflective Practitioner*.
27. Grocott, 'Design Research & Reflective Practice', 138.
28. Lisa Grocott, 'The Discursive Practice of Figuring Diagrams', in 'Drawing Knowledge', special issue, *Tracey Journal* (May 2012), http://www.lboro.ac.uk/microsites/sota/tracey/journal/edu/2012/PDF/Lisa_Grocott-TRACEY-Journal-DK-2012.pdf, accessed 18 October 2015.

29　Donald Schön, 'The Theory of Inquiry: Dewey's Legacy to Education', *Curriculum Inquiry* 22, no. 2 (1992); Cameron Tonkinwise, 'Subject of Practice Post Theory', Graduate Research Conference Address, RMIT University, Melbourne, October 2007; Lisa Grocott, 'Designerly Ways of Researching: design knowing and the practice of researching', *Studies in Material Thinking* 6 (2011), https://www.materialthinking.org/papers/60, accessed 18 October 2015.

30　Shana Agid, 'Worldmaking: working through theory/practice in design', *Design and Culture* 4, no. 1 (2012).

31　Donahue, 'Unmapping'.

32　Dan Hill, *Dark Matter and Trojan Horses: A Strategic Design Vocabulary* (Moscow: Strelka Press, 2012).

33　Ibid, 57.

34　Donahue, 'Unmapping'.

35　Jordan Litman, 'Curiosity and the Pleasures of Learning: Wanting and Liking New Information', *Cognition and Emotion* 19, no. 6 (2005): 801.

36　Wrzesniewski and Schwartz, 'The Secret of Effective Motivation'.

37　Hill, *Dark Matter and Trojan Horses*, 35.

38　Schön, *The Reflective Practitioner*.

The ghost of a practice
Matthew Galloway

In this essay, Matthew Galloway reflects upon his own education from the perspective of his then-recent appointment, in 2014, as a lecturer at the School of Design at Otago Polytechnic, Dunedin, New Zealand. Galloway discusses the central role played by both formal and informal studio-based conversation in his undergraduate educational experience, and describes how he now draws this to the surface in his teaching practice. Although studio-based conversation is often taken for granted, Galloway addresses its value as a generative act that, properly managed, allows students to negotiate and embrace ambiguity, fostering curiosity and life-long learning.

> I do some of my best painting in the wash-hand basin when I'm cleaning my brushes. — Philip Clairmont talking, as remembered by Julian Dashper in his book *This is not writing*.[1]

At the beginning of the term just gone, I shared a text from the book *This is not writing* with a group of my first-year students. It's a piece called 'Some of the things I can remember Philip Clairmont saying today' — a written record consisting of thirty-five sentences, extracted from a conversation between New Zealand painters Clairmont and Julian Dashper, in the latter's studio one day circa 1980. The text was first published as part of an exhibition catalogue in 1990, six years after Clairmont's death. Retold from memory by Dashper, the sentences vary in content, switching from the seemingly banal and everyday — 'Do you like my new sports jacket?' and 'We always like a roast on Sunday' — to some more curious and open — 'That was Allen' and 'You've got to burn all your bridges' — to those directly related to the act of painting itself — 'Saying you've got no money is not an answer to how's your painting going' and 'Thanks but that painting should have never left the studio'. But the overwhelming impression you get while reading this text is that, by recalling this conversation in such a straightforward and seemingly non-selective way, what Dashper is really hinting at is that it's *all* about painting, that the very act of the two of them engaging in conversation is a part of their practices. This is two painters discussing their daily lives, discussing their painting. We read them challenging one another's perceptions, giving voice to fears, questioning approaches and generally engaging in the practice of everyday life.

This obscure text might seem like an odd reading to share with a group of first-year graphic design students, especially those unaware of Dashper's practice, of his importance to the New Zealand art scene and of his lucid, conversational style of writing. But bear with me, because, through the manner in which Dashper recounts and connects anecdotes, conversation is positioned as a generative act, one that captures throwaway thoughts and meaningful articulations alike, and which breaks down the isolating existence of the creative practitioner (but perhaps this feels heightened in the New Zealand context). For those embarking on a course of study in any creative field, there is a simple yet important demonstration here of the significance of conversation in the development of a practice.

I first became aware of the late Dashper and his 'not-writing' while still a student myself. My lecturer, Luke Wood, was commissioned to design *This is not writing* and in the process of designing the book was so taken aback by the content that he ended up sharing it with us. Looking back now, I think the main points I took away from the book at the time were stylistic: Dashper's ability to write as if no one were reading — or, perhaps, without feeling the need to say anything to anyone particular. He was simply sure of his own voice, *his voice was the whole point*. Since then, I've come to see this observation about voice as a symptom of what's really playing out on the pages of the book. Through its varied records and conversations, we see the vague traces of how Dashper chose to operate. Published posthumously, the book acts as a ghostly portrait of a practice.

The fact that *This is not writing* was shared with us on the fly was typical of my education (a BFA, then an MFA, majoring in Design from the

Ilam School of Fine Arts, Christchurch, New Zealand). For the most part, my course of study was incredibly fluid. Projects would change from year to year, briefs were left intentionally vague and outcomes could be heavily moulded to suit each individual student's interests. Much of this could probably be traced back to the fact that classes were small — eight of us made it through in my year. Consider, for a moment, what eight people represents: at best, it's the size of a small dinner party; at worst, more like a large group of siblings. Essentially, I've come to see my BFA as a four-year-long conversation, and about halfway through this conversation we were introduced to the idea of practice-based research. From that moment on, most of our projects were filtered through this framework.

As a class, we met once a week for a few hours, and brought in new work. This was about *our* response to the given brief. We were each individually responsible for turning up with work to show, and that work was essentially viewed as a conversation starter. We would sit around as a group on the couches in the communal area of the Design Department and discuss our work. Usually, the best discussions occurred when work was unfinished. Questions would abound and, although we initially found these curveballs hard to deal with, somewhere along the way we became aware that what Luke and Aaron (Beehre) were trying to get us to do was get better at dwelling on these questions, as opposed to getting better at finding answers. This is consistent with the realisation I had about a year out from my BFA: that constantly questioning was the whole point; that constantly questioning might be a good definition of what it means to have a practice; and that to have some small understanding of what it means to have a practice might be a good outcome of four years of undergraduate study.

This also seemed appropriate when considering what and where it was we were studying. We were learning to be designers in the context of a fine art school. Through our conversations, we learned to view graphic design as inherently mouldable — responding to its surroundings and feeding off of content provided by others. We continued to use the modes and methods of graphic design, but were encouraged to embrace an expansive definition of the discipline. Design was a ghost, a meeting place, a grey area.[2] Its methods and its outcomes could be authorial. Our voice was important.

This grey area, as we experienced it, was a pedagogical tactic that fostered our understanding of practice as an ongoing, fluid process of questioning. Through the constant need to justify our work and its criticality, this also helped to galvanise our beliefs and, by extension, our interactions with the world. We became aware of our context as designers, realised the importance of locating our interests within that context, and began to define our respective practices. This had both philosophical and material implications. Dashper's writing was shared with us because of his underlying interest in distribution. His strategies to get his work out there, from a remote set of islands in the South Pacific to the rest of the world, resonated with us as designers, learning to deal with mechanical reproduction and distribution.

In many ways, this approach to education could be considered to be aligned with what Michel de Certeau, writing in *The Practice of Everyday Life*, referred to as 'ghostly voices'; informal modes of speaking and recording, dialectical in nature, at once embracing grey areas of thought, while central to the progression of collective understanding.[3] These 'voices' were in opposition to what he referred to as our modern 'scriptural' society — the (literally) black and white pages of written, recorded language that had become increasingly systematised over the course of the nineteenth and twentieth centuries, both through mechanical reproduction and through the centralised control of that production. To record in this manner, he wrote, was to normalise, to 'cut' the content for mass production in the way you might cut a record, leaving no space for the grey, shifting, fluid nature of the ghostly voice.

As de Certeau saw it, the production of words on a societal level had become a practice that dissolved ambiguity by deeply formalising thought, while in contrast the ghost might allow ambiguity to float out of your mouth, into the world, open to some manner of response. Was that what we were doing when we sat around on those couches in the Design Department of the School of Fine Arts? Were we being pushed to activate and embrace our ghostly voice? Was the fluidity of the course a reaction against the formal, concrete outcomes that characterise most of what would be considered commercial graphic design practice? And is this what makes Dashper's writing so interesting, those loose conversations formalised in a hardcover book, whose posthumous release added extra weight to what might otherwise be best understood as scribbled recollections of a studio visit? Perhaps it is this push and pull between the formal and the informal voice that added to our confusion as design students, but which ultimately helped us to understand the kind of practice we were being led towards during those critique sessions.

What I've been circling here is the idea that the informal, dialectical nature of conversation holds a seemingly disproportionate sway on the development of an understanding of practice because it models our experience of everyday life and forces us out of scriptural formality. When emphasis is put on our ability to think on the spot, to question and to speculate, our guards are down and something closer to our true thoughts are revealed. Looking back now, those critique sessions and conversations acted as a primer, emphasising the moment of articulation as a generative act that bridges inner thought with a public forum. We were being asked to present ideas and work that were half-formed, half-understood, and, in the process, we were talking our way into an understanding. Sure, we struggled with the vagueness of this approach. It ran counter to the 'stand and deliver' mode of education we'd experienced at high school and in the lecture halls of our theory studies. But this concept of speaking understanding into being has roots in early learning theory. In 'Thought and Word' (1934), Russian developmental psychologist and educational theorist Lev Vygotsky discusses 'the functional role of verbal meaning in the act of thinking'. The general idea is that one shouldn't view the *understanding of meaning* and the *articulation of that meaning* as two separate elements, but instead as partitioned areas within the same process. Seen in this light, 'meanings function in the living process of verbal thinking'.[4] Or, in other words, to speak is to think out loud. Speech becomes 'a tool for generating new ideas through the process of thinking'.[5]

Once you start thinking of speech as a tool for learning in relation to the informal conversations we had at design school, and as modelled by Dashper, it suddenly provides an expansive view of what is actually happening when half-formed ideas are let loose. By the simple act of forcing those ideas to be articulated, they must be internally moved forward, refined and critiqued in readiness for the world. In fact, it reminds me of something Stuart Bertolotti-Bailey said in a text/letter from *Dot Dot Dot #8*, which I can't ever seem to get too far away from:

> During the period when we met, I was generally meeting a lot of new people, doing non-stop talking, and realising it was crystallising unformed ideas. Talking to think, to clarify and to remember. It seems stupidly obvious now, but I'd never thought about it before. Thinking aloud. Thinking a-visible.[6]

'Thinking aloud' is another nice way to describe Dashper and Clairmont's conversation and, in turn, our critiques at design school. It was learning achieved through informal conversation. Through this approach, we came to understand practice as an ongoing conversation, and, by extension, our work became conversation pieces — not outcomes as such, but more like lines in the sand, or just articulations crystallised to a more permanent point.

Now — a number of years removed from my time as an undergraduate, and at a different design school — to sit around a table, with about fifteen of my own students holding handouts of the Dashper text, feels like a good way to start the term. Each year, while sharing the text, I'm acutely aware of the challenge I face in simply *starting* a conversation amongst a newly formed cohort. At this point, it's worth noting that my year group back at Ilam was, by all accounts, a bit of an anomaly, because, pretty much off the bat, we actually *spoke*. In many ways, we skipped the first and most problematic stage, one that I now face in engaging with the students I teach, and one that I know Luke and Aaron have faced with other groups at Ilam: how do you engender a culture of conversation within a group when it doesn't come naturally?

Thinking about my own studies and how they have shaped how I now teach design myself, one consideration comes before most others, namely the idea that I need to facilitate an ongoing, three- or four-year long conversation with my students and, in the process, convey to them that perhaps the best thing they can do to develop their own voice is simply open their mouths and start speaking. At Ilam, informal speech played a central role in engendering this type of sure-footedness. It was education through critique and, importantly, we were asked to critically engage not just with our own work and the work of our peers, but also to constantly ask how the work itself critically engaged with its audience or the public. I've come to realise that truly understanding what it means to have a practice is synonymous with the development of one's own voice, and that having a voice is a prerequisite for the kind of tactical engagement with society that de Certeau was talking about. Students should be continually asked to justify their thoughts and actions — to justify how they choose to engage with the *scriptural* — and they should be encouraged to fully understand and account for the implications of whatever it is that they, as designers, are sending out into the world.

In this light, sharing 'Some of the things I can remember Philip Clairmont saying today' with my students always feels like a good first step. More or less indicative of *This is not writing* as a whole, the text operates as a window onto practice, by modelling practice as a set of conversations one might have with others, with oneself, with one's work.

I introduce the text, we sit and read the thirty-five sentences together in silence, then share our favourite lines; we start a conversation.

1. Julian Dashper, *This is not writing* (Auckland: Clouds and Michael Lett, 2011), 27.
2. Stuart Bailey, 'Dear X', in *Dot Dot Dot* 8 (The Hague: Dot Dot Dot, 2004), 3.
3. Michel de Certeau, *The Practice of Everyday Life* (Berkeley: University of California Press, 1984), 131.
4. Lev Semënovic Vygotskij, 'Thought and Word', in *The Essential Vygotsky*, edited by V. R. W. Rieber, David Keith Robinson and Jerome S. Bruner (New York: Kluwer Academic, 2004), 72.
5. Ibid.
6. Bailey, 'Dear X', 3.

The Leipzig style
Constanze Hein

The origins of the Academy of Fine Arts in Leipzig date to 1764, making it one of the oldest art schools in Germany. Over the course of its history, the Academy has had a number of names, but, curiously, its English name is not a translation of any of them. Its current German name, Hochschule für Grafik und Buchkunst, can be literally translated as 'Academy of Graphics and Book Art', which represents the school's unique history and focus better than its English name. Best known simply as the HGB, the Academy offers no fewer than four discrete graphic design specialisations. In 2010, in collaboration with colleagues from the HGB, Brad Haylock ran an experimental publishing workshop there. Berlin-based designer Constanze Hein was a student at the school at the time, and a participant in the workshop. Haylock and Hein met again in 2015, at a mutual colleague's studio in London; their conversation at that time led to this text, in which Hein reflects upon how and why the HGB persists as a unique place for graphic design education — one that is resistant to homogenisation and instrumentalisation.

During a discussion with Brad Haylock about graphic design education at the Academy of Fine Arts (HGB) in Leipzig, a statement he made left me astounded: 'Leipzig seems very far away from the real world'. I had been a student in Leipzig and at this point was working in London. Leipzig and the Academy were already distant memories, but Haylock's comment pointedly raised the question of the relevance or importance of an institution like the HGB in a contemporary design education context. To impart anything about this education, two contextual stories need to be told: that of the city itself, in particular that of the impact of the city's history as a major centre for the book and graphics industries, and that of the Academy itself, with its particular academic structure. Only in this way does it become apparent why the HGB is a unique place for graphic design education.

The city
In 1989, Leipzig started to change dramatically. The beginning of the peaceful revolution started in the Nikolaikirche and on the surrounding streets of Leipzig, where inhabitants demonstrated for freedom of speech and freedom of movement. This and other protests eventually led to the fall of the German Democratic Republic. Leipzig was therefore a significant city for the 'Wende' — the period between the fall of the Berlin Wall on 11 November 1989 and the unification of East and West Germany in 1990.[1] But it is not only these relatively recent historical events that are important to the city's identity. Its history as a centre of trade and, more importantly for the current discussion, the tradition of bookmaking in the city, starting in the mid-nineteenth century, seem to be major factors contributing to its contemporary self-esteem.

Leipzig used to be an economic capital, particularly in terms of book production. In 1912 — the year when the German National Library was founded there — the book industry in the city comprised 300 typesetting and printing workshops, 982 publishers and bookshops, 173 bookbinders, 298 other graphic-based services and thirty-six print engineering companies.[2] These statistics demonstrate how significantly the industry has influenced the city's culture and identity over the decades.

To give an impression of the history of this industry, I would like to point out one example: the encyclopaedia publishing house Bibliographisches Institut, which was founded in 1826 by publisher Joseph Meyer (1796–1856).[3] Meyer encyclopaedias and dictionaries were published in Leipzig until a few years ago and still pile up on German bookshelves — along with Brockhaus encyclopaedias, which were also published in Leipzig.

The 1926 silent film *Geist und Maschine* (Mind and Machine) shows the stages of the production of a printed encyclopaedia.[4] The film starts with the physical parts of the book — the cover, binding and signatures — and the complex process of assembling such a tome. A Monotype machine in action shows the great efficiency that had already been achieved in typesetting in that era. Errors and corrections are taken in as part of the routine, in a supervised factory setting. The production of metal printing plates is difficult and laborious. After the sheets are printed, it takes more than twenty-five workers to fold them into signatures, partially helped by an industrial folding machine. A stapling machine staples book blocks, a guillotine trims them and another machine rounds the spines. The next machine stamps gold foil onto the covers, and so on. The film and its documentation of the elaborate process of the mass production of books during the early twentieth century in Leipzig makes you realise how important the book has been to the financial make-up of the city and to the identity of its inhabitants, employed in multiple roles, from writing and editing to producing and selling.

Today, the epicentre of the German book industry has shifted to Frankfurt and Berlin. The unification of East and West Germany in 1990 changed not only the political but also the economic system, affecting publishing: the former Eastern book industries, which were mainly publicly owned enterprises, suddenly became part of the free market economy. As a result, there were many closures, layoffs and restructures. In the end, it meant that a new structure, a new identity was needed.

Unofficially, the city still bears a strong association with its history as a centre of publishing: it is still referred to as 'Buchstadt Leipzig' (Leipzig, city of books). The annual Leipzig book fair is well known among publishers and booksellers, and it has spawned several independent publishing fairs and literature events. Evidence of a long trading tradition can still be seen in the city centre. For example, the big 'MM' sign on the tower next to the central train station stands for 'Mustermesse' (sample or trade fair), which remains one of the largest German trade fairs, and buildings such as the Städtisches Kaufhaus (city trade house) are architecturally prominent. The tradition of the book industry in the city can been seen in buildings such as the Haus des Buches (the House of the Book, which is now the House of Literature), the Graphisches Viertel (the graphic quarter) and the German National Library itself, which collects every book published in Germany, as it has done since 1913.[5]

Just outside the city centre, one finds some rather bizarre and idiosyncratic developments: abandoned houses next to huge supermarkets, next to bars or vacant land. At its peak in 1930, Leipzig had around 700,000 inhabitants. Since then, historical events such as the Nazi regime, the Second World War, and the German Democratic Republic and its fall in 1989, led to tremendous decreases of inhabitants. Today, however, Leipzig is one of the cities in Germany that is thriving, developing and growing rapidly, with a population of around 602,000 in 2018,[6] compared to a population of 524,000 in 2010.[7] There is still space for more people to come, space that is used by artists, graphic designers and other creatives. For a long time, it was easy to open up a bar, an artist-run space or a gallery. With only a moderate outlay, people were able to establish projects such as independent book fairs, including *It's a Book*,[8] for graphic design and art books, and *Millionaires Club*,[9] for illustration and drawing, or special-interest design bookstores, including MZIN and ROTORBOOKS. There was no need to hustle to find an affordable studio space.

The Academy

As one approaches the HGB, in the south of the city centre, the architecture makes an impact. There are buildings such as the Supreme Administrative Court, the German Institute for Literature and the large residential houses of publishers such as Karl Tauchnitz (1798–1884), from an era that embodied the

Entrance to the Mustermesse fair ground, Leipzig, Spring 1983. The MM logotype was created by graphic designer, painter and illustrator Erich Gruner in 1917. Photograph by Thomas Lehmann, Bundesarchiv image 183-1983-0315-111.

The atrium at Academy of Fine Arts Leipzig.
Photograph by André Köhler, from the book *Der Bau und seine Geschichte* (The Building and Its History), Institut für Buchkunst, Leipzig, 2014.

former wealth of the city of Leipzig. The HGB is located next to the Galerie für Zeitgenössische Kunst, aka GfZK (Leipzig Museum of Contemporary Art). This museum holds the Inform Prize,[10] which supports exhibitions and projects by international graphic designers with a conceptual practice.

Not only do the surrounding buildings have a high impact, but so too does the Academy itself. Its nineteenth-century architecture is massive and symbolises wealth and power. Above the main entrance, a stone carving reads 'Hochschule für Grafik und Buchkunst'. The name translates as 'Academy of Graphics and Book Art', which differs from its English name, Academy of Fine Arts, but which highlights its connection to the book-making tradition. The institution was called Zeichnungs-, Mahlerey- und Architecturakademie (Academy of Drawing, Painting and Architecture) when founded in 1764, and was renamed in 1876 to Königliche Kunstakademie und Kunstgewerbeschule (Royal Academy of Art and Applied Art), and again in 1900 to Königliche Akademie für graphische Künste und Buchgewerbe (Royal Academy for Graphic Arts and Book Technique).[11] After closing for two years at the end of the Second World War, the school reopened in 1947 and was given its present-day name in 1950. The imposing arcade lined with huge columns at the entrance leads to a grand atrium, connoting the 'greatness of the creation' that might happen there. The building's structure follows the purpose of combining workshops and educational programmes. From the basement to the fifth floor are artistic and technical workshops: letterpress, lithography, etching, offset, silk screen, xylography (lino- and woodcut), artistic offset, a 3D lab, bookbinding, papermaking, metalwork, woodwork, photo studios and darkrooms, and multimedia labs for sound, video and photography. Normally, the huge hallways are empty. Now and then, visitors might be able to glimpse into the artists' sky-lit studios in the top floors, or sneak into a lecture in the auditorium on the first and second levels. There are public events throughout the year, and a gallery space on the lower level run by a curator who implements internal and external exhibitions. The most interesting time to visit the HGB is in February, for the 'Rundgang'. As in almost every art academy, this annual exhibition opens up studios, workshops and bars to show a variety of questions, thoughts, results and progress.

Compared to the size and scale of the building, the number of students and programmes could seem rather small. There are around six hundred students in four programmes: Book Art/Graphic Design, Photography, Media Art and Painting/Fine Arts. Since 2009, the Academy has also offered a Master programme in 'Cultures of the Curatorial'. These departments are all located in the one building and are not separated onto specific discrete levels, which means that a graphic designer might study next door to a media artist. This chaotic mix benefits the interdisciplinary ethos of the programmes of study. If I had to describe the character of the graphic design department in one word, it would be *niche*. As a graphic design student at the Leipzig academy, you are only among artists: no architects, no fashion designers, no industrial or product designers, only artists. And so, unsurprisingly, a student here is more influenced by art than by design.

The Book Art/Graphic Design programme conforms to the Bologna model, which standardises educational qualifications within EU countries, but the HGB maintains its uniqueness through the Diploma degree structure, rather than a Bachelor and Master structure. This five-year programme is divided into two years of Foundation Course followed by three years of Main Course.

The undergraduate classes in graphic design are scheduled daily with intense deadlines, focused on the basics of graphic design, type design, typography and illustration. It is also mandatory to visit the artistic workshop and to take theoretical courses. The idea of interdisciplinary studies is implemented early on by mixing the students of the different departments, so that they come into contact with diverse ideas and approaches to art and design. The theoretical classes are as important as the practical. After two years of undergraduate study, there is an exam and an assessed exhibition for entry into the major programme.

The Graphic Design major is divided into four specialisations: Typography (currently taught by Ludovic Balland), System Design (currently taught by Maureen Mooren), Illustration (currently taught by Thomas Matthaeus Müller) and Type Design (currently taught by Fred Smeijers and Stephan Müller). A typical class takes place every two weeks for three days. On the one hand, semesters are usually arranged around topics within the classes, taking the form of research projects or applied design projects, on which students work individually or in groups, depending on the class and the teachers. On the other hand, there is a vast freedom to develop one's own schedule and skills. There is no obligation to adhere to a system of subjects, credit points or hours per week. For example, a student can choose to spend the whole semester in theoretical classes, working in the artistic workshops or collaborating with students from the other departments, as long as they complete the class projects and attend the tutorials. This kind of self-directed study is based on a time-honoured German university tradition in which students are responsible for their own studies. In general, students have a wide range of options, but they need to present their work at the end of each semester.

Students complete their studies with a diploma project to receive the degree. This project is split up into three parts: a theoretical thesis, a practical/artistic project and a diploma presentation. The work is shown to a colloquium comprising a general audience, other students and faculty. There can easily be fifty to one hundred spectators. Students in the design classes typically take a very conceptual approach to this presentation, going far beyond simple book projects. The System Design class over the last eight years has produced a wide variety of diploma presentations, often self-initiated research projects, such as performances, installations, photography exhibitions and live offset printing — and, of course, books, books and more books.[12] Driven by different approaches to text, images and topics, the students' work reflects deep personal interests that are rigorously researched, processed and materialised.

Conclusion

As I have described, there are two major factors that make graphic design education in Leipzig unique, and also important in a global context: the city's significant history in graphic industries, combined with contemporary economic conditions that provide freedom and possibilities for creative enterprises; and the academic structure at the HGB, which is driven by interdisciplinary learning and a keen focus on theoretical engagement with art and graphic design. From my perspective, the academic structure is the most important part of the equation.

As I have already pointed out, graphic design is the only applied programme at the academy. This unique position enables an expanded perspective of what graphic design can be, without necessarily being restricted by the requirements of applied design. For this reason, and because Leipzig is an affordable city, students can focus on their work, addressing conceptual and theoretical concerns and matters of authorship and production in great depth.

Furthermore, the focus of graphic design education at the HGB could be perceived to be nostalgic and traditional, given its focus on book design, typography and craftsmanship. In the contemporary context, which is characterised by digital media, this tradition-based graphic design is often considered antiquated. But, examined more closely, this alignment is much more visionary than it seems. To explain why tradition can be a motor for contemporary practice, I would like to quote Michael Giesecke's thoughts on 'preserving, accumulating, innovation'. He says: 'preserve the balance between tradition and progress by using old techniques beside contemporary ones and be open to recent developments'.[13] In Leipzig, tradition isn't interpreted as something antiquated or outdated. Instead, it is understood as a model to evoke new ideas. It opens up a new cosmos. The old is not only there to be preserved or maintained; rather, it is a source for transformation. Tradition can be rethought into something new, in order to change the present. The Leipzig style is one in which students are privileged rather than inhibited by history.

1   The German word 'Wende' translates simply as 'change'.
2   These impressive numbers can be seen on display as part of a city model in the German Museum of Books and Writing in the German National Library.
3   See: http://www.leipzig-lexikon.de/INDU HAND/biblinst.htm, accessed 18 March 2018.
4   *Geist und Maschine* can be viewed at the German Museum of Books and Writing online gallery: http://mediengeschichte.dnb.de/DBSMZBN/Content/DE/Industrialisierung/08-geist-und-maschine.html.
5   See: http://www.dnb.de/EN/Wir/wir_node.html, accessed 19 March 2018.
6   See: https://statistik.leipzig.de/statcity/table.aspx?cat=2&rub=4&per=q, accessed 3 May 2019.
7   See: https://statistik.leipzig.de/statcomp/table.aspx?cat=1&rub=2, accessed 3 May 2019.
8   *It's a Book* is an independent publishing fair for art and design books, which takes place every year at the Academy in Leipzig (as a side programme to the book fair). It was founded by Markus Dreßen with a group of HGB students.
9   *Millionaires Club* is an independent publishing fair for illustrated books and fanzines that takes place in various locations every year in Leipzig.
10 See: https://gfzk.de/en/aktivitaeten/kunstpreise/inform/, accessed 1 June 2020.
11 See: https://www.hgb-leipzig.de/index.php?a=hgb&b=gesch&l=1&, accessed 18 March 2018.
12 See: https://www.hgb-leipzig.de/systemdesign/#/category/final_projects/, accessed 19 March 2018.
13 Conference programme of *It's a Book* in 2016, IT'S A BOOK Independent Publishing Fair, Leipzig, 19 March 2016.

Norman Potter's teaching spaces
James Langdon

Norman Potter was an outspoken designer and teacher who left an indelible mark on British design education. In 1964, he led the development of the Construction School at the West of England College of Art in Bristol, which he imagined as the British successor to the Bauhaus. James Langdon has been researching Potter's legacy, in all of its complexity, for many years. Here, Langdon follows Potter's trail from the British Film Institute to Bristol and to rural France, in order to unearth some of the pedagogical persuasions of this influential but complicated figure.

Ten thousand students

At the British Film Institute in London, I have an appointment to view a film called *Art — To A Degree*.[1] Made for UK television and broadcast in 1976, it was part of the long-running 'Omnibus' series of arts-related documentaries. I collect the VHS tape from a kind man in a cramped basement office. Racking from floor to ceiling is loaded with the black casings of several generations of AV equipment. He shows me to the viewing room. A table against one wall runs the length of the room, leaving a narrow gap for two chairs. There are stacks of players and monitors and a tangle of cables. The machine that I am to use appeals against its redundancy on its case: 'VHS to DVD transfer' and 'HD up-conversion'.

A shimmy of static introduces the opening images. An announcer speaks to camera in a television studio. 'In tonight's film, by Philip Donnellan, two people take a journey through the labyrinth — and that's what it is — of British art education.' The film reports on the state of art and design education in the UK, particularly in light of profound upheavals that redefined the field in the 1960s. It is presented by a prominent English graphic designer, Ken Garland, and Lil Smith, a trade union convener whose role is to ensure the legibility of the report to the audience. 'She's our representative, asking the kind of questions the general public might want to have asked', the announcer says.

The journey begins in Bristol. Garland and Smith are driving a small beige Renault. Out of the window, the Clifton Suspension Bridge appears in the misty distance, spanning the Avon Gorge. 'What's the point of us coming on a wet day?' asks Smith, sarcastically. 'We are here to celebrate the great design achievement of Isambard Kingdom Brunel', replies Garland, glancing away from the road to admire the view of the bridge. 'This was put up in the 1850s. Brunel got his training on the job, never went to a design school.' 'When you see this', asks Smith, 'and when you imagine that this was built in the 1800s, you have to think to yourself, "What are our designers building today? Where are they going that is as far in the future as this bridge was when it was built?"'

The car speeds downhill into Bower Ashton, site of the purpose-built faculty for art and design at the West of England College of Art, opened in 1965. Garland sets Smith's expectations, 'The guy who runs this course, Norman Potter, has got some rather special ideas about education. I think we'll find this as something out of the ordinary.'

Apparently directed by Potter, the pair enter the building not through the main reception but by a stepladder that they find propped up to the window of a workshop. Smith jokes about this unorthodox entrance — 'What! Up and through a window?' — but it goes by without explanation. Inside, she and Garland climb down from the window ledge, walk through a studio of drawing boards and emerge into the open hall at the centre of the department. A second male voice begins to speak, on the voiceover: 'To me ... the enemy is paper-shuffling, and key-jangling. People who have emotional capital wrapped up in the business of closing doors rather than opening them.' I recognise the voice, and the metaphors, as Potter's.

As he speaks, we see a small group of mostly female students around a workbench, cutting and working with timber. The images synchronise with the voice and Potter appears. I have been researching his work for several

Ken Garland and Lil Smith enter workshops at the
West of England College of Art, Bristol. Still from
Art — To A Degree, directed by Philip Donnellan, 1976.

years, yet this is the first time I have seen him on film. He is seated, his head and torso tightly framed by the camera. His animation is composed; he looks hunched and solid. His body language positions the interviewers in the room. Smith is apparently seated to Potter's right. He twice turns to address her directly as he talks about the 'shop floor':

> There's a hell of a lot of difference between appointing a representative to go into a committee, for God's sake, and actually having a real-life situation — as *you* would know — on the shop floor that is making some sense. ... People are actually involved with controlling their own lives and making their own education. We have always seen this as our task, not to educate people, but to provide an environment, including the facilities that are necessary technically, in which people can effectively educate themselves.

Cut to a close-up image of a pad of writing paper on a workbench. In black ink, Garland begins to diagram the history of art and design education in the UK:

> Today, Lil, there are about ten thousand art and design students all over the country. Bristol is just one of a whole lot of centres. Let's see how things have developed. Starting with 1853. This is when the government set up a teaching and exam programme in the new schools of design that had sprung up in the enthusiasm of the Great Exhibition of 1851. In 1913, they instituted a drawing certificate, which held sway for a very long time. 1946, in fact, was the next development. We have a National Diploma in Design, 'NDD' for short. This is a thing I went through. Rather a gruelling affair, lots of exams, you had to do a certain thing at a certain time while somebody watched you. All rather unpleasant, none of us liked it very much.

Garland proceeds down the page, representing his chronology with a column of boxes into which he enters important dates and events. At the bottom of the page, he splits the column into two diverging paths:

> An outfit called the Coldstream Committee produced a report in 1960 suggesting a new approach. They proposed a Diploma in Art and Design — DipAD — which didn't have this exam structure, it was a rather freer structure and relied more on displays of work and portfolio demonstration, things like that. This was accepted and, in 1963, out of eighty-seven colleges of art and design that applied for the new diploma, only twenty-nine were approved. The rest — the fifty-eight who were rejected — had to go off and do their own thing somewhere.

The narrative is familiar to me — Potter wrote about it in *What is a designer*, a book on design (not only) for students, published in 1969. The DipAD split, and the long-running tensions between 'provincial' education and what was offered in the London schools, produced the opportunity that first brought Potter to Bristol. The West of England College of Art had failed to win accreditation for a DipAD programme and so, in 1963, Potter, then teaching at the Royal College of Art in London, was recruited to assemble a staff and establish a new course, initially as a vocational offering, with the hope that it would achieve accreditation for DipAD the following year. His proposition was to unite the existing interior design and furniture design courses with graphics as a single programme called 'Construction'. Potter brought with him colleagues from the RCA, including George Phillip, Robin Baker and Jim Wood. Richard Hollis was appointed to lead the graphics work. Some members of the old Bristol administration remained, their sceptical presence foreshadowing problems ahead. The first prospectus from the new course, a modest document typed on off-white foolscap, no images, set out a few critical formulations that Potter would later develop in *What is a designer*:

> Design is a field of concern, response, and enquiry as much as decision and consequence: to a known and defined sense of situation the student must bring an awareness of his position, a constant search for a place of value in a world of facts, and a full command of the tools and techniques with which he can validate his intuitions.[2]

Donnellan's overview does not have time to make this explicit, but, far from resolving the West of England College of Art's difficulties, almost from the outset Potter's course produced a new conflict with the National Council for Diplomas in Art and Design, the governing body set up to administer the DipAD system. The main point of contention was the name 'Construction' and the integrated approach it implied. The word 'interdisciplinary' is not much used in Potter's writing; I suppose he would have thought it an aggrandisement. His often-repeated maxim 'all designers are graphic designers' suggests a more everyday appreciation of the fact that many design processes have essential features in common — surveying the situation, writing and communication, graphic production (either as an output itself, or as a specification for further manufacture) and model-making. But the DipAD structure emphasised specialisation: furniture, interiors and graphics were recognised separately. Difficulties seemed inevitably to follow, and in 1966 accreditation was refused. The new course was in crisis already.

'The undersigned architects, designers, and others, express confidence in the Construction course at Bristol, endorse the professional relevance of its terms of reference, and would like to see the experiment receive positive support.' So begins the petition produced by Potter in reaction.[3] 'It is hardly possible for a degree-level course to vindicate its worth with a restricted student intake, and in an atmosphere of continuous preparation for annual re-assessments. We therefore urge the National Council to take a generous view of this matter in the spirit of the Coldstream recommendations; to rescind its refusal of recognition for DipAD interior design; and to give such recognition, whether provisional or not, for long enough to allow the course to show its potential.'

The conventional 'interior design' had apparently been adopted as a compromise. The petition was signed by a roster of celebrated designers nationally and internationally, including James Stirling, Aldo van Eyck, Edward Wright and Cedric Price. (And also Ken Garland.)

What is hard to reconcile now, from the documents I have seen, is the impression that, aside from tensions about naming and disciplinary boundaries, Potter's programme seemed in accord with the essential directives of the new national system. In 1960, Coldstream had criticised provincial schools for a lack of rigour. In response, Potter's programme was sophisticated and various, and, as anyone familiar with his writing would expect, it thoroughly synthesised literary and philosophical perspectives with practice and technical rigour. The lecture programme in 1964 included notable international designers and critics such as Paul Schuitema, Walter Segal and Kenneth Frampton, and titles such as 'Microscopic identification of timber', 'Origins of the modern movement' and 'The diagram as an analytic tool'. Potter himself struggled to explain their failure:

> We had a first-class and highly motivated staff, a most promising and enthusiastic first group of students, a brand new building, excellent technical facilities, and a most detailed academic programme and case in support, the substance of which has never been challenged to this day. All we wanted was permission to proceed. When it was withheld, I stormed about in London trying to find someone who would debate the issues with me... The only person who was helpful was Robin Darwin, who revealed the cabinet secrets (I cannot repeat them).[4]

Back to Garland's diagram, its path now split decisively in two. 'In 1968, there were ructions. We have the Hornsey/Guildford sit-ins...' The prosaic pacing of Donnellan's film is suddenly interrupted, cutting to a noisy, graphic montage in black and white. The footage is from Patricia Holland's 1970 film documenting the six-week occupation of Hornsey College of Art by students and staff. A female student is shown on the telephone in an improvised office. 'We are in authority. We have taken control of the college!' We see images of large groups of students and staff gathered in the college's main hall, debating. The sit-in attracted significant media attention for its longevity and for the constructive nature of its protest, which took the form of exhaustive discussions, and the formulation and publication of proposals for the reform of the college.

Potter reappears on the voiceover:

> I think the Hornsey students had a very rough time out of it. They suffered very greatly for being projected into the possibility of a marvellous dream that couldn't be sustained. ... I don't think myself that intellectually anything very substantial came out of it. I don't think it was that kind of thing. But it certainly brought forward, into conscious debate, whole numbers of issues of student participation in the way that courses are run, student representation and so on.

This statement hardly betrays the fact that these were painful events for him, which ultimately brought his 'Bristol experiment' to a premature end. Students at Bristol also protested in 1968, and an 'information room' was set up in the Construction department to document events and statements of protest nationally and internationally. Potter left Bristol soon afterwards, under threat of legal action from the college for his role in the protests. Some notes for a lecture from 1969 give a more emotionally charged picture of his experiences at Hornsey:

> I cannot describe to you how my whole heart reached out to the potential of this situation… There are some experiences to which, to know them, their truth or falsity, you must expose all your faculties. I shall not forget driving past the building the night the lights went out and the physical hurt I felt, the sense of outrage.[5]

Leaving Bristol, Garland and Smith continue their tour to Dundee, Bradford, Leeds, Birmingham and Middlesex. They find markedly different perspectives on recent history. At Dundee, an emphasis on traditional craft skills prevails. During a life drawing class, Smith asks a senior tutor if he thinks art education is going in the right direction. The pointed answer is 'no'. He thinks it's becoming too much about talking, not enough doing. In Bradford, a play performed by students echoes this sentiment. The performers revel in lines of dialogue mocking the professionalisation of art education: 'They may not be able to sing or dance very well, but they'll certainly be able to talk incomprehensibly about singing and dancing!' In Leeds, the camera captures looks of confusion and indifference on the faces of passers-by as a group of art students performs in the street. Smith and Garland are shown in a local pub with the performers afterwards, discussing what value for money public art represents for taxpayers. In Birmingham and Middlesex, these perspectives are countered by interviews with students on product and fashion design courses. 'Industry' is a pressing concern. Students are anxious about how they will find work after their studies. Smith, embodying the social conscience of Donnellan's film, asks a fashion student if she realises what her education will ultimately have cost the taxpayer and if her employment prospects could possibly justify it.

Their journey complete, Garland and Smith are walking, in reflective conversation, on a canal towpath beneath a network of sweeping flyovers. They are talking about what they have seen and speculating about the future. The tone is confused and doubtful. Smith feels overwhelmed by the disparities. Garland worries, conversely, that the most interesting work, at the edges, is being lost as courses are regulated and institutionalised. The camera pans away from them, through 180 degrees, and I think I recognise where they are: back in Birmingham, at the Gravelly Interchange, colloquially known as 'Spaghetti Junction'.

A week later I am there, a mile from my studio, looking to confirm if I've correctly identified the place. Spaghetti Junction is a central hub of England's transport network: the convergence of the M6 motorway — connecting London and the North — with arterial roads around the Midlands, built over the top of the existing junction of the Grand Union, Birmingham-Fazeley and Tame Valley canals, and the confluence of the Tame and Rea rivers. Opened in 1972, it remains as defining an icon of the industrial culture of its time as Brunel's Clifton Suspension Bridge. The two images bookend Donnellan's film. He takes us from a monumental, singular structure to a sprawling, convoluted network, the metaphorical labyrinth that the film's announcer promised.

Aerial photograph of 'Spaghetti Junction', circa 1972.
Original source unknown.

The place is not knowable on foot. It takes an hour of walking indirectly to find the position of the panning shot in the film. In the intervening years, trees have covered the banks and additional supports have been installed to accommodate the massive volume of traffic passing above. Standing beneath the junction, the vantage is incomplete. Unlike Brunel's bridge, which is an awesome spectacle from the valley in Bristol, Spaghetti Junction — as an image — can only be appreciated from behind the wheel of a moving car, sweeping over and under, or from a great height. Aerial photographs show its knotted vectors as they must have looked to its designers: a dizzying problem-solving exercise. Paths loop across each other, entering the fray, disappearing from view, then re-emerging on some unlikely trajectory. Back at the studio, I find a proud image of the junction at its opening — empty of cars — in a photographic history of Birmingham. I scan it, print it and pin it to the wall.

A family of students

Looking at this labyrinthine image, I am reminded of something. It is two years prior and I am in the French countryside, searching for an address. Following directions noted down over the telephone, I have difficulty finding it. I seem to be in the right place, but there is no apparent entry point. A thirty-foot wall of vigorously overgrown trees and thorny bushes obscures any view of the building within. To the side, the unhinged door of a small outbuilding facing the road is secured with a coiled bicycle lock. I peer inside, through a small window, and see piles of unopened post and a rusty scooter. Further around the side of the plot is a steep bank, and signs of a path through the tangle of green, soon to be overgrown again.

This small house, in the Charente region, was previously owned by Potter. He spent some of his later life in rural France and this was the last of a number of small properties he bought to renovate. He died in 1995 and the inertia of French inheritance law has left the house almost untouched for the intervening twenty years. Potter's family have recently been here to recover significant personal belongings, original papers, books and other things they thought relevant to Potter's archive. I am visiting at their invitation.

The house itself is in a state of irreversible decay. Its ceramic bricks are crumbling; rot is consuming its roof timbers. The roof at the back is partially collapsed. Inside, three tight spaces are lined by stacks of building materials and belongings spilling out of decomposing cardboard boxes. I find plastic bags containing books, damp and rotting. There is a rack for tools and fixings and, leaning against walls and clamped to beams, some simple material exercises. Hooks, handles and switches embedded in lengths of timber — preparations for Potter's planned renovation of the property. After a couple of hours poking around, I collect up the bags of books and take them to the cottage that I am renting a couple of miles away. I lay them on the stone floor in front of the fire to dry out. Amongst others, there are copies of A. N. Whitehead's *The Aims of Education*, Paulo Freire's *Pedagogy of the Oppressed*, John Holt's *How Children Fail* and Everett Reimer's *School is Dead*, all in 1970s paperback editions with bright graphic covers.

One bag also contains a pile of photocopied papers bound together by damp. By the fire overnight, the sheets turn soft and powdery and can be gently prised apart. There are ninety-two A3 photocopies, each reproducing a double page opening from what appears to be a book dedicated to labyrinths. No cover or title page is present to identify the book. Back at the studio, some weeks later, speculative research suggests a few possible titles, and I ultimately find a used copy of *Mazes and Labyrinths of the World* by Janet Bord, published in 1976. The book was printed in colour, but Potter's photocopies render its photographs, drawings and stone rubbings coarsely in black and white. Some pages show vast landscaped labyrinths and mazes, others symbolic representations of labyrinthine forms found on coins and tablets. Potter's books and papers are typically not annotated, and these sheets have no handwritten marks. The deterioration of the paper, though, has produced strange marginalia to the printed images. The wet paper had been infused with patches of mould. Some areas have soft, soaked expanses of colour, like washes of sepia ink, densely spotted with darker spores. The dankest sheets are painterly fields of blotchy growth, now irritating to the nose. These are marked with linear pathways projecting outwards from central nodes, intricate organic relatives of the graphic forms printed on the pages.

One labyrinth design is familiar. On page 27 of Bord's book is a constellation of dense spiral forms, a network of chambers and other isolated graphic forms resembling trees and arcs. The caption identifies the markings as ancient rock engravings found in Mogor, Spain. I recognise the design from *Models & Constructs*, the monograph on and by Potter, published by Hyphen Press in London in 1990. There it appears as a full-page monotone image, roughly enlarged so that its edges harden like crenellations. It is placed with a selection of Potter's poetry, prefacing the prose poem 'Daedalus, An act of creation'.

Potter began to write poetry seriously after 1968 and the labyrinth was an image that preoccupied him. The Cretan labyrinth and the Greek myth of Icarus are appropriated as the settings for his series of poems titled *In:quest of Icarus*, first published in 1975 and revisited frequently for the next two decades. The versions of these poems that appear in *Models & Constructs* are dramatically altered from their original publication as a handout given to the audience at the only performance of the poems during Potter's life. This took place at Bristol in December 1975 — shortly after Potter returned to the school for a second spell as its head — and took the form of a staged reading given by students and colleagues. In these poems, the mythological Minotaur is an incidental presence. The labyrinth itself is the threat, a metaphor for the prototypical institution, the oppressor of the spirit of youth that Potter identifies with the naïve energetics of Icarus. *In:quest of Icarus* is his portrait of the corruptibility of students. I take its language — at once tender and resentful — to be indicative of his state of mind in the period following his departure from Bristol in 1969, deeply dissatisfied with his experiences there, and at Hornsey. The work is dedicated to the international student movement.

In:quest of Icarus is not as exceptional as it may seem in Potter's output as a designer and educator. While it is his only body of published poetry, it reflects intimately on his experiences as an educator, and is itself highly designed, proposing a union of script and stage that Potter intended as an isomorphic relation of the constraining corridors of the labyrinth to the

[23] Ancient rock engravings in other parts of Europe sometimes include labyrinthine designs. The designs shown here are very similar to the cup and ring marks previously illustrated. They were found in Spain at Mogor, near Marin, Pontevedra Province.

Section of one of Norman Potter's photocopies from *Mazes and Labyrinths of the World*, by Janet Bord.

mechanisms of the typewriter on which the poems were written. The set was built by the student performers during the public rehearsal period. Immediately following the work's original performance, Potter led a seminar on the connections between poetry and design. A cassette recording of these proceedings still exists. During some opening remarks, Potter addresses what he presumably anticipated would be a confused response to his combination of these two activities:

> For years I had a block against poetry. Word poetry, that is. I chose to work as a craftsman and designer with my own workshop. How did I feel about it then? To write seemed not to do. To be somehow supplementary to what was done or, in that sense acted out. I felt that the act of making something was to have immediacy and concreteness. That it was treason to follow and to be wise after the event, to comment upon experience in the way that poetry seemed to me to do. ... Once you see that poetry is not something you do in church, or try to avoid doing in school, but is, in fact, the intensification of ordinary speech, and an effort to use words as tools to extend our humanity, then the barrier — we might say the wall — is breached.[6]

Earlier in 1975, Potter had been persuaded to return to Bristol after six years away. In his absence, the course had faltered, partly reverting to its previous administration, sinking into inertia without spirited leadership. Potter made his return conditional on the institution's acceptance of a radical reorganisation of the course. He proposed a new pedagogical model, its spatial plan borrowed from another classical archetype, the Roman arena:

> The structure is now replaced by four family groups, made up by first-, second-, and third-year students, with independent teaching methods, working environment, and course objectives, under the autonomous direction of the four full-time academic tutors in the school. ... The four groups relate to a central area called the Arena. Here all students meet in certain common projects, for specialised lectures or seminars, for extra-curricular activities which the Arena is concerned to foster, and for the exhibition of work from all four groups, whether for project criticism or for exhibitions of longer duration. In some of these respects the Arena is an area of critical disputation, in which work is examined by objective criteria, and if necessary, harshly; as distinct from the more subjectively orientated working ambience of the family groups. The Arena has no power to over-rule the academic autonomy of individual groups, but will freely criticise their positions, i.e. their assumptions and objectives, as much as their apparent performance.[7]

Potter's proposal combines the self-organised teaching forms that flourished during the Hornsey sit-in with an 'area of critical disputation' that he describes with a hint of menace. That Potter should adopt the spatial metaphor of the arena is telling. In the order of Roman public spaces, the forum was the general meeting place and the stage for political discussion and demonstration. The arena had more spectacular functions. Gladiatorial contests took place there, and theatre and performance — all troubling connotations to students for whom criticism was an intimidating prospect.

A single student

In June 2013, I met four former students — all male — from the first intake to the Construction course in 1964. Our meeting was an informal reunion for this group of friends, in the extraordinary home designed and self-built by one of the former students, Mike Harvey, in the St Weburghs area of Bristol. My notes remind me that in preparing for this meeting I had wanted to ask about one-to-one access to Potter, to understand how present he was in the everyday life of the school in that initial phase. The response that one of the group gave to this question left me with a mental image that, as I recall it now, conflates with the tightly framed, up-close image of Potter from Donnellan's film:

> There was a general office which had a library, and the secretary. Behind that was this dingy basement with a tiny skylight. He was there. He had this little office. He would chain-smoke Senior Service cigarettes. You walked in and you immediately had secondary cancer. He did a lot of one-to-one tutorials in that space. These were ... well, I found them quite gruelling. He usually gave me the third degree on anything I'd done. He would be hunched over, with a fag in his hand. If he didn't like what you were doing, a lot of growling noises would come out of him. Mhhrmmmr. Mhhhrrgghm. Then he'd draw some little diagram, just to show you how your idea could be sorted out. You could spend hours talking, if you wanted to. I would go over to his house at midnight sometimes, knock on the door, he would be awake. We'd just sit around having coffee and talking until three, four, five in the morning.[8]

I have encountered Potter's preference for tight spaces before, but this smoke-filled example seems particularly evocative of its era. But most telling is the association of this space with the late-night meetings in Potter's home, the suggestion that the conversation wasn't defined by the school building or its timetable.

Two archival boxes containing some of Potter's papers are temporarily residing at my studio. They have been in the care of his publisher since the production of *Models & Constructs* in the late 1980s. I recently brought them here for cataloguing, before they are reunited with a larger archive retrieved from France by Potter's family, which is presently in storage in London. Some of the material is divided into folders corresponding to the sections of *Models & Constructs*. There are autobiographical materials and correspondence, photographs and technical illustrations from projects produced in Potter's workshop, and poetry. Other folders contain documents related to the Construction course. One card binder has typed copies of the first year's teaching programme: dates and listings for lectures, and what seems to be a complete set of numbered project briefs. Another has copies of staff memos and student reports.

I am spending a day reading and making digital scans of these documents. At the computer, I label the scans and organise them for future reference. Beginning with the correspondence, I read a typed copy of a memo distributed by Potter to 'Members of academic staff in Bristol'. It is undated, but probably from January 1969, shortly before Potter's first departure from the college. In the upper right corner of the page, in Potter's handwriting, is the note: 'The legal game: move one on the board.' The memo reproduces a letter received by Potter — retyped, not photocopied — from a legal firm, Adams, Brown & Co.:

> We have been acting for the University of Bristol in connection with legal proceedings which have been brought against certain persons who were concerned in the recent occupation of the Senate House building. Our attention has been drawn to a Broad Sheet which was issued during the 'sit-in' under your name, which indicated that you were a supporter of the 'sit-in' and seems to suggest that you may have been one of the people who was actually involved in the unlawful occupation of the building. We feel it only fair to warn you that the University would consider commencing legal proceedings against you if it transpires that you did, in fact, trespass in the Senate House building.[9]

The second page of Potter's memo relays his response to Adams, Brown & Co.:

> I personally attended four such discussions, together with many members of staff from the Bristol Colleges (including the University). I did so for the obvious reason that my students were there; students whose judgement I have cause to respect, and for whose education I have a continuing responsibility under all circumstances. It is difficult, indeed absurd, to interpret this action as 'trespass' in any good sense at all. ... It is regrettable that those who deplored the students' conduct failed, as it seems, to exercise their own educational responsibility; first, by failing to conceive an imaginative and realistic educational structure in which such happenings would be unnecessary, and second, by failing, in the event of the sit-in, to argue coherently their case against it. To my mind, a teacher opts out of education if he fails to join with his students at crucial times in their academic life, whether or not he decides to support, or reasonably to oppose their conduct, by persuasion of its wrongfulness. I am not aware of a more basic principle on which to structure the pursuit of further education.[10]

There is nothing further from this correspondence in the material I have, and no copy of the broadsheet. Apparently legal action was not pursued, but I suppose Potter's motivation for distributing the memo was to display conviction to others who may have been present at the sit-in and received similar threats. The commitment is unflinching and the tone combative. As I work at the scanner, I rehearse an argument, clarified by revisiting the story of the dingy basement office and reading this memo. In my notes, I write, 'In Potter's writing for (and about) education there is a disregard for the institution and its implied boundaries: between personal and professional, between student and teacher.'

In the second archive box, the heroic rhetoric of this note is abruptly undermined. I find the contents of a folder with typed copies of sixty-six student reports, all from Potter's second phase at the school. Written directly to students, their tone is typically critical, anecdotal and generally encouraging. Until, about halfway down the stack, I find an extraordinary example. This report, from 1977, has six pages. The first two are administrative forms stating that the student is failing the course. The remaining four sheets resemble a letter more than a report. It begins:

> ...you must not go winey on me (or yourself) and pretend to be less intelligent than you are. If I were to say that your 'report' and the back-up of your portfolio, exhibit attitudes that are lazy, ignorant, bigoted, and selfish, and that you appear to be living in a soft-headed middle-class dream; you would probably burn with outrage and the injustice of it, and you would be right, and so would I be right, because your whole situation is in some sense an injustice to you; it is not, that is to say, sufficiently and usefully true to everything that you are, could be, and probably need to be; and someone has to say so at this point in time and it has to be me.[11]

These lines shock me, as clearly they were meant to shock the student. To describe them as offensive is redundant — the letter openly declares its intention to be taken this way, to outrage. This is compounded by the context: an on-the-record, formal communication that seems to acknowledge no responsibility to assume the depersonalised voice of the institution. The force of the criticism immediately confronts me with questions that I have never asked about Potter and the teaching culture that he produced.
I continue to read:

> If you cannot accept that the world makes demands on you and that these demands are inescapable, you should simply get married and be sheltered by money or God knows what for the rest of your life.

The letter was written to a female student. Reading it today, this sentence can only be interpreted as conforming to an abusive, patriarchal culture. I struggle to reconcile its exercise of male intellectual privilege with the image of Potter protesting with his students, and the letter he wrote in their defence that I handled only an hour earlier. The context — the student's situation and disposition — is unknowable to me in this moment, but my own investment in studying Potter as a teacher compels me to perceive a distinction between the cruelty and candour exhibited here.
Having taught in design schools, I think I recognise the dynamic that Potter seems so antagonised by. There exists in design education the possibility to simplify critical exchanges with underachieving students by offering non-committal commentary that permits the student to continue in a particular direction without confronting what, in the fullest sense, their work might lack. This practice is sometimes justified amongst educators with the excuse that work ought to 'deserve' criticism — that if it is below a certain level of sophistication or intensity, there is no point subjecting student work

to rigorous scrutiny. When he writes 'someone has to say so at this point in time, and it has to be me', I read Potter categorically refusing to take such an easy way out.

There is a sense, then, in which this candour might be constructive. Potter assumes a responsibility to be direct, to not allow the student to simply withdraw from criticism by failing the course. Momentarily, this interpretation feels believable. But the criticism continues, unrelentingly, over two thousand words:

> Of course the subjective experience of an education, particularly a self-education, is the heart of it, or the heart of the organic growth of understanding that an education is. Theorists of education, from Socrates to John Dewey, and field workers of which I am one, have urged this view along with many of its implications, and many of us in further education have battled for years to fight-off the counter claims of specialised training and more particularly, the spurious attention given to short-term results in education, to success criteria related solely to career prospects, and to every other sort of educational window-dressing.
>
> This is not at all what we are on about in asking for 'evidence of study'. The point is that this is the minimum that can relevantly be asked of you, to guarantee your own freedom of manoeuvre within the social facts that we must all live with. If you say of this 'it's not what you're doing that counts at all but your ability to write about it at some later date' this is such a crass misunderstanding and evasion of what is involved I can only assume that you are really talking about something else, some emotional problem in yourself; unless you simply do not realise that a creative challenge is here implied, on the one hand, and the first condition of freedom (the recognition of necessity) on the other.

By this point, the writing has become essayistic. I recall other occasions, when reading a report or staff memo written by Potter, that I have recognised fragments of prose from *What is a designer*. The process of writing to students was evidently productive for him, and that perhaps partly explains the length and range of this letter. These paragraphs I take as a response to the anti-academic sentiments expressed by the student performers in Donnellan's film (and presumably by the student in question here): 'They may not be able to sing or dance very well, but they'll certainly be able to talk incomprehensibly about singing and dancing!' The objection was that the DipAD — by 1976 in operation for almost a decade at Bristol — was too much about writing and critical reflection. On this point, Potter proceeds forcefully:

> This is a BA course and as far as I am concerned standards are involved. If you want to argue a case about education, I expect you to do your homework — as I have had to do — and I expect you to have sat up all night and several nights so that you actually know your Bantock and Peters and Holt and Illich and Reimer and Goodman and all the rest so that we can take all that for granted as common ground before we begin. And this applies to any other matter on which you are forming

> views. There is no point whatever in exchanging opinions at the level of a women's institute tea-party; if you want to be taken seriously as a degree level student — and may I say ... I would not go to the trouble of writing you this long letter unless I respected you and took you seriously.

The dismissively phrased suggestion that to be taken seriously a female student must have read a list of canonical male authors finally exhausts my motivation to reconcile this letter with my admiration of Potter's candour as a teacher.

The letter concludes:

> I think you should ask yourself a whole lot of questions including just what you are doing here; but also, what is blocking you and (apparently) clouding you. The message of your portfolio appears to be 'I hate to give' and the message of your report 'I live and love to take into myself, stop asking me to justify myself or to give you anything'. If this is so in any degree at all, then you ought, I think to take a radical view of your whole life situation and all I can do, helpfully, is to put up various mirrors around you. The nature and extent of the distortion in those mirrors, is for you to determine.

The mirrored enclosure completes this collection of spatial metaphors found in Potter's career as an educator: beginning with the unknowable labyrinth, proceeding through the publicly contested arena to arrive at this claustrophobic space. As a series, from the perspective of the student, they seem increasingly unforgiving.

In 1977, Potter finally left Bristol. His letter of resignation is amongst the documents I am scanning. In it, he wrote:

> In leaving, I am not particularly pleased with myself any more than many of the things and attitudes I see around me. On the other hand, education can become a bland pretence that all is right with the world, except just the little problem of apathy around the place, when religion, philosophy, art and design have been in a turmoil of crisis and despair about the meaning and direction of life, not to mention either the concentration camps of the near past, the apparently overwhelming survival problem for mankind, and the ominously growing world-wide use of torture as a normal feature of political life. One must see an education — however specific to nuts and bolts — in the full context of the culture that supports it, and to whose change it seeks to contribute. In 1977, a student who wants a cosy time wants to remain a child.[12]

One thing seems clearer, and important, in the presence of these documents. I think back to Garland and Smith climbing through the studio window at Bower Ashton. The meaning of Potter's staging device now appears plain: it was a subversion of the institutional pretence that there exists a threshold between education and life.

I return to the long student report to scan it. Its sheets are held together with a metal clip that has rusted and bound itself to the surface of the paper, making scanning difficult. I consider whether to remove the clip, probably tearing the corner of the paper but enabling a visually clearer scan, or to leave it intact and accept that the sheets will fan out beyond the edge of the scan in a distracting way. I opt for the former. I collect the scans of all of these documents in a folder and name it 'give everything expect everything'.

Images accompanying this essay are reproduced courtesy of Sally Potter and Charlotte Potter for the Norman Potter Archive.

1. *Art — To a Degree*, produced by Philip Donnellan, featuring Humphrey Burton, Lil Smith and Ken Garland, from the 'Omnibus' series (London: BBC, 1976), 55 min.
2. West of England College of Art, 'School of Design prospectus' (Bristol: West of England College of Art, 1964).
3. Typed copy of a petition addressed to The National Council for Diplomas in Art and Design, originating at West of England College of Art, June 1966, from the Norman Potter Archive.
4. Norman Potter, undated correspondence to 'David', from the Norman Potter Archive.
5. Norman Potter, 'box and fox: a personal comment on design and teaching', unpublished typed notes for a lecture given at the Royal College of Art, London, 27 November 1968, from the Norman Potter Archive.
6. Recording of a seminar given following the performance of *In:quest of Icarus*, undated, from the Norman Potter Archive, transcribed from cassette tape by the author.
7. Norman Potter, undated typed document titled 'Changes in academic structure and content', from the Norman Potter Archive.
8. Interview by the author with a past student of Norman Potter, 30 April 2013.
9. Norman Potter, typed copy of a memo sent to 'Members of academic staff in Bristol', undated, circa 1969, from the Norman Potter Archive.
10. Ibid.
11. Norman Potter, typed copy of a student report, July 1976, from the Norman Potter Archive. The excerpts following on pages 176–178 are also from this source.
12. Norman Potter, letter of resignation from West of England College of Art, 1977, from the Norman Potter Archive.

It's rather an attitude
Richard Hollis, interviewed by Brad Haylock

Richard Hollis is a graphic designer who is perhaps best known for his design of John Berger's book *Ways of Seeing* (1972) and for his work for the Whitechapel Gallery in London during the 1970s and 1980s, but he is also renowned for his work as a design educator and historian. Notably, in the mid-1960s, at the invitation of Norman Potter, Hollis was the inaugural head of the graphics programme in the School of Design at the West of England College of Art in Bristol. Hollis is also the author of *Graphic Design: A Concise History* (1994), which Brad Haylock has used as a textbook in his own teaching. In this conversation, Hollis and Haylock discuss the crafting of student assignments, the Bristol pedagogy, how and why to teach history, and other matters of enduring concern in graphic design education. This conversation took place in early 2016, in Hollis's studio in the basement of his London home.

BH   Richard, as well as being a practitioner, you've spoken about, written about, and worked in graphic design education at many points throughout your career. I know that you have a specific interest in the role of history in graphic design education. In 2014, you gave a keynote presentation at a conference titled 'Graphic Design: History and Practice', in Bolzano, Italy, in which you outlined some of your thoughts on education. Shall we take that paper as the starting point for our conversation?[1]

RH   Yes. I started off by listing all the things that I think are missing from graphic design education today. For example, too many courses focus on branding, so students are not actually learning enough about graphic design. Students think, 'if we know how to do branding, then we'll get a job'. But when the schools are graduating so many people, all that happens is that they turn out half-educated people. In my view, designers should be as well trained as doctors or surveyors or any such profession. Otherwise they're in the hands of clients who, these days, because of computers, think that they know as much about design as any professional designer.

There are many things that are missing from graphic design education today. Things that used to be done a few years ago have been forgotten. For example, designers at one time learnt how people interpreted words and images. One of the assignments that I set students was to give them six squares of six inches by six inches. In each of them, students had to convey the idea of the word 'fly'. They could use the letters 'F-L-Y', but they had to do something so that when somebody looked at it, they would understand the idea the student was trying to communicate.

With students we would go through all kinds of things, even optical illusions, so that they really understood how vision works, and how an image or sign communicates. One of the ways of doing this, of course, is by looking at things that have been done in the past, and not only in the field of design. For example, I always think that designers should understand things like heraldry, and how that sort of visual and verbal communication developed. After all, the contemporary idea of a slogan came from something that was yelled on the battlefield, and it was a certain length so it could be put on a banner. You would have to be able to distinguish one banner from another because you would need to be able to identify your comrade or your enemy. It's that sort of historical, traditional aspect that I find interesting, and I think that students can also be interested in it. Some training in the traditions and conventions of visual language should be an essential, natural part of designers' education.

Graphic design education should include the study of signs and language. Students should understand how the alphabet works and how it developed. To my mind, designers should have an academic background, which would then give them confidence when they're practising. Or, if they don't practise, because they won't all get jobs in the field, at least they will be leaving as educated people who have a rich range of experiences and knowledge, and they will be people who are curious about their subject — or so one might hope.

Because people are so used to looking at images online, in one of the assignments that I set recently, when I was teaching in Oslo, students were

Central School of Art & Design
Graphic Design Department . DipAD Course

Short Course in Visual Language

This course is intended to give an introduction to graphic language. The work produced should make an exhibition in the corridor by the end of the term.
It is easiest to think of 'graphics' as marks, which are made or chosen to convey a specific meaning. (These marks, which include continuous gradations of tone, like a watercolour wash or a photograph, make images.) When these images are part of a system of conventions, they are called signs – like a multiplication sign, for example, or a road sign. Letters of the alphabet, together with punctuation and numbers, form a system of alphanumeric signs.
Anyway, to get off to, or rather, on to a good start, can you please try to finish the job below, which deals with alphabet and image, by next Tuesday morning, and have your work pinned up, ready for you to talk about, in room 203 at 11am.

Job

Make six four cards, each 6"x6" to convey the meaning of the word 'fly'.

1. Use the word 'fly' only - this will form a title to the other three
2. Use an image to convey one meaning of the word, but do not use the word itself
3. Use an image together with the word 'fly' to suggest another meaning than that of 2, above
4. Use lettering of the letters 'f', 'l' and 'y' so that the form of the letters, or their position in the square, reinforces the meaning of the word.

Use any medium you like – photo / collage / montage / paint, pencil, felt pen

Richard Hollis

Introductory sheet handed out to each student, explaining the aims and premises of the Visual Language course, followed by a practical brief. Written by Richard Hollis for the DipAD course at the Central School of Art and Design, circa 1978.

asked to choose just six images from the web, randomly. Then they had to put them into context. I asked, which of these interests you most? They had to describe the image and try to understand why it is like it is — their curiosity about images is extraordinarily limited. Since these things flash by on the screen, there's very little concentration on a particular image or on what it is trying to do, who made it, why they made it, and so on.

BH   Curiosity is a very important quality in designers. But I wonder if what you're talking about here might also be a shared framework for thinking, or a shared disciplinary language? As educators, how might we begin to teach such things?

RH   In Bristol, we tried to use semiology as a framework, so that we were all using the same terms. But we found that it was really rather a dead end. It became too technical, and not something that you could discuss with students who hadn't been amongst the same staff, teaching with the same understood terms.
    There is also the need to understand things like motivation and perception, why people want to look at things, why the eye looks at a particular thing, why something is remembered. For example, students should look at experiments into the way our eye moves over images. At the Hochschule für Gestaltung in Ulm, they had an Ames room permanently set up, so students could understand how past experience conditions the viewer.[2] I think it helps if students can understand that whatever they're working on, they have to be using a language which is understood by the viewer. It seems crazy to set up something like an Ames room just so that people can learn one thing. But I think it's an important example, because as soon as students have seen it in person, they can understand that people see what they expect to see because of their previous experiences.

BH   Your visit to Ulm was clearly an important moment for you. For how long were you there?

RH   Yes, it was. Oh, a very short time, only a couple of days, maybe a bit longer. It was really talking to students there that was useful and interesting, and because the English typographer Anthony Froshaug was teaching there. I'd never met him before. It was very... what I would call 'scientistic'. It was very mathematical. In those days, about 1960, people believed much more in using mathematical methods in design. It wasn't so useful in graphic design, but possibly more so in product design.
    However, I think the notion of algorithms is important. When I was at the Central,[3] we reckoned that people had to understand the concept of the algorithm, because typographers often have to design forms. It's a very interesting challenge to design a form and get somebody to fill it in. A great many forms are very poor. My chequebook is very hard to fill in, presumably because the people who designed it do everything electronically. Things may yet get much worse.
    Ulm did impress me at the time. They did some very interesting work, for instance, with the analysis of advertisements. Do you know the stuff that they

did on visual rhetoric? The main thing was a magazine published here called *Uppercase*. By the way, do you know of Judith Williamson?

BH   Yes, I know the *Decoding Advertisements* book.[4] And I also see it on your bookshelf.

RH   She used a lot of that understanding of how people read words and images and how they might be persuaded to respond. And then there is Edward Tufte — and others, of course. Tufte was a pioneer of 'information design', which became popular in the print media.[5] In *The Guardian* newspaper, they used to have endless graphics explaining the proportions of this, that and the other, which often were so visually attractive that the information they were carrying was in fact very inaccessible. There was a course, which I think was very good, at what was then the London College of Printing — and of course the Typography course at Reading University used to be very good from that point of view. And there was the *Information Design Journal*. And the *Journal of Typographic Research*, which was something we all looked at. Does it still exist?

BH   Yes, but it's now called *Visible Language*.

RH   That's right, yes. I fear that many of today's books and magazines aren't very interesting. Too many are just picture books, which I think is a very sad thing, because it's very much like what happens online. It's just a series of images without any explanation of why or how they came to exist. Do you know that book on Helmut Krone, who was art director of the famous 1960s campaign for the Volkswagen Beetle?[6] It is, I think, a model book of graphic design history.

BH   No, I don't know that one. Why do you admire it so much?

RH   It explains how everything was done. Also, it fits the work into a social context, and an historical context of what the US was like then. I have to say that the author, Clive Challis, was a student of mine, but he worked in advertising. One instance in the book is where he draws a relationship between Volkswagen advertising and the Bauhaus, and the fact that the Beetle was the people's car. In a way, the book is too big, but it couldn't be anything else, because his research was extraordinarily deep and wide. He explains Krone's origins and his relationship with architects and so on. It is amazing because he published it himself, had it printed in China, and went to China to see every section of the book off the press. To get copies to Scandinavia, he filled his car up with books and then took the boat. Extraordinary. Some people are really committed.

BH   It is important to reflect on the role of publishing in the transmission of knowledge between generations of designers. But it seems to me that there is a consistent theme emerging here, namely passion. Is this kind of energy something you saw at Ulm, and which you sought to implement in Bristol?

RH I wouldn't put it like that, because the driving force in Bristol was really Norman Potter. I was working in Paris, and he wrote to me and said, 'I think we could make a more up-to-date course in Bristol'. He was applying to be head of what I think was then called 'interior design'. He also said that they needed a head of graphic design. 'If you apply you'll probably get it', he said, and so I did. So we worked together closely because three-dimensional designers were working mainly, in those days, by drawing. Everyone had drawing boards, so the first year of the course would be graphics students and three-dimensional design students together. They often worked alongside each other, and much of the course would be run jointly, which I think worked extremely well.

Also, we tried to do as much as was possible outside the school, going on visits and looking at things and making reports in common. You'll know from Potter's book *What is a designer* that most of the things that he devised were quite unconventional.[7] For example, he believed that a day a week should be spent learning or using English, learning how to write and deciding what was worth reading and that sort of thing, because a lot of the three-dimensional designers who were nearer to architects would be spending a lot of time writing reports over the course of their careers. This also applies to graphic designers, who work with words as much as images.

BH Can you tell me your thoughts on the balance between working as a design practitioner and working as a design educator? I understand that the Coldstream Report, which introduced the then-new model of the Diploma in Art and Design that was implemented in the UK in the 1960s, sought to require teachers to maintain a practice in their chosen field.

RH I haven't been to many schools where I've been deeply impressed, partly because they're not staffed by working designers, generally speaking. If designers can earn a living through design, they will often be doing so and not teaching. Having said that, of course, I was teaching for quite a long time, more or less until I finally thought I could be earning a better living by working as a designer, but the combination of working and teaching is very good, because the quality of my work dropped as soon as I stopped teaching. It's not that the students might see something terrible you've done, but you were somehow so much more engaged in thinking about the job.

BH Perhaps the task of having to articulate the way you work when you're teaching helps you to do better work?

RH I think so, yes.

BH The contrary challenge, of course, is that many practising designers don't have the understanding of theories such as semiology, for example, that you would hope to see.

RH Because they haven't had a good training.

BH   Well, this brings us back to your earlier comments regarding the things that are missing from contemporary design education. But changes in education mean that today we have larger student cohorts than Ulm or Bristol, or other schools of note in earlier eras, would have had. It can be a challenge to teach everyone the diverse range of things they need to know to be practising designers these days — semiology, for example, and history, not to mention the raft of technical skills they'll need. It is a lot of material to cover in a relatively short amount of time, and indeed the scope of knowledge required seems to be continually increasing.

RH   I used to try to teach history not by doing it chronologically, but by doing it thematically — how movement is represented, say, would be a whole lecture, and you would go through the topic historically, always showing examples. Also, I always give students notes, because if you're saying the word 'Tschichold', if they haven't got it written down, it's too confusing.

But, regarding Ulm again, let me share another anecdote. Before Froshaug went to Ulm, there was something playful about what he did. He did not do a great deal of work, but what he did was intuitive. As soon as he was at Ulm, he just ranged type left in a grid, and that was it, more or less. That was that intellectualised, 'scientific' attitude. Thinking back to Ulm, certainly I came back with maths books. I suppose it was just that people there thought much more about what they were doing, because while the graphics that they used could just as well have been Swiss, visually, the actual thinking behind it was much more rigorous. Although, having said that, Froshaug worked to quite an ordinary formula. Everything was rather dressed up somehow, as science and maths.

BH   This is why Ulm is important, of course, because it was an attempt to scientise design, but perhaps it went too far in that direction?

RH   It was more, I would say, sociological. They were interested in mass communications, in what was happening in American culture, such as planned obsolescence. That was a phrase of the period. Then, I suppose much later on, later in the 1960s, things like Schumacher's *Small is Beautiful* and ecological concerns became of interest to some students.[8]

I'm being really nostalgic about how teaching has changed. Froshaug was actually a very good teacher. For example, the first assignment he set for new students asked them to devise something that would explain to all the other students who they were. To give them an identity. There would be some limitations. For example, the format and the media — photographic, typeset, collage, etc. Some wrote CVs, others made self-portraits. It was an additional way for the group to get to know one another.

The second assignment was to get students to organise things in terms of various criteria. They would collect a number of objects and arrange them according to one set of criteria, and then have to arrange them again according to another, which helped people to get the idea of sorting out and categorising and relating and establishing a hierarchy of the information that you were going to present. I think that in typography that's a very good skill to learn.

One task I used to set for typography students involved giving them phrases from, say, Ruskin or somebody else who was using language in quite a precise way, and get them to, as it were, parse it typographically, so they would organise it according to the sense of it. Those are just some of the things that I remember, which may suggest something of the sort of thing that I feel is missing. Students are today only given assignments that are like jobs in the outside world, which these weren't. They were quite clearly exercises.

The other point about history is that writers learnt to write by reading. They read all the classics. I don't understand why students aren't presented with what are the established classics of graphic design and then asked to question why they are thought to be good. Of course, some things are difficult to understand. In fact, many of the aesthetics belong to a particular period, even to fashion, which has to be put in context, and which also demands an understanding of the technology that produced it, the printing technology, and so on. It's this sort of thing that I think is missing.

Incidentally, there's a book about the work I made for the Whitechapel Art Gallery, by Christopher Wilson.[9] The research he has done is just absolutely extraordinary, because it explains the relationship between an institution, the people who are working in it, the designer who is working for it, and the people they are communicating the information with. I sent to him yesterday a photograph of a printer that I must have taken — which I'd quite forgotten — at a guillotine, really to remind people that in those days everything was, as it were, hands-on, that it was such a different activity.[10] It was a craft activity — not so much an intellectual craft, but a physical one.

When work from a certain period is being looked at, students need to understand how it was made. There's a letterpress setup in many schools, so students can see how that worked, and sometimes an offset press of some sort. They can see those presses, but not the whole printing trade that was producing these things.

My generation was particularly lucky, because we started with only letterpress. I was lucky, one of the staff at the Central gave me work, because I needed to earn money, as a photo engraver's messenger. I spent a lot of time watching it all being done.

At one time, designers understood they had a trade, which was to do with the stages of production of what they were designing. They weren't sitting at a desk all the time. They ordered and oversaw typesetting, reproduction and printing, choosing suppliers and checking proofs. The relationship with clients, though, isn't that different, because talking with the client is probably very much the same, knowing what questions to ask, not forgetting to ask how much money is going to be available to produce something, and the deadline, and those sorts of things. You can establish checklists of questions. That's something that Potter discusses in his book.[11]

BH   Certainly, but what about teaching student designers to understand audiences? This, surely, is trickier. How have you approached the task of teaching an understanding of the people for whom one is designing?

RH   It's very funny you should ask that, because Wilson reminded me that one of my colleagues, who was teaching with me in Bristol, was asked to pretend to be an Italian businessman, for whom each student had to produce promotional material for a product he was marketing. It was a gadget that pumped air or carbon dioxide into a wine bottle, and this would force the cork out. I gave a talk about corkscrews, which raised all kinds of issues about the purpose and application of design. The students had to make some sort of promotion that would persuade people to buy this gadget. The whole exercise was intended to make the students critical of doing something that they thought was against their principles. It was supposed to make the question of professional responsibility an issue. Of course, the role playing was also fun.

BH   This is in the era of the 'First Things First' manifesto?

RH   Thank God I wasn't in London for 'First Things First'. I probably would have signed it and now I'm very glad I didn't. It's so pious.

BH   Would you often set assignments like the one for the carbon dioxide corkscrew replacement, putting students in a position where they were so manifestly challenged to think about their professional ethics?

RH   No. That would have been almost incidental, partly because I was particularly irritated by that corkscrew. It was just a waste of material.

BH   Can we talk more about Bristol? You were there only for a short period?

RH   Two years. Or just over two years — I went there a term before Norman Potter came. It was an extraordinary time, because we were really able to transform what went on there, against terrific resistance. 'Who are these people coming from London?', were the cries. Of course, we also had a lot of support. The whole design profession was behind the schools, and many senior designers spent time on committees, going around the schools, and these were people who we as young teachers respected greatly. They were very established people who, generally speaking, we admired, even if a few of them were still doing work we thought belonged to an earlier generation. They were serious people who were giving their time to the next generation. Because there were so few designers, the older designers were very good to the young designers. It was a very different atmosphere.
    Designers of every generation then all knew one another, because there were so few of us in London. I did one job for a client whose regular designer telephoned me to ask if I would be in London in August when he was away. Could I step in? I did, and that led to many other jobs for the same client subsequently. It was only because this camaraderie existed, whereas now I think designers are much more competitive. For example, when I was ousted from the Whitechapel, because they wanted a different approach to the design and not to deal with a 'one-man-band', the fellow who took over would — in the 1950s and 1960s — have rung me up and said, 'I've been asked to take over, you know? I'm sorry. Is there anything I should know?' There would have been an understanding that you might be taking the bread out of someone else's mouth. That always happened, it was absolutely normal.

Now nobody would do that, I think, because there are more designers than there is work.

BH   Can I ask why you left Bristol so soon?

RH   Why I left? Really there was a lot of opposition to new ideas, and some of the staff in my department were quite difficult. For example, if the students presented a design for a book jacket, there was a member of staff who would want it mounted like a watercolour, whereas I would want it put on a dummy book, wrapped around. Some of the older staff seemed unable to get their heads around different ways of doing things. On the other hand, I had people in the department who were very supportive, but, generally speaking, it was very difficult, and actually Potter was not easy to work with. He was a wonderful teacher, but he tended to attract acolytes, and Froshaug too. They were great buddies, and I invited Froshaug to teach in Bristol. He was extremely good, but he often pitched his talk to a level higher than the students could understand. When I shared a class with him at Central, I often had to say, 'What he means is…'.

BH   So, what worked well at Bristol? I ask because the Bauhaus is well known and well documented, and Ulm is relatively well documented, even though it is less well known than it perhaps should be, but the pedagogical approach at Bristol is not so well documented.

RH   Bristol was a very provincial place at the time, and they looked to us coming from London as having all the answers. Potter was very charismatic. He had a marvellously persuasive manner with almost anyone. He was very good with the students, but he was, in a way, too good to be a designer.
    We had good people who would come down, Froshaug amongst them, and the Swiss designer Emil Ruder would have come, but he became too ill. I've got the letter from him saying that he was sorry, that although he'd agreed to come, his doctor wouldn't let him.

BH   Was there something uniquely British about what you were trying to do in Bristol? You mention your attempt to have Emil Ruder come over from Switzerland — was Bristol looking to Switzerland, or to the Ulm model?

RH   It was fairly different. There were, I suppose, Ulm-ish elements — yes, slightly, perhaps you could say scientistic, but only very slightly. I think most of the pedagogical ideas came from Potter, and to some extent from Froshaug, who of course had the Ulm experience, but Potter's approach was much more home-grown. I think that comes across very clearly in *What is a designer*. He was actually not a very practical designer. He was somebody who really came out of the Arts and Crafts movement. He had that kind of very scrupulous mentality; everything had to be absolutely right.
    I probably told you about a time when we took all the students, the graphic and the interior students, down to Cornwall, which is a bit beyond Bristol, and we went to see artists like Barbara Hepworth, who invited us to tea — all the students. It was extraordinary, really. We went to the Camborne

Central School of Art and DEsign
Department of Graphic Design

BA(Hons) Course . First Year
One-day Job . 20 April 1978

0   This job is designed to show how you can change meanings
    and interpretations - by cropping images and editing words,
    and by changing the relationship of word to image, and by
    substituting new words and new images. (Normally, you work
    the other way round: finishing or making images and
    combining them with words to provide a specific meaning.

1   Using the two newspapers you have, from any part,

1.1 Cut out the same 6 photographs of your choice (12 in all)

1.2 Arrange one set of six photographs, as straightforwardly
    as possible, individually on A4 sheets of newsprint (you
    may also choose squares 210mm x 210mm or 297 x 297mm). Add
    the original caption or headline to the photograph.

2   Take each of the other six photographs, and

2.1 Crop one by ¼ area and paste down without caption
2.2 Crop one by ½ area and paste down without caption
2.3 Crop one down by as much as you like without caption
2.4 Paste one down uncropped with new caption
2.5 Paste one cropped as you like, but with original caption
2.6 Paste one freely cropped, with any free choice of caption

3   You will end with 12 same size sheets which may be stapled or fixed together

4   Criticism at 4pm room 203

Richard Hollis
20 April 1978

Duplicated assignment briefing sheet issued to each
student. The brief begins by stating the intention of the
job and ends with a clear deadline for completion.
Written by Richard Hollis for the BA(Hons) course at
the Central School of Art and Design, 1978.

School of Mines and to see Neolithic monuments, and to look at rock formations. The idea was to come back and give an account of what we'd done, based on the notion of granite, both the building material and because that's the underlying structure of the land. Anyway, we brought back stones and goodness knows what else, and took photographs, of course.

The students then had to design an exhibition on the subject 'Granite'. They each did a design for the layout. None of the students' designs were good enough, so something designed by one of the staff was used. It was constructed of sheets of building board, each measuring eight by four feet, on which images were placed, and objects were placed below them. Norman Potter was up a ladder, and this friend of mine, the one who did the... do you know this story?

BH   Yes, I do, but I like it very much. Please keep telling it.

RH   So this friend of mine, the one who acted as the Italian industrialist, was working with a graphic design student — and Norman was up the ladder — and he came and said, 'Norman, nobody's going to see it from up there'. Norman, wagging a finger, said, 'God will'. To Norman, in a sense, it wasn't entirely a joke. He did have that sense that there was something numinous about design. I don't know how you would describe it. I wouldn't say that they were Christian values, but they were to do with a job well done. They were Arts and Crafts values, I think.

For example, in one job he did — a haberdasher's shop in a small town in Wiltshire — when he showed me over it, he'd had all the steel joists painted with red lead. I asked him, 'Is this to protect them against rust?' He said, 'No, that's for God'. Even if you couldn't see something, he wanted it to be right or proper — I'm sure 'proper' is the word that he would use.

There was something slightly crazy about him, but endearing. Something slightly rogue, but admirable. He stayed on for many years in Bristol. I don't know how he managed it.

BH   Could we talk more about the importance of history in design education: the importance of teaching history, or of understanding one's place in it?

RH   I think, as I said before, if you learn from what people have done very well previously and try to reconstruct what was happening, both in their minds and at the time, and what technology was available, it helps you to understand the process of design. Even if it doesn't seem directly relevant to you as you sit in front of a computer screen, it builds an understanding of how things are produced and consumed visually.

I think it may also help to establish some standards. You have to ask yourself, why is it that these things have been preserved? What are the values that have worked, that were common at the time, that made people at the time reproduce these works, and then still think they're worth looking at? It's quite difficult to imagine what things were like, to imagine the historical period in which things were produced, but it's worth doing, partly because it takes you away from the screen and all the stuff going on in front of you — there's a lot of visual noise.

BH　How did you come to hold this opinion of the importance of history? Were there key works that you saw?

RH　No, there were key people. I was interested in the values of individuals. That's why I'm writing a biography of Henry van de Velde, who was a pretty hopeless graphic designer, and a paradoxical character, but someone who was admired for his ideas, his attitudes, which were derived from Ruskin and William Morris.[12] He's not a particularly original person, but he was extremely forceful in trying to understand what a terrible state things had gotten into, and in trying to do something about it. Potter was in this tradition too.

It's really the spirit of so many of the designers of the 1920s and 1930s that I admire, because they were trying to get rid of the ways in which things had been done previously and trying to make more rational design available to everybody. And, by the way, 'sweeping away' (the old styles and methods) and 'reason' were the essence of van de Velde's programme. It's only recently that I understood the part van de Velde played in discussions with Max Bill on planning the course at Ulm.

That's not to say there aren't a lot of creative things going on today, but I was interested in the ways in which things might be changed, so it's partly a political attitude. So many of the designers whom I admired were actually political people, like Bill, for example. Their work was really to do with trying to make things better. It's rather an attitude.

BH　That strikes me as a value system and a curiosity that one may or may not be able to teach.

RH　I think that sort of thing has to be implicit. I don't think it can be taught because it rests on an individual's personal attitudes and convictions. It depends upon their home life, so many things that determine their social attitudes. I think things have probably changed, because my generation, which was very young during the wartime, went through the period of austerity after it. It was then a sensation that things were gradually getting better. That atmosphere changed very quickly in the 1970s because the idealism disappeared. There are still movements that try to do something about it, but it is as though the world has been taken over by the whole business nexus and the idea of privatising everything, and so on. So I don't think that political values can really be taught. A knowledge of history might affect people's views, I don't know. It's probably dependent upon media. Fortunately there is a new generation, more alert to current distortions of the aims and values of design as professed by their predecessors.

1　The paper in question is now published in the book that is the proceedings of the conference. See: Richard Hollis, 'History and the Graphic Designer', in *Graphic Design: History and Practice*, edited by Antonino Benincasa, Giorgio Camuffo, Maddalena Dalla Mura, Christian Upmeier and Carlo Vinti (Bozen-Bolzano: Bozen-Bolzano University Press, 2016), 17–37.

2　An Ames room is a distorted, trapezoidal room that produces an optical illusion whereby things that are, in reality, the same or similar in size appear to a viewer to be very different in size. It was invented by American scientist Adelbert Ames Jr. in 1946. The room is viewed with one eye, through a peephole, from a specific viewpoint. The combination of the carefully constructed room and monocular vision tricks the viewer's brain: the brain assumes that the walls of the room are parallel, and so too the floor and ceiling, although this is anything but the case. The brain's learned assumptions about the rectangularity of rooms causes things to appear to be different in size at different locations in the room, or to change in size as they move around the room. The optical illusion is most profound when two people are seen standing in different corners of the room, or when someone walks around the room. To read more about the Ames room, see: Roy R. Behrens, 'The Life and Unusual Ideas of Adelbert Ames, Jr.', *Leonardo* 20, no. 3 (1987): 273–279.

3   The Central School of Art and Crafts was a school of fine and applied arts in London, founded in 1896. It was renamed the Central School of Art and Design in 1966, became part of the then-newly formed London Institute in 1986, and in 1989 merged with Saint Martin's School of Art to form Central Saint Martins College of Arts and Design, which is now known simply as Central Saint Martins and is often abbreviated to CSM. The London Institute became a university in 2003 and was renamed University of the Arts London in 2004. For a short history of the Central School, see: Jonathan M. Woodham, 'Central School of Arts and Crafts', in *A Dictionary of Modern Design* (Oxford: Oxford University Press, 2004). For a wider-ranging history of the London art schools, see: Nigel Llewellyn and Beth Williamson, eds., *The London Art Schools: Reforming the Art World, 1960 to Now* (London: Tate Publishing, 2015).

4   Judith Williamson, *Decoding Advertisements: Ideology and Meaning in Advertising* (London and New York: Marion Boyars, 1978).

5   Tufte's best known books are: Edward R. Tufte, *The Visual Display of Quantitative Information* (Cheshire, Conn.: Graphics Press, 1983); Edward R. Tufte, *Envisioning Information* (Cheshire, Conn.: Graphics Press, 1990); and Edward R. Tufte, *Visual Explanations: Images and Quantities, Evidence and Narrative* (Cheshire, Conn.: Graphics Press, 1997).

6   Clive Challis, *Helmut Krone. The Book. Graphic Design and Art Direction (Concept, Form and Meaning) after Advertising's Creative Revolution* (Cambridge: The Cambridge Enchorial Press, 2005).

7   *What is a designer* is Potter's best known book. It was first published by Van Nostrand Reinhold in 1969 as *What is a Designer: Education and Practice, A Guide for Students and Teachers*. In its revised and extended second edition, published by Hyphen Press, the book's title changed to *What is a designer: things, places, messages*. The current edition, which is cited in this volume, is: Norman Potter, *What is a designer: things, places, messages*, 4th edition (London: Hyphen Press, 2002).

8   E. F. Schumacher, *Small is Beautiful* (London: Blond & Briggs, 1973).

9   Christopher Wilson, *Richard Hollis Designs for the Whitechapel* (London: Hyphen Press, 2017).

10   The image in question is reproduced in Wilson, *Richard Hollis Designs*, 188.

11   See: 'Asking questions', in Potter, *What is a designer*, 133–138.

12   Richard Hollis, *Henry van de Velde: The Artist as Designer* (London: Occasional Papers, 2019).

**Stripping down and dressing up
Corin Gisel and Nina Paim**

In this parallel text, Corin Gisel and Nina Paim explore how what students wear might illustrate the ideologies of the schools they attend. For this, they compare and contrast two schools that are both historically significant but whose cultures could hardly be more different: Black Mountain College (USA, 1933–1957) and the Hochschule für Gestaltung Ulm (Germany, 1953–1968).

Two strings of leather, crossing in a zigzag from the big toe to the ankle. A simple design, reminiscent of ancient times, like the very first type of footwear made by humankind. This is what some of the sandals made by students at Black Mountain College looked like.[1]

There are numerous accounts of sandal-making at the college. Historian Martin Duberman speaks of two students at the school in its very beginning in 1933 — Nat French and Betty Young — who 'started a small sandal-making business when others had admired their homemade products'.[2] Meanwhile, student Patricia Gay Lynch, who entered the college in 1942, credits the endeavour to Mary 'Molly' Gregory, the instructor in woodworking. Gregory 'had a feeling for naturalness' and 'knew how to make things', says Lynch. She introduced 'very natural, nice fashions' and taught many of the students how to make their own sandals.[3] Another student, Hazel Brister Harris, attributes the sandal-making to the influence of Bernard and Berta Rudofsky,[4] who were guest teachers at the College for two weeks during the Summer Institute of 1944;[5] Berta Rudofsky also returned the next summer to teach a class in leatherwork.[6] As Harris remembers, the Rudofskys' class in 1944 addressed 'what would be a sensible form of dress', and taught the students how to make their own sandals, starting by tracing the shape of their own feet.[7] 'This was, mind you, considerably before people went in for thong sandals', Harris further explains.

It seems that the local folk of the surrounding area knew of the sandal-wearing people from Black Mountain. Kenneth Noland, who attended the college from 1946 to

Slim, narrow, with a straight edge. A simple design, ranging from shades of grey, to block colours, to delicate patterns, and usually made of unconventional materials. These were the neckties made by the student Susanne Eppinger Curdes at the Hochschule für Gestaltung Ulm (HfG).[9]

It was in 1958, during her foundation year at Ulm, that Eppinger Curdes started designing and producing neckties. She knew the trade already, as she had taught tailoring and sewing at a women's school. Making and selling neckties was a means to generate some income alongside her studies. 'How I decided upon neckties as something to make, I don't remember', she says. And as far as she could tell, no one else produced and sold clothing or accessories in the school. Eppinger Curdes' neckties cost between three and seven Deutsche Marks each — 'not so terribly much', as she points out. During her four-year stay in Ulm, she reckons she must have produced over five hundred of them. An impressive feat, considering that during its fifteen-year lifespan, the HfG had a total of 540 male enrolments.[10] Eppinger Curdes' customers were mostly her fellow students. However, not all were interested in her products, as many never wore a tie. She also sold items to friends of customers or even to guest teachers visiting the school. 'But no permanent teacher ever bought one of my pieces', she says, 'either because I was not part of his "crowd" or because they simply did not want to.'[11]

She usually opted for unique textiles such as double brocade, or modern synthetic fabrics such as trevira polyester or jersey. And she often made only two identical pieces

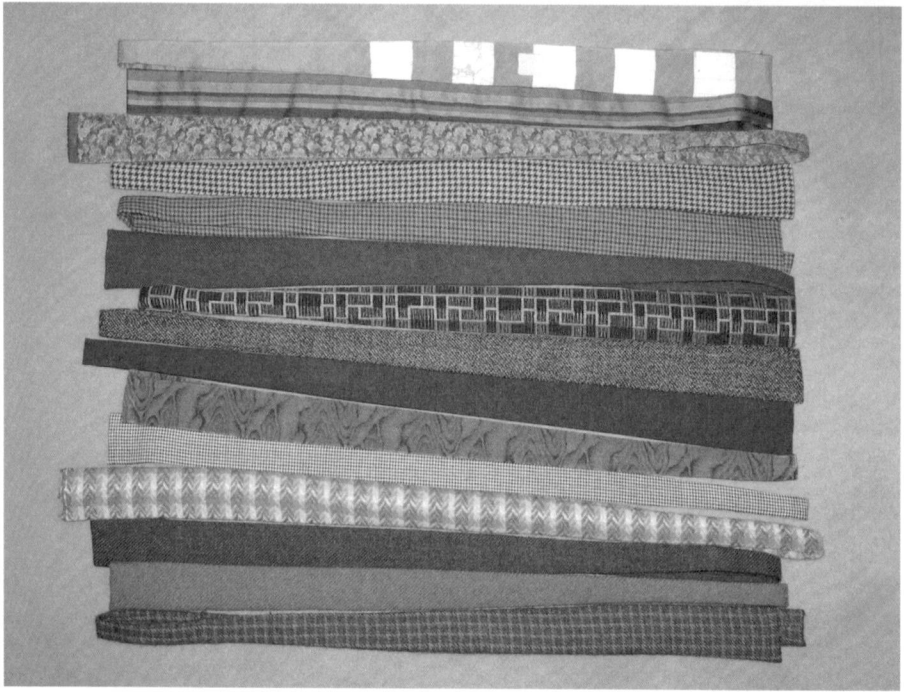

Top: Sandals of Shirley and Diane Moles at Black Mountain College, summer, 1946. Photograph courtesy of the Western Regional Archives, State Archives of North Carolina.

Bottom: Ties made by Susanne Eppinger Curdes during her time as a student at HfG Ulm, from 1958 to 1962, as part of her label 'Cravat Separat'. Photograph courtesy of Susanne Eppinger Curdes.

1948, remembers that before enrolling he was working in a clothing store in the nearby town of Asheville, when one day two young people wearing sandals came in. One woman, one man. When he asked them whether they came from the college, they said yes, proving his suspicion right. It was their sandals that gave them away as Black Mountain students.[8]

Usually worn as a casual item of clothing, sandals are among the oldest known types of footwear. In fact, the earliest evidence of footwear was a pair of sandals discovered in the Fort Rock Cave in the US state of Oregon, proven to be 10,400 years old.[13] Historically a unisex item, sandals can be described as a type of open shoe, which in their simplest construction consist of a sole tied to the foot with strings or straps. Their basic function is to protect the feet. In warmer climates they also allow the feet to move freely. Their form therefore derives foremost from practical considerations.

The sandal could be understood as a *pars pro toto* for the image we have of Black Mountain College itself. When characterising the college, the word 'experiment' is often used. Several publications have reinforced this perception in their titles: *Black Mountain College: An experiment in education* from 1968;[14] *Black Mountain College: Experiment in Art* from 2003;[15] *The Experimenters: Chance and Design at Black Mountain College* from 2014;[16] and *Black Mountain: An Interdisciplinary Experiment*, published in 2015 to accompany an exhibition of the same name at the Hamburger Bahnhof in Berlin.[17]

of each design. Sometimes even just one. One of her classmates helped her with an advertisement, which she was allowed to display in a case placed just opposite to the secretariat. She called her little venture 'Cravat Separat' — a rhyming name that refers to the singularity of her pieces. This attitude was further underlined by her slogan: 'the necktie of the individualist'.[12]

A single story

Usually worn as a formal item of clothing, neckties have their origins in military usage. During the Thirty Years' War, which lasted from 1618 until 1648, Louis XIII of France enlisted Croatian mercenaries, whose distinguishing red neckwear caught the attention of the French. With that, the necktie developed from a sometimes-seen item of military clothing into an often-seen fashion accessory, mostly worn by men.[21] It was the industrial revolution that finally simplified the form, leading to the narrow strip of fabric we know today.[22] In our times, ties are generally seen to symbolise formality, professionalism and authority.

The tie could be understood as a *pars pro toto* symbolising the Hochschule für Gestaltung Ulm itself. When characterising the school, the word 'model' is often used. One of the most popular books on the HfG is titled *Ulm Models – Models After Ulm*.[23] Released in 2003 on the occasion of the fiftieth anniversary of the founding of the school, the book accompanied an exhibition of the same name, which toured both in Germany and internationally, through more than ten different countries, including Spain, Australia, the Philippines, South Korea, India, Montenegro, Brazil and Argentina.[24]

In 2016, the Hammer Museum in Los Angeles hosted the first comprehensive American exhibition on Black Mountain College. Titled *Leap Before you Look*, the show was introduced by the following Josef Albers quote: 'We do not always create "works of art", but rather experiments; it is not our intention to fill museums: we are gathering experience.'[18]

Perhaps this oversimplification is also evident in the canon of works that have repeatedly been cited in accounts of Black Mountain College. One might think of Robert Rauschenberg's unicorn costume for his sister Janet, made of foliage and sticks, and designed for a Mardi Gras celebration at Black Mountain; or perhaps Xanti Schawinsky's multimedia, 'total experience' experimental theatre; or Willem de Kooning's abstract expressionist 'collage' paintings, densely layered and constructed from a variety of media; or Cy Twombly's early black and white paintings, made while he was a student at the college, which are equally considered as examples of abstract expressionism; or even the poems of Charles Olson, based on the poet's breathing, which favour sound and perception over syntax and logic. In a way, the canon of Black Mountain College seems to also be the canon of an avant-garde and expressive aesthetics.

It is clear that the understanding we have of how people dressed at Black Mountain College is shaped by the discourse that has built up depicting and characterising life at the college. Having flipped through numerous publications, the images that stayed with us were those of women and men sitting outdoors, in the grass, reading, studying, painting, drawing, relaxing.

In 2016, a new exhibition reinforced this idea. Presented at the Raven Row gallery in London, the show was once again titled *The Ulm Model*. Its curatorial text describes the HfG as a school that 'pioneered an interdisciplinary and systematic approach to design education — known as the Ulm Model — that was to become universal'.

Perhaps this oversimplification is also evident in the canon of works that have time and again been used to illustrate the HfG Ulm. One might think of the minimalist wooden stool designed by Max Bill in collaboration with Hans Gugelot and Paul Hildinger, which was later christened the 'Ulmer Hocker'; or perhaps the white, geometric, stackable porcelain tableware designed by Nick Roericht as a diploma project, and later manufactured exclusively for canteens; or the entirely modular and ever-growing maquette for space units for residential buildings, designed by students Bernd Meurer and Willi Ramstein under professor Herbert Ohl; or even the visual identity for Lufthansa, designed by Otl Aicher with the E5 development group as a complete and complex system and immortalised by a precise design manual. In a way, the canon of the Ulm School of Design is also the canon of a rational, functional and minimalist aesthetics.

It is clear that the understanding we have of how people dressed at the Hochschule für Gestaltung is shaped by the discourse that has built up depicting and characterising life at the school. As we browsed through books and walked through exhibitions, the images that stayed with us were those of male teachers in full suits and ties, and male students wearing mostly white shirts, sometimes

Indoors, groups of people are seen sitting on the floor of a classroom, in a circle, crouching down, discussing books or exercises. Many wear shorts, sandals or simple shoes. Often sleeves are rolled up, shirts wrinkled, collars left unbuttoned. There are also groups of men wearing jeans and heavy boots, sometimes shirtless, and women in headscarves, working outdoors, moving horses, ploughing the fields, farming, building. From this perspective, we picked up and stored only some snippets of information, which our minds forged into a simplified narrative, a coherent story — a 'single story', as the Nigerian novelist Chimamanda Ngozi Adichie calls it.[19] We were quick to create one image out of several, and thereby overlook important details and differences. 'The single story creates stereotypes, and the problem with stereotypes is not that they are untrue, but that they are incomplete', Ngozi Adichie says. 'They make one story become the only story.'[20] In order to understand the dress culture at Black Mountain College, we must therefore engage with a multiplicity of stories rather than accept a single unified myth.

finished off with a tie or covered with a sweater. Female students, often sporting short hair and sometimes wearing unisex clothing, appear considerably less often — which is no surprise, since they were a minority at the HfG.[25] We also observed students in workshops, wearing grey or white lab coats, captured in moments of extreme concentration. Although most photographs are in black and white, in the few colour reproductions an achromatic spectrum dominated. A lot of grey, some brown or blue, a few single-colour items, and almost no patterns. From this perspective, a simplified narrative is formed in our minds, a coherent story — a 'single story', as the Nigerian novelist Chimamanda Ngozi Adichie calls it.[26] We were quick to create one image out of several, and thereby overlooked important details and differences. 'Stories matter. Many stories matter', Ngozi Adichie says. And, for her, 'stories can also be used to empower and to humanise'.[27] In order to understand the dress culture at the HfG, we must therefore engage with a multiplicity of stories rather than accept a single unified myth.

A complex dress culture

Founded in 1933, Black Mountain College sought 'to develop the special function that a community can serve in general education', based on the idea that 'learning is not confined to classrooms but pervades daily life'.[28] With its beginnings coinciding with the Great Depression, the school was created by a group of professors and students who left Rollins College, a private educational institution and Florida's oldest recognised college, in an upheaval against their teaching policy. One of them, John Andrew

Founded in 1953, the Hochschule für Gestaltung was 'based on a moral justification', as design historian René Spitz says.[47] With its beginnings in the aftermath of the Second World War, the school was established with the conviction that the education of individuals for democracy would prevent a recurrence of the barbarism and inhumanity of the Third Reich. Otl Aicher and Inge Scholl, two of its founders, had been actively engaged in the resistance against the Nazi regime, defending values such as

Rice, was a firm believer in John Dewey's principles of progressive education and thereby the conviction that learning was best achieved by doing and making things.[29] As the first rector of Black Mountain, Rice wanted to educate better citizens for participation in a democratic society.

For that, the arts had not a supplementary but a central place within the education that this liberal arts college offered. Everyone was expected to attend fine arts classes. Apart from that, the college offered courses in classics, language, literature, history, social sciences and mathematics. Students could pick and choose classes, there were few tests and even fewer rules. It had none of the institutions of traditional American colleges: no fraternities, no sororities, no athletic team. And students would simply graduate when they were ready to graduate, or just leave whenever they felt like they had learned what they came to the school for.

Black Mountain College attracted students from all corners of the US. In a rural and tranquil environment in North Carolina, students and teachers all lived on campus, first in a building rented from the YMCA Blue Ridge Assembly south of the town of Black Mountain, and from 1941 across the valley on its own campus at Lake Eden, where it remained until its closure in 1957. Together they shared the responsibilities of living together. As an integral part of the programme, students and some teachers would work in the kitchen and on the grounds, helping out in the construction of new buildings or working on the school's farm. Mornings were usually devoted to classes, afternoons were dedicated to working on the farm or doing other personhood, freedom, human dignity and self-determination. Together with the Swiss designer and artist Max Bill, they initiated the HfG Ulm not simply to supply the design of common commercial goods, but actually to 'design society'.[48]

For that, the sciences had not a supplementary but a central place within the education that this design school offered. After a first preparatory year, students would choose between five specialisations: industrial design, building, visual communication, information or filmmaking. Apart from that, the school offered classes in sociology, economics, philosophy, psychology and politics, but also in topology, combinatorics, semiotics and ergonomics, amongst others. Former students would further develop their skills by joining in real-life 'development groups' led by staff members and working with industry partners.

The Hochschule für Gestaltung Ulm attracted students from all corners of Germany and the world — especially from Switzerland, the US, Japan, Austria, the UK and the Netherlands, but also from Brazil and Argentina. The overall percentage of foreign enrolment, 44 percent, was by far the highest amongst German colleges and universities at the time.[49] The school's campus was located on the top of Kuhberg, a small hill on the outskirts of the city of Ulm, where all students and teachers also resided. Mornings were devoted to work in the departments and workshops, in the afternoons seminars in technical, scientific and cultural topics were held, after dinner the students often returned to the workshops to continue work on their projects. Students and teachers frequently

Top: The Studies Building at Lake Eden campus, Black Mountain College, designed by A. Lawrence Kocher and built with the help of students in the early 1940s. Photograph courtesy of the Western Regional Archives, State Archives of North Carolina.

Bottom: The HfG Ulm building, designed by Max Bill, as seen from the west in 1956. Photograph by Wolfgang Siol, courtesy of HfG-Archiv / Museum Ulm.

chores, evenings were again occupied with classes. Students and teachers often shared meals and spent leisure time together. Such moments were frequently used as opportunities to continue the discussions beyond the classroom.

The way people dressed has only been marginally described in texts about the college. One of the first published accounts of the school is 'Education on a Mountain', written by Louis Adamic and published in *Harper's Magazine* in 1936. Even if the article doesn't specifically mention anything about clothing, Adamic talks about 'group influence' as a central aspect of the college experience. He writes that the community at Black Mountain 'psychologically strips the individual, and there he stands revealed to everyone, including himself — and finally likes it'. Yet he didn't relate this stripping-down of a constructed self to the stripping down of clothing.[30] This might be because at the time of his visit — the school had then existed only for three years — their way of dressing was not much out of the ordinary. A picture of the faculty and staff from 1933 shows them sitting on the stairs of the building all properly dressed in suits, with buttoned-up shirts and ties. Three women in the front are wearing long skirts and blouses. However, in *Black Mountain: An Exploration in Community*, the first comprehensive book about the college, from 1972, historian Martin Duberman writes that after only a few months, people from the nearby village were suspicious of the college being a 'Godless place' and even a 'nudist colony'. Duberman connects this outward image back to the fact that 'students often wore shorts in warm weather, and several appeared in shared meals and breaks in more informal settings and would even, on occasion, have classes outside.

The way people dressed has only marginally been described in texts about the school. One of the most extensive accounts was written by journalist Bernhard Rübenach upon his visit to the school in 1958–1959. His impressions were broadcast by the German radio station Südwestfunk Baden-Baden, and later published as a book with the title *The Right Angle of Ulm* in 1987.[50] In his account, Rübenach stresses the school's obsession with the rational and the logical and its connection to the architecture. 'It's remarkable — in the white building on Kuhberg, fear of the inexact, the vague, the rambling or, geometrically speaking, of swelling curves, undefinable turns, appears to have been replaced by worship of straight lines and right angles.' And he goes on to inquire: 'Is the right angle not only the basic architectural figure of the Ulm college, but also the symbol of their spirit?'[51] Rübenach describes the admission to the college as a rite of passage, an initiation: 'The haircut is the first stage of the initiation. A very short haircut.' Secondly, they 'stop using capital letters'. As the third stage, they 'drop last names, the burden of your origin'. And lastly, they 'change your way of thinking. To reassemble the way you think and feel.'[52]

Some of these notions are confirmed by other voices. Herbert Lindinger, who studied Industrial Design at Ulm and later was a Professor of Design at the school from 1962 to 1968, stated that 'group pressure was noticeable in matters of design and aesthetics: hairstyles, cars, clothing and choice of furniture were sanctioned, art and styling

Top: Black Mountain College faculty and staff upon its foundation, September 1933. From back to front, left to right: John Evarts, Theodore Dreier, Frederick Georgia, Ralph Lounabury, William Hinckley, Joseph Martin, Helen Boyden Lamb Lamont, Margaret Loram Bailey, Elizabeth Vogler and John Andrew Rice. Photograph courtesy of the Western Regional Archives, State Archives of North Carolina.

Bottom: HfG Ulm faculty meeting in the library, 1955. Clockwise from bottom left: Max Bill, Andrea Schmitz, Helene Nonné-Schmidt, Walter Zeischegg, Tomás Maldonado, Friedrich Vordemberge-Gildewart, Fred Hochstrasser, W. Florian Thienhaus, Cornelius Uittenhout, Otto Schild, Paul Hildinger, Fritz Pfeil, Otl Aicher, Inge Aicher-Scholl, Günther Schlensag. Photograph by Hans G. Conrad, courtesy of René Spitz.

204 Stripping down and dressing up

Top: Group photo taken at the entrance to the Studies Building at Lake Eden campus, Black Mountain College, Summer 1946. Photograph courtesy of the Western Regional Archives, State Archives of North Carolina.

Bottom: Students sitting on the terrace of HfG Ulm, circa 1960. Photograph by Peter Emmer, courtesy of HfG-Archiv / Museum Ulm.

town … wearing sandals that revealed *bare feet*.'[31]

The college's standard text in brochures for the summer session from 1944 onwards advised the participants: 'Clothing appropriate for walking in the mountains and for working outdoors should be provided, as well as ordinary city clothes suitable for this climate. Evening dresses are worn at dances and concerts.'[32] In 1949, in a brochure addressing students attending the full school term, the college added a sentence to this standard instruction: 'Since old clothes or work clothes are worn during the day, an extensive wardrobe is not necessary.'[33] The text is again slightly changed in 1952: 'Blue jeans and work clothes are usually worn during the day; however, it is customary to change for the evening meal.'[34]

Although the college underwent different phases and was influenced by larger changes in fashion during its twenty-four years of existence, two aspects seem to have been consistent throughout. For one, people dressed more casually during the day and more formally during the evening or on special occasions, such as the regular Saturday evening dances. For another, the casualness of the daytime clothing seems directly connected to spending a lot of time outdoors, and to working in the fields and in the construction of buildings and roads. This is summed up in an anecdote by John Reiss, a student at the college from 1944 until 1946. On his first day of school, he saw a man trimming weeds alongside the road. Later, at dinner, the same man appeared wearing a blazer — he turned out to be the English professor.[35] Underlining how the practicalities of work changed the way people dressed, William forbidden. Who did not within the first week drop all the remains of bourgeois dress was stigmatised. At first, the hairstyle was changed, then the fabric of the shirts and suits changed.'[53] Argentinian student Jeanine Meerapfel remembers that when she arrived at the school in 1964, she had 'a gray pullover with stripes: yellow, white and gray'. And then someone told her: 'one doesn't wear such a thing here'. She also had brought 'some strange little ladies' bag', which, too, felt out of place. 'But I quickly adapted', she continues to explain. 'And then I got the same hairdo and dressed in gray and soon you couldn't distinguish me from the others.' Other former students even say that patterned or frilly clothes were discarded, altered or dyed in a different colour.[54]

However, many voices disagree with this description of peer pressure. According to Susanne Eppinger Curdes' own memories and those of her husband Gerhard Curdes, who attended the school at the same time, 'there was little pressure to dress in a particular way'.[55] Former student Klaus Krippendorff, who studied Industrial Design in Ulm from 1956 to 1961, calls these recollections downright exaggerations. 'I did not experience a rite of passage or peer pressure to conform to dress codes and appearances. Most of us were revolutionaries who resisted being forced into a single mold.'[56] However, he does acknowledge that there was 'some drift to conformity', and points out that he himself still prefers to write in lowercase characters today. But for him the group influence 'focused largely on how we understood and could justify designs'.[57]

Even though it would be wrong to talk of an Ulm uniform, it is

Treichler, a student at the college from 1947 until 1948, and then a teacher in 1949, remembers another scene. A girl coming down the dormitory steps was wearing a beautiful and expensive sweater. As she was climbing onto a truck, the other girls said: 'You can't wear that; it will be ruined.' She had never imagined having to handle sooty chunks of coal.[36]

It seems that, over time, daytime clothing became more casual. In 1940, John Rice left the college, and a year later Josef Albers became the new rector. In 1944, the first summer programme was held. Temporary students and guest teachers flocked to the college. Roberta Blair, who attended the first summer session, recalls: 'That was the first year of the "natural look", and long hair with bangs, shirts, jeans, and sandals were standard dress.'[37] On the first day, she 'felt a little out of place among the casually dressed college students who were staying for the summer session'.[38] Patricia Gay Lynch remembers something similar happening to herself and her classmates when she came to the college in 1942: 'We weren't hung up any more about what was proper to wear to school, or what the proper way to wear your hair was, as you were in high school.'[39] She continues: 'I think the original hippies were there'.

In 1951, the poet Charles Olson took over the directorship of the college. 'We wore Levi's', Jorge Fick remembers of that time, having attended Black Mountain from 1952 until 1955. He would combine denim pants with a denim jacket with the sleeves cut off. His wife, Cynthia Homire Fick, who was there roughly at the same time, characterises the students as a 'rowdy bunch'.[40] According to scholar David Silver,

certainly possible to talk about a dress culture that was specific to the school. Ann Wolff, who came to Ulm in 1958, says that it was not only the actual exercises they had to do that influenced a certain aesthetic belief of Ulm, but also 'the environment, the building and its interior'. She talks not of an outward pressure to adapt aesthetically, but of an inward one. 'We solidified the "Ulm-style" within us', she says. 'Wooden sandals, grey sweaters, a minimalist way of life were just part of it.'[58] It seems as if, through the clothes they wore, the students and teachers of Ulm embodied the school's approach to design, which sought to replace ornament and personal expression with logic and functionality. The school wanted to train designers who were not to be driven by individuality or intuition, but by rationality and science.

However, this dress culture was certainly not a monolithic dress code. Rübenach himself talks about diversity in apparel and dress. Sitting at the school cafeteria, he describes different social groups, distinguished by the clothes they wore, how they appeared, how they behaved, and by the words they used. 'There are the blue jeans and coarse sweaters', he says, 'a bit uncertain and still unpolished, but endeavored'. Then there are the foundation year students: 'the new, the foreign, those who still enjoy freedom and full ideas'. He goes on to a third group: 'the gray pants, the anthracite-colored sweaters, the dark and vibrantly colored skirts, the strikingly tinted sweaters and shirts, a little exotic, understated, self-assured, industrious, the middle generation'. He concludes with 'finally the old: tight tube pants, refined unadorned clothes, strikingly unobtrusive,

Top: Taking a break from farming, Blue Ridge campus, Black Mountain College, circa 1936–1937. Photograph courtesy of the Western Regional Archives, State Archives of North Carolina.

Bottom: Walter Zeischegg, a teacher in the product design department at HfG Ulm, with students, 1962. Photograph by Wolfgang Siol, courtesy of HfG-Archiv / Museum Ulm.

'if you look at the pictures of the Olson years, it's almost like the exterior is irrelevant and they are busy finding their interior'.[41] It was the postwar period and the financial situation of the college was even tighter than usual. For Silver, that's when 'the college starts to literally go through systematic starvation'. He explains: 'everyone is so interested in poetry and finding oneself that they forget to do things that are communal, like feeding the cows and watering the garden'.[42]

Not everyone was happy with the increasingly slack dress culture that started to emerge at the college. In a school publication from 1948, the positive description 'sensible dress' can be read right next to the negative comment 'sartorial slouchiness'.[43] Another complaint came from teacher and then director Josef Albers. After having been away from the college for a short time around 1941, Albers set up a meeting to 'lament the disorderliness of the campus and to insist that trash be collected and a minimal dress code enforced'.[44] But even with Albers, 'people didn't have to come to class in suits', as his student Pete Jennerjahn reminisced.[45] Nevertheless, Albers expected a minimal amount of decorum from his students. As he later told his students at Yale — where he went on to teach — he was distressed by shirttails hanging out and students walking around barefoot at Black Mountain College. He would demand they tuck in their shirts and wear something on their feet when entering his classroom.[46]

otherwise very self-confident, very superior, very behaved'.[59] Another student, Gerda Müller-Krauspe, who attended the school between 1958 and 1962, says that it was a pity Rübenach never returned to the school in later years, because he would have witnessed even another wave of style: 'the metamorphosis from jeans to flannel'.

Generally, it can also be said that the teachers dressed more formally than the students. Müller-Krauspe describes them in 'conventional, mostly grey suits and white shirts'.[60] Krippendorff adds that 'most faculty wore ties'.[61] But on the student side, formality and informality of dress varied. Both Müller-Krauspe and Krippendorff remember information department students being more elegant and formal than the rest.

In all this, there were of course also those who had more signature elements of style. Günther Elstner, who attended the school from 1964 until 1967, remembers that Otl Aicher loved pink shirts and ties. There was even a rumour that he had a lamp with a pink shade standing on his bedside table.[62] Gerhard Curdes, who studied in Ulm between 1959 and 1963, remembers Hermann von Baravalle, who taught in the preparatory year, always wearing a dark blue blazer with golden buttons.[63] Klaus Krippendorff's preferred sweater, which he would wear leisurely over his pants, had a turtleneck-like collar and 'nobody objected or categorized me as deviant'.

Making clothes and thinking about dress

Josef Albers's classes dealt with the elements of form. Bringing his experience of similar classes from the Bauhaus, where he had studied

Klaus Krippendorff designed a suit for himself. 'I knew I had to wear a suit for several formal occasions and buying one from a store in Ulm was and taught before coming to Black Mountain, he published a text called 'Concerning Art Instruction' in the college's Bulletin of 1934. In it, he reinforces the philosophy of viewing the arts as an alternative and important way of learning about the world. The intention was not that all students became artists. 'But if they know', Albers posits, 'for example, the capacities of color they are prepared not only for painting but also for the practical use of color in interiors, furniture, clothes. These examples also illustrate the need of an understanding of materials.'[64] Beyond Albers's guided study of form and material through practical exercises, craftsmanship workshops in weaving and woodworking would bring the students into direct contact with materials. Students often built their own furniture. Working on the construction of new buildings was meant to teach students about architecture beyond the drafting of plans. And working on the farm was intended to give them a direct understanding of the realities of labour.

A certain maker culture that was in line with the college's pedagogy could therefore be described. However, the making of clothes was driven not only by ideology, but also by economic necessity. The college operated on a very small budget, tuition was low compared to other colleges, and the teachers earned almost no salary. The Great Depression and wartime meant that students had equally little money. Martha Treichler, who was at the college from 1948 until 1949, describes how her classmate Robert Rauschenberg would often lend his sewing machine to other students. 'I told him he should charge, and suggested something like something below the standard of a becoming designer.' As for the colour, 'it had to be gray, of course, which was the standard color of many products designed in Ulm'. Made from a new synthetic fibre called Dacron, his suit was a simplified shape with no lapels, hidden buttons and no breast pockets, no pleats, no cuffs or covers for pockets. 'You may recognize the philosophy of minimalism', he says, 'trying to remove everything that seemed unnecessary to me'.[75] He had it custom made by a tailor in town. 'I recall it took him a while before he understood the philosophy of the unusual design', Krippendorff explains, 'he was accustomed to making ordinary suits and frankly didn't understand why I wanted to deviate from what everyone was wearing at that time'.[76]

Klaus Krippendorff's suit and Susanne Eppinger Curdes' ties, however, remained exceptions. He was one of the only students to ever design his own clothing, and he did so out of necessity. For Eppinger Curdes, ties were a simple item she could make herself in order to earn a modest but much-needed income. Her enterprise lasted only as long as her studies. After graduating from the visual communication department in 1962, she never made a necktie again.

At Ulm, there were neither dressmaking classes nor a textile department. Only very rarely did assignments or projects refer to some kind of garments or accessories. In 1957, Hans Gugelot asked his students to design unisex and universal spectacles, and Herbert Lindinger responded with floating lenses held by a single metal rim on the top, which accentuated the brow line.[77] In 1960–1961, student Reinhard Butter designed a watch in the class twenty-five cents an hour', she remembers. 'Then, when I borrowed his machine to put a zipper in a dress, I hurried so much in order to save money that I put the zipper in backwards. He never got over razzing me about the backward zipper.'[65] Patricia Gay Lynch said that sandals were only one item amongst many examples of self-made clothing at the school. She and her fellow classmates bought fabric — monk's cloth, to be precise — and made straight dresses out of it, which would then be pulled in at the waist with wide leather belts. She talks further about how girls bought boys' shirts (or took their brothers', fathers' or even boyfriends' old shirts) and simply dyed them. 'This was how you got color, and you got colors that you liked and colors that looked nice on', she explains.[66] 'Everything was an opportunity to do something with that', Ati Gropius Johansen says about her time studying at the college from 1943 until 1946: 'Saturday night you wanna get dressed, what are you gonna wear for jewellery? Well, what do you put together that you can find, you know, of leaves, or pebbles, or whatever.'[67]

Apart from the dances on Saturdays, where people would often dress up in formal evening wear, there were also theme-based costume parties, for which both students and teachers would dress up in self-made creations. These costume parties evolved out of the theatre programme that was set up by Robert Wunsch in 1934. Students not only performed theatre pieces, but also created the sets and costumes for the productions. An important figure for theatre at Black Mountain was former Bauhaus student Xanti Schawinsky, who joined the faculty in 1936 together with of Bruce Archer, the industrial designer and theoretician who was a guest teacher in Ulm during those two years.[78] And in 1965, student Frank Hess designed, as his diploma project, a suit that would protect the wearer from radiation.[79]

However, people often wore, and even made, costumes for festive events. In a series of candid pictures documenting the 1956 edition of the carnival party,[80] characters include clowns, sailors, harlequins and prisoners. One man is wearing earrings and another is dressed as a woman. And one girl wore a self-made cylindrical paper hat with the inscription 'die gute form' — a humorous take on Bill's famous exhibition series. Students, teachers and local people alike attended these elaborate carnival festivities, which were traditionally organised by the first-year students.[81] Besides these annual 'Faschingsfeste', there were also spontaneous gatherings and parties.[82] These occasions were an important aspect of community life at the school. Through them, the different generations mingled and hierarchies were loosened.[83]

In the school year of 1960 and 1961, Horst Rittel, the mathematician and professor of methodology, together with Archer, conducted a statistical study with his students trying to verify if there was a specific type of tie at the HfG. From the data they collected, they concluded that there was no dominant style to be identified. Beyond this study, the school did not give much thought to clothing. Despite Ulm's universal view on the designed world, clothing was apparently not something they considered in their theoretical frame. 'Don't exaggerate the importance of clothing at the Ulm school', Klaus Krippendorff says,

Top: Saturday night dance, Dining Hall, Lake Eden campus, Black Mountain College, circa 1945. Photograph courtesy of the Western Regional Archives, State Archives of North Carolina.

Bottom: Costume carnival party at HfG Ulm, 1968. Photograph by Wolfgang Siol, courtesy of HfG-Archiv / Museum Ulm.

212 Stripping down and dressing up

Top: Irene Von Debschnitz Schawinsky (centre) teaching a dressmaking class at Black Mountain College in 1937. Next to her are Anni Albers and John Andrew Rice. Photograph courtesy of the Western Regional Archives, State Archives of North Carolina.

Bottom: Clog sandals by the German brand Berkemann, as worn by many people at HfG Ulm during the time that Susanne Eppinger Curdes was a student there, from 1958 to 1962. Photograph courtesy of Susanne Eppinger Curdes.

with his wife, Irene Von Debschnitz Schawinsky, who was a trained fashion designer and who gave a course in dressmaking during that time. Two years later, the couple moved to New York, and with their departure the dressmaking classes ended as well. Much of the college's curriculum depended on the teachers who came and went.

During their short visit during the summer session of 1944, Bernard and Berta Rudofsky not only taught the practical crafting of clothes. On a more critical level, they addressed the sad state of dress as a central problem of living. The Rudofskys had their students critically examine their own clothes. They were asked to draw the patterns of their garments, a task that was intended to alert them to the absurdities of modern fashion. Berta Rudofsky helped the students make their own clothing and accessories using different techniques,[68] and sandals were only one aspect of this hands-on investigation. Their class description in the brochure for that Summer Institute also mentions 'uncut types of clothes improvised by students', and 'headgear and footwear investigated'. As part of the class, Bernard Rudofsky held critical lectures with titles such as: 'Man's unwillingness to accept the anatomic form of the human body as satisfactory and definite'; 'Topography of modesty'; 'Corporal decoration among primitive and civilized peoples'; and 'Contemporary dress: anachronistic, irrational, impractical, harmful'.[69] As student Hazel Brister Harris remembers, the class addressed fashion that deforms the body with 'foundation garments, shoes that warp the feet and whatnot'.[70] She vividly recalls the two teachers describing the 'sixteen

'it was very informal and not much talked about'.[84]

Gerda Müller-Krauspe offers one explanation as to why the school challenged so many aspects of design but not those of dress. She speculates that 'one could also see it as smart tactics, to not bring oneself into the position of an eccentric outsider, which one already assumed in one way or another'. And that it would also convey an 'impression of "stable" conditions towards the students and guest teachers they were recruiting'.[85]

But could it be that an abstinence towards what is fashionable might be a key ingredient in the school's disinterest in clothing or dress? One of the reasons why Samuel Roth came to study at Ulm in 1955, after finishing an apprenticeship in the textile industry, was: 'I enjoyed the craftsmanship aspects and technical challenges of the profession, but I had my issues with the constant changing of fashion: what was good today, was outdated on the next day — out. That really annoyed me.'[86] Still today, Klaus Krippendorff wears the kind of turtleneck sweaters that he started wearing during his time at the HfG — and he also still prefers to write in lowercase letters.[87] Another favourite item of his was a pair of clog sandals, of a type worn by many people while he was attending the school. 'Regrettably, I had to give that up as I came to the US', he says about them, 'partly because I couldn't find them here and partly because they became impractical'.[88] Susanne Eppinger Curdes also vividly remembers these sandals. To her, they were 'the epitome of simplicity and avoiding the unnecessary'.[89] Krippendorff generally relates the way he started to shape his layers of cloth around a man's neck' — if one counts all the linings, inner-linings and foldings of a man wearing a dress shirt, a necktie and a coat.[71]

Shortly after the Summer Institute of 1944, Bernard Rudofsky opened his exhibition *Are Clothes Modern?* at the Museum of Modern Art in New York. The show started with the following wall text, a disclaimer of sorts: 'WARNING: This is not a fashion or dress reform exhibition. It aims to show how and why we dress as we do, and how greatly clothing influences our behavior.'[72] In the show's press release, Rudofsky questioned the reason why clothing, 'one of the essentials of life',[73] had up until that point resisted any rational investigation, unlike food or shelter had received in modern times. For him, this was especially puzzling considering 'certain striking similarities of dress and architecture'. He wrote: 'It is perfectly useless for us to invent new architectural organisms and new structures for houses, so that life may flow along in them with a new naturalness, if we persist in keeping the body imprisoned within the caprices of irrational fashion.'[74] Thinking about how we dress should precede thinking about the houses we live in. And with that thought in mind, Rudofsky designed an exhibition that intended to disturb basic ideas and conventions about the clothes we wear on a daily basis. The floor was purposely uneven, intended to reconnect the visitors with their own feet, and a mirror was placed at the exit, forcing the viewers to confront their own choice of clothing. Through its spatial experience, the exhibition confronted certain blind spots when it comes to the absurdities of dress.

appearance more to rational or practical considerations than to fashionable trends. Reasoning why he cut his hair short, for instance, he says that 'the philosophy of minimalism, the value put on not being pretentious, not to compete with fashionable appearances, and purely practical considerations made me do it'.[90]

However, in his 2006 book *The Semantic Turn*, Krippendorff writes that people often do not choose items such as cars, food or clothing because of their functional value, but because of their semantic value. Not for what they do, but for what they mean. 'What matters is whether one feels good in them or not', Krippendorff writes, 'and this feeling depends, at least in part, on expectations of what other people might say about how one looks in them'.[91] He goes on to mention the example of high-heeled shoes as something that women wear for reasons of presentation and not comfort: when a woman comes home from a formal occasion, the first thing she does is remove her uncomfortable shoes.

When he talks about our 'reliance' on objects, Krippendorff also offers a hint as to why we don't give much thought to our everyday items of dress. While we are using artefacts, they 'become background, like breathing, wearing shoes, and walking, which can be taken for granted in view of the activity that really matters', he writes.[92] After a while, these everyday artefacts become invisible.[93] Our concern for these objects fades, and so too our inclination to question them. Through this process, each and every one of us develops certain blind spots when it comes to the significance of dress.

Top: Lunch on the roof, Lee Hall, Blue Ridge Campus, Black Mountain College, circa 1939. Photograph courtesy of the Western Regional Archives, State Archives of North Carolina.

Bottom: Students in the mensa (canteen) at HfG Ulm, circa 1966–1967. Photograph from the estate of Herbert W. Kapitzki, courtesy of HfG-Archiv / Museum Ulm.

Looking back and moving on

We say that 'clothes make the woman or the man'. This means that people will judge you based on what you wear. Even though we use such idioms in everyday speech, and thereby implicitly acknowledge the importance of dress, it seems that we have a persistent blind spot when it comes to the social significance and normalised absurdities of dress in design and art education. We always communicate something through the clothes we wear. Whether consciously or unconsciously, our external appearance plays a crucial role in defining our personal identities within society. What happens in life in general, also happens in schools. They are, in many ways, microcosms that mirror the world at large.

Education is a complex phenomenon, but in many ways also an invisible one. The real changes that education fosters happen within us, hidden from easy detection. Yet, the clothes we wear can be viewed as indicators of what happens in this transformative process and context. They are visible signs that point to the exterior and interior circumstances of a school. They give hints about group assimilations that happen naturally. They can point to the invisible changes that take place when we become educated. But, beyond that, the clothes we wear to class might even have a reciprocal influence on the way we think.

We also say 'put on your thinking cap', hinting at how an item of clothing, even if imagined, might influence our cognitive abilities. In recent years, researchers have started looking into what they call 'enclothed cognition'— or how what we wear affects the way we think. In one study from 2015, for instance, a team of psychologists from California State University, Northridge, and Columbia University asked undergraduate students to bring in two sets of clothes. One set was to be more formal: 'clothing you would wear to a job interview', they directed the students. The other, more casual: 'clothing you would wear to class'. The students were asked to perform cognitive tests, once dressed formally, once casually. The results showed that wearing formal clothing can be associated with more abstract processing, making us think more broadly and holistically. This happens because formal clothing is usually worn in an environment that is less casual and familiar, a place with increased 'social distance'. This, in turn, makes us think with greater social distance.[94]

After screening his very successful documentary film *Helvetica* several times around the world, filmmaker Gary Hustwit remarked: 'One thing I discovered was that graphic design students are exactly the same in every country and even look exactly the same. They wear the same clothes. It is a truly global network of designers. I did feel very much like I was showing the film to the same group 90 different times.'[95]

But is that really true? Do graphic design students today really all look the same? Perhaps Hustwit too quickly formed a solidified image, a single story. But if Hustwit's perception is accurate, then what does that say about the current state of graphic design education? Are design schools around the world becoming increasingly similar? Or is it less the schools than the global pervasiveness of blogs, websites and social media that wields an increasing aesthetic influence? Is the design field feeling the ill effects of our living in what Marshall McLuhan described as a 'global village'? Rather than leading to cultural diversity, is this global village producing a global monoculture? Is graphic design turning into a single story? To examine this in all of its complexity, we would have to tackle our blind spot and follow the trails of influence that lie behind the clothes we wear. We would have to strip down our dressing up.

1   This description is based on a photograph belonging to the Black Mountain College Project Collection, Clifford Moles Series, photographs: image of Shirley Moles and Diane Moles sandals, available at the Western Regional Archives. From other descriptions, it seems credible that there were different styles of sandals.
2   Martin B. Duberman, *Black Mountain: An Exploration in Community* (New York: E. P. Dutton and Company, 1972), 38.
3   Patricia Gay Lynch interviewed by Mary Emma Harris, 20 January 1972. Available at the Western Regional Archives, North Carolina.
4   Hazel Brister Harris interviewed by Mary Emma Harris and Geraldine Berg, 27 October 1970. Available at the Western Regional Archives, North Carolina.
5   Black Mountain College Bulletin, Art Institute Summer 1944, 6–9.
6   Black Mountain College Bulletin, Art Institute Summer 1945, 6.
7   Hazel Brister Harris interviewed by Mary Emma Harris and Geraldine Berg.
8   See: https://black-mountain-research. com/2014/09/30/kenneth-noland, accessed 14 August 2017.
9   This description is based on a photograph provided by Susanne Eppinger Curdes. 'Hochschule für Gestaltung' translates as 'School of Design', but the German name and abbreviation are often used to refer to the school in English texts.
10 Of a total of 637 enrolled students, only 97 were women. See: René Spitz, *HfG Ulm: The View behind the Foreground: The Political History of the Ulm School of Design, 1953–1968* (Stuttgart: Edition Axel Menges, 2002), 19.
11 Susanne Eppinger Curdes in an email to the authors, 1 November 2016; own translation.
12 Own translation. Original: 'Die Cravatte des Individualisten', as viewed on the original document at the HfG Archive, ref. 'Dp 039.017'.
13 See: https://oregonencyclopedia.org/articles/ fort_rock_sandals/#.WZF09 MaB22w, accessed 14 August 2017.
14 Roger A. Wicker, *Black Mountain College: An Experiment in Education* (Nashville, TN: Southern Student Organizing Committee, 1968).
15 Vincent Katz and Martin Brody, *Black Mountain College: Experiment in Art* (Cambridge, MA: MIT Press, 2003).
16 Eva Diaz, *The Experimenters: Chance and Design at Black Mountain College* (Chicago: University of Chicago Press, 2014).
17 Eugen Blume, Matilda Felix, Gabriele Knapstein and Catherine Nichols, *Black Mountain: An Interdisciplinary Experiment, 1933–1957* (Leipzig, Spector Books, 2015).
18 See: https://hammer.ucla.edu/exhibitions/ 2016/leap-before-you-look-black-mountain- college-1933-1957/, accessed 20 December 2016.
19 Chimamanda Ngozi Adichie, 'The danger of a single story', lecture, available at: https://www. ted.com/talks/chimamanda_adichie_the_ danger_of_a_single_story, accessed 16 August 2017.
20 Ibid.
21 See: https://www.tiesncuffs.com.au/pages/ the-history-of-the-tie, accessed 14 August 2017.
22 See: https://www.youtube.com/ watch?v=oThApiIH7dM&feature=youtu.be, accessed 14 August 2017.
23 Dagmar Rinker, Marcela Quijano and Brigitte Reinhardt & Ulm Museum/HfG Archive, eds., *ulmer modelle – modelle nach ulm (ulm models – models after ulm): Ulm School of Design 1953–68* (Stuttgart: Hatje Cantz, 2003).
24 See: http://www.hfg-archiv.ulm.de/english/ exhibitions/past_exhibitions.html, accessed 20 December 2016.
25 Women represented only a little more than 15 percent of the enrolments, a rate that was lower than other German universities. See: Spitz, *View behind the Foreground*, 19.
26 Ngozi Adichie, 'The danger of a single story'.
27 Ibid.
28 Black Mountain College Bulletin of 1943, available at: http://toto.lib.unca.edu/ findingaids/mss/bmcmac/01_bmcmac_ publications/bmcmac_pub_10_1943-44/ bmc_10_catalog_1943-44/default_catalog_ 1943-44.htm, accessed 14 August 2017.
29 See: 'Louis Menand on John Dewey and Black Mountain College', https://www.youtube.com/ watch?v=D1RhAGgoRCE, accessed 14 August 2017.
30 Louis Adamic, 'Education on a Mountain: The Story of Black Mountain College', *Harper's Magazine*, April 1936, 523–525.
31 Duberman, *Black Mountain*, 38, italics in original.
32 Black Mountain College Bulletin, Art Institute Summer 1944, 11.
33 Black Mountain College Bulletin, 1949–1950, 11.
34 Black Mountain College Bulletin, 1952–1953, 26.

35 Mary Emma Harris, *The Arts at Black Mountain College* (Cambridge, MA: MIT Press, 1987), 66.
36 See: http://blackmountaincollegeproject.org/MEMOIRS/TREICHLERwilliam MEMOIR.htm, accessed 20 December 2016.
37 Roberta Blair, 'The First Day at BMC', in *Black Mountain College: Sprouted Seeds: An Anthology of Personal Accounts*, edited by Martin Lane (Knoxville: University of Tennessee Press, 1990), 134.
38 Ibid.
39 Patricia Gay Lynch interviewed by Mary Emma Harris.
40 Jorge Fick and Cynthia Homire Fick, interviewed by Mary Emma Harris, 4 February 1972. Available at the Western Regional Archives, North Carolina.
41 David Silver in a Skype interview with the authors, 4 November 2015.
42 Ibid.
43 'Opinions of former students: no agreement', in Black Mountain College Bulletin, vol. 6, no. 1, January 1948, 1.
44 Mary Emma Harris, *The Arts at Black Mountain College* (Cambridge, MA: MIT Press, 1987), 66.
45 Patricia Gay Lynch interviewed by Mary Emma Harris.
46 Frederick A. Horowitz and Brenda Danilowitz, eds., *Josef Albers: To Open Eyes* (London: Phaidon Press, 2006), 79.
47 Spitz, *HfG Ulm: The View behind the Foreground*, 40.
48 René Spitz and Jens Müller, *HfG Ulm: Kurze Geschichte Der Hochschule für Gestaltung: Anmerkungen zum Verhältnis von Design und Politik / Brief History of the Ulm School of Design: Notes on the Relationship between Design and Politics* (Zürich: Lars Müller, 2014), 26.
49 Spitz, *HfG Ulm: The View behind the Foreground*, 19.
50 Bernhard Rübenach, *Der rechte Winkel von Ulm: ein Bericht über die Hochschule für Gestaltung 1958/59* (Berlin: Verlag der Georg Büchner Buchhandlung, 1987).
51 Ibid., 47; own translation.
52 Rübenach, *Der rechte Winkel von Ulm*, 37; own translation.
53 Martin Krampen and Günther Hörnman, *The Ulm School of Design: Beginnings of a Project of Unyielding Modernity* (Berlin: Ernst & Son, 2003), 197.
54 See: Gerda Müller-Krauspe, *Selbstbehauptungen: frauen an der hfg ulm* (Frankfurt Am Main: Anabas, 2007), 147.
55 Susanne Eppinger Curdes in an email to the authors, 1 November 2016; own translation.
56 Klaus Krippendorff in an email to the authors, 1 November 2016.
57 Ibid.
58 Ann Wolff, in *Rückblicke: Die Abteilung Visuelle Kommunikation an Der Hfg Ulm 1953–1968*, edited by Barbara Stempel and Hochschule für Gestaltung Ulm (Ulm: Club Off Ulm, 2010), 121; own translation.
59 Rübenach, *Der rechte Winkel von Ulm*, 30; own translation.
60 Müller-Krauspe, *Selbstbehauptungen*, 148; own translation.
61 Klaus Krippendorff in an email to the authors, 1 November 2016.
62 Günther Elstner, 'Ein Blick zurück an die hfg ulm: Visuelle Kommunikation', in *Rückblicke: Die Abteilung Visuelle Kommunikation an Der Hfg Ulm 1953–1968*, edited by Barbara Stempel and Hochschule für Gestaltung Ulm (Ulm: Club Off Ulm, 2010), 188; own translation.
63 Gerhard Curdes, *HFG Ulm: 21 Rückblicke: Bauen, Gemeinschaft, Doktrinen* (Ulm: Club Off Ulm, 2006), 88.
64 Josef Albers, 'Concerning Art Instruction', in Black Mountain College Bulletin, series 1, no. 2, June 1934, available at: http://blackmountaincollegeproject.org/PUBLICATIONS/BMCB%20SERIES%201/BMCB%20SERIES%201%202%20ALBERS%201/BMCB%20SERIES%201%20 2%20ALBERS.htm.
65 See: http://www.blackmountaincollegeproject.org/MEMOIRS/RITTENHOUSEtreichlerMarthaMEMOIR.htm, accessed 20 December 2016.
66 Patricia Gay Lynch interviewed by Mary Emma Harris.
67 Interview with Ati Gropius Johansson by Sigrid Pawelke, 2010, available at http://black-mountain-research.com/2015/07/10/interview-with-ati-gropius-johansson/, accessed 20 December 2016.
68 Black Mountain College Bulletin, April 1944, vol. II, no. 6, 6.
69 Ibid.
70 Hazel Brister Harris interviewed by Mary Emma Harris and Geraldine Berg.
71 Ibid.
72 Museum of Modern Art, 'Are Clothes Modern?', press release, available at: https://www.moma.org/momaorg/shared/pdfs/docs/press_archives/963/releases/MOMA_1944_0049_1944-11-27_441127-41.pdf?2010, accessed 20 December 2016.
73 Bernard Rudofsky in Museum of Modern Art, 'Are Clothes Modern?'.
74 Bernhard Rudofsky, 'What's Needed Is Not a New Way of Building, What's Needed Is a New Way of Life (Comments on a design for a house on the island of Procida)', in Andrea Bocco Guarneri, *Bernard Rudofsky: A Humane Designer* (Vienna: Springer, 2003), 178. Originally published as: 'Non ci vuole un nuovo modo di construire ci vuole un nuovo modo di vivere', in *Domus*, no. 123, March 1938, 2–3.
75 Klaus Krippendorff in an email to the authors, 31 October 2016.

76 Ibid.
77 See: Herbert Lindinger, *Hochschule für Gestaltung Ulm: Die Moral der Gegenstände* (Berlin: Wilhelm Ernst & Sohn, 1987), 82.
78 Ibid., 94.
79 Frank Hess, 'Diploma projects: Protective Suit (1965)', in: *ulm 19/20: Journal of the Ulm School for Design*, August 1967, 64–5.
80 These pictures were viewed by the authors at the HfG-Archiv, ref. 'Kasten 3, 2.1.4.5, Feste'.
81 See: Gerhard Curdes, 'Industrialisiertes Bauen', in *HFG Ulm: 21 Rückblicke: Bauen, Gemeinschaft, Doktrinen*, edited by Gerhard Curdes (Ulm: Club Off Ulm, 2006), 89; and Klaus Krippendorff, 'Designing in Ulm and off Ulm: Die Abteilung Produktgestaltung: 39 Rückblicke*, edited by Karl-Achim Czemper and Club off Ulm (Dortmund: Verlag Dorothea Rohn, 2008), 55–72.
82 Krippendorff, 'Designing in Ulm and off Ulm'.
83 Gerhard Curdes, 'Einleitung', in *HFG Ulm: 21 Rückblicke: Bauen, Gemeinschaft, Doktrinen*, edited by Gerhard Curdes (Ulm: Club Off Ulm, 2006), 8.
84 Klaus Krippendorff in an email to the authors, 31 October 2016.
85 Müller-Krauspe, *Selbstbehauptungen*, 148–9; own translation.
86 Barbara Stempel and Hochschule für Gestaltung Ulm, *Rückblicke: Die Abteilung Visuelle Kommunikation an der HfG Ulm 1953-1968* (Ulm: Club Off Ulm, 2010), 60; own translation.
87 Klaus Krippendorff in an email to the authors, 1 November 2016.
88 Ibid.
89 Susanne Eppinger Curdes in an email to the authors, 1 November 2016; own translation.
90 Klaus Krippendorff in an email to the authors, 31 October 2016.
91 Klaus Krippendorff, *The Semantic Turn: A New Foundation for Design* (Boca Raton: Taylor & Francis, 2006), 48–9.
92 Ibid., 132.
93 Ibid., 133.
94 Michael L. Slepian, Simon N. Ferber, Joshua M. Gold and Abraham M. Rutchick, 'The Cognitive Consequences of Formal Clothing', *Social Psychological and Personality Science*, 6, no. 6 (2015): 661–668.
95 Virginia Postrel, 'What's in a Font?', *The Atlantic*, January/February 2008.

Two schools of thought
Fraser Muggeridge,
interviewed by Paul Mylecharane

Fraser Muggeridge is a graphic designer and occasional teacher, who leads a small but notoriously prolific team at his eponymous studio in London. He teaches on two very different university graphic design programmes — the BA Graphic Design at Camberwell College of Arts, University of Arts London, and the MA Book Design in the Department of Typography & Graphic Communication at the University of Reading. He is also the founder of Typography Summer School, an independent, week-long programme of typographic study for recent graduates and professionals, which has been held in London since 2010, in New York since 2013 and in Melbourne once (in 2015). In this interview, Muggeridge discusses his own education, the values of different pedagogies, the importance of independent education initiatives, and the ways in which one's practice as an educator can inform or be entwined with one's studio practice.

I first met Fraser Muggeridge in 2015, when he came to Melbourne to run Typography Summer School. I was unable to attend the workshop, but Fraser and I did spend some good times together and discovered that we shared a mutual interest in education and graphic design on the periphery. What I noticed most about him in the few days we spent together was his generosity and curiosity: his willingness to share his experience and knowledge, and his excitement for discovering new things. These qualities seem to drive his practice both as a designer and as an educator.

That same year, Fraser invited me to participate in a project during his design residency at the Barbican in London for Doug Aitken's thirty-day happening, *Station to Station*. The 'residents' were housed in a studio complex created to service the gallery space. Fraser had invited a few of his students from Camberwell College of Arts, as well as a cast of artists and designers, such as myself, to contribute to the public atelier model. It was a great way for me to see firsthand how Fraser operates in a workshop setting, focusing on making through an experimental approach. Most of the objects produced during the week were facsimiles of Fraser's past studio work, made using analogue techniques, a few plotting machines and a WaterColorBot. Some of the posters and record sleeves produced went on sale downstairs in the gift shop — these were the deliverables required by Doug and the Barbican — but the rest was freeform creativity.

Since that experience, I've been curious to find out more about Fraser's practice as an educator. I wanted to understand the duality of teaching in two institutions that are pedagogically very different, and how this experience might have informed the creation of a third, para-institution — Typography Summer School. I also wanted to find out how his approach in each of these educational contexts might in turn inform his studio practice, to understand how pedagogy might be embedded in his day-to-day graphic design work.

PM   Can you tell me about your own education at the University of Reading? And, given its reputation as a place of rigorous typographic training, how did you come to admire the approach of self-trained designers, such as Richard Kostelanetz, Pontus Hulten and Wolf Vostell?

FM   I had a privileged typographical education at the University of Reading. We were taught history, theory and the application of design through projects, workshops and 'real jobs'. For me, it was normal to attend a lecture by Robin Kinross, or a class with Gerard Unger, or Saturday morning sessions with James Moseley on the letter 'e'. We were exposed to Isotype, ephemera, legibility studies and print technology; it was a truly rich and thorough education that I refer back to almost every day.

But, after twenty years of practice, I also became interested in the figures who *haven't* made it into the canon of graphic design, for whatever reason: those figures who had no formal training, who didn't promote themselves, or who flew under the radar for other reasons.

I curated a show about this at the De La Warr Pavilion in 2015. It was a chance to share these outsider influences with a larger audience.[1] I think these lesser-known figures began to inform my work over a number of years as my approach shifted towards a disposition of 'un-knowing', or towards an experimental practice of making and doing that was less concerned with the end results. I've come to embrace both beauty and ugliness, legibility and illegibility, formality and chaos. The project *Shonky: The Aesthetics of Awkwardness* is probably the most ambitious and best realised result of this shift. It's the melding of both a rigorous, formal approach to typography and a desire to break the rules, to push the limits of what is acceptable in graphic design. *Shonky* takes a lot of risks in terms of legibility: both the letterforms and the layout (the centred arrangement, the placement of footnotes, and so on) are very unconventional. The integration of exhibition graphics and catalogue production, in terms of recycling and remixing, is also becoming an ongoing thread of exploration within my practice. At the root of it all is a desire to get out of my comfort zone, in order to push my craft and practice.

PM In terms of craft, can you talk about the fundamentals you learned at Reading and how they formed your understanding of detail in typography?

FM Early in my undergraduate studies, in the early 1990s, Michael Twyman gave a lecture titled 'Typography without Words', which used a simple notation to teach graphic variables and the basic hierarchy of typography.[2] Through examples composed of different combinations of 'x', 'o' and 'i' with varying indents and space around simulated headings and paragraphs, typography was simplified into an abstract graphic form and began to make sense to me: the use of positive forms and negative space to create structure, hierarchy and meaning. This became the real bedrock of my practice.

Another key element was understanding the relationship between type size, line length and leading. 'Dimensional relationships in the composition of text', published in The Stafford Papers in the 1970s, showed the same passage of text, set at the same size, with different line spacing (8-, 9-, 10-, 11- and 12-point leading) and different line lengths (27, 20 and 13 pica ems).[3] Through this example, I could immediately see the effect that each variable had on the others: the longer the line length, the more leading required. It highlighted the micro-detailing that makes a subtle yet recognisable difference when setting type. These two things are the framework that, in my opinion, underpins a solid typographic practice.

PM In terms of your own education, would you say it was a case of the sum being more than the parts? Or was there something or someone specific who made the experience so important and its influence so lasting?

FM The four basic beliefs that governed the course as it was set up by Michael Twyman in 1968 were:

> To communicate something using language.
> To understand the technical means at your disposal: print processes, computer and typeface technology.
> To respond to the needs of the reader, being able to read what you design.
> To plan in the context of a client, an organisation, a budget and a deadline.[4]

Without really knowing it, we were taken on a journey covering all aspects of graphic design and typography. My recent work as a typographer, however, intentionally reacts against contemporary norms and against a number of the conventions I learned at Reading — I have been trying to set myself apart from the mainstream by creating work that retains evidence of the designer's hand. In my recent work, I have intentionally used type design software the wrong way, or I have found typographic uses for software developed for other applications. This, coupled with a systems-driven approach, has led me to new ways of thinking about graphic design. I have been focusing on analysing and producing work through lenses that are not principally visual. I've been pushing back against the ubiquitous use of the computer in graphic design. I see these different forms of hacking type as a kind of 'digital analogueness' and as a reaction to perfectionism.

PM   Given how far you have been pushing these typographic experiments in your own work, would you say, in terms of your approach as an educator, that there is as much importance in 'un-learning' as there is in learning the technical details of typography? Should the two fit side-by-side as an approach to learning and teaching, or do you take a hierarchical approach and teach the fundamentals first?

FM   I would definitely teach the fundamentals first. And I wouldn't call it a process of 'un-learning', but rather one of learning to improvise once the fundamentals are fully understood. I still feel that the most important thing I teach in typography is the relationship between type size, line length and leading — the core concepts I took from Reading — and the importance of changing the little things in order to create the best typography for a given project. I'm less inclined to focus on graphic design as a big idea or concept. Learning the fundamentals is key to having the ability to experiment more.

PM   How do you take this focus on craftsmanship to your teaching at Camberwell? And, vice versa, do you try to introduce free experimentation into your teaching at Reading? Do you see a fundamental difference in the work produced by students at the two schools? And could you perhaps explain the differences between the two institutions?

FM   At Camberwell, we fully encourage the use of the print facilities — the letterpress, screenprinting, etching and stone lithography facilities. We often build these into projects, or they can be the entire focus of a project. I ran a project there called 'Type High', in collaboration with the letterpress technician James Edgar. I wanted students to explore the idea of image-making through letterpress printing — or maybe it was just a project that I wanted to do myself! The idea came to me at a karaoke bar in New York, on the last day of Typography Summer School in 2015. I found a huge bar mat that had holes in it, it was roughly A3 in size, and I thought, I really want to print that! So I stole it, took it back to the UK and printed it — that was my contribution to the project! So the project was actually not a typographic exercise per se, but it was about composition and the tension between

Barcelona Offset, 2017. Experimental offset prints made by Fraser Muggeridge in collaboration with Ariadna Serrahima at L'Automàtica, Barcelona. The effect is made by squirting water and/or gasoline onto the press while printing with multiple colours using a split fountain technique. Photograph by Fraser Muggeridge.

positive and negative space, which is so important to understanding how good typography functions. There were sixteen people in the workshop. Each was asked to bring in a random object that was 2.3 centimetres high, in order to be printable on the letterpress machine. These objects — a block of chocolate, a magnifying glass, a banana, and so on — were then laid out together on the press to form a 16-page section of a book (although the sheet also works as a poster). It was a collaborative design and making process, including the control of the press. The students' faces lit up when they saw that they had created something interesting and beautiful together — it was a magical moment.

To be clear, Camberwell and Reading are two different places, with different sets of tutors offering two very different courses. Reading is a serious research centre for the study of language and typography, and Camberwell is an art school in South London. But, over time, I have definitely been able to take parts of each into teaching at the other. It has also been a really important process for my own practice — to have the mix of formalism and experimentation at the root of what I do, whether in the classroom or in the studio.

PM   Are there specific ways in which you encourage students to break away from their preconceptions about typography and graphic design? Apart from experimenting with different modes of creation, is research or critique a part of that process?

FM   Briefs that explore an expanded vision of graphic design help to encourage this, such as the 'Fashion and Graphic Design' project that Robert Sollis and I have run at Camberwell since 2017. By introducing other elements such as fashion into the mix, students can become absorbed by the project while learning the fundamentals of graphic design along the way. Apart from creating their own fashion object or piece of clothing, the students created their own support structures for the exhibition. Every student had their part to play in the design, production, communication and organisation of the show. Their remit was also to produce an identity for the exhibition and all of the associated graphic outcomes, both print and digital.

In terms of critique, I'm probably quite hard on students! I think the process of a crit is actually a great learning experience for anyone. Often students think that when they come to a crit, it's like, 'oh, I'm going to hand in my work, someone is going to talk about it and hopefully they'll say something nice'. But, actually, I organise a crit so that it can be an opportunity for self-critique. I ask students to write down what they've learned during a particular project on a big sheet of paper and they stick these on the wall so they can all see each other's texts. That way, they become more aware of what they're learning.

PM   You've spent a significant amount of time teaching in these two institutions. Did this experience motivate you to start Typography Summer School? You obviously saw a space for an alternative education model outside of the academy?

FM   Absolutely. My main reason for initiating Typography Summer School was that I felt that students were graduating from undergraduate courses in graphic design still not having a strong sense of what typography is and how it functions — of all the moving parts. Recent graduates would come to see me in the studio and show me their research projects on 'dreams' or 'culture' or whatever, and expect to get a job based on self-initiated projects alone. I would be thinking, 'Well, if I gave you some corrections to do, firstly, would you be able to do the task, and, secondly, would you do it with a sense of pride, rigour and professionalism?' Much of graphic design is not about creativity — there are many pedestrian tasks to be done. Particularly in publishing, it's often about taking a style guide and applying it carefully.

   I also started to see that students had become pigeonholed by learning a particular style at a particular school, producing work that reflected a specific tutor's approach. I had a hunch that if I could get twenty-five recent graduates together in a room for a week with a revolving cast of professional practitioners, we could really teach them some useful things in a short amount of time. The most important thing was that I also wanted them to get a sense of how graphic design functions in the real world. That's something I learned early on at Reading. So much of one's practice as a graphic designer is about communication, not *through* design, but *in support of* design: one's relationship to the client and to the printer, creating and communicating budgets, etc. At Reading, we had what were called 'real jobs'. These were projects that would come into the department. They would often be really simple jobs, like designing a business card or a leaflet, or a little exhibition catalogue, or sometimes a book. We would have to organise and attend a meeting with the client, prepare a budget and a timeline that included revisions and a production schedule, along with the actual typographic work and presentations. It was a totally non-abstract process. We would have a supervisor, one of our tutors, and I personally learned a great deal about how to deal with clients, what finished artwork is, how it relates to getting something printed — it was sort of like a mini work experience. And, at the end of it, you had a project in your portfolio that was a result of your work with an actual client-led brief. I took this approach directly into the Summer School model because I found that it was such a valuable experience. A lot of summer schools tend to focus more on creativity and an expanded sense of graphic design, which is definitely important, but I felt that the mechanics of the process needed more attention.

PM   Can you speak a little about the progression of your approach to Typography Summer School over the years? How do you approach the writing of the briefs, and the choice of practitioners you invite to lecture and teach?

FM   For the first few years, I formulated briefs with existing clients of mine. We would workshop stuff through the week with different tutors, then the clients would come in and the students would present to them. I tried to find briefs that would be challenging in different ways — projects that students could take something away from, even if they were seemingly simple. The main impetus was to help students to understand the process of addressing a client's needs through typography. But I also tried to emphasise the fact that, sometimes, in order to make interesting work, you need to educate a client in how to participate in the design process.

 This has evolved over the last few years into a framework in which the first few days are about rigorous typesetting — line length, leading, hierarchy, footnotes, page numbers, that kind of stuff. And then we give a brief for a project that will be the main outcome, which also includes a type design project. So: application and structure, form and analysis, with critique along the way. In some ways, I'm also trying to bridge the gap between a typographer's way of thinking and that of a type designer.

 The choice of tutors was really influenced by the range of practitioners that I had access to through Reading. A variety in terms of age, gender and experience is really important, as is a diversity in terms of the type of work they do — a cross-section of teachers, artists and designers is best. I've always wanted the students to get a rich and diverse perspective of all aspects of typography — both the formal and the experimental.

PM What space do you see Typography Summer School filling in graphic design education?

FM Well, for one thing, I feel that students learn a lot in a very short amount of time. Their eyes are opened to new ways of thinking and new approaches. They are exposed to a number of different tutors in quick succession. This is very different to the universities' approaches to education. The fact of being independent means that we can be far more playful and flexible with how things flow. Also, almost everywhere in the world, studying graphic design at a university today costs a lot of money and takes a long time, and I think a lot of students are sick of that. So, a short-term, workshop-based model offers an important alternative to more bureaucratic forms of education. Typography Summer School is small-scale, homespun, and it has a personal feel to it.

 Because the Typography Summer School class sizes are relatively small, students get to spend valuable time with the tutors. They get to receive feedback from practitioners who they recognise and respect. A lot of students are surprised by the amount of time they get with the tutors — they're like, 'what do you mean they're going to stay after their talk?' This personal feedback and advice is really important. Class sizes are so big in the UK now that students don't get the kind of in-depth feedback I received when I was a student. These big classes can result in a very impersonal experience of learning.

PM This is something I've struggled with too. Large class sizes make it particularly difficult to focus on craftsmanship.

FM Yes, the craft aspect is really important — the word has two meanings that are significant. Firstly, 'craft' can refer to a manual process of some kind. It is important to follow a tradition of making, to learn how things are made, the reason why things are the way they are, and then how to actually make those things. And, secondly, there is 'craft' as it relates to typography — meaning the micro-typographic details in the crafting of a design. I might, for example, spend a relatively short amount of time designing the basic layout of a poster, but I will spend a lot of time finessing the small typographic details.

In my experience, students are not taught much craft these days — or attention to detail, in other words. It all feels very surface-based and aesthetically driven. I guess it also has a lot to do with attention spans being shorter, what with the world of Instagram, Tumblr and cut-and-paste culture in general. I find that a lot of students find the details boring and not 'creative' enough. I also find that they're reluctant to get messy and to let go of their preconceived ideas about what design is. They're worried about fitting into a mould of what they think the design community expects, or about what might happen if their work doesn't conform to the conventions of contemporary graphic design.

PM So, what, if any, are the differences between your approach in the classroom and in the studio? Does one feed the other?

FM I think that over time my approaches in the studio and in the classroom have melded into one. I feel like they feed into each other more and more. These days, I feel confident running workshops in which I don't quite know what the outcomes will be, whereas in the past I would've tried to dictate the outcomes. A lot of people talk about teaching outcomes these days, don't they? In the institution, many learning outcomes are dictated in advance. I personally never want to go down the road of teaching solely based on expectations from above. In the end, it has to be about the experience of the students, making sure they go away with some significant tools with which they can expand their practices in the future. I'm also seeing that now, more than ever, you have to make the briefs for students exciting, otherwise they're just not interested in participating.

In terms of the question of how running workshops has fed into my studio practice, a starting point for me was the Barbican residency. It was the first time in a really long time that I spent experimenting with analogue techniques. It felt like going back to art school. But, actually, I never went to art school! Learning typography at Reading was a serious business. I didn't get to throw paint around or dip my hair in acid or whatever. So, during this residency, I could start the day by saying 'hey, let's do some screenprinting using hair spray as a resist'. It was like a liberating art school moment for me, and it felt a bit like a foundation course — which, again, is something I didn't do. I guess I've started to approach my practice more like an artist, but I'm still very much what I'd call a traditional graphic designer, in the sense that my work is produced solely for clients. I feel privileged that I get to take as many risks as I do — but I should say that it doesn't always work out. Clients have understandably freaked out about some of the approaches I've taken in the past few years!

The question I'm constantly asking myself is: how can a 'knowing wrongness' with regard to typographic experimentation and print processes lead to new forms within typographic practice? Most designers employ the same tools, visual references and production techniques, so how can any new work contain elements of bespokeness and creativity? And can ugliness and beauty co-exist?

Fraser Muggeridge, interviewed by Paul Mylecharane

This interview was commenced over email and online chat, and was concluded in Tokyo in 2018, where Mylecharane and Muggeridge both attended the Tokyo Type Directors Club Annual Awards.

1 *Towards an Alternative History of Graphic Design*, curated by Fraser Muggeridge, De La Warr Pavilion, Bexhill-on-Sea, UK, 8 August – 4 October 2015.

2 A version of this material is published as: Michael Twyman, 'Typography without Words', *Visible Language* 15, no. 1 (1981).

3 Peter Burnhill, *Dimensional relationships in the composition of text* (Stafford: Stafford College of Art and Design: 1970).

4 See: Michael Twyman, 'Typography as a university study', an address given at the meeting of The Wynkyn de Worde Society, 17 September 1970 (Reading: University of Reading, 1970), also reprinted in this volume.

Typography as a university study
Michael Twyman

Design historian and educator Michael Twyman joined the staff at the University of Reading in 1959. He was founding Head of the Department of Typography & Graphic Communication, which was established in 1974 and which has long been recognised as a centre of excellence in graphic design education and research. Although he has now retired from full-time academia, Twyman continues to work in the department as director of its Centre for Ephemera Studies. 'Typography as a university study' was originally delivered as an address to the Wynkyn de Worde Society, in Stationers' Hall, London, on 17 September 1970, and was distributed as a pamphlet to members and friends of the society. The address reflected on the then-recent introduction — in 1968 — of the four-year BA programme in Typography & Graphic Communication at Reading, outlining its pedagogical principles and aspirations.

I must confess that I am talking about the typography course we have recently introduced at Reading University with some misgivings — partly because I am a little suspicious of innovations in education generally, but mainly, I suppose, because I am suspicious of those who talk about them publicly. Education is not fundamentally about courses, syllabuses, teaching methods and so forth, but is concerned with the interaction of people and the sharing of interests and experience; and such things have not changed much over the years. However, your Honorary Secretary invited me to speak, and tempted me with the carrot of joining this illustrious society, so how could I refuse? Those of you who share my suspicions must just switch off for a while.

Like many innovations, the new course owes a lot to the past. It seems that typography has been taught at Reading University for over half a century — though I can tell you little more than this. One thing at least that universities seem to have in common with the printing industry is a reluctance to preserve their own records, and probably for equally good reasons. All I can really tell you, therefore, is that my immediate predecessors were William McCance, who managed the Gregynog Press for a time, and, before him, Robert Gibbings. The background was one, as you might imagine, firmly based on the English Private Press tradition, and students practised a little typesetting and designing as part of a degree course in Fine Art. This was my own introduction to typography, and I am grateful for it. All the same, it has seemed clear to me for some time that things would have to change if Reading was to play a very useful role in relation to the needs of society generally and those of our own industry in particular.

Consequently, a four-year BA honours course in Typography & Graphic Communication was introduced in 1968. In fact, the new title ratified some of the studies we had introduced under subterfuge over the previous few years; and, because of this, students were allowed to change their course mid-stream. The first such hybrid students graduated this year, the first generation of students taking the full course has just completed its first year's study, and the first intake of students who have specifically applied to follow the new course will join us in a fortnight's time.

I suppose we could have called the course 'Graphic Design', but the word design is so misunderstood in schools and art schools that we settled for the rather cumbersome title 'Typography & Graphic Communication'. In our view typography is the fundamental area of graphic design through which design method in general can be taught in relation to an industrial process. The word 'typography' is, of course, variously defined and interpreted according to one's profession and country of origin. We use it in a very broad sense to include all design in relation to printing and allied graphic processes, and to include the design and use of letterforms, whether for printing or not. Moxon's hallowed definition of a typographer, updated to include subsequent developments, is not so very far off the mark, even today.

The structure of the course at Reading is governed by four basic beliefs. No doubt these will sound rather trite to those of you involved with design for printing day after day, but if I outline them you will at least know what we stand for, and this might help to explain the nature of the course. First, we believe that typography starts with a concern to communicate something — the 'message', to use a fashionable term, or the copy if we are talking in practicalities — and that the visual form of typography should closely relate to the language used and its organisation reflect and reinforce its meaning. Second, that typographic designers must have a general understanding of the technical means at their disposal and the ability to come to terms with any specific technical situations which affect them. Third, that the needs of the reader must be respected and, in so far as we know what they are, should be central in designing. (And here I might say in parentheses that it is a happy coincidence that, of all universities, the one associated with typography, or design for reading, should be Reading. In spoken language there is no ambiguity here, but in written language there can be; and every student of typography at Reading is brought face to face with this problem very early on. It provides a powerful demonstration of the value of having both upper- and lower-case alphabets, and also serves to underline that typography is an extremely subtle tool and is concerned, as Tschichold has pointed out, with the sum of minutiae.) Fourth, we hold that typographic design is planning in relation to these three considerations, and usually in the context of a client, an industrial organisation, a budget and a deadline.

If I may now return to these propositions one by one, I shall try to explain how they are taken into account in relation to teaching.

First of all, the concern for the message or copy. Here I think I have to stress the value of some aspects of a traditional university education; by which I mean the writing of essays, preparation of seminars, opportunities to work and browse in a good library. These activities help to create a respect for language and learning, and encourage a precision of thought and expression, which are essential for a typographer. In some quarters learning from books is held in low esteem, and it is true that some learning is very much better done in other ways, but of all people surely typographers must have a respect for the printed word; and if they do not, then in my view they ought not to practise. In this connection perhaps the most valuable part of the course is the dissertation which students prepare in their final year. This puts them in the position of originator of ideas and writer of copy, and they experience in a fairly modest way, but usually very forcefully, that the message is really very important when it is their own. This attempt to encourage a respect for the meaning of copy is largely a by-product of one of the teaching methods, but we also approach the problem directly through practical work done in the studio where we lay stress on the relationship between content and visual organisation.

Second, the need for a clear understanding of the means of production. The whole of the teaching of typography at Reading is rooted in the printing workshop, and this is the most important legacy of my predecessors. Though the facilities are extremely limited, and even old fashioned, they demonstrate well enough the principle of the relationship of design to production. Once this principle is understood, it can be applied to new and varied situations as they arise. We still, for instance, place great faith in the hand-setting of type as a means of introducing students to the subject — not for any purist or ideological reasons, but simply because it gets to the very essence of what typography is all about: the organisation of standardised units, letter by letter, word by word, line by line. And this applies whether the means is a setting stick or a computer. I should perhaps add that we do not stop there.

We regard familiarity with a keyboard as important for the same reasons, and instruct students in the use of an IBM composer and an Intertype composing machine. These composition systems are backed up by reasonable facilities for simple letterpress machining, and in the near future we shall be installing a small litho unit.

What we are able to offer ourselves in respect of machinery is very limited at present, though we make the most of what we have, and students really do become familiar with the limitations it imposes on design. In any case, we supplement this kind of instruction with classes in printing methods, visits to printing works, and the local College of Technology arranges special printing classes to fill the most obvious gaps in this field. At the other end of the technological spectrum, students attend a year's course of classes in the Applied Physical Sciences Department of the University where they are introduced to computers, programming, and a simple graphic display system. Governing our whole approach to the teaching of production methods is the belief that we should be mainly concerned with underlying principles and educating our students for change. Learning one system draws attention to the problems of working within another system, and, of course, makes it that much easier to learn about a new one when the need arises.

Third, under the heading needs of the reader, I would include the visual aspects of design. We approach these through the usual kind of studio work, through projects designed to explore particular problems, and real jobs which provide some kind of feedback. This occupies much of the greatest part of a student's time and is difficult to describe in a few words, but it includes drawing, photography, lettering, preparation of layouts, visuals, art work and so forth.

We accept that most visual judgements are largely subjective, and while we make every attempt to foster visual awareness, and are obviously concerned with the appearance of things and matters of quality, such issues are always raised in relation to particular situations. One other way we hope to encourage visual awareness is through classes in design criticism in which students themselves assess the value of a particular piece of design. Another is through classes in the history of typography and letterforms in which students are brought into contact with work of accepted quality, whether it is fashionable or not. And we are particularly fortunate in having recourse to good collections of original material in the University Library and elsewhere.

In addition to the more subjective aspects of visual judgement, which are faced empirically in studio work and design criticism, students take a course in perception in our Psychology Department and are introduced to legibility studies and experimental methods. We feel that students should know how to evaluate the effectiveness of particular kinds of work should this ever be necessary but, above all, that they should be able to assess the value of experimental work undertaken by others.

I suggested earlier that the typographer's consideration for the meaning of copy and the needs of the reader had to be considered in relation to an industrial organisation. This often calls for human qualities which it may not be in our power to do much about; but students are at least given modest experience of being in job situations while they are at Reading. They are quite used to being given the entire responsibility of meeting clients, seeing jobs

Top: Printing workshop at the University of Reading, 1970.

Bottom: University of Reading students on a fieldtrip, viewing the unseen lettering on the Column of Trajan, Rome, circa 1972.

through the press, and taking on all the administrative work in connection with them. One of those small privileges in teaching is to see young students handle their first clients, bring some semblance of order to a chaotic brief, and experience the pleasure of a successfully completed job. Printing still has a touch of magic about it for the beginner — even old Gutenberg's printing of the kind we practise. Experience of this kind is richly rewarding for students; it allows them to see that design is more than a drawing-board activity, and is concerned with human needs — and human limitations.

How, you may ask, does all this work out in practice? Like all acts of designing, planning such a course has to be done in relation to the hard realities: shortage of money, staff, equipment, accommodation and, of course, the existing structure of the University. What we have at Reading is by no means an ideal course, and I am not necessarily advocating its pattern elsewhere.

During their first year, students of Typography, like all other students in the University, read two other subjects for two terms. These can be chosen from the entire range of subjects offered by the Faculty of Letters and Social Sciences. In return, students of other subjects may take Typography if they choose to do so; and this might well have interesting repercussions.

After sitting the First University Examination at the beginning of the summer term of the first year, students spend their remaining three years in Typography. During the second and third years they combine their practical work in the studios with various courses of lectures and seminars covering printing methods, history of typography, perception and legibility studies, design criticism, theory of typography, and an introduction to computers. In this period they also opt for a special subject which is taught by another department. At the end of their third year students take five theoretical papers covering various aspects of typography and the special subject.

In their final year students begin to work much more independently. There is no threat of an examination of the traditional kind, and they concentrate their activities on preparing a body of practical design work and writing a dissertation on some aspect of typography. This work is submitted at the end of the fourth year and students are assessed in the light of this and their performance in the third year examination.

At some stage in their course a student is expected to work in industry for about three months. We cannot be too specific about these arrangements at present because of the difficulty of finding good firms, within easy travelling distance of Reading or students' homes, who are prepared to take on a student from time to time.

I should perhaps say a word or two about research work, which is, of course, a vital activity in any university department. Research into aspects of printing history has been undertaken at Reading for a good many years, and I hope this interest will continue. We also have a research programme centred on the design and use of graphic material in schools which we are undertaking in association with our own Psychology Department. Similar research in conjunction with other departments must be undertaken if Typography is to develop, as I feel it must, as an interdisciplinary subject. Here in particular lies the significance of some of the undergraduate teaching: we hope to be able to provide our students, or at least some of them, with sufficient understanding of other disciplines to enable them to undertake some kind of interdisciplinary research, whether in the field of psychology, linguistics, sociology, management, engineering, or whatever. It is my own belief that typography has missed out on research work of this kind largely because there has been no university providing undergraduates both interested in and capable of research work in such fields.

I notice from the announcement of this meeting that I am invited to offer hopes for the future. Looking into the crystal ball is discouraging for anyone in education today; there is usually much that one would like to do, and precious little to do it with. My view at present is that our major growth point should be in postgraduate work — in areas such as communication research, in the study of the function of design in an industrial context, the history of typography, and, what seems to me a most pressing need in the world today, a study of comparative typography.

I should also like to see a closer relationship between industry and ourselves at all levels. I have already mentioned at least one way in which industry can and does help by taking undergraduates for short periods, but I should also like to see the movement in another direction, and would welcome the opportunity, and would dearly like to have the financial means, to invite top people from industry to conduct seminars and contribute to series of lectures. Looking further ahead, it ought to be made possible to consider the secondment of interested parties in industry, who could be given an opportunity to recharge their batteries at a university by undertaking work of their own. We might not be able to help in a very positive way, but at least we could provide a good library, an environment which is conducive to study, and some very open minds.

I am often asked what areas of the industry we are aiming at in our new course. I believe that is the wrong question to have to answer. We are concerned with giving a broadly based education with typography at its core, and with producing graduates who can exercise independent thought and judgement and are capable of adapting to the changes which lie ahead.

It was only after the course was underway, and after talking to some of the students, that I realised to the full what an enormously rich subject ours is from the educational point of view. It certainly presents a solution to some of the educational problems of today: it is a rewarding subject in its own right, and yet offers career possibilities of many kinds, as well as an opportunity to serve a useful social purpose; it bridges the arts and the sciences and offers an introduction to the technological and business worlds of our own time; it opens up avenues to the past through the study of the history of writing and printing, which is after all the study of the history of the civilised world; it is concerned with the three languages of words, numbers and pictures, and gives great scope for the creative solution of problems which tax both mind and eye; it involves manual dexterity and qualitative judgement; and, above all, it is concerned with ordering and making something, which seems to me to be a basic need of humankind.

Though some may still view a university course in typography with the same kind of suspicion as the Oxbridge academic of the nineteenth century viewed science and history, I am bound to say, looking back, that it seems surprising to me that we have been prepared to wait so long. In short,

I believe we have been sitting on an educational bonanza — if that is not too crude a word to use in this context. We have been so concerned with the training of people for our own industry that we may have failed to see the educational potential of our own subject — a potential which, if realised, could do nothing but benefit the whole industry.

This text was originally delivered as an address to the Wynkyn de Worde Society, in Stationers' Hall, London, on 17 September 1970, and was distributed as a pamphlet to members and friends of the society. The text appears here almost exactly as it did when distributed as a pamphlet, but has been updated to include a few linguistic changes and specifically to remove instances of gendered language that were the norm at the time.

Communicating design studies: a peripheral dialogue about transnational design pedagogies
Noel Waite and Richard Buchanan, in conversation

This text is an edited extract from a previously unpublished, 21-page interview transcript. The conversation took place near Karitane Beach, Te Wai Pounamu, New Zealand, in 2006. Buchanan was then Head of the School of Design at Carnegie Mellon University, and Waite was a lecturer in the Department of Design Studies / Te Toki a Rata at the University of Otago, which began redesigning its undergraduate curriculum in 2004. During this redesign process, Otago hosted a diverse range of design practitioners and theorists, including Charles Owen, Barry Katz, Gui Bonsiepe, Roberto Verganti, Michael McDonough and Buchanan. This was a conversation born of curiosity: Buchanan's idea of design as a 'liberal art of technological culture' had informed the teaching of design at the University of Otago since the late 1980s, so Waite sought to understand the relationship between the Design Studies curricula at Otago and at Carnegie Mellon.

NW Can you tell me, what is the Design Studies curriculum at Carnegie Mellon University, and how does it contribute to the design programme overall?

RB Our beginning, of course, is the Design Studio. That's fundamental, and it is where everything is integrated in practice. The Studio programme is distributed over a four-year period for the undergraduates. It is also central for graduate students.

Beyond that, we have Ideas and Methods in Design, which is where we pull out special features that are relevant to practice and which support the Studio programme. For instance, human and cultural factors would be studied there, and issues of mechanics and electronics — how mechanical systems work, and so forth. Things like time, motion and animation, for instance, would also be covered in one of the Ideas and Methods courses — whatever idea, method or technique needs to be studied. We also run 'Special Topics', wherein we cover branding or logo development, and so on. These are all supporting courses, though. When you take a project in the Studio, you need this supporting knowledge.

The third part is Design Studies itself, which is about the history, theory and criticism of design — it's the liberal education component, seen from the point of view of a designer. And then there's a fourth part to our curriculum, which comprises courses taken outside the School of Design. They're also liberal education or general education courses, but Design Studies for us is the bridge between the university's version of liberal education and the design version of liberal education. So, we're practising a general education process with, as I said, history, theory and criticism, which involves a lot of reading and writing, as well as some project work when it's relevant. For instance, I teach a course in Reason and Emotion in Design, and the students will do a substantial essay, but the second part of the course is a project where they have to explore it in concrete form. So it does have a studio element to it sometimes, but it is different from our fundamental Design Studio. So, Design Studies is a special bridge for us.

NW If Design Studies is a bridge, a liberal education for designers, is there any equivalent for non-designers? A liberal education through design for non-designers?

RB A lot of students take the Design Studies courses. They're open to many people in the university. Some of the history courses, for instance, are open enrolment, and we take quite a number of students. But it's intended to operate within the structure of the four-year Design Studio. In the first year, there is an exploration of human experience in the contemporary world, while linking to the past, where we have students try to observe things that are made in the world and talk about them. So it is an introduction to what design could *be* — not in a studio sense, but in terms of a general perception of things around us. And technology comes into this too. We also teach a course in what has been called 'Art History' in the past, but it has become something different today, which I'm glad of. I teach a course that I like a lot called 'Learning to Look'. It's a course for advanced undergraduates and graduate students. I think it is important because we find that, in the haste to do design work, students don't spend enough time looking, and looking carefully — people can look and not see. They'll want to learn to look well, and so I'll spend a lot of time just talking about a very few images, or getting students to talk about them. Sometimes we'll sit for ten or fifteen minutes and not say a word. It's very popular with students. I want them to take time and have access to the things that we see. Sometimes they're from fine arts, sometimes they're from design, it makes no difference. Wherever there's an image that might come into a person's mind, we'll look at that, and just take the time to discuss its content and subject matter, how it's presented visually, and its formal qualities.

NW How much, then, does Design Studies actually comprise of the total programme?

RB Well, every student in the undergraduate programme has to take five courses per term (per fifteen-week period) and, of those, one or two are in the Design Studies track. There is at least one every semester, which means that the students have to reflect, in a sense. The Studio is about production, the Ideas and Methods part is a kind of specialist practice, and Design Studies is about reflection, where the students have to think and write, and try to make connections and explanations or stories, narratives, things like that. This focus on reflection works its way through, and it flows back and forth. These tracks pull out special points of focus, but in practice you'll find reflection and discussion inside the Studio course. And vice versa, you'll find a little Studio in some of the things we do in Design Studies.

NW Do you find the students make connections between Design Studies and Design Studio, or do they see them as a separate? Do they get the ideas out of the Design Studies courses into practice?

RB That's a really good question. I'd have to say that we've always felt that the students are the ones who make the connections across the areas of study and the disciplines, whether it's within design — communication or industrial or interaction — or between design and other subjects of study. But, to be honest, one of the problems of education is the difficulty students sometimes have in making these connections. You know, we're buried in facts and data — that's the character of our time. We're given tonnes of data, gazillions of facts, and the problems we face now are: how do we connect them, and how do we recognise what is significant in that flood? So the problem lies not with data and facts per se; the challenges lie in identifying connections, principles and significance. And so, with that in mind, I'd say that we find that teaching students to make connections is actually a key part of the educational challenge. In the beginning, they don't make connections. They have to learn how to make connections. The discipline of thinking and the capacity to make complex connections can be acquired and cultivated. It's a developed capability, and that's what an art is: it's an acquired way of thinking and practising and doing things. So our students gradually learn how to make the connections, and make the connections across the course, but it comes slowly.

NW What do you see is the role of understanding history in terms of design practice? I ask because I've used the term 'design precedent' before, where one looks to the past for precedents for future actions, but certainly not just as something you need to replicate. But some designers will reject that, saying 'all design is innovation'.

RB Well, there are many ways of practising design, but I would say that history plays a valuable role if it's understood properly. John Dewey is, for me, the guide in this, as he is in relation to so many things for designers. Whether we know it or not, Dewey's ideas played a deep role in design as it unfolded in the twentieth century. Dewey said that history is always told from the standpoint of the present, something he got into a lot of trouble for. There were a lot of debates around this,[1] but he gave a very powerful argument that it is our current interests, the problems that strike us today, that lead us to go back and tell the story of the past. And so we're constantly retelling the story of the past from the standpoint of our current problems. Now, what this means to me is that we look to the past to find out how they solved problems — not to replicate their solutions, but to see how they dealt with problems. And then we find our problems — which may be different, or may be similar, who knows? — but we learn from what has been done before. It doesn't keep us from doing other things, but it's valuable to understand those precedents. And, frankly, I think it's woven into human culture as a whole that we have this continuity with the past and the future.

NW It does help you understand your sense of place in the present if you understand history in that way.

RB Of course, the danger is that history becomes an encumbrance, and that's not what this is about.

NW I'm also interested in the distinction between how I see histories used in the North American design studies context, as compared to the British tradition of a more contained silo of design history. Can you tell me your thoughts on this tension?

RB This has been of great concern to me too. The British seem to have very much developed design history as a separate matter. I've talked to British design historian Jonathan Woodham about this before, and we've bounced these things back and forth, and I must say that I think his understanding is closer to a Deweyian pragmatic approach than a lot of the, I would say, technical design historians in the UK. It'd probably make them angry to hear me say that, but I do think it's a problem in the UK, and there would be greater benefit all around if history and historians were engaged with contemporary work, and then, likewise, if folks working in contemporary design engaged more with history. History is a kind of interrogation. It's a way of questioning the things we see around us and so much of what we see around us doesn't yield its understanding in our immediate context. Everything around us has some historical link, and so understanding that history is a way to interrogate our surroundings, to understand where things have come from, what they mean, and it frees us to create new meanings and new work.

NW   One definition of design is that it is a future-oriented activity. This frees up design history, to a degree. There's a sense that historians won't touch the last twenty years because it's too recent for them to have developed a significant amount of hindsight, but, in my opinion, design historians don't have the luxury of ignoring the last fifteen or twenty years, because that brings us to the present day. And if you don't deal with that, then you're not dealing with many significant changes in practice.

RB   This comes back also to the difference between history and criticism. History, I think, does deal with the past — maybe from the standpoint of the present, but definitely with the past. But criticism deals with the present, it deals with an assessment of the qualities of things as they are for us today. So a critical interpretation of a building or a product around us is not necessarily design history, but it's a critical view of a contemporary thing, and of its context, meaning, use and value. Theory is something different. I think theory is oriented towards the future, towards what could be, towards the possibilities. You would discover principles in order to understand the future. No doubt, principles are key to understanding the past, but history is a future-oriented enterprise too: how will we tell histories in the future? If you scratch the surface of any topic, you'll find philosophic problems just below the surface. People like to run away from those, and don't want to deal with them, or pretend they aren't there, but they're there. We make those decisions about philosophy knowingly or unknowingly, but we make them.

NW   Do you agree that design is an emerging discipline? And what does it mean for design to be a discipline?

RB   Those are two fundamental questions. Yes, I think design is an emerging discipline — or set of disciplines. Raymond Williams wrote a wonderful book on culture,[2] and one of the sections deals with how Marxist theory can account for changes in cultural periods. He developed the concept of *dominant*, *emergent* and *recessive* elements of culture. I've found this to be a very powerful tool, and a good dialectical distinction. I'd say that there are a number of *recessive* practices in design — practices that are really outdated in many ways. They're too comfortable. They're here with us, and they have some value for us, but they really belong to the past. To devote too much time to them is perhaps a mistake. And then there are *dominant* practices, and we find the dominant practices of design varying from country to country. I, however, am specifically interested in *emergent* practices, and there are two ways in which Williams articulates this category. He talks about 'novelty', and separates that from 'emergence'. Novelty will come and go. Novelty is around us all the time — we're in a culture of the new, of whatever's happening now — but true emergence refers to the things that are new and that will become dominant in their time, and will move us forward in different ways. I would think about design as a mix of dominant, recessive and emergent practices.

What are emergent practices today? Organisation design and service design are emergent practices. Interaction design, I would say, is still an emergent practice, but it's very close to becoming mainstream dominant, certainly in the digital domain. There is no question that there is an orthodoxy that has settled in, but, even within interaction design, user research is still an emergent practice. There are so many design schools that still don't understand the importance of user research for design work. These are schools that are often dominated by their art origins, and which think of design as a kind of self-expression. There are many bad consequences that follow — some good, but mainly bad, I think. So, user research is an emergent practice in design, and in design education too. It is not a novelty; it is emergent. You could ask variations of this question: what new kinds of user research might we need, and so forth? I see residual practices that survive today, practices that were dominant in the past and which help to illuminate where design has come from. But I see new practices arising, such as the convergence of communication design with industrial design and interaction design. These changes throw up a very complicated set of threads of past, present and future.

One of the matters I think is emergent, and that will become dominant in our understanding of design and design education, is design ethics. I have reached a point in my career where I'm writing a lot of encyclopaedia entries, and I was asked to do an article for an encyclopaedia of science, technology and ethics,[3] which intends to do for ethics around technology what a similar encyclopaedia did a few years ago for bioethics. As I got into working on this piece, I realised that design ethics did not exist before about the mid-1990s. Now, there'd be a gasp from some designers and design educators. Please understand that what I'm saying here is that the formal consideration of ethics in design is only so old as the mid-1990s. From the beginning of design practice, there have of course been considerations of ethical problems, dilemmas and values, that's clear. But I haven't found — and I looked hard for — serious, formal discussions of design ethics at the philosophic level, and there was nothing before the mid-1990s. People like Alain Findeli, Carl Mitcham and Victor Margolin had done some work in this area.[4] And I've done some on human rights and human dignity.[5] These pieces started coming out in *Design Issues* — this is one of the things I'm very proud of in the journal, namely that we found an emergent matter and started to give it greater shape.

NW There's an interesting distinction in this respect between communication design and industrial design. Engineers, for example, have had codes of ethics since the turn of the twentieth century, but they're different in that they emerge as professional regulations.

RB Yes, certainly. I'd characterise the encyclopaedia entry I wrote as a kind of inquiry,[6] rather than as a summary of ethical understandings of design. Encyclopaedia articles are not typically inquiries into a subject. They're usually a summary of existing knowledge on a topic, but I was shocked to realise that, to write this encyclopaedia entry, it would have to be an original inquiry. So, I mapped out the ethical dimensions of design, beginning firstly with personal ethics and values, and going on, secondly, to the ethics of practice and professionalisation. Design has often relied on engineering and architecture for its codes of ethics — ICSID, ICOGRADA and IFI all turned to architecture and engineering and other fields for their early statements on professional ethics.[7] The third dimension of design ethics, in my estimation, is product integrity, and that's where a lot of the complexity of design falls. Problems of form, formal structure, usability, desirability and identification — these are all ethical problems. Aesthetics, in the narrow sense of issues of beauty, becomes a part of the ethical integrity of a work of design too. Then, of course, the final dimension is: what is the ultimate purpose of design? That's an ethical matter as well, and there are many different positions on this. So, what I was trying to suggest, in this encyclopaedia entry, is that there are many different dimensions to the ethics of design, many ways of thinking about this matter, which would include but not be limited to professional codes of ethics. We still have much work to do on matters of design ethics. And design studies and design education will have a big part to play in this.

Coda

Richard Buchanan was one of a number of international keynote visitors who actively contributed to design discourse in the Department of Design Studies at the University of Otago between 2002 and 2008. The inspiration for this Karitane conversation was Buchanan's concluding keynote lecture, 'Design and the common wealth of nations'. It crystallised for me the difference between design studies as a 'liberal art of technological culture',[8] and our locally hybridised, bicultural model, in Otago, of an integrated discipline and critical practice of design.[9]

The Otago curriculum was premised on Buchanan's 'four orders' of design,[10] moving from design studio fundamentals in the first year, to communication and industrial design in the second year, to interaction and environmental design in the third year. Design studies, conceived of as an architectonic discipline and practice of design, placed equal weight on theory and critical practice, such that communication design consisted of linked Theory and Project courses. After the first year, we intended for students to specialise in one of two pathways: communication or industrial design. However, students quickly enrolled in a more immersive and intra-disciplinary programme of communication, industrial, interaction and environmental design, and also, from 2007, in a fourth year of four intra- and interdisciplinary collaborative design practice-led courses, with a two-semester capstone research project.

Because Design Studies was a major subject within a Bachelor of Consumer & Applied Sciences, it could also be taken as a major or minor subject by a Bachelor of Arts, Laws or Science student. This ensured that, depending on the degree, a Design Studies student could select a second major in any university subject from Anthropology to Zoology. In this way, Design Studies became interdisciplinary within the University's major/minor subject and double-degree frameworks.

Buchanan wrote that 'if one idea could be found central in design studies, it most likely would be communication'.[11] The centrality of communication was embedded in two core Design Visualisation courses, which could be taken in either the first or the second year of the major degree. Design Visualisation sought to integrate information, linguistic and numeric literacies through *graphicacy*, 'the competence in dealing with images',[12] in order to avoid any binarism between word and image, or research and practice.

Gui Bonsiepe, who gave an Otago Design Studies keynote lecture in 2004, proposed that *visuality*, or 'thinking in terms of images',[13] was one of six important values for the twenty-first-century designer. These critical visual literacies were foundational for design cognition, practice and propositional projects at Otago. This approach also allowed design, from its origins in Otago Home Sciences in 1911, to deviate from colonial applied arts models then prevalent in New Zealand and to move instead towards a more creatively challenging integration of design practice, theory and ethics in the late twentieth- and early twenty-first-century design education landscape of New Zealand.

This edited interview excerpt is dedicated to all of the creative Otago Design Studies teachers and graduates, who preferred to sustain a re-framed, bicultural, collaborative design practice and who learned the trick of standing upright there.

1   See: Donald Benander, 'Revisionist Criticisms of John Dewey's Theory of Schooling' (D.Ed. diss., University of Massachusetts, 1980).
2   Raymond Williams, *The Sociology of Culture* (Chicago: University of Chicago Press, 1981).
3   Richard Buchanan, 'Design Ethics', *Encyclopedia of Science, Technology, and Ethics* (Farmington Hills, MI: Thomson Gale, 2005), http://www.encyclopedia.com/science/encyclopedias-almanacs-transcripts-and-maps/design-ethics, accessed 9 June 2020.
4   See: Alain Findeli, 'Ethics, Aesthetics, and Design', *Design Issues* 10, no. 2 (1994): 49–68; Alain Findeli, 'Rethinking Design Education for the 21st Century: Theoretical, Methodological and Ethical Discussion', *Design Issues* 17, no. 1 (2001): 5–17; Carl Mitcham, 'Ethics into Design', in *Discovering Design: Explorations in Design Studies*, edited by Richard Buchanan and Victor Margolin (Chicago: University of Chicago Press, 1995); and Victor Margolin, *The Politics of the Artificial: Essays on Design and Design Studies* (Chicago: University of Chicago Press, 2002).
5   See: Richard Buchanan, 'Human Dignity and Human Rights: Thoughts on the Principles of Human-Centered Design', *Design Issues* 17, no. 3 (2001): 35–39.
6   Ibid.
7   ICSID (International Council of the Societies of Industrial Design) was established in 1957 and ICOGRADA (International Council of Graphic Design Associations) in 1963. Since 2008, IFI (International Federation of Interior Architects/Designers) has been a member of the International Design Alliance (IDA), together with ICSID and ICOGRADA, which holds joint meetings biannually. ICSID was renamed the World Design Organisation in 2017.
8   Richard Buchanan, 'Wicked Problems in Design Thinking', *Design Issues* 8, no. 2 (1992): 5.
9   Noel Waite & Cameron Ralston, 'The Education Model', in *Strips Club* 1 (Autumn 2014).
10 Buchanan, 'Wicked Problems in Design Thinking', 9–10.
11 Richard Buchanan, 'Declaration by Design: Rhetoric, Argument and Demonstration in Design Practice', *Design Issues* 2, no. 1 (1985): 4.
12 Gui Bonsiepe, 'Some Virtues of Design', a contribution to the symposium 'Design beyond Design...' in honour of Jan van Toorn, held at the Jan van Eyck Academy, Maastricht, November 1997, published 2 November 1998, 20, http://www.guibonsiepe.com/pdffiles/virtues.pdf, accessed 9 June 2020.
13 Bonsiepe, 'Some Virtues of Design', 19.

Problem formulation is the problem
Brad Haylock

It is often understood that graphic design, like other kinds of design, is concerned with problem solving. In this essay, Brad Haylock argues that problem formulation, aka problem definition, is a vitally important part of the design process, but one that has been historically under-recognised in graphic design education and practice. Here, he discusses ways in which graphic designers might become more sensitive to complexity, and, drawing from service design, strategic planning, entrepreneurship and innovation management, he considers a range of tools and methods that designers might employ to tackle the knotty task of problem formulation.

Most design problems, properly understood, are complex, not merely complicated. To utter or to write these words is one thing; to convey this idea to students, however, is quite another, not to mention the challenge of also equipping them with some means by which they might begin to contend with such complexity.

Many of the problems faced by designers are characterised by intractably interwoven forces that issue from labyrinthine constellations of social practices and technical systems so advanced they appear opaque. Each of these qualitatively dissimilar networks is discretely so complex that it is almost certainly unknowable in its entirety; the complexity of the situation is nonetheless compounded by the intersection of multiple such systems; and the whole enterprise is made more difficult still by the fact that design is concerned not only with the current but also with the future state of these systems and their intersections. All of this is a fancy way of saying that the circumstances to which a designer must respond are not easily understood. With this in mind, design education done properly must give to emerging designers a disposition and a suite of resources that will allow them not only to recognise complexity but also to be comfortable in the face of it and, further, to have some sense of how they might begin to tackle it.

'Rewrite the brief': unmasking the wickedness of design problems

My understanding of the problems faced by designers is informed by the concept of 'wicked' problems proposed by Horst Rittel, who was Professor of Design Methodology at the Hochschule für Gestaltung Ulm from 1958 to 1963 and Professor of the Science of Design at the University of California, Berkeley, from 1963 until 1990. The best-known explication of the concept of wicked problems is from an article by Rittel and Melvin Webber, then Professor of City Planning at UC Berkeley, published in 1973.[1] In that article, Rittel and Webber were concerned with the problems faced by professionals in the fields of social policy and planning, so some of the defining characteristics of wicked problems in their analysis are matters of scale and scope not typical of design problems in other fields, but the essential principles and most of the attributes of wicked problems in their definition are usefully transferable. Wicked problems are distinguished from 'tame' problems by their inscrutability. Tame problems — Rittel and Webber give the examples of mathematics problems and simple engineering problems — can be definitively understood and objectively solved using proven methods, and the correctness or otherwise of a given solution can be assessed according to commonly held criteria. Wicked problems, by contrast, resist any attempt at a singular definition, let alone an ideal solution.[2]

Rittel and Webber identified ten defining traits of wicked problems,[3] of which the first is perhaps the most essential: 'there is no definitive formulation of a wicked problem'.[4] There can be no definitive or objectively preferable definition of or solution to a wicked problem, not only because the variables in play are many and various — indeed, some of the forces at work may persistently evade recognition entirely — but also because, inevitably, there are different stakeholders and stakeholder groups involved whose needs and values differ dramatically, often to the point of being irreconcilable.[5]

Richard Buchanan brought the concept of wicked problems into contemporary design discourse.[6] Buchanan uses the terms 'determinacy' and 'indeterminacy' to respectively describe the definability or otherwise of tame and wicked problems. The 'wicked/tame' and 'indeterminate/determinate' pairs have useful qualities, but, when I am introducing these concepts to students, I prefer to describe wicked or indeterminate problems as 'complex', and tame or determinate problems as merely 'complicated'. The 'complex/complicated' pair is, in my experience, a little more easily acquired by students when they are coming to these ideas for the first time, and, in this context, I hold that the choice of signifiers and their provenance matter less than does the intelligibility of the distinction between the two classes of problems. With the exception of a brief mention of the term 'wicked' for the purposes of citation, I specifically prefer to avoid this word when teaching because of its moral overtones, which can be misleading for all students and particularly confusing for those whose first language is not English.[7]

Rittel and Webber observe of wicked problems that 'problem understanding and problem resolution are concomitant to each other'.[8] In other words, 'wicked problems have no definitive formulation, but every formulation of a wicked problem corresponds to the formulation of a solution'.[9] Buchanan draws out the implications of this when he asserts that 'there is a fundamental *indeterminacy* in all but the most trivial design problems — problems where, as Rittel suggests, the "wickedness" has already been taken out to yield determinate or analytic problems'.[10] This is a key insight to be drawn from a wicked-problems approach to design thinking: every definition of a problem already suggests a solution; or, conversely, in every proposed solution there is always an implicit and unavoidably *partial* definition of the problem under consideration. (In my use of 'partial' here, I deliberately mean to evoke two senses of the word: *incomplete* and *biased*.) One important practical implication of this is that *most design briefs remove much of the wickedness of a design problem*. Most design briefs render a complex problem as merely complicated, and in this way presuppose certain kinds of solution and foreclose others.

A past colleague of mine in design education had a rallying cry to students: 'rewrite the brief!' (Actually, it was typically rather more emphatic: 'rewrite the brief, rewrite the brief, *rewrite the brief!*') Although my colleague did not, to my knowledge, explain it in this way, this mantra was nothing other than a call to unmask the wickedness of a design problem that had otherwise been suppressed. The difference between a good brief and a bad brief is that the good brief makes *better* — or, preferably, *fewer* — assumptions in the process of reducing a complex problem to a complicated one, but all briefs are always already a reduction of the problem. There is no one right way of approaching such a reduction, and indeed any such reduction is undesirable, since any formulation of an indeterminate problem as a determinate one necessarily forecloses some courses of action that might otherwise have been possible. In other words, in the writing of a brief, important parts of the design work have already been done, and there is no guarantee that they have been done well. The 'return brief' or 'reverse brief' — that practice whereby designers restate to a client their understanding of a job, perhaps partly or significantly reframing it in the process — is a right-minded but typically inadequate attempt to reinstate some of the complexity of a given design problem.[11] It must be said that formal, written design briefs are today relatively uncommon, but whether the instructions from a client to a designer take the form of email exchanges, a verbal conversation, a widely circulated invitation to tender or otherwise, the dangers in the reduction of a problem so formulated remain the same.

Civic-scale questions, such as where to build a freeway, how to reduce crime or how to set a tax rate, are wicked problems of the type with which Rittel and Webber were concerned.[12] Very knotty, polysystemic, national or global social problems like homelessness, intergenerational poverty and climate change are clearly also wicked problems. But the value of a wicked-problems approach to design is diminished if we associate it only with these very large challenges whose full complexity is minimally comprehensible at best. A wicked-problems mindset is valuable and applicable to design challenges of all scales. In her conversation with Bonne Zabolotney in this book, Laurene Vaughan offers the example of a hypothetical client who seeks to commission a complex digital outcome when in fact a relatively simple solution would probably be better.[13] I have colleagues who work in digital development; new clients frequently come to them looking to have an app built. When asked why they want an app, these would-be clients often answer with little more than the refrain, 'because everyone else has one'. The we-need-an-app phenomenon is so commonplace today that it has become a cliché in the industry. A sensitivity to complexity, i.e., a wicked-problems mindset, fosters an interrogative disposition: instead of simply doing what is asked, first inquire into what it is that really needs to be done — and *for whom*. Time and budget constraints will necessarily also come into play, but these are relatively mundane inevitabilities of practice, like the proverbial death and taxes.

To better understand the phenomenon of wicked problems in graphic design, let's consider a more detailed example: a hypothetical art museum that needs a new visual identity. On what media must the identity appear? In which visual landscapes must it stand out? What kinds of imagery need to be accommodated? Identity design is, on one level, already a challenging task, on account of the standard of visual craftsmanship required for the design of such systems, but behind these formal tasks lies a wicked communication design problem. To whom does the organisation need to communicate today, to whom will it need to communicate in the future — for the foreseeable life of the new identity — and what does it need to say to these audiences, publics and stakeholders? Because of the design labour and the roll-out costs involved, a rebrand is an expensive exercise, so a current-state analysis is not sufficient to understand the problem; future user scenarios must also be taken into account. Current audiences, those new audiences and publics with whom the museum aspires to engage, and government and corporate stakeholders will all have different expectations of the organisation. A single visual language that would speak to all equally well would be a difficult proposition, if not an impossible one. How might we speak to new audiences without alienating current stakeholders? How might we reach a large number of people if we have only a limited budget to work with? How might we communicate appropriately to local and national audiences whilst benchmarking against international best practice? Should we prioritise digital, print or signage applications to help audiences navigate the physical premises? Should funds be diverted from the advertising budget to make staff more available to answer telephone inquiries, because research suggests that a significant portion of the current audience still prefers to pick up the phone to find out about upcoming events? If the solution is not good enough, will some corporate sponsorship be lost? What are the implications for future generations of audiences if government funding for the museum's programming or operations is thus also diminished? Small and large questions arise, one after another. Some cascade, others take forking paths, but these constituent problems seem to unfold endlessly.

Yet imagine now that our hypothetical museum is not an art museum but an ethnographic one, whose collection is partly comprised of colonial spoils. How might a graphic designer confront the moral and political demands for the restitution of stolen artefacts? An individual designer or agency might avoid such a conundrum by refusing the commission, but opting out does not make the problem go away. Should the museum simply close its doors? Could an ethnographic museum in the twenty-first century communicate with stakeholders and publics in a way that would reconcile its civic role with the historical traumas in its DNA? Wicked problems are, according to Rittel, problems that are 'ill-formulated, where the information is confusing, where there are many clients and decision makers with conflicting values, and where the ramifications in the whole system are thoroughly confusing'.[14] Our hypothetical rebrand of a museum is clearly a wicked problem. What might have started as a seemingly simple request for a new logo has snowballed, apparently out of control.

Diagramming definition: the Double Diamond in design education

If design is a problem-solving process, then problem formulation, aka problem definition, is, as we have seen, an immeasurably important part of the process.[15] Certain schools at certain moments in history have done a very good job of training students in problem definition. The pioneering methodological work undertaken at the Hochschule für Gestaltung Ulm must be acknowledged here, however it must also be pointed out that 'the Ulm model' has had a much greater influence in industrial design education than in graphic design education, and that, seemingly in spite of its progressive political roots and its sociological leanings, which ought to have led to a sensitivity to diverse audiences' needs, Ulm perpetuated a decidedly undifferentiated, universalist formal language.[16] Closer to home, relevant to the present volume, and surely unusual in the antipodes at the time, Max Hailstone taught a graphic design curriculum that was strongly concerned with problem definition — although he might have called it 'diagnosis' — in the School of Fine Arts at the University of Canterbury in Christchurch, New Zealand, from the late 1970s until the 1990s.[17] These examples notwithstanding, I maintain that problem formulation has been too often under-recognised in graphic design education.[18]

In recent years, I've tried to redress this gap in my own work as an educator by bringing the Double Diamond into the classroom and into curriculum development. The Double Diamond is a non-discipline-specific model of the design process, developed by the Design Council in the UK and launched in 2004.[19] It identifies four key phases in the design process, a quartet of alliterative verbs: *discover* and *define*, *develop* and *deliver*. These are two pairs of divergent and convergent processes, which, when mapped from left to right, from problem to solution, make a pair of diamonds.[20] The point at which the two diamonds meet is the moment of agreed problem definition — the design brief. There are, of course, other models of the design process, such as the Stanford d.school model of design thinking, which comprises five 'modes': *empathise*, *define*, *ideate*, *prototype* and *test*.[21] Is the Double Diamond the best model of its type? Probably not. Is it an extraordinarily useful teaching tool? Yes, I think so. I particularly like the Double Diamond as a tool in graphic design education not only because it makes visible to students both the problem definition and the problem solution phases of the design process, but also, importantly, because it gives equal visual weight and therefore equal conceptual weight to each. In this way, it makes it clear that a whole raft of work lies behind — or *should* lie behind — a design brief. It also concisely shows that the tasks of problem definition and problem solution both require divergent and convergent thinking processes — exploration and refinement, respectively. By taking a wicked-problems approach as a starting point and then deploying the Double Diamond in the classroom, I aim to instil in students an awareness of the significance of problem formulation and an appreciation of those many constituent tasks that might not be conventionally understood as design.

I don't want to labour the point or fetishise the diagram, but I will briefly say that graphic design education has too often focused mostly on the first three quarters of the second diamond in the Design Council model. That is to say, education in the discipline has for many years focused a lot on design development and a little on the formal refinement that goes into delivery, but few schools have offered much training in the technical and industrial processes that make up the latter part of the delivery phase in graphic design (admittedly because the costs involved in doing so well are typically prohibitively high), fewer have focused on frameworks for the evaluation of impact or success at the end of the delivery phase (i.e., testing how well a solution delivered against its stated aims, or didn't), and fewer still have given due emphasis to the vast and important matter of problem formulation.[22]

It is all well and good, I hear you ask, to point students towards this whole other diamond, but how are they to navigate this? 'How will this intelligence of the invisible be taught?', Alain Findeli asks.[23] I am not suggesting that we should push emerging designers into the void of wickedness and hope for the best. If we expect that our graduates should be able to tackle complexity, then we must offer them some tools, methods and models with which they might begin to negotiate this terrain (even if we also expect that they will need to become, in time, their own methodologists in this domain). Just as we guide students to develop proficiency in, or mastery of, the tools and methods of design development and delivery — including but not limited to sketching, prototyping, benchmarking, coding, preparing finished art, and so on, not to mention the tenacious triumvirate of Photoshop, Illustrator and InDesign — so too must we train them in the use of tools and methods for discovery and definition.

Despite its value as a tool in design education, some potential shortcomings of the Double Diamond diagram must be pointed out. The convergence of the right-hand side of the right-hand diamond into a single point unhelpfully connotes a singular solution — one that will presumably be successful if all four phases of the process have been carried out adequately well, and which would in any case appear to be static thereafter. Contrary to the singularity and the closure implied by the diagram at that point, it must be reiterated that there may be many possible solutions to any given design problem, that a solution is likely enduring only in respect of the most determinate of problems, that post-delivery evaluation ought to be carried out, and that periodic reviews or the continuing refinement of any so-called solution will probably be necessary. Indeed, from a wicked-problems standpoint, the very concept of a solution is something of a misnomer, since the networks of systems and actors affecting any complex problem are invariably characterised by flux, such that any would-be solution stands to be more or less obsolete so soon as it is deployed. Rightly, then, the Design Council's later 'evolved' Double Diamond model of 2019 speaks not of 'problems' and 'solutions' but instead of 'challenges' and 'outcomes'.[24] In order to acknowledge and accommodate the inevitable contingency of outcomes that address complex challenges, we might fruitfully look away from the Double Diamond and instead towards Agile approaches drawn from software development, or we might imagine diamonds that segue into participatory action-research cycles — but these are questions for a different essay.[25]

If you're not part of the problem, you're part of the solution: service design, strategic planning and entrepreneurship tools

'I'm worried', said Richard Buchanan, 'about graphic design. It's at a critical turning point. The window of opportunity is about to close.' This prognosis, no doubt intended to provoke, is from Buchanan's closing keynote at 'New Views 2: Conversations and Dialogues in Graphic Design', a conference convened by Teal Triggs and Laurene Vaughan at London College of Communication in 2008.[26] Part of the root of the fear at the time — or, rather, part of the alibi of the hyperbole — was the rise of the field of service design. Luke Wood was in the audience that day. His disbelief in the forecast demise of graphic design and his general scepticism towards 'design thinking' and service design led to the project *(Graphic) Design School School*, to the many conversations we've had about graphic design education over the years, and so to this book. Service design (SD) and other human-centred design (HCD) disciplines, commonly known by their initialisms, such as customer experience (CX) design, user interface (UI) design, user experience (UX) design and interaction design (IxD), were rapidly growing in visibility and influence in 2008. These then-emergent spheres of practice would, it was feared, make graphic design redundant. The doomsaying has thus far been unfounded, but it cannot be denied that the changing landscape of practice has given the discipline of graphic design a good kick in the ass along the way.

What of the relationship between graphic design and these newer, now-established disciplines, today and into the future? It is not an either/or scenario, despite what some pessimistic or provocative prophets might have us believe. Graphic design persists as an essential part of these newer modes of practice, too often under the clumsy moniker of 'visual design'. But I am more interested here in the converse: the place of HCD thinking and SD tools in graphic design education and practice.[27]

User-centred thinking is not a recent development in graphic design. To offer but one example, book typographers have for centuries held user-centred thinking close to their hearts. Wisdom regarding the proper relationship between line lengths, type sizes, contrast, spacing, and so on, was handed down from one generation of practitioner to the next, all in the service of readability. Beatrice Warde's concept of the 'crystal goblet' is surely the best-known call for best practice in this domain.[28] Developments in eye-tracking devices over the course of the twentieth century added substance to these received practices, and *The Journal of Typographic Research*, founded in 1967, gave a voice to these concerns and a platform for rigorous inquiry in the field. In the intervening years, however, other kinds of questions have prevailed, and some of the discipline's sensitivity to end users' needs was sidelined along the way.[29] Design authorship, deconstructivism and a fascination with vernacular typography, for example, were all, in their own ways, important developments in the recent history of graphic design discourse and practice, but I think it's safe to say that user-centred thinking wasn't at the forefront of the discipline's collective consciousness as we ran into the new millennium.[30] Today, however, in a climate of rapidly developing adjacent discourses, graphic design cannot shy away from user-centredness.

The emergence of these newer varieties of design practice — SD, HCD, UI/UX and other incipient initialisms — has forced graphic designers to articulate the significance of their discipline anew. More importantly, however, these new fields also offer a rich repertoire of tools and methods upon which we might draw in order to prepare emerging graphic designers for the demanding work of problem formulation. Specifically, tools and methods drawn from service design can be fruitfully combined with others from the fields of strategic planning, entrepreneurship and innovation management. This repertoire of resources can be used to foster an understanding of users' or audiences' experiences, needs and expectations. They can also enable a systems-level view of communication design problems, and they allow an appreciation of the relationship between user-centric considerations and questions of feasibility and viability.[31] At this point, however, I should emphasise that, while a number of the tools I discuss here are borrowed from the world of business, they can be used to understand socio-technical systems and to empathise with the needs of various audiences and publics *not only in the service of capital*.

Some of these methods are ethnographic or autoethnographic in nature.[32] Although not new, these methods are enjoying a renewed visibility in design practice.[33] These include *interviews* with end users or other stakeholders, which might be structured, to facilitate comparison between different participants' responses, or unstructured, to facilitate deeper inquiry and the exploration of emergent topics. *User diaries*, in which users maintain a record of their interactions with an organisation or their habits in relation to a particular kind of practice, give designer-researchers an insight into user needs or expectations that might otherwise be opaque. *User shadowing*, an observational method, can similarly reveal insights about behaviours or immanent needs that participants do not self-report in interviews. *Service safaris*, meanwhile, involve designer-researchers themselves engaging with an organisation, interface, service, etc., in order to better understand the strengths and weaknesses of an existing offering. These are just a few of many useful discovery methods; although they are not easily mastered, the basics are taught and learned readily enough.

Other tools are valuable for developing empathy with audiences and users in different ways, or for visualising systems and processes. These include *user personas* and *archetypes*, which give human attributes and relatable traits to otherwise impersonal trends in data. Some of the most valuable tools that graphic designers might borrow from service design and experience design are *journey maps*, aka *experience maps*. Such maps allow relatively complex systems and sequences of interactions to be clearly visualised, and so they can help designers and others involved in decision making and problem formulation to better understand the human dimension and the polysystemic aspects of wicked communication design problems. In these maps, end users' actions, thoughts and feelings can be understood in relation to organisational touchpoints, and certain external influences can also be identified. More specialised tools can also be brought into the graphic design classroom, such as *service blueprints*, which can help students to recognise, among other things, the 'line of visibility' that distinguishes front-stage activities from back-stage processes — for example, the distinction between the work of a maître d' and that of a chef, or between the user interface of an e-commerce app and the picking and packing protocols in a warehouse.

Strategic planning tools also have a place in graphic design education. A *stakeholder map* affords an overview of the various persons and groups that influence or are affected by a given product, service, organisation or system. A *SWOT analysis* is a time-honoured tool that allows a structured view of the strengths, weaknesses, opportunities and threats that will support or impede an objective. A SWOT analysis is typically a matrix of favourable and unfavourable factors on one axis and internal and external factors on the other, but, abandoning the internal/external distinction, it can also be used to distinguish favourable and unfavourable *current-state* factors (strengths and weaknesses) from favourable and unfavourable *future-state* factors (opportunities and threats) — this temporal distinction is particularly useful for designers.

Another suite of tools can be drawn from the fields of entrepreneurship, product management and innovation management. *Competitor audits* can be used in the classroom to help students think through the complexity of competitive environments from various audiences' and stakeholders' points of view. The *Business Model Canvas* is a lightweight replacement for the traditional business plan;[34] it is a lean startup tool typically used to rapidly ideate a new business, but it can also be used as an analysis tool in order to gain a structured overview of an existing business or organisation, particularly with a view to understanding the relationships between operational matters and the value that a business or organisation represents to different audiences or customer segments. When used in the design classroom, the Business Model Canvas can foster a multifaceted understanding of an organisation's value proposition(s) — it encourages designers to assess an organisation or product from multiple stakeholders' perspectives.

This list is not exhaustive, but I hope to give an insight into the variety of tools and methods with which we might equip students, to help them navigate the complexity of wicked communication design problems. The appropriate combination of tools and methods and the sequence of their use will differ from project to project. When delivering short and fast assignments, I typically ask students to use a specific set of methods in a specific order. In longer-duration projects, students may assemble their own toolkit and approach from a variety of possible methods arranged in a sequence they determine. The goal is that emerging designers should become adept at choosing the right tools for a given job — they should become independent methodologists in discovery and definition work, in the same way that we would expect them to make informed choices about tools, methods, production processes, and so on, during the development and delivery phases.

If you're wondering how graphic design students react to all of this, let me assure you that I've consistently seen fantastic results. To give but one example, I've seen great outcomes from undergraduate students who, working in teams of two or three, can undertake a body of fieldwork and produce a sophisticated strategy document in a five-day intensive workshop despite having no prior knowledge of these concepts and no prior experience using these tools. They undertake various fieldwork activities and come back to the classroom where we work together to interpret data, sift for insights, pore over diagrams of processes, plot diverse touchpoints on experience maps, and so on, until they eventually have a convincing, user-centred and multifaceted grasp of the communication problem in hand, incorporating multiple stakeholders' viewpoints and at least a rudimentary understanding of other forces in play, such as matters of feasibility and viability that might suggest or preclude certain possible solutions. The level of detail required and the number and variety of tools and methods employed in the discovery and definition phases will be largely determined by the time available for the assignment. But only when the problem has been formulated in a considered way might we begin to talk about colours, typefaces, or any of the other matters of concern typically associated with graphic design reductively understood.[35]

Although my focus in this essay lies with accessible tools for problem formulation in design education, I should point out that the ways in which these tools and methods might be deployed by students will probably differ in one important regard as compared to their application by practising designers: students, especially in fast-paced undergraduate assignments, are unlikely to have access to clients and other hard-to-reach stakeholders, whereas practising designers should consult closely and regularly with all persons who have an interest in a problem or project as well as those who stand to be impacted by it. Clients and others, including users and publics, are all, in different ways, problem-owners who have a stake not only in solutions to problems but necessarily also in their definition. The principle here is one of *co-design* in all phases of the design process, a principle that is perhaps summed up best by the product development mantra 'share early, share often' (which is, in turn, closely related to the software development mantra 'fail fast').[36] Although designers might bring a toolkit of methods to the table, they are not heroic seers who alone have the power or the right to untangle complexity. Similar principles underpin participatory design in the Scandinavian tradition, which has much in common with a wicked-problems mindset, since it is concerned with democratic participation in the design of complex sociotechnical systems, such as late-industrial workplaces.[37]

Conclusion

I have sought to argue in this essay for a greater emphasis on problem formulation in graphic design. I have discussed some tools and methods drawn from service design, strategic planning, entrepreneurship, product management and innovation management that, in my experience, can be fruitfully brought into the classroom — and into practice — to help designers navigate complexity. I have spoken a lot about design processes in the abstract, and about tools and methods for problem definition. It is true that I am very interested in methodological matters, but if it has seemed that I am an advocate of social research methods, strategy, process diagrams, and so on, at the expense of graphic artistry, heuristics and visual play, allow me to say that this could hardly be further from the truth. I am also a pedantic typographer — frustratingly so, some of my collaborators and students might say — and a staunch advocate of learning through trial-and-error. As I have argued above, the relationship between graphic design and newer, more expressly human-centred design disciplines is not an either/or situation. Today, I expect graphic design graduates to be as conversant with touchpoints, pain points, value propositions and the Business Model Canvas as they are with type anatomy, print processes, Bézier curves and the Pantone Matching System.

I would like to make some concluding remarks about the broader importance of teaching designers to be sensitive to complexity through human-centred approaches and systems thinking. The concept of wicked problems was born in the wake of massive social upheaval and the rise of multiculturalism in the US throughout the 1960s. Rittel and Webber forecast that postindustrial society was 'likely to be far more differentiated than any in all of past history'.[38] Three decades later, the American graphic designer and educator Katherine McCoy noted that a 'renewed celebration of ethnic diversity counterbalances the long American tradition of assimilation', compelling designers to concern themselves with the needs of heterogeneous audiences and diverse communities.[39] Although the concept of a 'mass market', misguided from the outset, has been well and truly overturned, and despite the fact that universalist approaches to design hold less sway than they once did, there is still much room for improvement.[40] Through human-centred and situationally aware principles and practices, we can better understand the complexity of the challenges we face as designers and as citizens, and this would be a vast improvement on the old paradigm of the designer as *auteur*.[41] Today, however, in the face of persistent challenges to the teleological narratives of modernisation and neoliberalism, not least of which is the increasingly pressing reality of climate change, we are also beholden, as never before, to attend to the needs and influences of non-human actors and ecosystems. In design education, the concept of wicked problems is one means by which we might broach a conversation about the need for a sensitivity to polysystemic complexity and ecological equilibria. We must not shy away from the potential of graphic design as a critical practice.[42] We must, as Donna Haraway would insist, stay with the trouble, and foster such a sensibility among emerging designers too.[43]

Lastly, if you disagree with anything I have said here, I hope that you will let me know. If you wish to offer some criticism or feedback, 'constructive' or blunt, please reach out — because education doesn't end when one graduates, and I, too, am always eager to learn.[44]

1 Horst W. J. Rittel and Melvin M. Webber, 'Dilemmas in a General Theory of Planning', *Policy Sciences* 4, no. 2 (1973).
2 The title of this essay echoes Rittel and Webber's proclamation: 'The formulation of a wicked problem *is* the problem!' Ibid., 161. The present title also echoes — but does not answer — the title of a public lecture I gave on 16 July 2014 at The Physics Room, Christchurch, New Zealand. That lecture, titled 'What is the problem in "problem solving"?', marked the beginning of *(Graphic) Design School School*, the project that led to this book.
3 In different papers and presentations, Rittel proposed slightly different sets of the defining qualities of wicked problems. In the article he co-authored with Webber, they are: 'There is no definitive formulation of a wicked problem'; 'Wicked problems have no stopping rule'; 'Solutions to wicked problems are not true-or-false, but good-or-bad'; 'There is no immediate and no ultimate test of a solution to a wicked problem'; 'Every solution to a wicked problem is a "one-shot operation"; because there is no opportunity to learn by trial-and-error, every attempt counts significantly'; 'Wicked problems do not have an enumerable (or an exhaustively describable) set of potential solutions, nor is there a well-described set of permissible operations that may be incorporated into the plan'; 'Every wicked problem is essentially unique'; 'Every wicked problem can be considered to be a symptom of another problem'; 'The existence of a discrepancy representing a wicked problem can be explained in numerous ways. The choice of explanation determines the nature of the problem's resolution'; and 'The planner has no right to be wrong'. Ibid., 161–66.
4 Ibid., 161.
5 The abstract for Rittel and Webber's article summarises matters well: 'The search for scientific bases for confronting problems of social policy is bound to fail, because of the nature of these problems. They are "wicked" problems, whereas science has developed to deal with "tame" problems. Policy problems cannot be definitively described. Moreover, in a pluralistic society there is nothing like the undisputable public good; there is no objective definition of equity; policies that respond to social problems cannot be meaningfully correct or false; and it makes no sense to talk about "optimal solutions" to social problems unless severe qualifications are imposed first. Even worse, there are no "solutions" in the sense of definitive and objective answers.' Ibid., 155.
6 Richard Buchanan, 'Wicked Problems in Design Thinking', *Design Issues* 8, no. 2 (1992).
7 On their choice of the term 'wicked' and its moral connotations, see: Rittel and Webber, 'Dilemmas in a General Theory of Planning', 160–61.
8 Ibid., 161.
9 Rittel, cited in Buchanan, 'Wicked Problems in Design Thinking', 16.
10 Ibid., 15–16.
11 Alain Findeli describes the systematic questioning of the design brief as 'the complexification of the problem into *problématique*'. Alain Findeli, 'Rethinking Design Education for the 21st Century: Theoretical, Methodological, and Ethical Discussion', *Design Issues* 17, no. 1 (2001): 14.
12 Rittel and Webber, 'Dilemmas in a General Theory of Planning', 160.
13 See pp. 263–264 in this volume.
14 Rittel, cited in Buchanan, 'Wicked Problems in Design Thinking', 15.
15 The definition of design as a problem-solving process is itself debatable, however that is a question for another time.

16   Bernhard E. Bürdek observes of HfG Ulm that 'already by the 1970s, … serious questions were being raised about a methodology whose supposed objectivity actually led to very uniform design results', and 'the Ulm methodology, as functionally oriented as it was, was only marginally concerned with the user, aside from ergonomic studies arising in the context of "engineering"'. Bernhard E. Bürdek, 'The Ulm School of Design: Methodology and Results', in *Ulm: Method and Design / Ulm School of Design 1953–1968*, edited by Dagmar Rinker, Marcela Quijano and Brigitte Reinhardt (Ostfildern-Ruit: Hatje Cantz, 2003), 52–55.

17   Hailstone taught both Luke Wood and Jonty Valentine. For an insight into Hailstone's understanding of design and design processes, including his process diagram that compares the work of a designer to that of a doctor, see: Max Hailstone, 'What Is Design?', in *Design and Designers* (Christchurch & Wellington: The Griffin Press and The New Zealand Industrial Design Council, 1985), 20. See also the reproduction on page 16 in this volume.

18   Audrey Bennett has discussed the use of empirical methods in graphic design education, however she focusses on the use of such methods in what would be the *development* and *delivery* — problem *solution* — phases of the Double Diamond, namely in the form of co-design or participatory design methods during ideation, in user testing of prototypes, and in evaluation. By contrast, I am concerned with the use of strategic and empirical methods in the problem *formulation* phases. See: Audrey Bennett, 'For the Sake of Humanity: Teaching Cross-Cultural Design with Empirical Enquiry', in *The Education of a Graphic Designer*, edited by Steven Heller (New York: Allworth Press, 2003), 275.

19   For an overview of the Double Diamond process model, its embedded methods and their applications, see: Design Council, 'Eleven Lessons: Managing Design in Eleven Global Brands', (London: Design Council, 2007).

20   For more on divergent and convergent thinking in design, see: Tim Brown, *Change by Design: How Design Thinking Transforms Organizations and Inspires Innovation* (New York: HarperCollins, 2009), 66–68; and Darrel Rhea, 'Bringing Clarity to the "Fuzzy Front End"', in *Design Research: Methods and Perspectives*, edited by Brenda Laurel (Cambridge, MA: MIT Press, 2003), 148–49.

21   Scott Doorley, et al., 'Design Thinking Bootleg', Stanford d.school, https://dschool.stanford.edu/resources/design-thinking-bootleg.

22   While acknowledging the importance of studies of design process, Alain Findeli holds that the 'problem' is inappropriately considered a given in design education and practice, and so argues: 'if we are interested — and designers should be interested — in the origin and the destination of their projects, then the complexification of the process and the product should be completed, on one hand, by the complexification of the problématique (or problem-setting), and, on the other, by the complexification of the impact of the project'. Findeli, 'Rethinking Design Education for the 21st Century', 12.

23   Ibid.

24   Design Council, 'What Is the Framework for Innovation? Design Council's Evolved Double Diamond', Design Council, www.designcouncil.org.uk/news-opinion/what-framework-innovation-design-councils-evolved-double-diamond, accessed 11 June 2020.

25   See: Martin Fowler and Jim Highsmith, 'The Agile Manifesto', *Software Development* 9, no. 8 (2001): 28–35; and William Foote Whyte, ed., *Participatory Action Research* (Thousand Oaks, CA: Sage, 1991).

26   'New Views 2: Conversations and Dialogues in Graphic Design' was held at London College of Communication, 9–11 July 2008. These comments by Buchanan are preserved in: Rick Poynor, 'It's the End of Graphic Design as We Know It', *Eye* 18, no. 69 (2008).

27   For another perspective on the place of service design in graphic design and vice versa, see Jakob Schneider's text 'Graphic Design: Providing Visual Explanation', in Marc Stickdorn and Jakob Schneider, *This Is Service Design Thinking: Basics, Tools, Cases* (New Jersey: Wiley, 2011), 68–79.

28   Beatrice Warde, 'The Crystal Goblet, or: Printing Should Be Invisible', in *The Crystal Goblet: Sixteen Essays on Typography* (London: The Sylvan Press, 1955).

29   The term 'end user' is a strange one. It is part of the common parlance in the field, but it is somewhat problematic on account of its functionalist overtones, which run contrary to its empathic intent. It does have the benefit, however, of unambiguously directing designers' thinking towards their clients' clients' needs, perhaps allowing one to recognise such things as biases towards operational matters or feasibility concerns, which might otherwise plague a design brief. By way of comparison, consider the concept of the 'Voice of the Customer' (VOC) and its related tools, which play a similar and important role in process optimisation methodologies such as Six Sigma.

30 In particular, debates about the designer as author in the 1990s were, it must be pointed out, markedly anachronistic in light of the very public pronouncement of the death of the author some three decades earlier. Roland Barthes's pivotal essay 'The Death of the Author' was first published in 1967. The English translation was actually published some months before its 1968 French debut, so there was no excuse for anglophone readers to be late to the party on this occasion. Today, the essay is most readily available here: Roland Barthes, 'The Death of the Author', in *Image, Music, Text*, edited by Stephen Heath (New York: Hill and Wang, 1977), 142–48. The key text in the design authorship debate is: Michael Rock, 'The Designer as Author', *Eye* 5, no. 20 (1996).

31 IDEO's triad of desirability, feasibility and viability is a valuable model that is readily acquired by students. See: Brown, *Change by Design*, 19.

32 For an instructive discussion of many of the tools and methods I mention here, and others, see: Stickdorn and Schneider, *This Is Service Design Thinking*.

33 For a discussion of social research methods in design education, see: Alex Wilkie, 'Learning Design through Social Science', in *About Learning and Design*, edited by Giorgio Camuffo and Maddalena Dalla Mura (Bozen-Bolzano: Bozen-Bolzano University Press, 2014).

34 Alexander Osterwalder and Yves Pigneur, *Business Model Generation: A Handbook for Visionaries, Game Changers, and Challengers* (Chichester: John Wiley and Sons, 2010).

35 When teaching these tools and methods to students for the first time, I draw a firm line between problem formulation and problem solution activities, in order to support students' acquisition of concepts and techniques in the sphere of problem formulation, but for advanced students and in professional practice the processes may be much less linear. For example, graphic ideation may fruitfully happen early on, so that sketches and prototypes can prompt conversations with internal stakeholders or decision makers, or because such ideation may lead to a better understanding of the problem. Recall Rittel and Webber's observation that 'problem understanding and problem resolution are concomitant to each other' — there is no definitively correct sequence of steps through which experienced designers ought to approach this dialectical pair.

36 Jim Shore, 'Fail Fast', *IEEE Software* 21, no. 5 (2004): 21–25.

37 Pelle Ehn, 'Scandinavian Design: On Participation and Skill', in *Participatory Design: Principles and Practices*, edited by Douglas Schuler and Aki Namioka (Hillsdale: Lawrence Erlbaum Associates, 1993), 41–78.

38 Rittel and Webber, 'Dilemmas in a General Theory of Planning', 167.

39 Katherine McCoy, 'Maximize the Message: Tailoring Designs for Your Audience in a Multicultural Era', in *The Education of a Graphic Designer*, edited by Steven Heller (New York: Allworth Press, 2003), 279.

40 For a concise discussion of the connection between the rise of research in design practice and the rise of multiculturalism, see: Christopher Ireland, 'The Changing Role of Research', in *Design Research: Methods and Perspectives*, edited by Brenda Laurel (Cambridge, MA: MIT Press, 2003), 22. For an overview of persistent problems and urgent opportunities in design education, see: Danah Abdulla, 'Sleep Faster, We Need the Pillows', in *Design as Learning: A School of Schools Reader*, edited by Vera Sacchetti (Amsterdam: Valiz, 2018).

41 The concept of 'designer as auteur' is drawn from Michael Rock's thinking on authorship: Rock, 'The Designer as Author'.

42 I do not deploy the term 'critical' lightly. For my thoughts on the matter, see: Brad Haylock, 'What is critical design?', in *Undesign: Critical Practices at the Intersection of Art and Design*, edited by Gretchen Coombs, Andrew McNamara & Gavid Sade (London & New York: Routledge, 2019), 9–23.

43 Haraway is a renowned feminist scholar in the field of science and technology studies. See: Donna J. Haraway, *Staying with the Trouble: Making Kin in the Chthulucene* (Durham: Duke University Press, 2016).

44 For their feedback on a draft of this essay, I would like to thank Adam Cruickshank, Ella Egidy, Stuart Geddes, James Langdon, Fraser Muggeridge, Megan Patty, Jael Rincon and Žiga Testen. For his leadership of a collaborative teaching activity in 2015 that consolidated my interest in the value of various service design and design strategy tools and methods in graphic design education, I would like to thank my colleague Jeremy Yuille.

What matters for future practice?
Laurene Vaughan and Bonne Zabolotney,
in conversation

In this exchange, two senior design academics discuss the changing state of design practice and the demands that might be placed on graphic design education in the future. Speaking from Australian and Canadian perspectives respectively, Laurene Vaughan and Bonne Zabolotney consider the impact of globalisation, the challenges of cross-cultural communication, the importance of locality, the promises of co-designed curricula, and the potential threat of machine learning to the discipline.

LV   What are the core issues, challenges or transformations that are happening in graphic design education now, from your perspective?

BZ   I think that graphic design students increasingly face the challenge of developing a visual language that is rooted to place, rather than being influenced by established corporate visual languages that permeate cultures around the globe. Consider the example of Starbucks, whose visual identity doesn't shift or change anywhere. Whether it's a remote city in Canada or a very busy European hub, you can expect to see the same visual identity. It doesn't draw from local cultures, it doesn't draw from local knowledge, and there are few signifiers of regional culture in its design. It seeks to dominate as its own culture. Starbucks is an extreme example, but I think a lot of graphic designers are too heavily influenced by that kind of approach, rather than recognising it as something they can react to, in opposition to which they could develop their own visual language, or to which they could bring their own backgrounds and local cultures.

LV   It's true, the same styles of graphic identity are permeating across sectors and across cultures, such as Facebook-style identities that start to appear on other platforms. There are particular shades of blue that we see consistently on web interfaces or in apps, and there seem to be consistent visual styles for similar services. There is a degree of sameness in the marketplace. I'm not sure if it is laziness, or if it is the result of an expectation on the part of companies that their product or service will have a graphic relationship to its competitors. Perhaps it is being driven by designers thinking that there is a need for visual alignment within a sector. But, from an education perspective, this opens up opportunities for us. When we're teaching students, we need to teach them to adopt a responsive, project-by-project approach, rather than following stylistic tropes for certain kinds of products and services.

BZ   I wonder if we're seeing the results of the last fifteen years of templates, which began to replace customised graphic design when people started to get a lot leaner and meaner in business. For example, you don't have to hire a designer to create a customised website anymore, you just have to choose a WordPress template. WordPress still needs designers to develop different options for their clients, but these solutions are more widespread, and they're generic enough to cover a broader ground.

LV   I think that this is one of the challenges we face when we're teaching graphic design. We need to help students understand the possible value of templates, but also how to go beyond templates in order to deliver design solutions appropriate for specific clients or contexts. It is difficult to strike a balance between ease and efficiency on the one hand, and craftsmanship on the other. The changes in technology are really highlighting this for us in a way that perhaps wasn't the case prior to the current era of digital practice. These technological changes have prompted a transformation in how designers practice and therefore we need to continue to change how we teach. We're more obliged than ever to teach basic design principles that will enable good design outcomes, in order to overcome the ease of lookalike solutions.

BZ   In the past few years, I've wondered if we were witnessing an impoverishment of visual vocabularies, but I'm now wondering if it's instead a systematic loss of an appreciation of the importance of the context of design. Through sites like 99designs and others, where you can buy a logo for a dollar or fifty dollars or whatever, you have people who are just churning out images without knowing the context for the work. One rebuttal from experienced designers is that if you don't know the intended use of a logo, you can't be sure that it will be fit for print or web use or whatever application is required, and the client may be left with a design that still needs to be fixed, which is to say adjusted for its purpose. But I'm less concerned with the technical considerations than the missing cultural context: the need for a fit between a message and its audience. With crowd-sourced graphic design, it seems like the client can forget about context as well — they get lost in the visual form.

LV   Perhaps because of globalisation and the fast pace of digital technologies, we have many international design trends emerging that are aligned to business and nothing else. In terms of design education, it's also important for us to come back to teaching the value of the design process and the value of the exchanges that happen in the making — to teach students to be attentive to the unexpected things that can lead to great design outcomes. Great design can come about even when designers use pre-made, off-the-shelf things but customise them for a particular use. But this brings us to the question of the ways in which automation might make graphic designers redundant, because anyone will be able to easily generate things that look nice, things that are styled appropriately for their use. As you've recognised, the argument in support of the future of the discipline is that automated solutions won't have the impact or value or meaning that we would expect from current modes of practice. But I'm left wondering: do we even know if that's true? In a recent article in *Wired*, Jason Tselentis presents examples of design studios that are developing their AI capacity to the point where websites will soon be able to design themselves.[1] There has been a level of comfort in the design fields to date because we have assumed that, because we are 'creative', we will be spared from the major disruptions that machine learning could bring, but what if algorithms are actually smarter and more creative than us? We don't know yet what all of this means — but it is developing fast.

When we're thinking about future practices and the future of design education, how are we preparing students to work at a speed that wouldn't have been possible fifteen or twenty years ago? The old finished art processes and typesetting processes took a long time, so graphic designers produced work at a slower speed. It's easy to think that it was better before, or that things should at least remain how they are now, but how can we maintain an open mind about the possibilities that might emerge? Does this go back to the core question of the value that a graphic designer brings to a client or to a given design problem?

BZ   I used to refer to a book about cognition and concepts in my teaching that used the Greek myth about the hero Achilles as a lesson about form versus meaning. It recounted the story of Patroclus, who wore Achilles's armour into battle, but was killed once the Trojans discovered he was not Achilles.[2] It is an exemplary case of mistaken identity: the form of the armour was not a substitute for the substance of a warrior. The story is a metaphor to warn against superficiality in design, to warn of the dangers of things that appear to have strength and integrity but which in fact lack substance.

If we're saying we have to combat the encroachment of artificial intelligence into graphic design, we have to be able to identify the human value in the work we're doing. What are the more authentic kinds of knowledge that we are working with? And — coming back to the question of context again — how do we facilitate conversations with people to bring out that knowledge, in order to make it visible?

LV   One of my colleagues tells a story about how he was once commissioned to design a website for a company. When he was doing the pitch to the board, showing the preliminary work from the person who commissioned him, it turned into an almighty fight in the boardroom that had nothing to do with him. They were fighting about what the business was actually about, and there were many different perspectives around the table. At that moment, he realised that he was being used as a pawn to facilitate change in the organisation.

This is a very interesting anecdote for us to keep in mind when we think about what a designer is doing when she or he is having a conversation with a client. In book cover design, a designer is trying to communicate what a novel is about, being sympathetic to what the author thinks the book is about and what the publisher knows will sell, and in the process endeavouring to synthesise all of this into something that a reader might also find interesting. Such a task demands a very complex negotiation between different stakeholders with different expectations. Perhaps some AI cover generator could come up with a solution if you put enough variables in, but perhaps not. We really have to educate our students to be able to articulate their value in these complex negotiations — the value that they bring to the conversation.

This leads us to a really hard part of design education that we don't often talk about: how do we educate a student to become a practitioner? We talk about professional practice, we might teach students to write business cases, we might teach them how to fill in their tax return, but we don't necessarily teach enough about teamwork, about conversations, about negotiation, about listening, about ways of giving feedback. These are core skills of professional practice.

BZ   That's true, we don't talk enough about those conversations and their role in the iterative process of going from concepts to a solution.

LV   It's through those conversations that clarity emerges. A client might say, 'I need a brochure', but then you realise they don't need a brochure, they need something quite different to meet their communication needs. Or that, despite their desire for a certain kind of complex digital outcome, they just need a very simple format. That process of working *with* someone to establish their communication requirements is the real skill of a good designer.

As we move into new areas of practice, such as service design and design strategy, this is even more clearly the case. Quite often, the designer isn't presenting an actual 'thing' to the client, they are talking through needs and experiences and the design work might be more methodology than artefact. We have to find a means for teaching students how to have these *design conversations* in practice. This is an expertise that a designer brings to a project — they build up relationships, they listen, they engage, they propose ideas. This skill set is essential for the future of design and design education. We need to see these conversations as design acts.

Often, we think that when you study professional practice, you need to look to organisational studies or another discipline instead of actually thinking about this as a design activity. Some of Bryan Lawson's propositions, in *How designers think* and *What designers know*, are alluding to this.[3] These are issues that can be brought into design curricula and courseware. We could use these ideas with students as a fundamental part of their education and practice development. This is something that we should be introducing in the first year of undergraduate studies, at the beginning of a designer's education and not at the end. It is a way of actually developing students' understanding of the field. Teamwork and collaboration are similarly important — the myth of the solitary designer working on their own or only in their own discipline is flawed. Most of the time, designers are actually working across disciplines and working in teams. Knowing how to articulate their value in those contexts will serve graduates well. These are transferable, lifelong skills.

BZ What you're saying is making me think about the importance of iteration. Design is not a science; it's not a linear process. Prior to being so heavily dependent on computers, software and very sophisticated output devices, we would still have some happy accidents. There would be a level of surprise in the discovery process, and you would happen upon good developments through a glitch in technology, through an unexpected conversation, because you'd run out of certain supplies, because you'd accidentally cut a photo the wrong way, or something else had happened that made you reconsider how you were going about a particular creative task. So, I wonder: do we have to build that back in?

LV I think we do. But this also makes me think of all of those classic design phase diagrams, based on problem solving and iterations. They describe linear processes that are solution-oriented — this is also part of the phenomenon of design thinking. These diagrams presume that there is only one good outcome, when in fact we know that there is no *one* ideal outcome. You can keep designing and you can keep iterating, allowing for the messiness of the creative process and the uncertainties within it, and the multiple iterations and the time it takes, and I think that this is one of the real challenges we face as educators — I don't know how we prepare students for this aspect of design practice, but perhaps we need to push back against the speed with which design outcomes are expected to be delivered today. Because, of course, automation could do much of this work quickly, and so we need to be able to evidence the difference that a human makes — if indeed humans do make a difference.

This is an area that we need to think about more: how do we confront that 'five-step' model of doing everything, the expectation that we're all agile, that we can all be effective startups, and that we can produce lots of things really quickly? How do we find the balance? This is a real opportunity for us as educators, and I suspect that working on this challenge with our students is actually the way forward, rather than us feeling like we have to have models to deliver to them.

This is where we can think about co-design as a pedagogic approach — not just in terms of co-designing assessments. Perhaps we also have to rethink the authority of teachers, whilst also respecting their expertise. Building on the work of Carol Dweck, Lisa Grocott emphasises the importance of *mindsets* in design education.[4] We need to prepare students to have a mindset of learning to learn. We also have to work on the educator's mindset, enabling them to see the value in co-production and co-learning, rather than focusing only on the dissemination of their own expertise. This would mean establishing a mutually trusting and respectful learning environment, as opposed to a master-apprentice studio model.

BZ   That's a very good point. Our international students are coming with specific approaches to interacting with technology, and different traditions of visual language. They're not willing to forsake that knowledge just to gain a new approach to design. The modernist idea that we might have a universal visual language is definitely out of date.

LV   Design education — well, education generally, but design education in particular — has become globalised, in that schools everywhere have students from somewhere else, yet, too often, we're still teaching a one-size-fits-all, modernist, European curriculum. But we've also seen the rise of the 'decolonising design' movement, which emphasises the fact that there are other ways of thinking about what design is. It is time for us to let go of the patriarchal and European model of design, and to really think about what a more pluralistic understanding of good communication might be.

New communication technologies and globalised patterns of work also demand that we cultivate in our graduates a capacity for intercultural communication and a respect for diversity. We need to embrace intercultural awareness, not just in projects that explicitly focus on design for social innovation, but also in corporate work.

BZ   You've mentioned the participatory or co-creational aspect of experienced designers working with students, which leads me to think of the cliché that you can only get good output if you have a good input. Specifically, I'm thinking about the kinds of cultural information that we are exposing students to, and I hope that, in the future, this will include more indigenous knowledge. We will need to be wary of cultural appropriation, but a diversity of influences will be increasingly important for the future of design practice.

We also have many international students who have a lot to tell us about contemporary manufacturing, and about what it's like to come from countries where technological development is progressing in leaps and bounds. We have an opportunity to learn from our students and to co-develop curricula with them.

LV Some of my colleagues in Melbourne have been looking at ways to link design education with Indigenous cultures and Indigenous practices of various types.[5] The aim is to identify how Indigenous forms of knowledge can inform the ways in which one practises as a designer. Instilling a broader cultural awareness and richer relationships to these cultures has to become a core part of design education.

BZ I agree. We work from a set of twentieth-century assumptions and principles, such as the way the eye scans a page from left to right and top to bottom, or, in the case of poster design, the way one might lead a viewer from perception at a distance to cognition at close range. But we don't test these assumptions enough.

LV The ways in which people read information will differ depending on their cultural background. So the idea of universality is problematic — we can't design something that addresses everyone equally. We need to examine these assumptions. It may be that we need to encourage students in the future to think fundamentally differently about what design is and what it can do.

[1] Jason Tselentis, 'When Websites Design Themselves', *Wired*, 20 September 2017, https://www.wired.com/story/when-websites-design-themselves/, accessed 19 December 2018.

[2] Gilles Fauconnier and Mark Turner, *The Way We Think: Conceptual Blending and the Mind's Hidden Complexities* (New York: Basic Books, 2002).

[3] Bryan Lawson, *How designers think: the design process demystified*, 4th edition (Oxford & Burlington, MA: Elsevier/Architectural Press, 2006); and Bryan Lawson, *What designers know* (Oxford & Burlington, MA: Elsevier/Architectural Press, 2004).

[4] Carol Dweck, *Mindset: how you can fulfil your potential* (London: Constable & Robinson, 2012).

[5] Yoko Akama, Peter West and Mark McMillan, '"I was worried about insulting Indigenous communities with my designs": shifting from fear to recognition to create a meeting place of sovereigns' (paper presented at ACUADS Annual Conference, QUT Creative Industries Faculty, Brisbane, 29–30 September 2016).

Contributor biographies

Paul Bailey is an Irish graphic designer, researcher and educator based in the UK. He is currently Course Leader for MA Graphic Media Design at London College of Communication, University of the Arts London; a member of Supra Systems Studio, UK; a committee member of the Graphic Design Educators' Network; and a fellow of the Higher Education Academy in the UK.

Stuart Bertolotti-Bailey is a graphic designer, writer and publisher based in London and currently working as Head of Design at the Institute of Contemporary Arts in London. He is one half of the artist duo Dexter Sinister along with David Reinfurt, and a quarter of archiving/publishing platform The Serving Library along with Reinfurt, Francesca Bertolotti-Bailey and Vincenzo Latronico. He co-founded and co-edited the left-field arts journal *Dot Dot Dot* in 2000, and continues to edit its successor *The Serving Library Annual* (formerly *Bulletins of The Serving Library*, since 2011).

Sheila Levrant de Bretteville is the first tenured woman at the Yale University School of Art, where she is the Caroline M. Street Professor, a title she accepted because city streets are where her site-specific installations have taken place. Her work is in the special collections of libraries and museums, including: the Umea Museum, Sweden; Victoria and Albert Museum, London; and Centre Pompidou, Paris. Her work has been shown in: *California: Designing Freedom*, at the Design Museum, London; *Graphic Design in America* and *Hippie Modernism: The Search for Utopia* at the Walker Art Center, Minneapolis; *Now Dig This! Art and Black Los Angeles, 1960–1980* at the Hammer Museum, Los Angeles and MoMA PS1, New York; *WACK! Art and the Feminist Revolution* at Los Angeles Museum of Contemporary Art and MoMA PS1; and galleries in Poland, Vienna and Stockholm. She has been designated a Distinguished Alumna by Barnard College, where she received her BA degree in the History of Art, and a Design Legend by the American Institute of Graphic Arts, she has been awarded honorary doctorates from five universities of art and design on both coasts of the United States, and she has been recognised with a Lifetime Achievement award from the Women's Caucus for the Arts.

Richard Buchanan is Professor of Design, Management and Information Systems at the Weatherhead School of Management, Case Western Reserve University. Before joining the faculty at Case Western, he was Professor of Design and former Head of the School of Design at Carnegie Mellon University. He is also Chair Professor of Design Theory and Practice at the College of Design & Innovation at Tongji University, Shanghai, China. At the Weatherhead, he is involved in introducing the concepts and methods of design into management, extending traditional areas of design theory and practice in innovative new applications such as Interaction Design and Organisation Design. He is a frequent speaker in venues around the world. Among his numerous publications are: *Discovering Design: Explorations in Design Studies*, *The Idea of Design* and *Pluralism in Theory and Practice*. He is co-editor of *Design Issues*, an international journal of design history, theory and criticism published by MIT Press. He is also a former President of the Design Research Society, the international learned society of the design research community based in the UK. He received his AB and PhD from the Committee on the Analysis of Ideas and the Study of Methods at the University of Chicago.

Vincent Chan is a graphic designer based in Melbourne who specialises in type design. Under the moniker Matter of Sorts he makes work that revolves around notions of commoning, design, pedagogy and type, and where they might overlap, co-mingle and meld. He has created original typefaces for clients as diverse as the Bob Dylan Center, Pitch Music and Arts Festival and Australia Post, and offers a changing library of retail typefaces through Matter of Sorts. He is a sessional lecturer at RMIT University and course coordinator of Typography 1 at Monash Art Design and Architecture. He is also a PhD candidate at Monash University, where his research is concerned with the idea of productive discursiveness in typographic practice.

Tony Credland is a Senior Lecturer on the MA Graphic Media Design programme at London College of Communication, University of the Arts London. He co-founded the *Cactus Network* and the poster magazine *Feeding Squirrels to the Nuts*. He continues to be involved with radical media projects, he co-edited *We are everywhere: The irresistible rise of global anti-capitalism*, and he is a member of the Design Activist Research Hub.

Europa is a graphic design studio interested in all forms of culture. Their approach to design is collaborative — believing that the constraints that a project brings can be both liberating and joyful. Europa has a particular interest in architecture, urbanism and the role that graphic design can play in a place's identity. They look for moments when graphic design and architecture overlap, and create opportunities for their work to play a more supportive and less top-down role in framing a place. Europa was founded in 2007 by Mia Frostner and Robert Sollis. Gareth Lindsay joined the studio in 2013 and Alice Vodoz in 2019. Alongside the studio, Sollis is a Senior Lecturer at Camberwell College of Arts, University of the Arts London, where he runs the second year of the BA Graphic Design course. He was head of the BA in 2018–2019 and led the revalidation of the current course. His project briefs range from a rigorous type design course to forming an independent state in Camberwell.

Katie Evans is a London-based graphic designer. She is ½ of Open Practice, ¼ of Words Don't Come Easy and ⅛ of Fraser Muggeridge studio.

Matthew Galloway graduated with a Master of Fine Arts (Distinction) from the University of Canterbury's Ilam School of Fine Arts in 2012, and since 2014 he has held the role of Senior Lecturer at the Otago Polytechnic School of Design. His research-based practice employs the tools and methodologies of design in an editorial way, and within a gallery context. This way of working emphasises design and publishing as an inherently political exercise and involves an interdisciplinary approach to producing publications and art objects. In 2016, he was a selected participant in Talente International Craft Fair, Munich, Germany, and ARTifariti 2016, Tindouf, Algeria. He was presented with a Merit Award at the 2016 National Contemporary Art Awards for *Fountain is a Copy?*, a collaboration with Ella Sutherland.

Rob Giampietro is Director of Design at the Museum of Modern Art in New York, leading a team of designers and producers at the museum and design store on projects across all media. From 2015 to 2018, he was Creative Lead at Google in New York, managing projects that included: four SPAN Design & Technology Conferences; the launch and relaunch of the Google Design website; an overhaul of the Google Fonts directory, including new typeface commissions; a brand-focused expansion of the Material Design system; a visual update for Google's do-it-yourself AI kits in Target stores; and contributions to the People + AI Research outreach efforts at Google. He is Senior Critic at RISD's MFA Graphic Design programme, and has been Executive Board Member and Vice President of AIGA/NY. From 2010 to 2015, he was Principal at Project Projects, whose work was recognised with the National Design Award in Communication Design in 2015. He is the recipient of a 2013 MacDowell Colony Fellowship and the 2014–2015 Katherine Edwards Gordon Rome Prize at the American Academy in Rome.

Corin Gisel is a Swiss writer, researcher and designer. Their writing has been published by Lars Müller Publishers, Diogenes, Spector Books, Occasional Papers, Walker Art Center and Valiz, and has covered topics such as design education, dress culture, the digitalisation of the museum, LGBTQIA+ button badges, and money as a medium for political opposition. In 2018, they co-founded the non-profit design research practice 'common-interest' with Nina Paim. Alongside their design work, Gisel is also active in LGBTQIA+ community organising and activism.

Ricardo Gonçalves is a Portuguese graphic designer currently based in London. His research practice aims to produce critical visual narratives that investigate tensions related to contemporary politics and network culture.

Lisa Grocott was once a graphic designer but nowadays mostly avoids finding a name for what she does. She is most excited about being the Director of WonderLab, a research lab operating at the nexus of design, learning and play. WonderLab, a platform for collaborating with social psychologists and educators, learning scientists and actors, has Grocott working on a range of experiential and playful projects designed to support people through the tough challenge of shifting mindsets, beliefs and practices. Grocott is a Professor of Design at Monash University. Before that, she was a Dean at Parsons in New York, where it meant nothing that she had once co-founded a design consultancy called Studio Anybody in Melbourne.

Brad Haylock is a designer, publisher and educator. He is an Associate Professor of Design at RMIT University, where he is Coordinator of Higher Degrees by Research in the School of Design. He previously managed the RMIT Master of Communication Design programme, a major redesign of which he led in 2015. His research and practice spans book design, publishing and the sociology of critique, and he is founder of Surpllus, an independent, para-academic imprint focusing on critical and speculative practices across art, design and theory. His recent curatorial projects include *Experimental Jetset: Superstructure* (2018) and *Metahaven: Field Report* (2020), both with Megan Patty, and his recent editorial projects include *Distributed* (2018), with David Blamey, and the present volume, with Luke Wood.

Constanze Hein is a Berlin-based graphic designer who teaches typography at the University of the Arts Berlin. After starting the studies of 'Integrated Design' at University of the Arts Bremen, she continued with undergraduate classes in Book Art/Graphic Design at the Academy of Fine Arts in Leipzig, followed by the design major in the System-Design class, then run by Oliver Klimpel. At the Academy, she met Jan Blessing and Felix Walser. Together they founded the graphic design studio 'Book Book' in Berlin, with a focus on publications, websites and ephemera. In 2016, Blessing and Hein received the Walter Tiemann Prize for designing the publication *Tutti* for media artist Anahita Razmi. At the University of the Arts Berlin, Hein collaborates with the illustration programme, run by illustrator Henning Wagenbreth.

Richard Hollis has been a freelance graphic designer since 1957. He has been on the staff of several London art and design schools, was art editor at *New Society* in the 1960s, and since that time has designed mostly art catalogues and books, the best-known being John Berger's *Ways of Seeing*. As a design historian, his books include *Graphic Design: A Concise History*, *Swiss Graphic Design: Towards an International Style 1920–1970* and *About Graphic Design*. His most recent book, *Henry van de Velde: The Artist as Designer*, was published in 2019.

Na Kim is a graphic designer, currently based in Seoul and Berlin, and a member of Table Union. After studying product design and graphic design in Korea, Kim participated in Werkplaats Typografie in the Netherlands. She focused on the visual language of autonomous works as well as various cultural commissioned projects. She was responsible for the concept and design of *GRAPHIC* magazine from 2009 until 2012, and has initiated a series of projects based on her monograph, *SET*, since 2015. She has held solo exhibitions, such as *Black and White* (2019), *Red, Yellow, Blue* (2017), *SET* (2015), *Choice Specimen* (2014), *Found Abstracts* (2011) and *Fragile* (2006). In addition, Kim has been a curator for Brno Biennale, Chaumont Festival, Seoul International Typography Biennale and Fikra Graphic Design Biennial. Her works have been included in international exhibitions at MMCA, V&A, MoMA, Milan Triennale Museum, Die Neue Sammlung and elsewhere.

James Langdon is an independent graphic designer and writer and professor for communication design at the Hochschule für Gestaltung Karlsruhe. Since 2004, he has worked closely with many artists on graphic design for publication and exhibition. From 2008 to 2018, he was a founding director of the artist-run space Eastside Projects in Birmingham. He is presently working on a biography of English designer Norman Potter (1923–1995) as a teacher.

Lu Liang is a graphic designer working between Rotterdam and Shanghai for her design practice The Exercises, which was established after she received her MA degree from Werkplaats Typografie, Arnhem, in 2011. Prior to that, she received her BA from the Gerrit Rietveld Academy, Amsterdam, in 2008. The Exercises works with a great variety of institutions, artists, designers and companies, engaging with clients and collaborators, finding strategic and creative solutions in the interactive process. The Exercises focus on visual identity, art direction, exhibitions, printed matter and online applications. Liang's commissions include the visual campaign and art direction for the Shanghai Project Chapter 1 & 2, exhibition design for *Wat is Nederland* at Het Nieuwe Instituut, and the visual campaign for the 10th Shanghai Biennale. In 2017, Liang co-founded Tools For Progress, a design collective that creates jewellery and centrepieces inspired by the timelessness of architectural and monumental elements. She is also the co-founder of Agency Agency, Practice for Strategy and Design.

Ellen Lupton is a writer, curator, educator and designer. She is founding director of the Graphic Design MFA Program at MICA (Maryland Institute College of Art) in Baltimore, where she has authored numerous books on design processes, including *Thinking with Type*, *Graphic Design Thinking*, *Graphic Design: The New Basics*, and *Type on Screen*. She also serves as Senior Curator of Contemporary Design at Cooper Hewitt, Smithsonian Design Museum in New York City. Recent exhibitions include *The Senses: Design Beyond Vision*, *Beauty: Cooper Hewitt Design Triennial*, *How Posters Work* and *Beautiful Users*. Her book *Design is Storytelling* was published by Cooper Hewitt in 2017. She received the AIGA Gold Medal for Lifetime Achievement in 2007, and was named a Fellow of the American Academy of Arts & Sciences in 2019.

Gabriela Matuszyk is a London-based designer, writer and researcher. Currently teaching on the BA Graphic Design at Kingston University, she focusses her collaborative practice on navigating through and between the polarities of contemporary conditions. She participates in Words Don't Come Easy, writes for *Eye* magazine and co-runs Open Practice Studio.

Fraser Muggeridge is a graphic designer, and director of Fraser Muggeridge studio, based in London. Throughout a wide range of formats, from artists' books and exhibition catalogues to posters, marketing material, exhibitions and websites, the studio prioritises artists' and writers' content over the imposition of a signature style. By allowing images and texts to sustain their own intent and impact, each project is approached with typographic form and letterforms playing a key role in arriving at a sympathetic yet subtly alluring object. Muggeridge founded and is a tutor at Typography Summer School, a week-long programme of typographic study for recent graduates and professionals, held in London since 2010 and in New York since 2013. He is a visiting lecturer at The University of Reading on the MA Book Design course (since 2003) and at Camberwell College of Art, London, in the second year of the BA Graphic Design (since 2011).

Paul Mylecharane is a graphic designer and educator whose practice focusses mainly on the intersection of physical and digital publishing and its relationship to the archive. He works collaboratively under the name Public Office with people and organisations doing non-profit work in the arts, culture and education.

Nina Paim is a Brazilian researcher, curator and designer. She has taught and lectured in Aruba, Brazil, the Czech Republic, Germany, Denmark, Estonia, France, Italy, Portugal, the UK, the US and Switzerland. In 2014, she curated the exhibition *Taking a Line for a Walk* at the 26th Biennial of Graphic Design Brno, Czech Republic, for which she received a Swiss Design Award in 2015. She co-conceived and edited the book *Taking a Line for a Walk*, published by Spector Books in 2016 and supported by the Graham Foundation for Advanced Studies in the Fine Arts. In 2018, she co-founded the non-profit design research practice 'common-interest' with Corin Gisel. In 2019, common-interest received a Swiss Design Award in the category of design mediation for curating the exhibition *Department of Non-Binaries* at the inaugural Fikra Graphic Design Biennial in Sharjah (UAE).

Megan Patty is a publisher, writer and curator. She is Publisher, Head of Publications, Photographic Services and Library at the National Gallery of Victoria, and Curator of the annual Melbourne Art Book Fair. She has worked across the museum and arts sector to develop new publishing propositions for museums, artists, and private and public collections for the past twelve years. Through the NGV's imprint, Patty has published over four hundred titles on Australian and international art and design, ranging from artist monographs, exhibition publications, scholarly journals, children's art books and young adult non-fiction. Patty has acted as publisher, editor and writer for many notable award-winning titles including, most recently, *NGV Triennial*, a 688-page volume of critical essays on contemporary art and design, and *Some Posters from the NGV*, an edited volume of Australian poster design for art exhibitions.

Radim Peško is a designer and typographer. In 2010, he established his digital type foundry RP, which specialises in typefaces that are both formally and conceptually distinctive. He has created original typefaces for the visual identities of institutions such as Boijmans Museum in Rotterdam, Eastside Projects in Birmingham, the Stedelijk Museum in Amsterdam, Aspen Art Museum, the Graham Foundation in Chicago, Fridericianum in Kassel and *Berlin Biennale 8*, as well as for fashion brand Paco Rabanne, among many others. In 2011 and 2012, he was a chairman of the International Biennial of Graphic Design in Brno and co-curated two of its editions: the 26th Brno Biennial in 2014 and the 27th Brno Biennial in 2016. He has lectured worldwide. From 2006 to 2012, he taught at the Gerrit Rietveld Academie in Amsterdam. He currently teaches at the Royal College of Art in London and on the Master in Type Design programme at ECAL in Lausanne.

Joe Potts is a graphic designer, educator, artist and writer working with found and synthesised images, sound, typography and language. He teaches typography and graphic design at Otis College of Art and Design and the University of Southern California, and is founding director of the Southland Institute (for critical, durational and typographic post-studio practices).

Bryony Quinn is a writer, editor and lecturer based in London. Her research falls in the intersection between visual culture and literature, and focusses on figurative and spatial obliquity — things that lean, slopes, diagonals, digression, etc.

Carlos Romo-Melgar is a graphic designer and researcher based in London. He is currently a tutor on the MA Graphic Media Design at London College of Communication, an occasional writer and an intermittent publisher. He is a co-founder of SPREEENG, a 'studio' enacting diverse methods of cooperation to interrogate the forms, places and intersections that make up design working formations in the present.

Naomi Strinati is a designer, based between London and Limerick. Her background is in graphic design and her research has a particular interest in the connection between the built environment and collective amnesia.

Jon Sueda is a graphic designer and currently the Chair of the MFA Design programme at California College of the Arts. He is the founder of the design studio Stripe, which specialises in print and exhibition design for art and culture. He curated the exhibitions *Work from California* for the 25th International Graphic Design Biennial in Brno, Czech Republic, in 2012 and *All Possible Futures* for SOMArts Cultural Center in San Francisco in 2014.

Lucille Tenazas is an educator and graphic designer based in New York. She is the Henry Wolf Professor of Communication Design at Parsons School of Design, where she is currently the Associate Dean in the School of Art, Media and Technology. Previously, she was the Founding Chair of the MFA programme in Design at California College of Arts and Crafts in San Francisco, where she developed a graduate curriculum with an interdisciplinary approach and a focus on form-giving, teaching and leadership. Originally from Manila, the Philippines, she has taught and practised in the United States since 1979. Her first experience of living in a design environment was as a graduate student at Cranbrook Academy of Art in Michigan in the early 1980s. She is the recipient of the AIGA Medal in 2013, the most prestigious in the field, awarded by the American Institute of Graphic Arts for her lifetime contribution to design practice and outstanding leadership in design education. From 1996 to 1998, she was the National President of the AIGA, the organisation's first appointment outside of New York in the organisation's history. Her work has received numerous awards and has been featured in many publications and exhibitions nationally and internationally, including a retrospective of her work from the permanent collection of the San Francisco Museum of Modern Art (SFMoMA), as well as in exhibitions at the Cooper-Hewitt National Design Museum and the Los Angeles County Museum of Art (LACMA). She was awarded the National Design Award for Communication Design by the Cooper-Hewitt National Design Museum in 2002.

Teal Triggs is Professor of Graphic Design in the School of Communication at the Royal College of Art, London. As a graphic design historian, critic and educator, her writings have appeared in numerous edited books and international design publications. Her research focusses primarily on design pedagogy, criticism, self-publishing and feminism, with recent projects exploring a history of graphic design exhibitions and the role of design in the future of the library. She is Associate Editor of *Design Issues* (MIT Press) and was founding Editor-in-Chief of *Communication Design* (Taylor & Francis/ico-D). Her recent books include: co-editor of *The Graphic Design Reader* (Bloomsbury), and author of *Fanzines* (Thames & Hudson) and the children's book *The School of Art* (Wide Eyed). She is a Fellow of the International Society of Typographic Designers, Royal College of Art and Royal Society for the encouragement of Arts, Manufactures and Commerce.

Michael Twyman is a design historian and educator. He joined the staff at the University of Reading in 1959, where he was founding Head of the Department of Typography & Graphic Communication, which was established in 1974. The department has long been recognised as a centre of excellence in graphic design education and research. Although he has now retired from full-time academia, Twyman continues to work in the department as director of its Centre for Ephemera Studies.

Jonty Valentine is a graphic designer, lecturer and sometimes a curator and writer, based in Auckland, New Zealand. Alongside his day job teaching, he runs the design studio Index with Amy Yalland. His main area of research is New Zealand graphic design history, with significant outcomes including: co-editing of the periodical *The National Grid* with Luke Wood, first published in 2006; authoring the book *Mark Cleverley: Designer*, published by David Bateman in 2014; curating the graphic design exhibitions *Mark Cleverley: Designer*, *Printing Types* and *Just Hold Me*, all at Objectspace, Auckland, and *Design and Designers: Artefacts from The National Grid* at Ramp gallery, Hamilton. Valentine received an MFA from Yale University and a BFA from University of Canterbury, both in graphic design.

Laurene Vaughan is Professor of Design at RMIT University, where she serves as Dean in the School of Design. She was invited to the position of Neirenberg Chair, Distinguished Professor of Design, at Carnegie Mellon University, 2012–2013. She is on the Advisory Board of the Centre for Design Research, Norway. Internationally recognised as a leader in interdisciplinary and applied design research, she investigates in her research the interactive and situated nature of cultural production and the practices that enable this, both analogue and digital. She was a lead researcher on the Circus Oz Living Archive Project and co-editor of *Performing Digital*, published by Palgrave. She has recently edited *Practice-Based Design Research* and *Designing Cultures of Care*, both published by Bloomsbury.

Noel Waite is a Senior Lecturer and Program Manager of the Master of Communication Design at RMIT University in Melbourne. He taught in the Department of Design Studies at the University of Otago from 2002 to 2015, and acknowledges all the colleagues and students who participated so enthusiastically in the antipodean design studies experiment there, in particular the initiator and facilitator of Design Studies at Otago, Nick Laird. He also acknowledges the importance of an interdisciplinary doctoral performance workshop run by Greg Dening and Donna Merwick in 1999 at the University of Otago, and the value of the beach crossing documented in this volume, in 2006 at Karitane, with a very generous Richard Buchanan.

Luke Wood is a graphic designer and musician, currently employed as a Senior Lecturer at the University of Canterbury's School of Fine Arts. He has taught on and off at various design schools around New Zealand since the late 1990s, while working as a graphic designer for museums, galleries and the occasional studio. In 2006, he and Jonty Valentine co-founded *The National Grid*, a journal with a focus on shining a light into the margins of New Zealand's graphic design history. In 2011, he and Stuart Geddes co-founded *Head Full of Snakes*, an experimental publication that focused on manual labour through the guise of a motorcycle magazine. In 2010, he and Aaron Beehre set up the Ilam Press, a print publishing research workshop at the University of Canterbury. Most recently, in 2017, he established Ilam Press Records, a project designed to explore the potential for the physical distribution of music and sonic arts in a predominantly digital future.

Jia Xiao was born in China but is currently living in London. She is an MA participant at the London College of Communication. With a background in industrial design and graphic design, she has an ongoing interest in proposing problems and seeking out connections from the mould of everyday life.

Bonne Zabolotney is a designer, researcher and educator from Vancouver, Canada. She holds a Bachelor of Design from Alberta College of Art and Design, a Master of Arts in Liberal Studies from Simon Fraser University, and a PhD in Design from RMIT University. She began working as a communication designer and art director in 1993 and began teaching at Emily Carr University of Art and Design in 2001. During this time, she has held the positions of Dean of Graduate Studies, Dean of Design and Dynamic Media, and Vice-President Academic and Provost. Her current research focusses on Canadian design history and the political economy of design.

Roxy Zeiher is a designer, based between London and Berlin. Particularly interested in critical and contemporary subject areas communicated through design, she pursues a multidisciplinary creative practice. She interrogates culture with her research-driven design practice that investigates how the designed world, especially new technology, is shaping our behaviour, perception and understanding.

Colophon

*One and many mirrors:
perspectives on graphic design education*

Edited by Luke Wood and Brad Haylock

With contributions by Paul Bailey, Stuart Bertolotti-Bailey, Sheila Levrant de Bretteville, Richard Buchanan, Vincent Chan, Tony Credland, Europa, Katie Evans, Matthew Galloway, Rob Giampietro, Corin Gisel, Ricardo Gonçalves, Lisa Grocott, Brad Haylock, Constanze Hein, Richard Hollis, Na Kim, James Langdon, Lu Liang, Ellen Lupton, Gabriela Matuszyk, Fraser Muggeridge, Paul Mylecharane, Nina Paim, Megan Patty, Radim Peško, Joe Potts, Bryony Quinn, Carlos Romo-Melgar, Naomi Strinati, Jon Sueda, Lucille Tenazas, Teal Triggs, Michael Twyman, Jonty Valentine, Laurene Vaughan, Noel Waite, Luke Wood, Jia Xiao, Bonne Zabolotney and Roxy Zeiher

Designed by Brad Haylock
Copy-editing by Brad Haylock, Lily Keil and Occasional Papers
Proofreading by Melissa Larner
Typeset in RH Inter
Cover image by Rida Abbasi
Printed by Die Keure
Published by Occasional Papers and The Physics Room

Supported by The Physics Room, University of Canterbury College of Arts Contestable Research Fund and RMIT University School of Design

© The authors, Occasional Papers and The Physics Room, 2020

All rights reserved. No part of this publication may be reproduced or transmitted in any form or by any means, electronic or mechanical, including photocopy, recording or any other information storage and retrieval system, without prior permission in writing from the publisher. Every effort has been made to trace copyright holders, but if any have been overlooked we will make the necessary accreditations at the first opportunity.

ISBN 978-0-9954730-1-0
www.occasionalpapers.org

The cover image by Rida Abbasi, one of a series of three printed variations, is a contemporary take on an elementary composition exercise of the type commonly associated with Johannes Itten's Basic Course at the Bauhaus, here executed algorithmically using Processing. Generative processes that take a human input to create a variety of outputs are becoming increasingly enmeshed in graphic design practice. Using systems that require the designer to relinquish control, they can reveal genuinely novel, surprising and self-renewing outcomes and compositions.